Praise for
Satan and the Problem of Evil

"In his new book, *Satan and the Problem of Evil: From the Bible to the Early Church Fathers*, published by Fortress Press, Archie T. Wright masterfully guides his readers through a complex web of literary sources pertaining to one of the thorniest and most enigmatic characters of early Jewish and Christian etiologies of evil—Satan. Wright's book admirably succeeds in a thorough and meticulous exploration of the origins and early history of this elusive antagonist in the literature of ancient Israel, of various texts from Second Temple Period Judaism(s), the writings of the New Testament, and the literature of the apologists and theologians of the early church. Although Wright's book deals mainly with the figure of Satan, it provides important methodological lessons for understanding other antagonists of early Jewish mythologies of corruption, including Melchiresha, Mastema, and Belial. A remarkable study, rigorous in character and judicious in quality throughout, it demonstrates Wright's philological depth, historical prowess, and highly nuanced theological sensibilities. It is indisputably the definitive work on Jewish and Christian demonology in modern scholarship and will long hold that position. Methodological insights of this portentous study will continue to have a profound impact in upcoming decades on the field of early Judaism in general and on studies of Jewish demonology in particular. This brilliant, nuanced, and thought-provoking study is a must-read for everyone who is interested in the theology and history of early Judaism and early Christianity."
—Andrei A. Orlov, professor of Judaism and Christianity in antiquity at Marquette University; author of eighteen books, including *The Enoch-Metatron Tradition* and *The Glory of the Invisible God: Two Powers in Heaven Traditions and Early Christology*

"Archie Wright offers a valuable study taking an in-depth look at the various iterations of 'Satan' from the ancient Near East through the Patristic Era. Whether scholar or student, anyone interested in the reification of evil as figured in the ultimate baddie will benefit from this fine book."
—Benjamin Wold, associate professor of early Judaism and Christianity, Trinity College Dublin; specialist in Second Temple Judaism and the Dead Sea Scrolls

"The basic questions of religions are: 'What is man?' and 'Where does evil come from?' In addition to the tradition of physical evil, the Judeo-Christian traditions have identified, understood, and transmitted the tradition of a personified ethical evil, most commonly known as the *satan* or Satan. The figure of Satan, representative and instigator of the ethical evil in the world, has been the subject of several books and studies in recent decades.

"Wright's extensive study explores the three-millennia Judeo-Christian traditions and examines how the ideas about this personified evil were identified and understood, and how the tradition associated with it has evolved. The author provides a detailed analysis of all the relevant texts in the Old Testament (Hebrew Bible and Septuagint), corpuses of the Second Temple Period such as the Dead Sea Scrolls and Pseudepigrapha, the writings of the New Testament, and the literature of the apologists and theologians of the early church. Wright's book opens new horizons, showing that significant changes in interpretation—a shift in the theological understanding of the role or function of the satan or the devil in the world—have taken place in the Dead Sea Scrolls and Pseudepigrapha. This interpretation led to the characteristics of early Christian literature, the period of the apostolic and early church fathers, in which the biblical opponent, the investigator satan, became the capital-S Satan, the heavenly evil being in direct opposition to the God of Israel and the church, and in some worldviews nearly as powerful. I warmly recommend this book to anyone who wants to get to know the worldview and the problem of evil in the Old Testament, the literature of the Second Temple Period, and early Christianity through in-depth analysis."

—Ida Frölich, professor emerita, Pázmány Péter Catholic University, Budapest

"Brilliantly interweaving concerns for exegesis and theology, Archie Wright offers an illuminating survey of ancient perspectives on the problem of evil. Wright's book makes scholarly findings on the fascinating history of Satan accessible and engaging, powerfully demonstrating how ancient discussions of the demonic can resound with sharp relevance in our own difficult times."

—Annette Yoshiko Reed, professor, department of religious studies and Skirball Department of Hebrew and Judaic Studies, New York University; author of *Demons, Angels, and Writing in Ancient Judaism* (2020)

"Archie Wright provides a learned, yet also accessible, examination of the development of the figure of Satan in early Jewish and Christian traditions as well as plausible reasons for this evolution. The result is a fascinating study of a figure who turns out to be remarkably versatile. Biblical scholars and students alike will enjoy reading this fine book."

—Cecilia Wassen, Uppsala University, Sweden

"How does Satan's presence reconcile with God's absolute sovereignty and human responsibility? Different groups, including the nascent Christian movement, clashed and separated on this issue from Second Temple Judaism. Wright's analysis is a fascinating look at the eternal human quest for an answer to the 'problem of evil.'"

—Gabriele Boccaccini, professor of Second Temple Judaism and Christian Origins, University of Michigan; founding director of the Enoch Seminar; and author of *Paul's Three Paths to Salvation* (2020)

Satan
and the
Problem of Evil

SATAN
and the Problem of Evil

FROM THE BIBLE TO THE
EARLY CHURCH FATHERS

Archie T. Wright

Foreword by
Loren T. Stuckenbruck

FORTRESS PRESS
MINNEAPOLIS

SATAN AND THE PROBLEM OF EVIL
From the Bible to the Early Church Fathers

Copyright © 2022 Fortress Press, an imprint of 1517 Media. All rights reserved. Except for brief quotations in critical articles or reviews, no part of this book may be reproduced in any manner without prior written permission from the publisher. Email copyright@1517.media or write Permissions, Fortress Press, PO Box 1209, Minneapolis, MN 55440-1209.

Unless otherwise noted, Scripture quotations are from the New Revised Standard Version of the Bible, copyright © 1989 by the Division of Christian Education of the National Council of the Churches of Christ in the USA and used by permission. All rights reserved.

Cover image: iStock/duncan1890, Token of Michel Fexandat, Printer of Paris, 1552
Cover design: Kris Miller

Print ISBN: 978-1-5064-3249-6
eBook ISBN: 978-1-5064-8465-5

This book is dedicated to those working to confront the darkness of the human-inflicted evils of genocide and human trafficking.

Contents

Foreword	ix
Acknowledgments	xi
1: Origins of Evil	1
2: Satan and the Devil in the Hebrew Bible and Septuagint	11
3: The Satan Figure in the Dead Sea Scrolls	51
4: The Satan Figure in the Second Temple Period Pseudepigrapha and Other Jewish Writings	61
5: Satan and His Other Names?	89
6: Satan in the New Testament	147
7: Satan and the Devil in the Early Church	197
Conclusion	245
Bibliography	253
Subject Index	271
Scripture and Ancient Text Index	281

Foreword

In this book, Archie Wright takes readers on a tour of ancient sacred texts and cultures to address the origin and development of belief in a satanic figure. As Wright's discussion amply demonstrates, emerging discourse about "Satan" in antiquity was far from theoretical. Every step of the way, it was dictated by attempts to come to terms with the malevolent and, indeed, commonly shared vicissitudes of human experience. As such, the question is larger in scope than the Jewish, Christian, and related traditions that could be mentioned and explored here. What is it that drove speech about evil to assume a personifying dimension? Would it not have sufficed to think of evil in principled terms, and does belief in God require (a) subordinate or equivalent counterpart(s)? Or, when considering ancient worlds, do we rather formulate the question the other way around: What would have driven anyone to think of evil in principled rather than personifying terms? The boundaries between principle and person may have been fluid. Thus, at what point does evil, when regarded as a destructive force with a certain logic to "how it works," acquire a name?

While Wright does not ultimately answer questions put this way, his work covers an array of views in written sources whose authors conceive of powers adverse to human flourishing that operate between the poles of divine authorization, on the one hand, and independent activity, on the other. Readers of the treatment in this volume will find a general trend from the former (ancient Israel, Second Temple Jewish tradition, including New Testament writings) to the latter (writings from the patristic period, including "gnostic" sources), though diversity will have persisted. Reverberating throughout is the conviction that, whatever God's role may be, evil is here and cannot be wished away. Thus, and perhaps more importantly, Wright recovers for us a wide array of issues that shaped and conditioned explanations for why and, more importantly, *how* the world is not what it ideally should be. In biblical and related traditions, we therefore do not so much encounter a series of illusionary ideas as realistic attempts to grapple with real problems that vex and complicate human longing for a better world. With this in mind, discourse about figures presiding over evil would have served attempts to manage adversity, the experience of which not only evoked explanation but also inspired the search for mitigating strategies to curb evil's baffling effects.

While for many today the very idea of believing in or conceptualizing a "satan figure" constitutes unnecessary baggage from a bygone era, there remains an undeniable continuity with the past. Humanity, whether then or now, knows all too well the problems posed by natural disasters, suffering of all kinds, repressive impositions of social order, individual acts of wrongdoing, and activity that undermines human dignity. Readers will find many contemporary issues and efforts to come to terms with them among the expert readings Wright offers in the pages that follow.

Loren T. Stuckenbruck
Munich, Germany

Acknowledgments

Doctoral studies can be dark days, not least in the midlands of an English winter. But I was intrepid when I began my doctoral work at Durham University, so I chose a dark topic in any climate: the origin of evil spirits. When I subsequently took up a position at a conservative evangelical university, I was not done with the topic, which eventually would take on an even darker hue in what would become this book, *Satan and the Problem of Evil*. Part of my fascination with this subject, which would spur me to continue along this trajectory, was the way in which some of my colleagues and students were blaming or rebuking Satan for what seemed to me to be unadulterated human evil. So off I went on a second journey into darkness, this time to explore the intractable relationship between human evil and what might be deemed Satan-inspired evil. My study is, of course, historical, but I would be remiss not to mention the impetus a conservative, evangelical environment had upon the questions I became increasingly compelled to pose.

I owe a debt of gratitude to the many who encouraged me to follow the evidence regardless of what others may think or say, not least Loren Stuckenbruck, my dissertation supervisor, colleague, and cherished friend. Brad Embry, Ron Herms, and Jack Levison offered untold encouragement throughout this ten-year project. They are dear friends, each of them. I especially want to thank Kaitlynn Merckling, who pushed me the last few months to finish the project.

I want to offer my gratitude to the United States Conference of Catholic Bishops for their generous Confraternity of Christian Doctrine grant that allowed me the time and opportunity to cut back on my adjunct teaching to finally finish this book. Without this funding, I can imagine I would still be writing the volume now, in the fall of 2021.

Neil Elliott, who at the time was with Fortress Press, took on this project and offered keen encouragement along the way. He claimed it is an important volume, and I hope to prove him right. Fortress Press, in particular Ryan Hemmer, has been extremely professional throughout the production of this book.

There is also the untold number of colleagues and friends in the academy whose sustained encouragement never waned, even if my enthusiasm for the topic did. I am grateful to them too.

Finally, a word to my readers. I hope, once you have read this volume, that you will reckon with darkness, take it seriously—though a book is hardly necessary to make the case that evil is rife in our world—and attempt to make life better for those around us and to be that shining light upon the hill.

Archie T. Wright
Norfolk, Virginia
2021

Chapter 1

Origins of Evil

Introduction

The "Problem of Evil" has been an issue plaguing humanity since the earliest days of its existence on the earth. Individuals, peoples, and nations of various religions and cultures have asked the question, "Why does evil exist in our world?" Theists might have asked (and still do), Why does God (or the gods) allow evil to exist? Judeo-Christians may wonder if the so-called first couple, Adam and Eve, were responsible for its beginnings, or was (or is) there some malevolent force in the world that is responsible for it? Religions and civilizations have offered many explanations through the millennia, but none of the accounts they have offered provide any consolation to suffering humanity in God's creation.

In the twenty-first century, some form of what we call evil has manifested itself among various radical religious groups—Christian, Jewish, Islamic, and others. However, these types of groups have been operating for centuries: the Sicarii, Christian Crusaders, Guy Fawkes, the Iron Guard in 1930s Romania, the Nazis led by Hitler, the Stalinist regime, the Red Brigade, the Shining Path, the Ku Klux Klan, the Islamic State, the Taliban, and al Qaeda; the list is endless. One might then ask, "Is there some evil force behind those who take part in these groups, or is it simply the free will of the members driven by an ideology?" Others also blame natural disasters on this evil force (or, at times, God), and there are many other scenarios in which an evil force is blamed for suffering. Stories in the newspapers or online portray too many examples of evil being perpetrated by these groups, who, knowingly or unknowingly, are playing an active part or tool in the manifestation of evil and the suffering of humanity or the environment.

Among the three "theistic" religions—Judaism, Christianity, and Islam—the manifestation of the problem of evil is often articulated in relation to the expression theodicy. The word comes from the Greek *theos* ("god") and *dikē* ("justice"), meaning "just God," and, as mentioned, relates to how one explains the goodness of the Judeo-Christian God and his sovereignty coexisting alongside the presence of evil. The term was coined by Gottfried Leibniz (1646–1716) in his work to demonstrate that the evil in the world does not contradict that God is good.[1] The concept of theodicy attempts to deal with how bad things happen to good people.[2]

Why must people suffer? It has been recognized throughout history, in every culture and religion, that the human condition is defined by suffering. It is a condition that all of humanity confronts and accepts each day. Its presence and purpose are and have been beyond our comprehension throughout history because suffering appears to often strike the people who have done the least to merit it.

The philosophical view of the problem of evil offers various responses as to why evil exists in the world; three merit recognition. The first response suggests that God allows evil in the world because evil allows opportunity for virtue to flourish. This solution might argue that the Nazi death camps existed so that a heroic figure such as Anne Frank could emerge.[3] The second response endeavors to explain why God might be justified in permitting evil while at the same time suggests this is no reason to deny the existence of God or some higher power. The third response is that the problem of evil and suffering is a good reason that there is no theistic God; thus, it is all up to individuals to make the right choices. Amid the ongoing attempts to answer the question of the problem of evil, some argue it is a result of free will in which humanity functions.[4] But if it is a result of free will, why would one choose to do evil rather than do good or at least be neutral about things? Is there something in the world that influences people to do evil? A solution to this question, offered by the majority of those who hold some form of a theistic worldview, is the existence of a character who has been accused of being the first creature to choose his/its free will to oppose the will of God; this being has been identified, rightly or wrongly, as the satan figure or devil who is deemed to be a malevolent, autonomous or semiautonomous, anti-God figure.

The question that always arises concerning theodicy is, If God is good, omniscient, and omnipotent, why is there evil in the world? We are told in the Jewish Scriptures that God, at times, appeared to be the cause of evil—he hardened Pharaoh's heart and then killed him and his army, he became angry at King David for taking a census and killed a number of the Israelites, and he caused the primordial Flood, which killed all but a handful of people on the earth, just to name a few of the incidents. However, the evolving religion of Israel in the postexilic period began to separate God (YHWH) from evil and the responsibility for evil's origins. During this period, we see the

---

1. See Gottfried Leibniz, *Theodicy: Essays on the Goodness of God, the Freedom of Man, and the Origin of Evil*, trans. E. M. Huggard (London: Routledge & Kegan Paul, 1951).
2. See Harold S. Kushner, *When Bad Things Happen to Good People* (New York: Schocken Books, 1981); Steven Weinberg, *Dreams of a Final Theory* (New York: Pantheon Books, 1992).
3. See N. T. Wright, *Evil and the Justice of God* (Downers Grove, IL: InterVarsity, 2006), 28.
4. See Alvin Plantinga, *God, Freedom, and Evil* (Grand Rapids, MI: Eerdmans, 1977).

emergence of the satan figure, who became a prominent character as the perpetrator of evil. However, the figure performs this function while operating under the authority of God (see, e.g., Job 1–2).

Some in Christianity argue that the satan figure is autonomous and acts independently of God's will, but if that is the case, then it becomes difficult to argue that God is all-powerful. If the satan figure is acting under the authority of God, then the question remains, Why is there evil in the world? If God is perfectly good, then evil should be contrary to his nature, not, as some might argue, connected to it (see Isa 45:7). As a result, individuals may arrive at several conclusions: (1) God is not perfectly good, (2) God is not all-powerful, (3) God is not all-knowing, or (4) God does not exist. An analysis of these responses goes beyond the scope of this volume, but as one can see, these are difficult issues to address, particularly for those with an (Evangelical) Christian, or even a general Judeo-Christian, worldview. However, an examination of the history and understanding of the satan figure may assist in guiding a future discussion of these larger issues.

So where does this satan figure fit into this big picture of good versus evil? To determine satan's role in God's plan, one must ask, Who or what exactly is this being (or, possibly, *beings*)? What are the origins of this creature? Is he/it part of an ancient myth or a compilation of mythical traditions? Or, as some have suggested through the ages, is he/it a very real being who is determined to stop the goodness and love of God from being perpetrated in creation, especially among humanity? In addition, one must ask, what is the literary or even scientific evidence for the reality of this being, what does the Bible say about him/it, what do texts from other ancient cultures offer concerning the emergence of such a character, and what do Jewish and Christian extrabiblical texts have to say in relation to the satan figure?

Influential Cultures

As mentioned, other cultures and religions likely influenced various ideas within the Israelite religion, and the satan character would have been no exception. Scholars have argued that the religious ideas of Egypt, Canaan, Mesopotamia, Persia, and Greece played some role in the emerging satan tradition found in the Israelite religion and later Christian tradition.[5]

---

5. Jeffery Burton Russell, *The Devil: Perceptions of Evil from Antiquity to Primitive Christianity* (Ithaca, NY: Cornell University Press, 1987). For example, the Babylonian creation myth Enuma Elish depicts the struggle of a new, younger god, Marduk, with the older primordial gods, Apsu and Tiamat, who were often understood as "watery chaos." Once he defeated the older gods, Marduk was appointed king of the gods. Later he became responsible for creating the world. During the struggle, Tiamat took Kingu as her partner and gave birth to monster serpents and dragons—an impressive evil force, according to the myth. See L. W. King, *Enuma Elish: The Epic of Creation* (Whitefish, MT: Kessinger, 2010). Cf. Canaanite Ba'al myth. See, for example, Stephen C. Russell, *Mighty Baal Essays in Honor of Mark S. Smith* (Leiden: Brill, 2020).

In the Israelite exilic and postexilic periods, we see sectarian divisions developing among the various groups in (what would become known as) Judaism(s), and at the same time, one can observe the emergence of apocalypticism among the diverse Jewish worldviews and the literature created by these groups. In what follows, we will examine the problem of evil and the "evil" figures that played a major role in perpetuating this malevolent problem within the various cultures.

Persia

This issue of the problem of evil (and the *satan* figure), in relation to Judeo-Christian traditions, most likely originated during the Babylonian exile, when the Israelites came in contact with the Zoroastrian religion. Some suggest that the Israelites had considerable interaction with the religions of these cultures.[6] In Zoroastrian texts, possibly dated to the Babylonian/Persian era (although extant manuscripts are dated from the ninth to tenth century CE), one discovers the problem of evil was not unbeknownst to the authors of the literary works that emerged from these nations.

In 539 BCE, Cyrus, king of Persia (a Zoroastrian), conquered Babylon. As a result, Zoroastrianism began to infiltrate Babylonian culture, and as participants in that culture, the Israelites likely came in contact with the cosmology and theology of the Zoroastrians and were to some degree impacted by it. It should be noted that this exchange of ideas was likely not unilateral. The (perhaps best described as henotheistic) Zoroastrian religion has at the head of its pantheon the "Wise" or "Good" Lord, Ahura Mazda. From Ahura Mazda, a duality of two spirits emerges, Spenta Mainyu (the Holy or Bountiful Spirit) and Angra Mainyu (the Destructive or Opposing Spirit). The two are often identified as good and evil spirits, but more precisely, they are two notions that represent the opposites of life; thus, a strong notion of dualism exists within Zoroastrianism.

In this dualistic worldview, human beings have the free will to choose between the two forces or paths. Spenta Mainyu, the Bountiful Spirit, upholds the principle of righteousness (*asah*) that guides the cosmos. Operating under Spenta Mainyu are the Amesh Spentas, or the "Holy Immortal Ones" (angelic or archangel-like figures). Each is said to represent some characteristic of Ahura Mazda, and they are the custodians of nature. Angra Mainyu, the Opposing Spirit, attempts to disobey the principle of *asah* and, at the same time, endeavors to influence

---

6. See, for example, Erhard Gerstenberger, *Israel in the Persian Period: The Fifth and Fourth Centuries B.C.E.*, trans. Siegfried S. Schatzmann (Atlanta: SBL, 2014); Susan Niditch, *The Responsive Self: Personal Religion in the Biblical Literature of the Neo-Babylonian and Persian Periods* (New Haven, CT: Yale University Press, 2015).

humanity to do the same. Humans then have a choice between the two paths set out before them, good and evil. Within Zoroastrianism, Angra Mainyu is identified as the adversary of Ahura Mazda and is the spirit or a (minor) god of destruction, death, and darkness. One might argue that within the characteristics and actions of Angra Mainyu, one can recognize some of the traits and the role of the satan figure that emerged in the Christian tradition.[7]

Mesopotamia

The religious tales of these ancient Near Eastern cultures included the development of supernatural evil beings and adversaries of the gods. One of the major texts discovered among these tales is the Mesopotamian Epic of Gilgamesh, written in Akkadian, the ancient language of Babylon.[8] The epic tells the story of the protagonist Gilgamesh, who is the king of Uruk. He has a traveling companion named Enkidu, with whom he traverses the landscape encountering monsters, the cave of the sun, goddesses, men who appear as scorpions, and an assortment of unchaste women. The epic offers some of the same early traditions that we find scattered throughout the Bible, including several motifs that may have impacted the development of a satan-type figure in the ancient world. In the story, Gilgamesh and Enkidu encounter a supernatural opponent that they confront in the Cedar Forest where the god Enlil goes to rest. Here, the monster Humbaba emerges to block the entryway into that paradisiacal place of refuge for Enlil (cf. Gen 3:23–24 and the cherub guarding paradise's gates).

Similar to the later Christian satan figure, Humbaba is the guardian of the dark places and is meant to terrify humans. Humbaba is associated with fire and death; however, it must be made clear that Humbaba is only a possible symbolic representation of the type of adversary that emerges in later Christianity, not necessarily the origin of that figure. The satan figure of postexilic Judaism did not necessarily possess these specific characteristics of Humbaba. Nevertheless, it is possible that some of the characteristics of this creature were adopted by authors in the development of the later satan figure or some other heavenly being.

A further possible source on a developing satan tradition may be found in the Epic of Gilgamesh's god Enki (Ea), who is a member of the divine court (cf. Job 1–2) and continually attempts to rebel to some degree (against Enlil?). He breaks ranks with his fellow court members and warns Utnapishtim of the coming of a flood event that will destroy the world (cf. 1 En 10.2, in which Sariel warns Noah of the coming Flood).

---

7. See Mary Boyce, *Zoroastrians: Their Religious Beliefs and Practices*, 2nd ed. (London: Routledge, 2001).
8. Morris Jastrow and Albert T. Clay, *An Old Babylonian Version of the Gilgamesh Epic: On the Basis of Recently Discovered Texts* (Cambridge: Cambridge University Press, 2015).

Canaan

The Ras Shamra manuscripts, discovered at the site of the ancient Canaanite city of Ugarit, offer a view into the religious world of the Canaanites.[9] Their gods included Ba'al (god of fertility) and Mot (god of the underworld; death personified),[10] among others, who are mentioned in the biblical text (e.g., Ba'al is referenced in Num 25:3; Judg 2:13; 1 Kgs 16:32; 22:53; Ps 106:28; Rom 11:4; and Mot in Hab 2:5; Job 18:13). However, the Canaanites did worship a supreme god, El, who is likely related to the Mesopotamian god Enlil and the Hebrew God Elohim.

The god Mot is the primary character who conceivably played a role in the later emergence and elaboration of a satan-type figure. He is the god of the underworld who represents death and infertility, and he resides in the city of "the Pit." Mot, like Enki in the Epic of Gilgamesh or Ahura Mazda in Zoroastrianism, is a bit of a rebel. It appears one of his primary tasks was to terrorize the earth and its inhabitants (cf. Job 1–2; 1 Pet 5:8). However, he apparently exceeds the boundaries of this task, and so Ba'al goes down to the underworld to correct the situation. A fight ensues, in which Ba'al is killed by Mot. Ba'al's sister, Anat, decides to take revenge for her brother and kills Mot. As a result, Ba'al is brought back from the dead, and he then restores fertility to the land. Surprisingly, Mot is also resurrected and the two gods begin another deadly battle that will last for eternity.

From the Canaanite accounts, three themes emerge that perhaps are echoed by the Christian view of the satan figure: (1) he is the god of the underworld; (2) he is identified as evil in his battle with Ba'al who, in his action to try to stop Mot from terrorizing the earth, is understood to be good; (3) Mot is categorized as a son of the god El (the satan figure is called a "son of God" [*bene haElohim*], in Job 1:6), and (4) Mot is understood as an adversary of good (a theme that has been assumed, rightly or wrongly, of the satan figure in the New Testament [NT]).

Another Ugaritic text that perhaps contributes to the development of the later satan figure is called the Lovely Gods.[11] During the god El's drinking party, *mrzḥ*, he encounters the creature Habayu, who is depicted in the text as "lord of horns and tail," a common image for the Christian satan figure. Unfortunately, Habayu is not found in any other Ugaritic text, so little is known about him or his role. Some have suggested that he is related to the god Resheph, a West Semitic god known for his destructive acts and associated with death and the underworld

---

9. Michael Coogan and Mark S. Smith, eds., *Stories from Ancient Canaan*, 2nd ed. (Louisville, KY: Westminster John Knox, 2012).
10. It may be possible to suggest a similar hierarchy to the Zoroastrian pantheon, in which the two spirits, Spenta Mainyu and Angra Mainyu, operate under the leadership of Ahura Mazda.
11. See Coogan and Smith, *Stories from Ancient Canaan*, 167–69.

(or possibly Humbaba in the Epic of Gilgamesh). Resheph has been portrayed as a creature with a tail, and its counterpart Nergal is described as "lord of horns."[12]

Egypt

The problem of evil in Egyptian culture takes on a slightly different perspective. Egyptian gods and goddesses were expressions of the god Aten, the one true god. All things originated from Aten, including both good and evil. However, it was clear that evil forces caused disorder in the cosmos. Humans were also responsible for their decisions and actions and had to answer for them after death: following their time on earth, each individual would enter the underworld (*tuat*) to be judged by the god Anpu. Persons considered to be evil were tortured and burned or devoured by demons. *Tuat* becomes an ethereal place of the dead (cf. Sheol in the Hebrew Bible).

The Egyptians also had a god who was considered wicked. Set was an immortal being branded as the god of blazing heat and usually portrayed as being red in color. Set is known to have battled with his brother Osiris and his nephew Horus in a struggle of good versus evil. In the early days of the Egyptian dynasties, the god Set and his nephew Horus were worshipped together, each representing one aspect of the deity. This may have a parallel within the biblical text (cf. the Canaanite texts from Ras Shamra) in which God is known to have created both good and evil (Isa 45:7), but, in later Christianity, evil became personified in the satan figure.

Greece

The deities of Greek mythology possess both good and evil traits, which, like in Egyptian mythology, originated from a one true god. This dualistic nature of the gods and goddesses can be seen in divine beings such as Pan, Hermes, and Hades, which, as some argue, influenced the emerging satan figure.[13] Hades is the god of the underworld in Greek mythology, and he may perhaps correspond to the Canaanite god Mot. As the god of the underworld, Hades (also known as Pluton) is the giver of all the blessings that come from the earth: he is the possessor and giver of all the metals, including gold and silver, and he is a god of the earth's fertility. Hades also causes infertility, he can become invisible by a special headdress, and he dwells in the place of torment for the wicked souls of the dead, where we also find demonic figures (*erinnyes*). However, Hades knew little of the events taking place in the human realm or on Olympus. In later times, the name Hades was transferred to his kingdom so that it became a name for the underworld itself.

---

12. See Coogan and Smith, 169.
13. See T. J. Wray and Gregory Mobley, *The Birth of Satan: Tracing the Devil's Biblical Roots* (New York: Palgrave Macmillan, 2005).

Substantial Shaping of the Satan Figure?

As noted in the discussion above, some points of contact, although no direct parallels, in the literature and imagery suggest that the cultures of the ancient Near East (ANE) may have played a role in the development of the satan figure in later Jewish and Christian traditions. It seems possible, if not probable, that some of these ideas were known to later Jewish and Christian authors and conceivably adopted in some form. Many of the figures mentioned struck fear into the hearts of humanity because they were in conflict or battled with one or more of their cultures' "good" gods. In addition, some of the functions or activities of these "evil" figures seem to have been developed further by the Jewish and Christian traditions of the satan figure. More importantly, we see connections between these gods, beings, or creatures and the problem of evil. The stories in which we find these figures attempt to answer such questions as, Why is death part of the human existence? Why do people suffer? and Who or what is responsible for this suffering? As such, it seems that these figures helped the people of those cultures contend with the ideas of suffering, evil, and sin. Is it possible that this was also a reason for the emergence satan figures in Second Temple Period (2TP) Judaism?

What's Ahead?

We must note that possible influences of other ANE cultures can be observed in the representation of the satan figure in the Hebrew Bible (HB). However, as we will discuss below, one facet of the Persian religion and its influence appears to have had a greater effect than others on the development of the satan tradition in Judaism and Christianity (although not precisely to the same extent): Zoroastrian dualism. This dualism, or at least the version of it adapted by the Jewish and Christian worldviews, seems to have played a role in the early stages of separating YHWH from the responsibility for evil in the world.

A likely result of this separation was the emergence of a heavenly being, perhaps even a minor deity, that appeared to be responsible to some extent for evil and suffering (although not necessarily by its own authority). As in other cultures, this being, which we call satan, or hasatan, emerged in the ancient world as a divine being who undertakes certain actions for God (the gods) in an effort to "test" members of the human community, or, as we will see, bring affliction and destruction upon individuals.

Considering this figure's role in the "problem of evil," we began this study with a brief review of the possible influences of the cultures of the ANE. In what follows, we will explore the development of the satan/hasatan tradition(s) in light of the question of the problem of evil. We will begin with a study of the use of the term(s) in the HB and its various translations in the Greek Septuagint (LXX), Jewish literature from the 2TP and the late first and early second centuries CE, and the Greek NT. The study will conclude with an examination of the writings of early church theologians beginning in the late first through fourth century CE. This last period is particularly important, as it presents a shift in the understanding of this heavenly figure. As I will argue, his/its treatment is significantly different in these later texts than it is in the Jewish Scriptures, the extrabiblical Jewish literature (e.g., Jubilees, 1 Enoch, etc.), and even the NT.

Chapter 2

Satan and the Devil in the Hebrew Bible and Septuagint

Introduction

Rivkah Schärf Kluger contends, "In the world of the Old Testament, names are not 'sound and fume,' but they have magic power; they are . . . substantial and therefore, in effect, identical with the nature of their bearers."[1] This looks to be the case with the Hebrew terms השטן/שטן (satan/hasatan). Peggy Day examines the etymology, meaning, and use of the noun *satan* in the HB/LXX, focusing on Numbers 22:22–35; Job 1–2; Zechariah 3:1–7; and 1 Chronicles 21:1–22:1. She concludes that there "is not one celestial satan in the Hebrew Bible, but rather the potential for many."[2] Others (scholars and laypeople alike) have argued that its use in the HB is that of a proper name, connecting it to the later Christian Satan figure,[3] a semiautonomous evil being who apparently opposes everything that is the will of God.[4] However, as will be argued below, that does not appear to be the case; the latter portrayal differs from that found in the HB or LXX.[5]

In addition to the well-rehearsed passages, we will examine three other texts in which early church interpreters identified the "satan" figure, even though the term, or any of its cognates, does not appear in the episodes in question. These texts include Genesis 3:1–15, the story of the serpent in the Garden; Isaiah 14:12–17, in which early Church Fathers identify the "Lucifer"

---

1. Rivkah Schärf Kluger, *Satan in the Old Testament*, trans. Hildegard Nagel (Evanston, IL: Northwestern University Press, 1967), 25.
2. Peggy L. Day, *An Adversary in Heaven: Satan in the Hebrew Bible* (Atlanta: Scholars Press, 1988), 15.
3. See, for example, Kurt Galling, *Die Bücher der Chronik, Ezra, Nehemia* (Göttingen, Germany: Vandenhoeck & Ruprecht, 1954), 61; Jacob M. Myers, *1 Chronicles*, ABC 12 (Garden City, NY: Doubleday, 1965), 145; H. G. M. Williamson, *1 and 2 Chronicles* (Grand Rapids, MI: Eerdmans, 1982), 143.
4. See D. Kinet, "The Ambiguity of the Concepts of God and Satan in the Book of Job," in *Job and the Silence of God*, ed. C. Duquoc and C. Floristán (Edinburgh: T&T Clark, 1984), 30–35. Kinet argues, "Satan is the real instigator . . . [who] . . . acts more or less as an independent agent, thereby exonerating God from sole responsibility" (31).
5. See Sara Japhet, *The Ideology of the Book of Chronicles and Its Place in Biblical Thought* (Frankfurt: Peter Lang, 1989). Japhet argues that *satan* was not being used as a proper noun in 1 Chr 21:1. Cf. Ryan Stokes, "The Devil Made David Do It . . . or Did He? The Nature, Identity, and Literary Origins of the Satan in 1 Chronicles 21:1," *JBL* 128, no. 1 (2009): 91–106, here, 99–100.

figure as the "satan" in what they describe as the story of "the satan's fall from heaven"; and finally, Ezekiel 28:11–19, which, again, early church theologians understood as describing the fall of "the satan" figure.

Prior to a close examination of these passages, we will determine the various definitions and uses of the term *the satan* in the HB and the corresponding Greek translations in the LXX.

The Term *Satan*

It is suggested that the term originates from the Hebrew root שטן, "to persecute, oppose, or be hostile toward," or more specifically, "to accuse."[6] שטן or a cognate form appears twenty-eight times in the Hebrew Bible. It first is used in Genesis 26:21, in the story of Isaac reclaiming the wells of his father, Abraham, in the Valley of Gerar, ruled by Abimelech, king of the Philistines. The Philistines had filled in these wells, and when discovered, Isaac's servants redug them and found the spring water. However, the herders of Gerar fought with Isaac's men, claiming the water was theirs. Because of the opposition, Isaac called the well "Sitnah" (שטנה; the first well he called Esek [עשק], "contend with") from the root שטן. Though here used as a proper noun, it likely suggests "accusation or opposition" in the context of the passage.

The root is used in a similar way, "to act as an adversary," in 1 Samuel 29:4, which identifies David as a possible "adversary" of the Philistines; here, they are leery of David fighting alongside them against Israel. They fear that David may be "an adversary" to them (ולא יהיה לנו לשטן) if he is allowed to enter the battle. The commanders of the Philistine armies question the presence of the Hebrews; here it is used in a disparaging sense for the Israelites, David and his men, as foreigners.[7]

Similarly, in 2 Samuel 19:23 (Masoretic Text; hereafter, MT), David calls the sons of Tseruyah his adversaries ("for you will be to me this day an adversary" [כי תהיו לי היום לשטן]) when they ask for the death of Shimei, who has accused David of killing Saul. In particular, Abishai is labeled a "satan" (שטן)—"an adversary"—for calling for the death of Shimei. Day argues that in this case, *satan* should be understood as a "legal accuser."[8] Abishai subsequently assumes the role of royal court accuser although he is only identified as a commander of David's armies; thus the term should be considered a function rather than an office in the court. It should also

---

6. Francis Brown, S. R. Driver, and Charles A. Briggs, *The Brown, Driver, Briggs Hebrew and English Lexicon* (1906; repr., Peabody, MA: Hendrickson, 2005), 966.
7. Cf. 1 Sam 4:6, 9 (used to mean "camp of the Hebrews"); 13:9; 14:11 (used by the Philistines to identify the Israelites); 13:3 (used by Saul to identify the Israelites); see also 14:21 (used by the author to identify the Israelites).
8. Day, *Adversary*, 25. See also her further argument in "Abishai the Satan in 2 Sam 19:17–24," *CBQ* 49 (1987): 543–47.

be understood that the term *satan* here, based on the narrative in 2 Samuel 16:5–7, has no slanderous connotations, as Abishai is correct in his accusation against Shimei.

In 1 Kings 5:16–20, at the end of military campaigns of Israel, we are told that Solomon has no "satans" (i.e., military foes) and is able to live in peace and build the temple. In 5:18, God grants rest to Solomon and removes the adversary (MT, שטן; LXX, ἐπίβουλος, "plotter") from the land. This period of peace ends for Solomon in 1 Kings 11, in which YHWH raises up military "satans" against him. The two occasions of a human adversary occur in 1 Kings 11:14–25. The first is Hadad the Edomite, in verse 14: "The Lord raised up a satan (שטן; LXX, σαταν) against Solomon, Hadad the Edomite, the king's offspring who was in Edom." Hadad had fled Edom to Egypt at the time in which David slew every male in Edom. He was granted favor by Pharaoh until the time that David died, along with Joab, the commander of David's army. The second occasion is in verse 23 (MT), in which God raises up Rezon, son of Eliada, king of Damascus.[9] In verse 25 (MT), we are told he is an adversary (שטן) to Israel all the days of Solomon.[10]

שטן occurs in verb form in the book of Psalms five times: Psalms 38:21 (MT, ישטנוני, *yestenuni*; LXX [37:21], ἐνδιέβαλλόν, "to falsely accuse"); 71:13 (ישטני, *sotenay*; LXX [70:13], ἐνδιαβάλλοντες, "ones falsely accusing"); and 109:4–6 (ישטנוני and שטן; LXX [108:4–6], ἐνδιέβαλλόν, διάβολος). In these instances, cognates of *satan* appear as personal foes or accusers of the speakers in the biblical text. In Psalm 109:1–6, the psalmist complains to YHWH of being attacked by slanderous enemies who are identified in 109:4 as "the ones accusing me" (ישטנוני; LXX [108:4], ἐνδιέβαλλόν). Leslie Allen suggests that the setting for the psalm should be "reconstructed as a religious court where the psalmist claimed his innocence before priestly judges as representatives of Yahweh."[11] In verse 6, the author of the psalm asks the Lord to set an accuser (*satan*; διάβολος in LXX 108:6[12]) against his enemy (note the shift to singular) that would stand at the right hand of his enemy to accuse him.[13] Finally, Psalm 109:20 and 29 use the terms שוטני/שטני (*sotenai*; LXX [108:20, 29], ἐνδιαβαλλόντων με, ἐνδιαβάλλοντές με), "the

---

9. 1 Kgs 11:23: "God raised up an adversary (שטן; no LXX) to him [Solomon], Rezon, son of Elyada, who fled from his lord Hadadezer, the king of Tsovah."
10. LXX does not include the passage concerning Rezon found in verses 23–24 in MT.
11. Leslie C. Allen, *Psalms 101–150*, WBC 21 (Waco, TX: Word Books, 1983), 75. Psalm 109 is quoted in Acts 1:20, in which it is used to echo the suffering experience of Christ.
12. We find a reference in LXX Esth 7:4 that translates the Hebrew term הצר (adversary) as ὁ διαβόλον. The context may be describing an individual or possibly a troublesome situation, while the Ps 109 reference is describing an accuser who is identified as an "evil one" or "wicked one" in the initial phrase of verse 6. In both occurrences, the Greek term used in the LXX is διαβόλον.
13. We find similar legal language and setting in the Zech 3:1–7 passage in which the "satan" stands at the right hand of Joshua to accuse him. N. H. Tur-Sinai suggests that the satan figure in Job may simply be a human "spy" of God who was invited to come to the heavenly court to give his report. See N. H. Tur-Sinai, *The Book of Job: A New Commentary* (Jerusalem: Kiryat Sefer, 1981), 45.

ones opposing me" / "the ones falsely accusing me." The psalmist is asking the Lord to act on his behalf to protect the Lord's name from slander and to show his love is steadfast and good.

A further instance of שטן occurs as an infinitive verb in Numbers 22:22, in the story of Balaam's ass, describing the actions of the שטן. Because of Balaam's disobedience, God sends a שטן (an "adversary") to stand in his way as he journeys toward Moab. The "satan" in this case is מלאך יהוה (*malach Yahweh*), the/an "angel/messenger of YHWH." This heavenly figure is "to act as an adversary toward Balaam" on his journey to Moab; thus, in this case, a שטן can be understood as a messenger of God who has been sent to hinder or obstruct an individual's plans.

The Term *Satam*

A secondary form of the term שטן is the root שטם, found five times in the HB, which gives the sense of "to persecute, to pursue, to entrap, or to hate."[14] The term וישטם (LXX, ἐνεκότει, "to be indignant") first appears in Genesis 27:41, where it is used to describe the animosity between Esau and Jacob. Esau "bore a grudge" (hated) Jacob because his father's blessing was passed to the younger son due to Jacob's trickery. Genesis 49:23 describes the hatred of Joseph by his brothers with the form וישטמהו, "to bear a grudge" (ἐνεῖχον, "to bear a grudge against"), and a third occurrence is Genesis 50:15, in which the form is ישטמנו, "to bear a grudge" (μνησικακήσῃ, "to bear malice"); here Joseph's brothers fear that he will remember their deeds following the death of their father. A further occurrence appears in Psalm 55:4 (MT) in the form ישטמוני (πλεμοῦντές, "ones waging war"); here the author fears his enemies hate him or bear a grudge against him. The final occurrence is found in Job 16:9—ישטמני—"he holds a grudge" or "he hated me."[15]

So as one compares the MT and LXX, it appears there is no suggestion of a clear connection to the figure of satan or *diabolos* in the use of this Hebrew root שטם. However, the basic meaning can be related in Hosea 9:8, with the noun משטמה, *mastema* (μανίαν, "insanity"), "one who is hostile toward (hates) someone or something." The term *Mastema* will, at times, be identified as personified "evil" and gain prominence in the book of Jubilees in the second century BCE, and this figure has a connection to the evil spirits of the Watcher tradition.

---

14. Kluger, *Satan*, 27.
15. Interestingly, we find here the term צרי, "adversary," in the same line as ישטמני—which produces the combination "my adversary holds a grudge against me."

Other Hebrew Root Words

Some scholars have argued that the root of the term *satan* may be one of several second or third weak consonant Semitic verbs.[16] A form of the verb שׁוש (שׁושׁם), "to roam about looking," is used in Job 1:7 (LXX, περιελθών, "roaming about"—cf. 1 Pet 5:8, the *diabolos* "goes about," περιπατεῖ); 2 Chronicles 16:9 (מְשׁוֹטְטוֹת, *meshottot*; LXX, ἐπιβλέπουσιν, "to look on with care"); and Zechariah 4:10 (מְשׁוֹטְטִים, *meshottim*; LXX, ἐπιβλέποντες, "looking upon with care"). N. H. Tur-Sinai argues that this may be the root from which *satan* is derived. If this is the case, then we see no clearly negative connotation with the term's use in the Hebrew nor with the Greek. If Tur-Sinai is correct, this may suggest the satan figure should not necessarily be understood as one in opposition to God.

We find in Zechariah 4:10 the interpretation of part of Zechariah's vision, which reads, "These seven are the eyes of the Lord; they are going to and fro (מְשׁוֹטְטִים) upon all the earth."[17] Tur-Sinai argues these seven eyes are like the individuals described in the fifth-century BCE Greek historian Herodotus's *Histories* 1.114 as the "eyes and ears of the king,"[18] individuals recognized as inspectors or overseers in the Achaemenid Empire.[19] Tur-Sinai suggests this definition places the "satan" figure in the HB in the service of God as his "eyes and ears" upon the earth. Thus, this roving character soon became known as an "adversary or accuser" (not of God) because he would make reports to God about the actions of individuals upon the earth. In addition, Tur-Sinai argues that if the "satan" did not find fault with an individual, he would provoke them to commit an offence,[20] hence the stories in Job 1:6–12 and 1 Chronicles 21:1 (the census of David). For Tur-Sinai, the description of the task of the satan in Job 1:7 and also in 1 Peter 5:8 suggests that the function of the satan figure is to go about the earth looking for someone to entrap.

Day suggests that Tur-Sinai's explanation that "satan" returned to Hebrew from a related dialect rather than retaining the original "on" ending—*shaton*—is vague, and his work lacks

---

16. See Marvin H. Pope, *Job: A New Translation with Introduction and Commentary*, ABC 15 (New Haven, CT: Yale University Press, 1973), 10–11. Possible roots include שׁוש, שׁיט; the final *nun* (*n*) was considered a suffix. N. H. Tur-Sinai argues that the original term would have been pronounced *shaton* rather than *satan*, a *shin* (שׁ) not a *sin* (שׂ). He defines *shaton* as "the one who goes to and fro"; see Tur-Sinai, *Job*, 41–44. Cf. W. W. How and Joseph Wells, *A Commentary on Herodotus* (Oxford: Clarendon, 1912).
17. LXX avoids the use of the "roaming about" verb and instead translates it as ἐπιβλέποντες, "to look on with care."
18. See A. D. Godley, trans., *Herodotus, with an English Translation* (Cambridge, MA: Harvard University Press, 1920).
19. H. Zimmern, *Die Keilinschriften und das Alte Testament* (Berlin: Reuther und Reichard, 1902), 2:461–63. Zimmern proposes the "satans" from Job and Zechariah are related to the Mesopotamian figure of *bel dababi*.
20. Tur-Sinai, *Job*, 43.

sufficient support for this proposal.[21] In addition, Day contends there is no substantiation for Tur-Sinai's suggestion that there would have been no differentiation between *shin* and *sin* in biblical Hebrew; if this were the case, there would have been no need for the distinction in the later Masoretic system.

Day does suggest that Tur-Sinai's argument may help explain the use of the verb שׂוט in Job 1–2; however, she contends the changes he notes, from *shaton* to *satan*, are likely accounted for through the influence of "folk etymological tradition."[22] From this tradition, we know that the authors of the HB attempted to explain the names of individuals or places with the use of words that were clearly understood. Therefore, Day, among others, argues the root is שׂטן, a simple QAL form meaning "to be an adversary." Day and others may be correct in identifying the root of the term, but this does not eliminate the tradition of the "overseers in the Achaemenid Empire" having some influence over the satan figure in the HB and later in 1 Peter.

Foreign Origins of the Term *Satan*

Ludwig Diestel argued that the satan figure was adopted from the Egyptian tradition's god Seth.[23] Through this comparison, we see how Egyptian dualism may have played a part in the development of dualism among the people of Israel following the Exodus. The god Osiris is understood as the guardian deity of Egypt, while Seth is the god of foreign nations. Kluger argues that at some point, Seth moved his worship center to Palestine and Syria.[24] Diestel identifies Seth/satan as the "fire of God," which may offer a connection to the "wrath of God" in 2 Samuel 24 / 1 Chronicles 21.[25] Interestingly, the god Seth has two animals closely related to him, the crocodile and the hippopotamus, which are themselves related to the two beasts that appear in Job: the Leviathan and Behemoth. Another biblical sea monster, Rahab, serves as a personification of Egypt in Isaiah 30:7; 51:9; and Psalms 97:4 and 89:10—the turbulent sea, which may reflect a connection to the other sea monsters found in Job, Leviathan and Behemoth. Diestel argues that the god Seth is identified in Plutarch as the bringer of disturbance and destruction,[26] which he contends are clear characteristics of the satan figure in the Hebrew Bible. In addition, he suggests that the name *satan* is undoubtedly connected to Seth: the middle weak verbs, שׂוט or

---

21. Day, *Adversary in Heaven*, 21–24.
22. See Day, 21–22. See also Kluger, *Satan*, 31.
23. See Kluger, *Satan*, 83–86; Ludwig Diestel, "Set-Typhon, Asahel und Satan: Ein Eeitrag zur Religionsgeshichte des Orients," *Zeitschrift für die historische Theologie* 30, no. 2 (1860): 158–217.
24. Kluger, *Satan*, 84.
25. Diestel, "Set-Typhon," 210.
26. Plutarch, *De iside et Osiride* 33.

שׂים, were adopted by the Israelites due to their similarity in sound to Seth. Kluger contends, "Nothing could be less likely, however, than just this, that satan, should, because of similarity of sound, be an arbitrarily selected covering name for Seth."[27] It should be asked, What is the purpose of the satan figure's connection to the name Seth in the HB? The satan that appears in Job is not tied to the two beasts in that book, nor does he arbitrarily bring disturbance and destruction; he only does this through the authority of God in Job.

While others argue for a Babylonian origin of the satan figure, he/it was likely incorporated into the Jewish worldview in the postexilic period in the book of Job. Kluger contends that the satan figure emerged from the "Poem of the Righteous Sufferer," also known as the "Babylonian Job."[28] The story tells of a king who is stricken with physical torment and claims, "All day the persecutor followed me, at night he granted me no respite whatsoever; through wrenching, my joints were torn apart; my limbs were shattered and rendered helpless."[29] However, Simon Landersdorfer contends that the author of this poem and the author of Job were familiar with a folk tale rather than Job having a literary dependence on the Babylonian poem.[30]

This "persecutor" in the Babylonian poem may be identified as the "sickness demon" who followed the king. Gustav Hölscher argues that based on this "parallel," one must conclude that the "Satan in Job is a demonic figure who is thought of as the originator of all evil, especially sickness."[31] However, as the satan figure is observed in Job, one can see that the figure is not simply a demon of illness. In fact, there is no hint of the Joban satan belonging to or functioning in the demonic realm; he is operating as one of the *bene ha'elohim*.

Following the discussion of the possible foreign terms that may offer some parallels to the satan terminology, we will now turn our attention to the uses of the terms in the biblical text. We will begin our discussion with an examination of Numbers 22, followed by 1 Chronicles 21, Zechariah 3, and finally Job 1–2. These texts will be followed by a further examination of Psalms 38:20; 71:13; 109:4; 109:20; 109:29; 1 Samuel 29; 2 Samuel 19; and 1 Kings 5, 11. Our final analysis will focus on the texts that interpreters have attempted to connect to the "satan" figure: Genesis 3:1–15; Isaiah 14:12–17; and Ezekiel 28:11–19.

---

27. Kluger, *Satan*, 85.
28. Kluger, 87–88.
29. See translation in Marcus Jastrow, "A Babylonian Parallel to the Book of Job," *JBL* 25 (1906): 135–91.
30. Simon Landersdorfer, "Eine babylonische Quelle für das Buch Job?," *Bibl. Studien* 16 (1911): 55–59. See also Samuel Terrien, *The Book of Job: Introduction and Exegesis* (Nashville: Abingdon, 1954), 3:881.
31. Gustav Hölscher, *Geschichte der israelitisch-jüdischen Religion* (Leipzig: Alfred Töpelmann, 1922).

Satan in the Biblical Text

Numbers 22

The first passage in this examination is Numbers 22, which provides an interesting possibility of relating the satan figure to an/the Angel of the Lord, perhaps, characterizing the satan's role as an officer of the heavenly court. The angel comes out as "an adversary" (שטן) against Balaam to prevent him from going with the Moabites. Similar to what we find in 1 Chronicles 21 and 2 Samuel 24, in Numbers 22:22 (MT), the anger of the Lord begins the series of events because of the sin of the main character—Balaam. Because of the anger of the Lord, God sends a satan to inhibit Balaam—"to be a satan to him" (MT, לשטן לו; LXX, ἐνδιαβάλλειν—"to falsely accuse"). The adversary comes from the divine realm and appears in a different sphere than Balaam, one that only the donkey can see. In this context, *satan* is a functional concept and not a proper name. It could mean a task that is characteristic of the Angel of the Lord.

Interestingly, the Angel of the Lord acts as an impediment to a satan figure in Zechariah 3:1, where *hasatan* stands before Joshua *to be a satan* but is rebuked by YHWH (through the Angel of the Lord) for accusing Joshua of being unworthy of the priesthood. It appears the Angel of YHWH may function as an emissary of the Lord and often functions as YHWH, or at least speaks as/for YHWH. The angel appears to speak as God in the story of Hagar in Genesis 16:10 ("I will greatly multiply your offspring"), and in Genesis 31:13, he identifies himself as the God of Bethel when speaking to Jacob.[32]

Kluger argues that the Angel of YHWH in Numbers 22 reveals a dark aspect of God (in fact, she argues it is God himself), one that is a threat to human life.[33] This dark aspect of YHWH may be reinforced here in this passage. Balaam does not appear to have done anything wrong; in fact, God grants him permission to go on the journey in verse 20: "If the men have come to call you, rise up, go with them; but only the word which I will speak to you, this you will do." Nevertheless, for some unspoken reason, verse 22 declares that the Lord is angry with Balaam for going. One finds further confusion in verse 32, in which the Angel of the Lord declares he has come out as an opponent, or adversary (satan), "because the path *was precipitated* [forced upon him?] in front of [him]" (strangely, the LXX reads, "because the path *was not beautiful* [ἀστεία—'planned well'?] before [him]"). But in verse 35, rather than

---

32. Cf. Judg 2:1–3; 13:17–18; Gen 32:29. In Judg 6:22, Gideon fears he will die, for he has seen the Angel of YHWH face-to-face: might this suggest the Angel of the YHWH is in some way a part of the Godhead?
33. Kluger, *Satan*, 75–76. Kluger suggests that in the story, one sees the significance of human existence. Only in coming up against the divine will can a human know that they have their own will, thus gaining self-consciousness.

force Balaam to return to his home, the angel permits him to go on with the same warning that God gave Balaam in verse 20. It is difficult to sort out why the Angel of the Lord came out as a "satan" to Balaam, save to say he was trying to stop him from continuing down the physical path he was on.[34]

Interestingly, this adversary, the Angel of the Lord, who stands in the way of Balaam wielding a sword is present in 1 Chronicles 21:16 and 2 Samuel 24:16–17; there, the Angel of the Lord (or *an* Angel of the Lord) is sent against Israel wielding the sword to carry out God's plan of punishment. One should ask if in these two passages, the Angel of the Lord is fulfilling the office of the/a satan, as he did in Numbers 22. If so, the satan figure may be used by YHWH to fulfill multiple tasks: as a vehicle of divine judgment, as we have here, and as an opponent in the case of Numbers 22. Whether the figure be human or divine, the satan figure operates at the behest of God.[35]

One might argue that the satan figure in Numbers 22 has a limited function in relation to the "problem of evil" in the biblical world of the author, as will be the case in most occurrences in the HB. In this case, the adversary may be attempting to prevent evil from occurring in Balaam's life, though in the eyes of Balaam, the satan is acting as a hindrance to his mission and thus (what he believes to be) God's plan.

Zechariah 3

In Zechariah 3:1, the author describes the incident in which the high priest Joshua is standing before the Angel/Messenger of the Lord, and "the satan" (הׁשׂטן; LXX, ὁ διάβολος)[36] is there to accuse him. The reason for this "court scene" is somewhat hidden in the text but is suggested by the language used. First, the high priest Joshua is set to be charged by the accuser for being unworthy of the position of high priest, exemplified by the filthy garments he is wearing (Zech 3:3).[37] The language in verse 3:1 clearly reflects a legal setting with the use of the terms עמד לפני ("standing before") and עמד על ימנו לשטנו ("standing at his right-hand to accuse him").[38] This

---

34. Day suggests the confusion in the story between the two sections, verses 2–21 and 22–35, is a result of two different sources; see Day, *Adversary in Heaven*.
35. See Day, 32.
36. *Diabolos* (διάβολος) is one of the LXX and Greek NT terms for the Hebrew *satan*, which refers to an "accuser" or "adversary" in court. It is rarely discovered outside of the LXX and NT; Wis 2:23–24 identifies the serpent of Eden with the term *diabolos*, where it could be understood as an adversary. The autonomous nature of *diabolos* as an evil power is not found in the HB but is an apparent development from the 2TP or early Christian period. This shift may be due in part to the effort in Jewish/Christian theology to remove God from the presence or cause of evil in the midst of the covenant people.
37. Marvin Tate suggests this is due to the time spent in exile, which would have corrupted the purity of the priestly line. See Tate, "Satan in the Old Testament," *Review & Expositor* 89, no. 4 (Fall 1992): 461–74.
38. Cf. Ps 109:6–7.

language may suggest that the satan is acting as a heavenly prosecutor whose task is to bring charges against those considered unworthy or unfaithful.[39]

As the scene begins, even before the satan has an opportunity to speak,[40] he is rebuked by the Lord (through the Angel?): "YHWH said to *the satan* (הַשָּׂטָן; LXX, διάβολε, vocative), 'May YHWH rebuke you [jussive in context] hasatan, YHWH who has chosen Jerusalem! Is this not the firebrand pulled from the fire?'" (Zech 3:2). Joshua is redressed in fine linens, thus exemplifying his worthiness and representing the priestly side of the diarchy symbolized by the two olive trees in 4:3 (Zerubbabel representing the royal side of the pair). This willingness of YHWH to act so quickly to rebuke the satan suggests that the satan has no grounds upon which to accuse Joshua of being unworthy. The use of the definite article here indicates that "the satan" is likely not a proper name, but perhaps indicates a title or an office that the heavenly being holds in the court of YHWH.[41] However, Day contends that there is no textual support for an "office of accuser" in the Israelite religion; similarly, she argues, no extant evidence exists in the literature of Mesopotamia. However, the lack of an existing figure in previous ancient literature does not disqualify the use of "the satan" in the postexilic HB as an "accusing officer," particularly if, as suggested, the authors of various texts are implementing a plan to separate YHWH as the perpetrator of evil. Tate suggests that the article in this particular case indicates an "appointed satan."[42] If this is correct, one may suggest that there are multiple "satans" working under the auspices of God's sovereignty (as we later find in 1 Enoch 40:7 and 65:1, in which there are multiple "satans" functioning in the hierarchy of heaven), or perhaps some of the *bene ha'elohim* from Job 1–2 may fall into this category (these may be the others present in Zech 3:4).

The satan figure in Zechariah 3 may take on a significant role in the "problem of evil" in the postexilic period of 2TP Judaism. Due to the apparent need or at least desire to separate God from suffering and evil among the people of Israel, the authors may have begun to introduce a character to take up this responsibility, even if at the behest of God. As can be understood

---

39. Meyers suggests a second issue that may be at hand in the passage: the reconstruction of the Jerusalem temple, which God declares he has chosen. Although unlikely, this is something to which the satan may be opposed. Carol Meyers and Eric Meyers, *Haggai, Zechariah 1–8*, ABC 25B (Garden City, NY: Doubleday, 1987), 185.
40. It may be possible that the words of the satan have been purposely omitted by the author, although there is no evidence of this in the text.
41. A. Cohen and A. J. Rosenberg argue that *satan* is not a proper name but is the function of the messenger. See Cohen and Rosenberg, *The Twelve Prophets*, vol. 8 of *Soncino Books of the Bible* (Brooklyn, NY: Soncino, 1994), 279–80; see also Day, *Adversary in Heaven*, 41–42.
42. Tate, "Satan," 472n5; Meyers and Meyers have suggested that the role of the satan figure is that of "the Prosecuting Attorney"; see their *Haggai, Zechariah 1–8*, 183–85. See also Paul Joüon, *Grammaire de l'Hébreu biblique* (Rome: Pontifical Biblical Institute, 1923), 137. Joüon notes the articular satan may be understood as a "certain satan"—that is, any heavenly being may act as a satan at the command of YHWH. Thus, one may suggest that these are similar circumstances to those found in Numbers 22 and the Angel of YHWH.

from other postexilic Jewish texts, this figure continues to function only under the authority of God but seemingly can be blamed for the evils perpetrated upon individuals and the nation.

JOB 1–2

Job 1–2 are likely the most familiar passages that contain the term *hasatan* (LXX, ὁ διάβολος). However, before one approaches an understanding of this text and the satan figure in it, one must set aside any presuppositions of the later Christian figure of Satan. What is found here, with the use of the term *hasatan* (השטן), is the function of the heavenly adversary of humanity, in this case Job's adversary. As will be seen, this satan can only act with God's permission and only within the boundaries of God's command.[43] This episode then begs the question in relation to the problem of evil, Who caused Job's suffering? Was it the satan? Or was it YHWH? In the worldview of 2TP Judaism, are the "heavenly beings" extensions of or manifestations of YHWH's personality?[44]

The first mention of the satan is in 1:6,[45] in which he comes to the court of heaven to present himself before YHWH along with the בני האלהים (*bene ha'elohim*), who appear to be serving in the capacity of agents of YHWH.[46] One may advocate the idea that the *bene ha'elohim* are the Watchers, whose task it was to watch over the earth and guide all humanity in the growth of civilization.[47] They may also be the minor deities (אלים) who are part of the heavenly divine council;[48] quite conspicuously, the satan figure joins them in reporting to YHWH. The language

---

43. See David J. A. Clines, *Job 1–20*, WBC 17 (Nashville: Thomas Nelson, 1989), 20. A. B. Davidson has argued that the satan is "rigidly subordinated to heaven, and in all he does subserves its interests." See Davidson, *A Commentary, Grammatical and Exegetical, on the Book of Job, with Translation*, vol. 1 (London: Williams and Norgate, 1862) for a discussion of the satan's role in Job cited in Clines, *Job 1–20*.
44. See Meir Weiss, *The Story of Job's Beginning: Job 1–2: A Literary Analysis* (Jerusalem: Magnes, 1983), 46–47.
45. Hebrew in Job 1:6 reads, "ויבוא גם השטן בתוכם" (And came also the satan in the midst of them); the LXX of 1:6 reads, "καὶ ὁ διάβολος ἦλθεν μετ' αὐτῶν" (And the *diabolos* entered with them). John Gammie argues the Greek suggests, a bit more forcibly, that the satan is one of the *bene ha'elohim*; see Gammie, "The Angelology and Demonology in the Septuagint of the Book of Job," *Hebrew Union College Annual* 56 (1985): 1–19, here, 7. One must keep in mind that LXX use of ὁ διάβολος falls in line with *hasatan* in Hebrew—a human or heavenly adversary.
46. The *satan* appears to be a member "from among" the *bene ha'elohim*, but it is not clear from the text what his task is exactly. Clines argues that the name here identifies his function rather than a title; see Clines, *Job 1–20*, 20. Norman Whybray argues that one may presume that the satan is one of the *bene ha'elohim* that has a specialized function upon the earth to report the actions of humans. See Norman Whybray, *Job* (Sheffield: Sheffield Academic, 1998), 30.
47. See Archie T. Wright, *Origin of Evil Spirits* (Minneapolis: Augsburg Fortress, 2015).
48. See 1 Kgs 22:19–23; Isa 6; Ps 29:1; 89:7; 82:1; Dan 4:13 (10 in MT), 17 (14 in MT), 23 (20 in MT); 7:9–14. On the divine council in Israel, see Frank M. Cross, "The Council of Yahweh in Second Isaiah," *JNES* 12 (1953): 274–77; R. Norman Whybray, *The Heavenly Counselor in Isaiah xl 13–14*, SOTSMS 1 (Cambridge: Cambridge University Press, 1971); H. W. Robinson, "The Council of Yahweh," *JTS* 45 (1943): 151–57; in the ANE, see Marvin E. Pope, *El in the Ugaritic Texts*, VTSup 2 (Leiden: Brill, 1955), 48–49. Compare also Lowell K. Handy, "The Authorization of Divine Power and the Guilt of God in the Book of Job: Useful Ugaritic Parallels," *JSOT* 60 (1993): 107–18; Handy, "Dissenting Deities or Obedient Angels: Divine Hierarchies in Ugarit and the Bible," *BR* 35, no. 1 (1990): 18–35. Handy argues that the satan in the prologue of Job should be understood as an obedient lower member of the bureaucratic divine realm of Syria-Palestine.

of the conversation between the satan and YHWH appears to be one between equals. This may suggest that the *bene ha'elohim* and the *satan* were in fact minor deities on the divine council who could speak openly with the chief deity of Israel's henotheism. This would fit well if one considers the scene in Zechariah 3 as a similar situation—that is, the satan has come to report on Joshua to YHWH. In addition, 1 Kings 22:19–23 offers a parallel of the scenes in both Job and Zechariah: YHWH is convening the celestial court to determine the destiny of Ahab.

The Job passage suggests this is a prearranged, regular reporting session (also 2:1) in which this group of heavenly beings "present themselves" (להתיצב) before YHWH.[49] One may submit that the *bene ha'elohim* and the satan are appearing at a time of the year for a regular reporting session to YHWH: the Targum of Job 1.6 asserts that this is "the day of judgment at the beginning of the Year." Céline Mangan suggests this is Rosh Hashanah, New Year's Day, "on which all good and evil deeds were brought before the Lord to be judged."[50] Targum of Job 2.1 reads, "Now on the day of great judgment, the day of the remission of offences," suggesting this may be the Day of Atonement on which all the sons of God, including the satan, "come before the Lord to stand in judgment." The use of the term היום (LXX 1:6, ἡ ἡμέρα αὕτη, "this day"; also 2:1) may support this idea; however, it is most often translated as "one day" rather than "today" or "this day," despite the evidence that it is likely pointing toward a specific day.[51]

The Job passage hints at the purpose of this "call before YHWH" in a way that might suggest the satan would bring certain individuals before the council of YHWH as their adversary and report their wrongdoing. Job 1:6 describes a discussion between YHWH and the satan in which YHWH asks the satan where he has come from and the satan states that he was roaming about the earth. Targum of Job 1.7 states that the satan was "Roaming the earth to *investigate the work of human beings* [sons of men]."[52] This response brings to mind the passage from 1 Peter 5:8, which states, "Be sober and keep watch; your enemy the *diabolos* (*satan* in Peshitta) as a roaring lion is walking about seeking someone to devour."[53] Here, the term can be taken to mean "accuser" or "adversary" but does not necessitate the figure being autonomous. In Job 1:8, YHWH asks

---

49. The verb להתיצב, "to present oneself," occurs on two occasions in which the person (or persons) has been called before YHWH to report to him: 1 Sam 10:19, in which the Israelites are told to present themselves before YHWH by their tribes and clans; and Deut 31:14, in which Moses and Joshua are told to present themselves before YHWH in the tent of meeting. See Whybray, *Job*, 30; also Tate, "Satan," 462. An Akkadian term, *manzaz pani*, suggests a royal official; in this case, they have come to report their actions and to get new orders from the king. A similar use of the verb is found in Zech 6:5; cf. also Prov 22:29.
50. Céline Mangan, trans., "The Targum of Job," in *The Targums*, vol. 15 of *The Aramaic Bible*, ed. Kevin Cathcart, Michael Maher, and Martin McNamara (Edinburgh: T&T Clark, 1991), 24–27.
51. Cf. Clines, *Job 1–20*, 19.
52. Mangan, "Targum of Job," 24 (translator's emphasis).
53. The language used here, along with the Christian tradition, suggests this heavenly being is free to do what he wants to humanity; however, through the lens of 2TP literature, he might be understood quite differently.

satan if he has considered his servant Job. The satan's response in verse 9 is quite interesting and suggests he is very much aware of who Job is and may have thought about attempting to persuade Job to stop worshipping YHWH.[54] However, Job has recognized that YHWH's hand is upon him and his family and all he owns (Job 1:10). The satan appears to challenge YHWH to remove his blessing and in fact to strike out at Job, saying that Job will turn from worshipping and serving YHWH. However, as Clines argues, the abrupt "imperative language is not the mark of disrespect, but the idiom of colloquial speech."[55] The satan is not attempting to bully YHWH, but rather the author is simply using the necessary syntax to heighten the drama and answer the question, Does piety equal prosperity?[56] This understanding would certainly reflect the blessing of the righteous of YHWH found in Deuteronomy 28:1–2.

The author states that the satan is given the power to strike Job's family and possessions (Job 1:12), and he proceeds to do so in verses 13–19, although the attribution of the catastrophic events to the divinely ordained work of the satan is only implied. Despite the catastrophe, Job does not turn his back on or curse YHWH; in fact, the author relates that he falls to the ground in worship and blesses YHWH for his life (vv. 20–21).

Job 2:1–3b offers a similar scene; in fact, the wording is nearly verbatim with that found in 1:6–8. This repetition perhaps reflects that both are from a periodic "reporting session" for the divine council. As in chapter 1, the *bene ha'elohim* come to present themselves before YHWH, and the satan comes with them also to present himself before YHWH (verse 1:6 does not include the language of "presented himself before the Lord," but it can be assumed). This second occurrence appears to be a follow-up to the satan's previous visit in chapter 1; again, YHWH asks the satan if he has considered Job. This is a strange question to ask. Jokingly, it may suggest (1) God has forgotten their previous conversation in Job 1:8, (2) YHWH doesn't know of the events that have occurred in Job's life, or (3) he wants to verify what the satan's actions have been toward Job. However, in 2:3c, YHWH challenges the satan and accuses him of attempting to ruin Job without just cause (v. 3). Does this suggest there was some doubt as to what Job's reaction would have been to the attack of the satan? The satan, recognizing the initial efforts have not brought about the desired result, responds by declaring that Job will

---

54. Although the term *satan* means "adversary" or "opponent," it is clear that his task, with permission from YHWH, is only to allure or entice individuals (Job 2:3). This task, interestingly, fits well into the role of the satan figure in the Dead Sea Scrolls, which we will discuss below.
55. Clines, *Job 1–20*, 27.
56. Clines, 28. Clines suggests that the point of contention in the prologue of Job is "the validity of the principle of reward and of the causal nexus between ethics and success." One is attempting to discover whether Job's piety is a direct result of his prosperity or genuine. Or is it possible that God is trying Job's piety in an effort to test or refine the faith of Job? If one considers the task of the satan in 2TP literature, this is a possibility.

give up his worship should his physical well-being depend on it (after the first challenge has failed!). The satan then challenges YHWH to stretch out his hand against Job's health, saying that Job will then curse YHWH (2:5). The satan is then given the power to inflict sickness upon Job, but he must not kill him. Unlike in Job 1, in 2:7, the reader is told that the satan is the one who causes the physical affliction of Job, while YHWH remains out of the picture.[57] Like Job 1, this passage suggests that the satan is a member of the divine council that functions upon the earth at the behest of YHWH and is only allowed to interfere with a human life with God's permission. In Job, the satan figure is not an evil being, but rather he is one who is, as is his task, out to defend the Torah, and he believes that there are no blameless people; all are corrupt. The author of Job goes as far as to suggest that God does not oppose the satan (see 1:12, 2:6) but, in fact, trusts him to obey the command of YHWH.

Chapters 1 and 2 serve as a prologue that offers two key theological and ethical questions that are answered in the remainder of the book: Are human concepts of justice the same as God's, and how should one react to unexplained misfortune? The satan figure plays an important role in answering these questions and the emerging responses to the "problem of evil" in the postexilic period. The story of Job continues the evolving efforts of the Jewish authors to separate God from the suffering of the people by increasing the visibility of the adversary of humanity, the satan figure. One also recognizes the place of human choice in the response to the problem of evil: Will a person turn their back on God when evil is apparently knocking at the door?

Excursus: Job 4:12–19: Satan as a Deceiver?

One may suggest that hasatan makes another appearance in the book of Job outside of the prologue. In Eliphaz's response to Job beginning in 4:1, the author suggests through Eliphaz's words that Job is not innocent before God by stating, "Who that was innocent ever perished?" (4:7). In verses 12–21, Eliphaz contends that he received a word in the night from a whispering spirit that asked a similar question: "Can mortals be righteous before God? Can they be pure before their Maker? Even in his servants he puts no trust, and his angels he charges with error [perhaps an allusion to the Watcher tradition of

---

57. Job 2:9 in the MT reads that Job should "bless God and die" (ברך אלהים ומת), while the Greek, with a significant addition to the passage, translates the Hebrew in LXX verse 9e as "εἰπόν τι ῥῆμα εἰς κύριον καὶ τελεύτα" (speak a certain word to God and die). Several English translations (e.g., NRSV) read "curse God and die"; this is significantly different from the MT and a questionable translation of the Greek.

1 Enoch]." This spirit (of fear?) came to speak to Eliphaz, gliding past his face and causing his bones to shake and his hair to stand on end. He was unable to make out its appearance even as it stood before him. The spirit seems to be speaking for God; perhaps it is the hasatan who has come to test Job through the message of his compatriot Eliphaz. The term used in verse 15, רוּחַ (*ruach*), is normally understood as a feminine singular noun, but in this occurrence, it is the subject of a masculine singular verb, יַחֲלֹף, "passed by," the same verb used to describe God passing by Job in 9:11. רוּחַ is also the subject of the verb יַעֲמֹד in verse 16, in which the spirit stands still before Eliphaz. A similar spirit is found in 1 Kings 22:19–23; in this case, it too is a spirit of deception, "standing before YHWH" in the assembly of the divine council. The message from the spirit to Eliphaz is then understood to be one that is untrue in 42:7, which suggests the spirit was a lying spirit from the divine council or perhaps, as suggested, hasatan.

1 Chronicles 21

The next reference to שָׂטָן (satan) is found in 1 Chronicles 21:1, which is a retelling of 2 Samuel 24:1. This passage is very important to the development of this figure in that it appears to be the first overt attempt to separate God from an evil act by introducing a satan (LXX, διάβολος; no article in either case) to take the place of God's wrath against Israel, as found in 2 Samuel 24:1 (אַף יהוה, LXX, ὀργὴ κυρίου).[58] In both passages, the anarthrous satan figure misleads/incites (MT, וַיָּסֶת; LXX, ἐπέσεισεν) David to take a census of the people of Israel and Judah for what appears to be preparation for war with the Philistines. In both passages David turns to Joab, his commanding general, to count the people, again suggesting this is likely related to a forthcoming military action. Joab questions the call for a census by intimating that it will bring guilt upon the people. It might be suggested that the sin of the action of David was his need to see if the forces were numerous enough for war rather than simply relying on YHWH for the victory over the enemy. One might instead argue that the sin is from the hand of Joab, who failed to report to David the number of the tribes of Levi and Benjamin. As verse 7 states, immediately following the comment concerning Joab's failure to include them, he (David or Joab?)

---

58. See, for example, Stokes, "Devil Made David Do It," 95; see also Kluger, *Satan*, 159. Day argues against the idea the Chronicler is attempting to separate God from evil. Day, *Adversary in Heaven*, 134–36. See, for example, the story of Micaiah ben Imlah and the lying spirit in 2 Chr 18:18–22 and the story of Rehoboam in 2 Chr 10:15. Day argues for a divine accuser who is a member of the divine council rather than a "terrestrial or celestial adversary." See Day, 144.

had committed evil in the eyes of YHWH: וירע בעיני האלהים. One may consider the actions of the satan figure to encourage the census as adversarial in relation to David and Israel and in fact as being used to test David and his faith in YHWH to deliver Israel from the Philistines.

The history of the interpretation of שטן in 1 Chronicles 21 depicts the figure as a proper noun, like the "Satan" of later Christianity—the "archenemy" of YHWH.[59] Other scholars less inclined to apply the anachronistic view of the figure suggest that he/it is a foreign adversary who has stood up against Israel in a military confrontation (see, e.g., the use of ויעמד על in 2 Chr 20:23 in a military context). Others suggest the figure is referring to an adversary of the human sort, as is seen in previous occurrences in the HB (e.g., 1 Kings 11:14, 23–24).[60]

Here, the satan character possibly can be understood in a similar fashion as found in the Job passages—that is, the figure is here to test David by misleading him or inciting him to go against God's will for Israel. The term *satan* is used in 1 Chronicles 21 without the definite article, which has caused several scholars to suggest this is a proper name.[61] But this is not necessarily the case; it is possible that the text should be read as "a satan"—one of the divine beings used by God to, in this case, come against Israel, and David and Joab in particular. However, the most likely scenario in the case of 1 Chronicles 21 is that this is not a heavenly being at all but rather is a military adversary of David and Israel. The verse reads, "And a *satan*

---

59. Day contends *satan* used as a proper noun does not occur until the mid-second century BCE, in Jub. 23:29 and As. Mos. 10:1; both, she suggests, are dated around the time of the Maccabean Revolt against Antiochus IV in 168 BCE. The occurrence in Jub. 23:29 does not necessarily need to be understood as a proper noun; rather, it can be read as *a* satan. It first occurs in Jub. 10.11, in which it is read as *the* satan by VanderKam in *The Book of Jubilees*, 2 vols. (Leuven, Belgium: Peeters, 1989). However, there is no article, definite or indefinite, used in Ethiopic Ge'ez; thus, here also, it could be *a* satan and not a proper noun. Of the three occurrences in the Dead Sea Scrolls—1QH 4.6; 45.3; and 1QSb 1.8—there is no clear indication that the term is used as a proper noun. Perhaps more significant is the term's use in the plural, *satans*, in 1 En. 40:7, dated to the Herodian period. As for the Assumption of Moses passage, the dating of this text is much debated. Most scholars date the text to the first century CE or perhaps the first century BCE, but even then, 1 En. 10:1 is thought to be a later interpolation from the late first century CE. Thus, there is little indication that the term *satan* was being used as a proper noun prior to later Christian literature. Further evidence for the use of *satan* in 1 Chr 21 as a proper noun may be found in the LXX translation, which uses the noun διάβολος rather than a Greek transliteration of the Hebrew; this is one of the rare occasions in which the term διάβολος is used without an article; see Day, *Adversary in Heaven*, 129.
60. Day (*Adversary*, 144–45) notes that one might draw a parallel between the divine wrath of Num 22 and the Balaam story and the divine wrath of 2 Sam 24. In Num 22, the result of God's wrath against Balaam is the sending of a satan, Angel of YHWH, while the Chronicler, perhaps in response to the presence of God's wrath against Israel, sends a satan against Israel. Interestingly, in 1 Chr 21:15–16, God has sent the Angel of YHWH against Jerusalem (and Israel) in a similar fashion to that in Num 22. In this case also, the Angel of YHWH speaks for God in rebuking of David and the elders of the nation.
61. For arguments for a proper name in this instance, see Ralph W. Klein, *1 Chronicles* (Minneapolis: Augsburg Fortress, 2006); Peter B. Dirksen, *Historical Commentary on the Old Testament: 1 Chronicles* (Leuven, Belgium: Peeters, 2005); H. G. Williamson, *I and II Chronicles* (Grand Rapids, MI: Eerdmans, 1982). For arguments against a proper name in this instance, see Day, *Adversary in Heaven*; Sara Japhet argues that the lack of proper noun indicates *satan* is *not* a proper noun. See the commentary by Sara Japhet, *I and II Chronicles: Old Testament Library* (Louisville, KY: Westminster John Knox, 1993); Heinrich Kaupel, *Die Dämonen im Alten Testament* (Augsburg, Germany: Benno Filser, 1930); N. H. Tur-Sinai, *The Book of Job*, rev. ed. (Jerusalem: Kiryat Sefer, 1967).

stood up against Israel," suggesting that God has sent a human adversary against Israel (based on the parallel in 2 Sam 24:1—"God's wrath"), which resulted in David taking a census of the military power and readiness of his army to go to war against this adversary. John Sailhamer argues that God's wrath (*satan*) "meant the threat of foreign invasion," thus requiring David to take the military census.[62] A similar situation, in which God sends a military adversary against Solomon, can be found in 1 Kings 11:14. Hugh Williamson argues that the reason for God's wrath (*satan*) was that David was turning away from absolute reliance on God. This reliance is usually a characteristic of Israel's success in battle and overcomes any numerical advantage the enemy might have (see 2 Chr 14:9–15). Conversely, Jacob Myers argues that the lack of article with the term *satan* indicates the figure is an opponent to God because he/it incites evil. As such, he/it has a personality with a will and purpose of his/its own.[63]

OTHER SUGGESTED OLD TESTAMENT PASSAGES
Genesis 3 and the Alleged Satan Figure

In Genesis 3:1–19, which introduces the story of the temptation of Adam and Eve in the Garden, the serpent has often been understood as the satan figure, the archenemy of YHWH, despite the fact the story does not contain the term *satan* (שטן). The text only describes the characteristics of the serpent (MT, נחש, *nachash*; LXX, ὄφις), calling it the "craftiest" or "wisest" (ערום, φρονιμώτατος) of the wild animals that YHWH created,[64] so it is at least troubling to understand the creature as a heavenly being rather than an earthly creature.[65] Genesis 3:14 speaks to the mortality of this creature; in speaking the curse against it, God states, "And dirt you shall eat all the days of your life." The language here suggests the insignificance of the creature, removing any sense of power granted in the narrative and any sense of personified evil.

The history of interpretation of the Genesis 3 passage reveals a transfixed Christian tradition that contends the serpent in the story is "the Devil" or "Satan"; the serpent, and thus satan, is a liar and a deceiver; the serpent is one of God's earthly creatures; and the serpent is

---

62. See John Sailhamer, "1 Chronicles 21:1—a Study in Inter-biblical Interpretation," *TJ* 10 (1989): 33–48; also John W. Wright, "The Innocence of David in 1 Chronicles 21," *JSOT* 60 (1993): 87–105.
63. Jacob M. Myers, *1 Chronicles*, ABC 12 (Garden City, NY: Doubleday, 1965).
64. Gerhard Von Rad, *Genesis: A Commentary*, trans. John H. Marks (London: SCM, 1961), 85. Here Von Rad contends that "[in] the narrator's mind it is scarcely an embodiment of a 'demonic' power and certainly not of Satan."
65. Marvin Tate maintains, "The serpent is not a celestial or angelic being in the manner of the references to *satans* in Num. 22; Job 1–2; Zech. 3:1; 1 Chron. 21:1, or in the later sense of a divine creature who is constantly at war with the purposes of God." Tate, "Satan," 466. It should not be a surprise that the animal speaks to the woman, as this was a development in literature of the ANE and the Israelite religion; see, for example, Num 22:28 and the speech of Balaam's donkey. However, Tate notes that the devil does speak to Eve through a serpent in the Apocalypse of Moses 17:4–5 (ca. 100 BCE–200 CE). Tate, 467. In addition, the satan figure comes in various other disguises in the T. Job 6:4; 17:2; 20:5; 23:1; and 27:1.

responsible for sin and death entering into the world.⁶⁶ One may ask how this created creature has been identified as God's enemy in Christian tradition. One approach suggests the history of interpretation of the serpent symbology presents a connection to foreign gods or deities in and around the Israelite religious cult. Many archaeological discoveries near foreign temples or cultic epicenters indicate a connection between the serpent and foreign deities, whether it be an object of worship or symbolic of a divine protector.⁶⁷

In other ancient traditions, the serpent certainly symbolizes evil. In the Babylonian myth Enuma Elish, Tiamat is the goddess of saltwater and chaos, and takes on the form of a dragon or serpent in a battle with Marduk, a creature with close ties to the pantheon of Babylon. In Greek mythology, the story of Cadmus, the founder of the city of Thebes, describes how he has to battle an evil serpent in order to establish the city. Upon doing so, he is named king of Thebes by the goddess Athena. He reigns there with his queen Harmonia, and interestingly, upon their deaths, they change into serpents and are carried off to paradise by the gods. In the Israelite biblical tradition, a chaos myth containing a serpent is found in Isaiah 27:1, in which God punishes Leviathan, the fleeing serpent, and destroys the dragon that is in the sea. Some have argued that there is an allusion to this myth in Revelation 12.

The understanding of a serpent as a divine protector or healer may lie behind the story in Numbers 21, in which the serpent pole is crafted by Moses in the wilderness. This wilderness account is noted in the text of John 3:14–15, in which the author states, "And just as Moses lifted up the serpent in the wilderness, so it is necessary for the Son of Man to be lifted up, in order that all who are believing in him may have eternal life." The author of John is drawing a clear parallel between the "healing" or "protective" nature of the serpent in Numbers 21:8–9 (YHWH instructs Moses to make the pole with the serpent upon it) and the "healing" and "salvific" nature of Christ (the cross with him upon it). How could the author create such a parallel between the serpent and Jesus if the former can only be understood as evil? Our scriptural support for this evil understanding of serpents is of course Genesis 3 and the suggested parallels in the scenes from John's Apocalypse (John 12:1–9). Here, the author describes a creature, a "great red dragon" (δράκων)—serpent—who swept down a third of the stars from heaven and cast them to the earth and then waited for the birth of the child of the "woman clothed with the

---

66. See further discussion in James H. Charlesworth, *The Good and Evil Serpent: How a Universal Symbol Became Christianized* (New Haven, CT: Yale University Press, 2010), 278–79.
67. Martin Noth contends the serpent represented a god of healing in the ANE. Noth, *Numbers: A Commentary*, trans. James D. Martin (Philadelphia: Westminster John Knox, 1968), 158. Milgrom notes that serpents had a distinctive healing feature in the culture of ancient Egypt and that the pharaoh used symbols of the serpent for the purpose of protection. Jacob Milgrom, *Numbers*, JPS Torah Commentary (Philadelphia: Jewish Publication Society, 2003).

sun." Immediately following the rescue of the child, the archangel Michael wages war against the Great Dragon and his angels. In verse 9, the author of the Apocalypse identifies this Great Dragon as the "Serpent of Old," which is "the one being called the devil" (ὁ διάβολος) and the satan (ὁ σατανᾶς).[68] The Revelation passage appears to have had a great influence upon the early Christian understanding of the serpent in Genesis 3, as this understanding of the serpent is ambiguously alluded to only in a single Jewish text, Wisdom of Solomon 2:24, prior to the late first century CE. However, Isaiah 65:25 appears to also make an allusion to the serpent of the Genesis account in the Garden. The author states that although former foes of the animal kingdom shall live in peace, the serpent (MT, נחש; LXX, ὄφις) shall have dust as its food (per Gen 3:14, when the Lord, in speaking to the serpent, says, "Upon your belly you shall go, and dust you shall eat all the days of your life"). Micah 7:17 may also be alluding to Genesis 3:14 as well when the author speaks of the response of the nations to the work of YHWH: "They shall lick dust like a snake (כנחש), like the crawling things of the earth."

How then does one arrive at the presupposition that the "serpent denotes only evil or Satan"?[69] James Charlesworth contends that commentators of John's Gospel assume the serpent to be a negative symbol. He offers an example of how some examine John 13:21, the entering of the satan into Judas, in parallel with the serpent story in Genesis 3:15.[70] As a result, Judas becomes "by the possession . . . the seed of the serpent, Satan, the son of perdition."[71] Other biblical "understandings" of the serpent add to its negative nature. For example, Leviticus 11:41–43 states that creatures that swarm the earth on their belly or on all fours "shall not be eaten . . . for they are detestable." Charlesworth states that 4 Maccabees 18:8, a text roughly contemporaneous with John's Gospel, presents the serpent as "a pejorative symbol of the phallus"; the mother of the seven martyred sons claims "the 'destructive, deceitful snake' did not spoil her virginity."[72]

The term *serpent* has limited use in the Jewish Scriptures. It appears in Genesis 49:17 in a description of the tribe of Dan: "Dan shall be a snake by the roadside, a viper (MT, שפיפן; not

---

68. Note here the use of the definite article with διάβολος and σατανᾶς, which may then be understood as "the adversary"—that is, one that carries out a particular task. The events depicted here may be the final fall of the satan figure as he realizes his time as the adversary of humanity has come to an end. One must keep in mind the chronological aspects of this story; how does one place the serpent in the Garden as an adversary of God when it is only now, in Rev 12, that he/it appears to be in a state of rebellion? As mentioned, a Jewish text, Wis 2:24 (late first century BCE), is likely the first Jewish text that alludes to the serpent of Gen 3 as *diabolos* with the phrase "φθόνῳ δὲ διαβόλου θάνατος εἰσῆλθεν εἰς τόν κόσμον" (envy of [the/a] devil *death entered the world*). This is a somewhat vague allusion to the Gen 3 story.
69. Charlesworth, *Good and Evil Serpent*, 20.
70. See David Simpson, *Judas Iscariot: The Man of Mystery, History, and Prophecy* (Waterloo, IA: H. Cedarholm, 1943), 48.
71. Charlesworth, *Good and Evil Serpent*, 20.
72. Charlesworth, 21.

in the LXX) along the path, that bites the horse's heels." In a narrative describing the tribes of Israel, Dan's description appears to be one of strength, in a positive sense, for the nation, perhaps in a sense of being able to protect the people. In Exodus 4:3, the staff of Moses turns into a serpent, again in a positive sense, in order to convince the people to believe that YHWH had appeared to Moses. The author of LXX Exodus 4:17 adds the phrase "the one that turned into a serpent"; it is used similarly in Exodus 7:15 in the MT and LXX: "take the staff, the one that turned into a serpent." In 2 Kings 18:4, the author speaks of the "serpent pole" Moses had made in Numbers 21; here the pole is cast in a negative light. King Hezekiah destroys the "bronze serpent" (MT, נחש הנחשת; LXX, τὸν ὄφιν τὸν χαλκοῦν) because the people had been offering sacrifices to it. *Serpent* is used in Isaiah 14:29 to refer to Israel. The oracle warns the Philistines not to rejoice that Israel has been broken, "for from the root of the snake (MT, נחש; LXX, ὄφεων, 'of the serpent') will come forth an adder (MT, צפע; LXX, ἀσπίδων) and its fruit will be a flying serpent (MT, שרף מעופף; LXX, ὄφεις πετόμενοι)"; although cast as a negative force toward the Philistines, Israel is portrayed as a positive force in the various forms of a serpent.

Other passages from the Jewish Scriptures present more ambiguous portraits of the serpent whether it is cast in a negative or positive light, mostly with the serpent as an earthly creature (MT, נחש; LXX, ὄφις): for example, Jeremiah 8:17; Proverbs 30:19; Ecclesiastes 10:8, 11; Amos 5:19; Psalms 58:5 (MT); 140:4 (MT; both speak metaphorically: venom of the snake like the words of the wicked); Job 26:13 (God pierces the fleeing serpent; MT, נחש; LXX, δράκοντα); and Proverbs 23:32 (speaks of the sting of wine as that of a serpent or adder). From this scant use of the Hebrew and Greek terms for serpent in Scripture, it is difficult to establish a distinctly negative portrayal of the creature in the understanding of the Israelites concerning the serpent in the Garden scene in Genesis 3.

Other New Testament passages are used to identify the serpent of Genesis 3 as the "lying" autonomous Christian Satan. In John 8:44, the author describes the devil as the "father of lies": "ὅτι ψεύστης ἐστιν καὶ ὁ πατὴρ αὐτοῦ" (because he is a liar and the father of his [lie]).[73] One might ask, What specifically is "his lie"?[74] From the context of the passage, it appears the lie may be that if the Jews (οἱ Ἰουδαῖοι; interestingly, these are Jews who had believed in him)

---

73. Many English translations (e.g., NRSV) read this as "he is a liar and the father of lies," but that is not what the Greek states.
74. C. K. Barrett suggests a reading of "he is a liar and the father of it [i.e., of the lie or falsehood]." Barrett notes that the difficulty of the Greek may be a result of the author of John's attempt at "forcing the negative parallel with Jesus and his Father" and the Jews and their father, the devil. See C. K. Barrett, *The Gospel according to St. John: An Introduction with Commentary and Notes on the Greek Text*, 2nd ed. (London: SPCK, 1978), 349.

kill Jesus, their problems with him will go away. In John 13:2, Judas is deceived by the devil, and here, the devil is understood as one who betrays and works deceptively, which is one of the primary images of the serpent at work in the Garden. Acts 13:10 describes Elymas the magician as one who is a son of the devil, full of deceit, which of course enforces the deceptive nature of the serpent in the Garden. First Timothy 3:6 portrays an individual who can be easily deceived through pride by the devil; this, of course, reinforces the tempting nature of the serpent in the Garden. The author of 1 John 3:8 states, "The devil has been sinning from the beginning," likely an allusion to the serpent narrative in Genesis 3. Acts 5:3 states that Satan has persuaded Ananias to lie to the Holy Spirit—again, adding to the lying nature of the serpent in Genesis 3. Romans 16:20 also offers a vague allusion to the Genesis 3 narrative; here, the author states the God of peace will shortly crush Satan underfoot and is perhaps referring to Genesis 3, although the Genesis passage suggests the offspring of the earthly creature will be struck by the offspring of the human woman, as YHWH, speaking to the serpent, stated, "I will put enmity between you and the woman, and between your offspring and hers; it will bruise your head, and you will strike its heel" (3:15). Some suggest a metaphoric reading of the passage, but one must ask, "Can there be an offspring of the satan figure?" Finally, Revelation 12:9 and 20:2 appear to establish a correlation between the serpent of Genesis 3 and the "great dragon" (ὁ δράκων ὁ μέγας), the "ancient serpent" (ὁ ὄφις ὁ ἀρχαῖος), and the devil (διάβολος) and the satan (ὁ σατανᾶς).

An important textual note in Genesis 3:1 is the use of the interrogative τί in the LXX translation. The serpent's approach to the woman in the LXX reading should be understood as a question: "Why is it that God said, 'Do not eat from every tree in paradise'?" (Gen 3:1b).[75] The woman's response to the serpent does not appear to be the answer for which the serpent is hoping:

---

75. E. A. Speiser, *Genesis: Introduction, Translation, and Notes*, 3rd ed., ABC 1 (Garden City, NY: Doubleday, 1983), offers a very interesting reading of the passage:

> Now the serpent was the sliest of all the wild creatures that God Yahweh had made. He said to the woman, "Even though God told you not to eat of any tree in the garden . . ." The woman interrupted the serpent, "But we may eat of the trees in the garden! It is only about the fruit of the tree in the middle of the garden that God did say, 'Do not eat of it or so much as touch it, lest you die!'" But the serpent said to the woman, "You are not going to die. No, God well knows that the moment you eat of it your eyes will be opened and you will know the same as God in telling good from bad." (Gen 3:1–5)

This is certainly an eisegetical reading of the passage, in which Speiser appears to purposefully cast the serpent as a deceiver and the woman as knowing the correct commandment given by God concerning the fruit of the trees in the Garden.

But the woman said to the serpent, "From the fruit of the tree(s) of paradise, we shall eat." But from the fruit of the tree, the one that is in the middle of paradise, God said, "Do not eat from it, neither may you touch it, in order that you may not die." But the serpent said to the woman, "Surely you will not die! For God has known that in whichever day you may eat from it, your eyes may be opened, and you will be as gods knowing (כאלהים ידעי; ὡς θεοὶ γινώσκοντες)[76] good and evil." (Gen 3:2–5)

In the occurrences of אלהים thus far, the LXX translator has used θεός; on this occasion, he uses the nominative masculine plural form θεοί, "gods." It may be best to identify these θεοί as divine beings along the lines of what are currently called "angels." This use of the plural "gods" may reflect the earlier passage in Genesis 1:26 in which אלהים or θεός is the subject speaking, "Let *us* make humankind in *our* image." The LXX translation of the Hebrew participle ידע in Genesis 3:5 with the Greek pluperfect ᾔδει may suggest that God knew and was perhaps expecting that the humans were going to eat from the tree and that what we have here is simply the testing of them through the words of the serpent.

Thus, the story in Genesis 3 is not about the satan bringing death and sin into the world but rather about the trial and testing of humanity that God had planned. Some traditions read the Wisdom of Solomon 2:24 as an allusion to Genesis 3 and the satan being the cause of death in the world. However, this is not exactly what the Greek text reads: "φθόνῳ δὲ διαβόλου θάνατος εἰσῆλθεν εἰς τὸν κόσμον" (and by the envy of an adversary [διαβόλου], death entered the world). Note that there is no definite article with the term διαβόλου, which would suggest this is not speaking of "the devil" but simply an adversary—in this case, perhaps the author is speaking of Cain, the first one to kill.

Von Rad contends the narrator does not want to shift the blame from humanity in the Genesis 3 story to the serpent, thus the "mention of the snake here is almost secondary."[77] The test or trial of the humans was not going to come from an internal source, within the heart; thus, the introduction of an external source becomes a necessity. One should note a point often overlooked in discussions of this passage: the serpent always poses his questions or comments in the plural,

---

76. The use of the masculine plural participle "knowing" in the Hebrew and the Greek is of particular importance. Does it refer to those whose eyes will be opened or, as the Greek suggests, to the "gods" whom they will be like? Speiser contends that the context here suggests "distinguishing between" moral matters of "good and evil" (cf. 2 Sam 19:36; 1 Kgs 3:9); see Speiser, *Genesis*, 26. Speiser suggests a parallel story in the Gilgamesh epic, in which Enkidu is similarly tempted, with the result that "he now had wisdom, broader understanding," and the courtesan states, "You are wise Enkidu, you are like a god." See tablet I, col. iv, lines 16–34, ANET, 75, in Speiser, 26.
77. Von Rad, *Genesis*, 86.

perhaps suggesting that Adam, the male, is present throughout the conversation. Initially, the serpent draws the woman into the conversation through a distortion of God's commandment not to eat of any tree in the Garden. The woman subtly corrects the serpent, noting that God said they could not eat of the tree in the middle of the Garden, but she also adds that they were not allowed to even touch the tree, perhaps an addition of the commandment relayed to her by her husband (see 2:17). Thus, the serpent is testing the obedience of the woman according to the command of God. What we see in the story is not the so-called lying or half-truth of the serpent but rather the choice made by Eve to disobey God and seek her own fulfilment.

Von Rad argues that "knowing" here is not just intellectual knowledge; it is a sense of "experiencing" or "becoming acquainted with." The implication here is that the "knowing" takes Adam and Eve beyond the limits of knowledge set for them by God, granting them the knowledge of the "gods."[78] The concept of the "gods" (here, angelic beings) having such knowledge of good and evil is found in 2 Samuel 14:17, in which David is said to have the wisdom "as a messenger of Elohim . . . discerning good and evil" (הטוב והרע כמלאך האלהים . . . לשמע). After assessing the tree in Genesis 3:6, not only does the woman see the tree as good to eat; she also sees the tree as a source for wisdom, ונחמד העץ להשכיל—"and the tree was desired in order to be wise." Nahum Sarna contends that the phrase "your eyes will be opened," in verse 5, suggests humanity is "endowed with new mental powers" that will allow them "to make decisions independently of God"—that is, through their free will.[79]

Through this discussion of Genesis 3 and the "Temptation in the Garden," we've determined that the text makes no mention of the figure of the satan and only through later anachronistic readings of the passage can one align the serpent with the satan. We will return to the interpretation of this passage in the chapter concerning the satan in the writings of the early Church theologians.

Isaiah 14:3–21—the Fall of Satan?

In Isaiah 13–14, we observe the prophet proclaiming an oracle against the nations, in particular against Babylon. Within this oracle, we find a graphic description of the coming judgment of Babylon on the "Day of the Lord" (13:6–16) in which, through the army of the Medes (vv. 17–22), the nation will fall along with its self-exalted leader. This leader, identified in chapter 14 as the king of Babylon (מלך בבל), has been understood for centuries by scholars and preachers as

---

78. Von Rad, 86.
79. Nahum Sarna, *Genesis*, JPS Torah Commentary (Philadelphia: Jewish Publication Society, 1989), 25. Cf. Gen 21:19.

the satan, Lucifer, or the devil. This understanding has led many to suggest that Isaiah 14:3–21 is describing the "fall of Satan."

The origins of this understanding began in the fourth century CE with the early Church theologians. Jerome, in his *Commentary on Isaiah* on 14:12–14, translated the Hebrew *Helel Ben-Shahar* (הילל בן שחר) as "Shining One, Son of the Dawn," which is translated as "Lucifer" in the Latin Vulgate.[80] The term *Lucifer* means "light bearer" and was used to identify the planet Venus from the time of the Vulgate in the late fourth century until the early 1600s. Interestingly, Jerome only used this term to personify the satan, while in other Old Testament (OT) passages, he uses the phrase to simply refer to the "morning" or "daylight."[81]

Origen argues that the term *Helel* (הילל) should be understood as the proper noun "Lucifer," the "light bearer," whom he identifies as the satan in *On First Principles* 1.5.[82] Augustine perhaps offers the clearest identification of this figure in Isaiah 14:12 as Satan: "Statements [i.e., 'How he is fallen from heaven, Lucifer, son of the morning'] in that context that speak of the king of Babylon are of course to be understood of the devil."[83] However, none of these early Church theologians offers much of an explanation as to how they reached their conclusions about this text. As we will see in chapter 7, one of the likely reasons was to battle the Gnostic ideas of the satan figure being created evil. Another possible explanation may be that these great men of the Church did not want to recognize the possibility that a myth may have influenced the writings of Scripture (or at least this particular text), as may be implied by Origen's statement, "How can we possibly suppose that what is said in many places in Scripture . . . about Nebuchadnezzar is said about a human being? For no human being is said to have 'fallen from heaven.'" However, as a result of these traditions, Lucifer became synonymous with Satan in the Christian tradition. In what follows I will attempt to put the passage in its proper context to suggest that this "king of Babylon" is a mere human king.[84]

---

80. See CCL 73:168–69; also the summary of the Church Father's interpretation in Steven A. McKinion, ed., *Isaiah 1–39*, Ancient Christian Commentary on Scripture, Old Testament 10 (Downers Grove, IL: InterVarsity, 2004), 115–25.
81. See, for example, Job 11:17; 38:32; Ps 109:3; 2 Pet 1:19. It is interesting to note that we find the term *morning star* in Rev 22:16 (ὁ ἀστὴρ ὁ λαμπρὸς ὁ πρωινός, "bright star of the morning") referring to Jesus, although the Greek text in Isaiah reads differently (ἑωσφόρος). We also find in 2 Pet 1:19 a similar term that may be referring to Jesus, φωσφόρος. Each of these terms or phrases represents the idea of "morning star." How then can this same idea be understood as Satan in the Isaiah text?
82. See also Origen, *De Prin.* 4.3.9. Origen, *On First Principles*, trans. G. W. Butterworth (London: SPCK, 1936).
83. Augustine, *Christian Instruction* 3.37, in P. Schaff et al., eds., *A Select Library of the Nicene and Post-Nicene Fathers of the Christian Church* (Peabody, MA: Hendrickson, 1994), 1:8:117 (brackets mine).
84. John Watts notes that the dirge in Isa 14 could be appropriate for other leaders of the ancient world: "It is not specifically tailored for the king of Babylon. It is a masterful poem to be sung over a tyrant who has fallen victim to his ambition and pride." See John D. W. Watts, *Isaiah 1–33*, Word Biblical Commentary 24 (Waco, TX: Word Books, 1985), 212.

Context of Isaiah 14

The story of chapter 14 is set in a broader context of oracles against the nations who have in the past not followed God, but these same nations have been used in the past by God to punish Israel for her apostasy:

> Wail, for the day of the Lord is near; as destruction from the Almighty will come. Therefore, all hands are helpless. Every man's heart melts. And they will be terrified. Pains and agony will take hold of them; like a woman in labor they will anguish; they look aghast at each other, their faces aflame. Behold, the day of the Lord is coming, cruel, with wrath and burning anger; to lay waste the land and destroy the sinners within it. The stars of the heavens and their constellations will not give light; the sun is dark when it rises, and the moon will not give its light. And I will punish the world for its evil and the wicked for their guilt. I will put an end to the pride of the arrogant, the pride of the ruthless I will make low. I will make men rarer than gold, humanity rarer than gold of Ophir. Therefore, I will cause the heavens to tremble and the earth shall be shaken from its place by the wrath of the Lord of hosts on the day of his burning anger. . . . Behold, I am stirring up against them the Medes, who think nothing of silver and take no delight in gold. And the bows of the young men will slaughter, and the fruit of the womb they will not show compassion, nor for the children will they have pity in their eyes. (Isa 13:6–13; 17–18)

The oracles are given due to the pride of the nations. The nation chosen by the author to highlight is Babylon. Babylon, in the late 700s BCE, was the pride and strength of the ancient world. She is culturally and economically superior to the Assyrian empire to her west. The author of Isaiah is using her to contrast the greatest human glory against the Holy One of Israel. The oracle makes clear God's sovereignty over human pride and the arrogance of every nation.

The "oracle against the nations" of Isaiah begins to narrow its focus from a general description of the coming Day of the Lord in verses 6–18, which describe how the past enemies of Israel are used to bring about the destruction of Babylon, to an oracle that focuses directly on the nation of Babylon in 13:19–22:

> And Babylon, the glory of kingdoms, the glory and pride of the Chaldeans, will be like Sodom and Gomorrah as God overthrew them. It will never be inhabited

> or lived in for all generations; Bedouin will not pitch their tents there; shepherds will not make their flocks lie down there. But desert-dwelling animals will lie down there, and their houses will be full of screeching creatures; children of ostriches will live there, and hairy goat beasts will dance there. Hyenas will cry in its towers and jackals in the pleasant palaces; its time is close at hand, and its days will not be prolonged.

Here we see that Babylon becomes a deserted nation in which various wild beasts, some possibly related to demonic beings, take the land as their place of habitation, including the abandoned homes of the people and the places of the former kings and leaders.

Interestingly the author offers a short respite from the oracle against the nations with the insertion of 14:1–4a. The interlude proclaims the compassion of God upon his people, which likely reveals the restoration of Jacob (Israel) into the land following the Babylonian exile. Strangers who will attach themselves to the House of Israel will join them, and they will be an inheritance to Israel as servants. Those who once held Israel captive will be under the rule of Israel in the Lord's land. There is no clear reason the author placed this brief pause here other than to establish a bridge, which will shift the focus of the previous oracle against the nation of Babylon to the king of Babylon beginning in 14:4.

It is at this point that the passage takes on the characteristics of a funeral dirge for the king; however, scorn and relief at the passing of the tyrant replace the sorrow and grief expected in a typical dirge.[85] This difference may be hinted at by the author's use of the term *mashal* (משל), typically a "proverb," which can also, as may be the case here, carry the understanding of a satirical song.[86] In doing so, the author has made a major shift from a scene of reunification and praise in Isaiah 1–12 to a scene of judgment of the nations in 13–23. Some scholars argue that this section was part of a smaller booklet of apocalyptic material that was added to the book of Isaiah just prior to the Christian era.[87] However, with the discovery of the Isaiah Scroll at Qumran, which is dated to approximately 100 BCE, some doubt may be cast on that particular theory, which would require moving the date of this apocalyptic material into at least the second century BCE.

---

85. See Walter Brueggemann, *Isaiah 1–39* (Louisville, KY: Westminster John Knox, 1998), 126. Brueggemann characterizes verses 4–7 as a celebration if not a song in which the voices seem to be gloating rather than groaning over the loss.
86. See I. W. Slotki, *Isaiah* (London: Soncino, 1967), 4.
87. See, for example, George R. Berry, "The Apocalyptic Literature of the Old Testament," *JBL* 62, no. 1 (March 1943): 9–16; Patricia Tull Willey, *Remember the Former Things: The Recollection of Previous Texts in Second Isaiah*, SBLDS 161 (Atlanta: Scholars Press, 1997).

The highly focused "taunt against the king of Babylon" describes, as Tate notes, "the king's fall . . . in almost cosmic terms: a descent from heaven to the netherworld in Sheol."[88] The dirge begins in 14:4b with a declaration of the end of the oppressor's rule: "You will take up this *mashal* against the king of Babylon and you will say 'How the oppressing one ceased oppressing, the boisterous one ceased being boisterous.'" The agent that is used to end his tyranny is declared in 13:17: "Behold I am going to stir up the Medes against them"—that is, against Babylon and the other nations who have oppressed Israel. The king is one who previously shook the earth and its kingdoms (v. 16); he overthrew its cities, turning the world into a desert (v. 17). But the author states in verses 14:5–6 that the former tyrant is no longer a threat; he has been brought low by the arm of God—in this case the Medes: "The Lord has broken the staff of the wicked, the scepter of rulers, that struck the peoples in unceasing anger, ruling the nations in anger with unrestrained persecution." From the language of the taunt against the king, it appears clear this is not describing the satan figure of the later Christian tradition. If not satan, then who is this seemingly "cosmic" being?

Much discussion has been offered as to the identity of this individual. The language describing his hubris and demise suggests possible connections to ancient myth in the cosmology of the ancient world. In verse 14:8, an interesting inclusion presents a possible allusion to the Garden of God found in the Canaanite religious traditions: "The cypresses rejoice on account of you, the cedars of Lebanon: 'Since you were laid low, the hewer does not rise up against us.'"[89] A possible connection may be found here to the oracle in Ezekiel. In 31:8–9, we find another reference to the Garden of God, Eden, in Lebanon, which contains the cedars and cypresses mentioned in Isaiah 14:8. Ezekiel 31:8–9 reads, "The cedars in God's Garden could not compare; the cypresses could not compare with its boughs . . . and all the trees of Eden, which were in the Garden of God, were jealous of it." As we will see below, this may be significant in light of the "Garden" language in Ezekiel 28 and the interpretation of the individual in both these passages as the satan.

However, even though there is no clear consensus on the name of the king, it is clear that the individual is a human king.[90] The Pesher on Isaiah from Qumran (4Q163 frag. 8–10) describes the end of the tyranny of this individual, citing Isaiah 14:8 in a mocking tone: "The very cypresses [laugh at] you, and the cedars of Lebanon. Since [you laid down the hewer will

---

88. Tate, "Satan," 468.
89. This may also be considered a reference to the kings of Assyria, who wreaked havoc on Lebanon. Cf. Hab 2:17.
90. See Tate, "Satan," 468.

not rise up] against them."⁹¹ The end of this person has brought rest (נחה) and quiet (שקטה) to the earth and great joy in the hearts and songs of humanity: "All the earth rested and was quiet, they broke out in joyful song" (Isa 14:7). Further evidence to the nature of the king is offered in Isaiah 14:9. The king is told that he is on his way to Sheol, where he will be met by those kings that he likely warred against on the earth: "Sheol, beneath, shakes on account of you. Calling you to enter, the *reph'aim*⁹² are arousing for you; all the leaders of the earth rose up from their thrones, all the kings of the nations." Sheol is the Hebrew realm of the dead. It is a place reserved for the souls of the human dead where they live on in a shadowy existence.⁹³ There is no authority figure in Sheol, as in the Christian concept of Hades, which is overseen by the figure Satan. Rather, its occupants are waiting for the Day of Judgment.

Isaiah 14:10–11 further support that the king in question is a human king. The king of Babylon will suffer the same fate as other kings that rise to meet him in Sheol, some of whom he was likely responsible for the deaths of. "All of them answer and say to you, 'Also you are made weak like us; you are mocked [spoken of] like us.'" He has been destroyed by the strong arm of the Lord like many of those present in Sheol. His flesh will be destroyed by the maggots and worms of the human grave. All these descriptions point to his very fragile humanness.

Verse 11 again presents some difficulty as to the identity of the king as the satan figure. It appears that he will likely die the death of a mere human: "Your exaltation has been brought down to Sheol *and* the sound of your harps. Maggots are spread out beneath you; worms are your covering." Some may argue that here we find a reference to the satan figure's role as the "chief musician" in the heavenly courts based on the presence of "the music of your harps"; however, this is of course an idea or role for the satan from Church tradition that has its basis on the understanding that this chapter in Isaiah is describing the fall of the satan figure. He has been assigned this function as the heavenly music director based on the early Church theologians understanding of this passage alongside the Ezekiel passage, which we will discuss shortly.

O Shining One, Son of Dawn

Isaiah 14:12a contains the focal point of this passage from which the early Church Fathers drew their understanding that the author was referring to the "fallen angel," the satan figure. Verse 12 reads, "How you fell from heaven, *O Shining One, Son of the Dawn*. You were cut down

---

91. Targum of Isaiah 14:4 reads, "How the mastery of him who enslaved us has ceased, the strength of the sinner has come to an end," perhaps alluding to King Nebuchadnezzar. Cf. Dan 2:38.
92. The *reph'aim* are understood as the "powerless ones." See Slotki, *Isaiah*, 68.
93. See Job 7:9; 17:16; 26:6; Pss 6:6; 31:18; 88:12, 13; 115:17.

to the ground, O conqueror of the nations."[94] *O Shining One* is translated from the Hebrew הילל (*Helel*), found only here in the Hebrew Bible,[95] which, as mentioned above, Jerome saw fit to translate as the Latin term *Lucifer*. The LXX use of ἑωσφόρος (*heosphoros*) is significant in that it is found in Hesiod's *Theogonia* 378 to identify Venus.[96] As a result, some have attempted to draw a parallel to the Greek story of Phaeton.[97] The myth describes the efforts of the "hero" of the story to secure proof of his divine lineage from his father. He requests permission from his father, Helios, to drive the solar chariot for a day, something his father attempts to dissuade him from doing. However, he fails to change his son's mind and, in the end, can only counsel him on steering the horses: Phaeton is to avoid flying too low so as not to burn up the earth, and he is not to fly too high as he may burn up the skies. As he sets off, the young Phaeton fails to control the mighty steeds and sets fire to the sky and earth. As a result, Zeus is forced to strike him from the chariot, at which point his body, burning with fire, falls to the earth as a star from heaven. The myth is primarily a lesson on the dangers of hubris and the divine punishment for human pride—the same crime that the king of Babylon is guilty of in Isaiah 14.

This Greek myth is not the only possible background to the fall of the king of Babylon in Isaiah 14. There is a close parallel in the Canaanite myth of the god Athtar, who was also known as the "Luminous One."[98] This hubristic god went to the mountains of the north (Tsaphon), where Ba'al lived, and attempted to take his throne upon his death. However, his plan failed as his feet could not reach the footstool, nor could his head reach the top of the throne. He could not rule from the heights of Tsaphon and instead became king over the whole earth. There is no real sense of a rebellion by Athtar[99] in this myth as there seems to be with the king of Tyre in Isaiah 14. Additionally, Athtar is not referred to as "son of Shahar"; rather, he is the son of Ba'al and Athirat, the mother of gods (probably related to Asherah or Astarte in the Canaanite

---

94. Italics mine. Targum of Isaiah reads, "How you are cast out from the height, you that were resplendent among sons of men as the bright star among the stars! You are banished to the earth, you that were a slaughterer among the peoples!"
95. See Brown, Driver, and Briggs, *Brown, Driver, Briggs*, 237.
96. See W. G. E. Watson, "Helel," in *Dictionary of Deities and Demons in the Bible*, ed. Karel van der Toorn, Bob Becking, and Pieter W. van der Horst (Grand Rapids, MI: Eerdmans, 1999), 392–94. See also Tate, "Satan," 468.
97. See J. W. McKay, "Helel and the Dawn Goddess: A Re-examination of the Myth in Isaiah XIV 12–15," *VT* 20 (1970): 451–64; John C. Poirier, "An Illuminating Parallel to Isaiah XIV 12," *VT* 49, no. 3 (July 1999): 371–89. The essential text of the Phaeton myth can be found in Ovid's *Metamorphosis* 1.747–2.400—probably a late first century BCE or early first century CE text.
98. Tate, "Satan," 469. Several scholars argue for the coming together of the Canaanite and Israelite religions. See, for example, Mark S. Smith, *The Early History of God: Yahweh and the Other Deities in Ancient Israel* (San Francisco: Harper & Row, 1990); Johannes C. DeMoor, *The Rise of Yahwism: The Roots of Israelite Monotheism* (Leuven, Belgium: Leuven University Press, 1990), cited in Tate, "Satan," 473n20.
99. *Athtar* is known as "the Terrible One" or "the Awesome One" in the Ugaritic account; see Michael Coogan, *Stories from Ancient Canaan* (Philadelphia: Westminster John Knox, 1978), 111.

religion). Some have suggested that there has been a mixing of the myths of Phaeton and Athtar in the Isaiah passage.[100]

Julian Morgenstern argues that two late Jewish/Christian texts support the idea that the king of Babylon is indeed the satan figure.[101] He suggests that, based on similar language, 2 Enoch 29.4–5 and the Life of Adam and Eve (LAE) 13–16, which describe some of the activities of the satan figure (for example, his fall), are presenting the same story found in Isaiah 14 (and Ezek 28).[102] Morgenstern argues both these early Jewish writings (with Christian interpolations) contain wording that is drawn either directly from the Isaiah text or from an oral tradition still circulating in Judaism. Morgenstern argues that 2 Enoch 29.4–5 describes the attempt by the satan figure "to place his throne higher than the clouds above the earth," while LAE 13–16 follows the wording of Isaiah 13–14 even more closely: "I will set my seat above the stars of heaven and will be like the Highest." "Highest" here is likely the translation of the Hebrew *Elyon*. Perhaps Morgenstern is making significant assumptions here by relying on the church tradition that the Latin translation of *Helel* as "Lucifer" indicates that this is in fact the satan figure. He then goes on to suggest an *undeniable* link to the words of Jesus in Luke 10:18: "I beheld Satan falling as lightning from Heaven."[103] All of this "evidence," he argues, affirms "with absolute certainty" that the myth found in Isaiah 14 (and Ezek 28) describes the "fall of Satan and his associate angels from heaven to earth."[104] What he does not consider is the idea that both texts he is suggesting support this reading are possibly from the early second century CE and so had been influenced by traditions similar to those of the early Church theologians.

Isaiah 14:13 appears to support the early Church interpretation of the rebellion of the satan figure. Although this may appear to be the case, there is evidence that this is simply the language of a self-deified king speaking in his hubris.[105] The passage reads, "You said in your heart [this phrase is an idiom for speaking in pride], I will go up to the heavens, above the stars of God [אל]. I will set my throne and I will sit on the Mountain of the Assembly in the heights of the

---

100. See P. Grelot, "Isaïe XIV 12–15 et son Arrière-plan Mythologique," *RHR* 149 (1956): 18–48. Cf. McKay's critique of Grelot in "Helel," 454–56. See a third possible explanation of the presence of a Greco-Ugaritic myth in Isa 14 in McKay, 463–64.
101. Julian Morgenstern, "Mythological Background," *Hebrew Union College Annual* 14 (1939): 108–11.
102. The Life of Adam and Eve is likely dated between 20 BCE and 110 CE; the dating of 2 Enoch varies widely from the first century BCE (Robert H. Charles) to the ninth century CE (J. T. Milik), but it is likely from the same period as the LAE.
103. See Morgenstern, "Mythological Background," 108–9.
104. Morgenstern, 109.
105. Aphrahat, a fourth-century CE Syriac church theologian, states in his *Demonstration of Wars* 5.4 that the individual making these comments is King Nebuchadnezzar.

North."[106] All this language is, of course, familiar to us from the lives of the Babylonian and Assyrian kings who exalted themselves to divine status in the eyes of their people and perhaps also in the surrounding nations. The mountains of the north of each particular country (Babylon, Greece, Mesopotamia, and Israel) are familiar sites for the gods in the ANE, as is the case with Mount Zion in Psalm 48:3 (MT): "A beautiful high view, Mount Zion in the far side of the north; the city of the great king is the joy of all the earth."

It is clear that this king was not satisfied with earthly power granted him by God; rather, he wanted to plant himself in the "assembly of the gods." In fact, he desired to make himself "like the most high" (Psalm 48:14). This would have been familiar to the audience from Genesis 14:19–22, in which Melchizedek and Abram called the God they served Elyon, a name that would be later identified with the God of Israel. In addition, this language draws an immediate parallel to Ezekiel 28:2, in which the falling king states that he is god and he will reside in the dwelling place of the gods. The author is certainly alluding to Psalm 82 or at least the tradition that lies behind the psalm. In addition, as Slotki argues, this is a familiar setting of the gods in Babylonian literature, in which the mountain is identified as Aralu.[107]

The author of Isaiah 14 makes it clear in verses 15–16 that all this prideful talk is for naught. This once powerful king of Babylon will be cast down just as those kings who await him in Sheol were. He will die the simple death of a man, "a man who made the earth tremble and the kingdoms quake." In death, he will no longer hold this divine status and power and will spend his time in Sheol awaiting judgment.

This passage is a poetic work of art that describes the failed lofty ambitions of the once divine king of Babylon. The poem reveals the temporary nature of a human's time on earth, even for those who desire to reach the heights of the divine. The king is met by the "great leveler" of human history—death. The passage continues with other descriptive language about the death of the king and his sons. These verses serve to further support the idea that the individual in question is just a human and not a divine being—that is, not "the fallen angel," the satan.

Ezekiel 28:2–19: The Fall of Satan

Ezekiel 28:2–10 contains language very familiar to the reader of Isaiah 14 and it appears that it is for this reason that some of the early Church theologians thought to connect the

---

106. This is the place in which the pantheon of the Canaanites resided, led by their god Ba'al. It is believed that the head of the pantheon in Canaan was El. See John Watts, *Isaiah 1–33*, WBC 24 (Waco, TX: Word Books, 2005), 207; also Slotki, *Isaiah*, 68.
107. See Slotki, *Isaiah*, 68.

two passages as a description of the fall of the satan figure.[108] It is important to offer a brief description of the dating of Ezekiel prior to any further discussion on the subject. The author of the book of Ezekiel identifies himself as a Zadokite priest named Ezekiel ben-Uzi, who lived as a deportee in the land of the Chaldeans, and contains for the most part the words of the prophet but may contain portions of a later prophetic school.[109] Based on the internal dating in the book, it has been suggested it was written sometime between 593 and 571 BCE. Others have suggested a date between 500 and 400 BCE,[110] while others, in particular C. C. Torrey, suggest the whole of Ezekiel comes from the third century BCE,[111] a date now thought plausible for the book of Daniel. The events described in the book appear to take place in the Babylonian exilic period, which would suggest the book is historical prophecy—that is, it is written after the events but as though it is prophetic in order to give it some authority in its particular community.

There is, as you can imagine, much debate about the content of Ezekiel, as with most of the other prophetic books. The second section, chapters 11–19, is likely the only piece that can be attributed to the original author of Ezekiel with any confidence. The first portion of Ezekiel, chapters 1–10, is possibly an addition by an editor, although we cannot rule out that it is original; the last two sections of chapter 28 are almost certainly additions by an editor. However, though scholars feel some sections of Ezekiel may be additions, we should not be tempted to remove chapter 28 from the context that is established in chapters 26–27. In fact, it appears chapter 28 is a more compact version of the two chapters (perhaps an oral tradition) although directed toward an individual rather than the nation.

As with Isaiah 14, the question that arises is who is the king in the passage. In the case of Ezekiel, who is the king (prince) of Tyre? Tate contends the passage contains a historical reference that speaks overtly of the ruler or the leader of the city.[112] As Hector Patmore has proposed, the imagery portrayed by the author of the main character fits not "an earthly monarch" but rather some other figure.[113] It may prove difficult to identify who the character is specifically, but it may be possible to determine the likelihood that he is or is not the satan

---

108. Although there are striking similarities between the Ezekiel and Isaiah passages, it is evident, as Tate notes, that "there are major differences in features and details." See Tate, "Satan," 470–71.
109. Joseph Blenkinsopp, *Ezekiel* (Louisville, KY: Westminster John Knox, 1990).
110. Walter Zimmerli, *Ezekiel 1: A Commentary on the Book of the Prophet Ezekiel, Chapters 1–24*, Hermeneia (Philadelphia: Fortress, 1979); Zimmerli, *Ezekiel 2: A Commentary on the Book of the Prophet Ezekiel, Chapters 25–48*, Hermeneia (Philadelphia: Fortress, 1983).
111. C. C. Torrey, *Pseudo-Ezekiel and the Original Prophecy* (New Haven, CT: Yale University Press, 1930).
112. See Tate, "Satan," 470.
113. Hector M. Patmore, *Adam, Satan, and the King of Tyre: An Interpretation of Ezekiel 28:11–19 in Late Antiquity* (Leiden: Brill, 2012), 3.

figure (as Christian tradition has suggested). There are several theories as to the identity of the king:[114] (1) some scholars suggest he is representative of the nation and not a specific individual,[115] (2) others argue he is to be identified as a fallen angel or the satan figure, and (3) a third consideration identifies him as the deity Melqart, who was the god of the city of Tyre during the first millennium BCE. Concerning the third theory, there are strong links to Greek mythology and the hero Heracles in the Melqart myth.[116] Second Maccabees 4:18–20 describes a second-century BCE celebration of the god of Tyre, Melqart/Heracles. Melqart is also connected to the god Ba'al found in 1 Kings 18:20–40.[117] In 1 Kings 18:27, we read the words of Elijah: "Perhaps he is asleep and must be awakened"; this statement is perhaps alluding to the cultic practice of "awakening" the god Melqart during worship. Josephus in *Jewish Antiquities* 8.141–49 suggests that Hiram, king of Tyre, erected temples to Heracles to worship him as a god.[118] However, as you can see, none of these suggestions are very helpful in identifying the king. A close examination of the text may help determine the identity of the king of Tyre.

Ezekiel 28:1–10

The first clue is found in verse 2 with the Hebrew term נגיד, *nagid* (LXX renders the Hebrew ἄρχοντι, *archonti*, "ruler"). *Nagid* is used most often in the HB to identify the human political leader of a nation—for example, the king.[119] The term is also used to refer to an official connected to the temple—possibly the reason for the "precious stones" language in verse 13.[120] Some scholars have suggested that the *nagid* is the angel of the nation,[121] appointed to watch over Tyre. However, there is no evidence that this word refers to an angel anywhere in the HB. Verse 28:2 reveals the hubris of the king in that he declares himself a god (ותאמר אל אני, "and you said, 'I am [a] God'"; LXX, καὶ εἶπας θεός εἰμὶ ἐγώ) and that he sits in the seat of the gods (probably a throne in the temple of Ba'al or Heracles); however, the author clearly identifies the *nagid* as

---

114. See the discussion of possible "kings" in María E. Aubet, *The Phoenicians and the West: Politics, Colonies, and Trade* (Cambridge: Cambridge University Press, 2001).
115. See Walther Eichrodt, *Ezekiel: A Commentary*, trans. Cosslett Quin (London: SCM, 1970), 390. See also Anthony J. Williams, "The Mythological Background of Ezekiel 28:11–19?," *BTB* 6 (1976): 49–61.
116. Herodotus describes Heracles as the "Hero of Tyre."
117. See Daniel Block, *The Book of Ezekiel Chapters 25–48* (Grand Rapids, MI: Eerdmans, 1998), 95.
118. "He both built the temple of Hercules and that of Astarte, and he first set up the temple of Hercules in the month Peritius."
119. See 2 Chr 32:21; 1 Chr 13:1; 1 Sam 9:16; 13:4; 1 Kgs 14:35; Dan 9:25 (used to refer to a king of a nation); 2 Chr 11:11 (the commander of a city); 19:11 (a court official).
120. See Jer 21:1; 2 Chr 31:12; Dan 11:22; 1 Chr 9:20.
121. See Deut 32:8: "When the Most High divided the nations, when he separated the sons of Adam, he set the bounds of the nations according to the number of the angels of God."

a man: "Yet you are a man and not a god."¹²² It should also be noted that this individual is addressed as a *melech* (מלך) in verse 12, a term that the author or editor of Ezekiel only uses to refer to an earthly king and not a divine being.¹²³ In verses 1–10, we have read the oracle to the *nagid*, which describes the sin of hubris ("an elevated heart"), and the consequences of the sin are clearly spelled out in verses 6–8, in which God declares the coming of his wrath against this leader and his nation. The king is accused of comparing his heart (possibly his mind) with the heart of a god (אלהים). Thus, he will be cast down by strangers into the Pit and meet the death of a human. From this brief discussion, it is plausible to suggest the *nagid* of Ezekiel 28:1–10 is human and not divine in the mind of the author, although it is clear from 28:2 that the *nagid* thought he was a divine being with the use of the Hebrew אל in his self-portrait and the translators use of the Greek θεός.

Ezekiel 28:11–19

This section of chapter 28 offers various interpretive encounters, including likely allusions to ancient myths, that make an exegetical analysis of the passage difficult. As mentioned above, it is possible that the section of the passage that follows is an addition by a later editor that further details the fall of this once highly esteemed king. The author's switch from *nagid* to *melech* indicates that verses 11–19 may be an addition to verses 1–10. The mythical language contained in these verses reveals the position this historical figure once held among the rulers of the world. He is the ruler of a powerful and prosperous kingdom, which, of course, does not reflect the sin, but perhaps led to it. Beginning in verse 28:12, we find the prophet is called to offer up a lament to the king due to his apparent fall from grace because of his pride. However, before describing the fall of the king, the author first sets out the prestige the king once held as the אתה חותם תכנית (*ata chotem tochnit*). This phrase has been primarily translated as "you are (or were) the seal of perfection." The term *perfection*, תכנית, is used only here and in Ezekiel 43:10, where it suggests a measurement. Walter Zimmerli has argued a broad range of meaning here while suggesting "correctness" may be suitable.¹²⁴ I would suggest that based on the possible allusion to the story of the origin of humanity, it should perhaps be translated "you were the perfect form [of humanity]."¹²⁵

---

122. ואתה אדם לא אל (*Ve'atah 'adam lo 'El*). He is also identified in verse 9 as a mortal, using the same phrase found in verse 2.
123. See Ezek 17:12; 29:2; 27:33; 28:17; 34:24; 37:25. These terms are also used together in Ps 76:13. See the discussion in Block, *Ezekiel*, 93–103.
124. Walter Zimmerli, *Ezekiel 2: A Commentary on the Book of the Prophet Ezekiel, Chapters 25–48*, Hermeneia (Minneapolis: Fortress, 1983), 81.
125. See Solomon Fisch, *Ezekiel* (London: Soncino, 1950). Targum of Ezekiel understands the phrase as "like the sculptural mold"—that is, "the Primal Adam." According to Samson H. Levey, the rabbis understood this to be Adam; see *b. B.B.* 75a; *Eccl. R.* 7:36; *Pes. R.* 14:10; see also Levey, *The Targum of Ezekiel* (Edinburgh: T&T Clark, 1999).

It has been argued that what is found in verses 12–15 is a parallel to the Genesis Adamic myth[126] presented through the lens of the Ugaritic Adapa myth.[127] In the Ugaritic myth, the man, Adapa, is the son of Ea, the god of wisdom. Ea had created him "as the model of man" and granted him wisdom but not eternal life. Adapa is created in perfect beauty and wisdom, and he is the king of Eridu in Mesopotamia, thus a possible connection can be made to the king in Ezekiel 28:12.[128] The Adapa myth does not, however, state that Adapa is the original human, as is the case with Adam in Genesis. Nor do we see any hint that Adam is perfect in wisdom apart from the episode in which he names the animals.[129] Erich Ebeling equated the name Adapa etymologically with the Hebrew Adam; if this is the case (although, dubious), the Adapa myth is about the first man, witnessing to the highly esteemed position of the king in Ezekiel as the first man.[130]

Verse 28:13 has created many exegetical problems for interpreters. Nancy Bowen describes verses 13–14 as "hopelessly obscure";[131] though, granted, the challenges of interpreting and understanding the text are significant, they are perhaps not hopeless. The author of Ezekiel 28:13 locates the king in Eden,[132] the Garden of God, perhaps giving credence to the connection to the Adamic myth, while in verse 14, he parallels Eden with the "holy mountain of God," likely an allusion to a northern Canaanite myth about Al'eyan, Ba'al, and Mot, which is represented also in Isaiah 14:13 and Psalm 82. The Canaanite myth describes a "divine" being who was perfect in his service to the deity until he thought to make himself ruler of the cosmos (cf. Isa 14:13). He was then cast off the mountain of the gods (Mount Tsaphon?), home of El and Elyon (see Ps 82:1), perhaps intimated in Ezekiel 28:8 when the *nagid* is cast down to

---

126. See Blenkinsopp, *Ezekiel*, 123–24. Blenkinsopp contends there are several suggestive parallels to the Gen 3 Garden narrative and the Ezek 28 11–19 account. See also Nancy R. Bowen, *Ezekiel*, Abingdon Old Testament Commentaries (Nashville: Abingdon, 2010), 169–74.
127. See Niels-Erik Andreasen, "Adam and Adapa: Two Anthropological Characters," *Andrews University Seminary Studies* 19, no. 3 (1981): 179–94.
128. "He [Adapa] possessed intelligence. . . . His command like the command of Anu. . . . He [the god Ea] granted him a wide ear to reveal the destiny of the land. He granted him wisdom, but he did not grant him eternal life. In those days, in those years the wise man of Eridu, Ea had created him as chief among men." Robert W. Rogers, trans., *Cuneiform Parallels to the Old Testament* (New York: Eaton & Mains, 1912).
129. Blenkinsopp, *Ezekiel*, 123.
130. See Erich Ebeling, *Tod und leben nach den vorstellungen der Babylonier* (Berlin: Walter de Gruyter, 1931), cited in E. A. Speiser, "Adapa," in *Ancient Near Eastern Texts Relating to the Old Testament*, 3rd ed., ed. James B. Pritchard (Princeton, NJ: Princeton University Press, 1969), 101n27, 101n27a.
131. Bowen, *Ezekiel*, 169–73.
132. Bowen, 165. Bowen suggests, "Eden is probably a metaphor for Tyre"; although plausible, her suggestion seems somewhat simplistic for such a complex text.

the Pit.¹³³ The second part of verse 13 leaves us with the imagery of the priesthood in Exodus 28:17–20 and the precious stones of the priestly vestments; however, Genesis 2:12 states Eden itself was filled with gold and precious stones. The question arises, "Was there such a Gentile king who could be paralleled with a priest?" Tradition suggests that Ethba'al, the king of Tyre (ca. 915–847 BCE), was considered the high priest of Astarte in the cult of the city, while during the Early Dynastic Period in Mesopotamia, the kings often functioned in a priestly role. The Canaanite priestly king Melchizedek also comes to mind. Nonetheless, it is likely the author of Ezekiel is using the language found in the Canaanite Adamic myth to refer to the king figure in Ezekiel 28. The close of 28:13 suggests a further connection to the Adamic creation myth with the language, "On the day of your creation they [settings and engravings] were prepared."

Ezekiel 28:14 contains the controversial description of the king את־כרוב ממשח הסוכך (*at cherub mimshach hasochech*). It is from this verse that many argue that the king of Tyre is none other than the satan figure, the fallen angel. This supposition has developed from the exegesis of the Hebrew phrase, translated as, "You are the anointed guardian cherub." First, it can be argued that the "anointed guardian cherub" is not the problem; it is clear from the text this can be the reading. The problematic portion of the verse is the first word in the Hebrew text, אַתְּ. The first point to note is that originally the Hebrew text was unvocalized—that is, without vowels. It would have appeared as simply את־. The Masoretic text reads a *patach* vowel with the *Aleph* consonant (א) and a nonvocal *sheva* with the *Tav* consonant (ת). If אַתְּ is the accepted reading of the text, as a pronoun, then it would in fact be the second feminine singular (2fs) form of "you,"¹³⁴ which in my estimation would not correspond with the rest of the passage. We do, however, have the LXX to help with the translation. The LXX has translated the את־ with the preposition μετά, or "with," and is read "with the anointed Cherub . . . I have set you upon

---

133. Cf. 1 En. 18:6–8: "I saw the paths of the angels. I saw at the end of the earth, the firmament of the heaven above. And I proceeded and saw a place which burns day and night, where there are seven mountains of magnificent stones, three toward the east, and three toward the south. And as for those toward the east, one was of colored stone, and one of pearl, and one of jacinth, and those toward the south of red stone. But the middle one reached to heaven like the throne of God." See also 24:1 and 25:3. John L. McKenzie has suggested there is a parallel here to Mount Tsaphon in the Canaanite myth of Ashtar also alluded to in Isa 14:12–14; see McKenzie, "Mythological Allusion in Ezek 28:12–18," *JBL* 75, no. 4 (December 1956): 322–27.
134. James Barr argues that it is possible that this is an extremely rare form of the 2ms pronoun found in only three places in the HB—Ezek 28:14; Num 11:15; and Deut 5:24. Barr states that the Greek and Syriac translations of "with" are due to the translators' inability to identify this rare form of the pronoun. Interestingly, the two other places where the rare form appears, both the LXX and Syriac texts, translate it as "you." Barr suggests that the mistranslation here is due to the obscurity of the passage. See James Barr, "'Thou Art the Cherub': Ezekiel 28:14 and the Post-Ezekiel Understanding of Genesis 2–3," in *Priests, Prophets and Scribes: Essays on the Formation and Heritage of Second Temple Judaism in Honour of Joseph Blenkinsopp*, ed. Eugene Ulrich et al., JSOTSS 149 (London: Bloomsbury, 1992), 212–23, here, 215–17.

the mountain of God." This would be a more natural translation considering the use of the *metheg* to connect את־ to the following כרוב.

In 28:15 the author states that the king of Tyre was created "blameless" until "iniquity was found in you," perhaps alluding to the fall in the creation narrative. The verb used by the author ברא, to create, is used only with God as its subject, again perhaps alluding to the Adamic myth.[135] The iniquity (עוולתה) of the ruler reveals his true nature. A related form of the noun (עול) is used in Leviticus 19:15 in the sense of injustice toward the poor and possibly deferring to the rich or powerful of society (cf. Lev 19:35; Deut 25:13–16; Ezek 18:8). Concerning the king, verse 28:12 states, "You were the perfect form"—he was formed in the image of God, but now the king has spoiled that image with his iniquity, with his misuse of power and prosperity. He has previously thought himself to be capable of being like God, having the same mind as God. His self-proclaimed divine status in 28:2, like other kings of the ancient world, has done little to save him from God's wrath. Consequently, he has been cast from the "Holy Mountain of God," perhaps a metaphor for divine protection over his kingdom or the ability to hear the voice of God as Moses did on the holy mountain of Sinai in Exodus 3:1 and 24:13. This metaphor of "hearing the voice of God" may be alluded to in 28:3 with the comment, "You are indeed wiser than Daniel, no secret is hidden from you." The story of Daniel depicts the hero as an individual who hears from God, whether through the voice of the spirit or through an angel. The king of Tyre is no longer granted that divine wisdom due to his sins of injustice and pride.

Verse 28:16b is an extremely complex verse that contains a similar Hebrew problem with the phrase "anointed cherub." Some translations (e.g., KJV, ESV) read, "So I cast you in disgrace from the mountain of God and drove you, O guarding cherub, from among the fiery stones." Although the Hebrew of the MT can be read as "I drove you out" (וָאַבֶּדְךָ), a first common singular (1cs) Piel perfect, a variant Hebrew reading of וַיְאַבֶּדְךָ, a third masculine singular (3ms) Piel perfect verb, along with the LXX reading, are understood as "a guardian cherub has banished you from among the fiery stones."[136] Of course, both these verses would recall the Adamic story of the Garden of Eden (see Gen 3:24). It should be mentioned that כרוב is never used in the HB to refer to the Christian image of the satan figure; one might go so far as to say there is no fallen satan figure in the HB or LXX. *Cherub* is used to describe the angelic

---

135. Bowen, *Ezekiel*, 131.
136. The variant is supported by the reading in the LXX: "καὶ ἤγαγέν σε τὸ χερουβ ἐκ μέσου λίθων πυρίνων" (And the cherub banished you from the midst of the stones of fire).

figures that make up the throne of God.[137] A further troublesome phrase in 28:16 is אבני־אש, *avnai esh*, "stones of fire." It is a phrase created by the author of Ezekiel but may be tied to the Moses/Sinai tradition in Exodus 34. Exodus 34:1 reads, "The Lord said to Moses, 'Cut two tablets of stone like the former ones, and I will write on the tablets the words that were on the former tablets, which you broke.'" Although there is no mention of creation of stones of fire in the Exodus tradition, in Exodus 24:17, the top of the mountain, the place to which Moses took the tablets of stone upon which God wrote the commandments, is said to be consumed by fire (Exod 34:1). The suggestion may be made that the king of Tyre once walked obedient to the laws of God (following the stones of fire) until iniquity was found in him. The term תמים (*tamim*) in Ezekiel 28:15 may offer further support to this reading. It is used on multiple occasions concerning the "blameless" who walk in obedience to God, such figures as Noah (Gen 6:9) and Abram (Gen 17:1). Throughout Leviticus, it is used to describe the perfect sacrifice, "one without blemish." In Joshua 24:14, Joshua is told to serve the Lord "blameless" and in faithfulness—that is, walking in obedience to the commandments. Perhaps what we see is a "pagan" king who had at one time followed the voice of the God of Israel, YHWH, but due to his great prosperity and success, he began to rely on his own abilities and ceased to seek out and to hear the voice of divine wisdom, and his pride caused him to fall from his royal position. The remainder of the passage describes the further destruction of the human king because of his pride and sin.

The preceding discussion has identified key components of Ezekiel 28 that use mythical language related to the Canaanite Adapa myth, which includes language that recalls the Genesis narrative about Adam and his sin. At the same time, the author has used language that clearly identifies the figure as a human king or prince of the city rather than the "fallen angel" figure, satan. If one looks at the chapter in context and its literary setting, one can surmise that the author is referring to an earthly king and not a "fallen angel." One question could be asked at this point: If the author of Ezekiel 28 is describing the fall of the satan figure, is it a futuristic event or something that occurred in the primeval history? If the figure is the satan and it does describe his fall from heaven, whether primeval or after the author's life, why is he not dead and in his grave in Sheol? The answer perhaps is that the figure is the king of Tyre, who is in Sheol, a place reserved for "human" spirits, not "angelic" spirits.

---

137. See 1 Sam 4:4; 2 Sam 6:2; 1 Chr 13:6; 2 Kgs 19:15; Isa 37:16; Ps 80:2; 99:1; Exod 25:18–22; 37:7–9; Num 7:89; they are described in Ezek 1:5–28; 9:3; 10:1–20 as "four living creatures with four faces and four wings and with the figure and hands of a human and the feet of a calf."

Summary

The preceding discussion has identified the major passages that include the terms שטן (satan) or διάβολος (diabolos) in the Hebrew and Greek Scriptures. The four major texts addressed included Numbers 22:22–35; Job 1–2; Zechariah 3:1–7; and 1 Chronicles 21:1–22:1. As discussed, scholars have argued for and against the idea that the "satan" in each of these passages is in some way related to the later Christian Satan figure, which is understood as a somewhat semiautonomous evil being who apparently opposes everything that is the will of God. Within the presentation of these texts, a brief etymological study of the relevant terms has been offered that defines the terms *satan* and *devil* as "one who persecutes, opposes, or acts as an adversary." The results reveal that the terms used in these passages can identify either a heavenly being or a human in the various contexts. The terms are used in other biblical texts—including Genesis 26:21; 1 Samuel 29:4; 2 Samuel 19:23; 1 Kings 5:16–20; 11:14–25; and Psalms 38:21; 71:13; 109:4–6; and 109:20, 29—to identify a human adversary. In addition to the obvious linguistic roots, other possible origins of the term were identified such as the verb שוט, "to roam about looking," and ש׳ט, a term adopted from the Egyptian deity that may have had a role in the emerging dualism of the Israelite religion. The final portion of the discussion focused on three texts that interpreters have attempted to connect to the "satan" figure: Genesis 3:1–15, Isaiah 14:12–17, and Ezekiel 28:11–19. A plausible conclusion from this examination suggests that within the worldview of the Israelites in preexilic and postexilic biblical texts (the Hebrew Bible or LXX), there is no "Satan" figure similar to that which is portrayed as an autonomous or semiautonomous figure, as found in the later Christian tradition.

The discussion will now move forward to a collection of texts known as Second Temple Period Jewish literature, which includes the Dead Sea Scrolls, the Pseudepigrapha, and the deuterocanonical texts. Within this variegated collection of texts, the trail of the "satan" figure travels a winding path, and he/it is identified with a variety of monikers by the authors and communities connected to these texts.

Chapter 3

The Satan Figure in the Dead Sea Scrolls

Introduction

Similar to the situation in the HB and LXX, one encounters some difficulty when trying to identify the "satan" figure in the Dead Sea Scrolls (DSS). Only a few fragmentary references to satan are extant amid the collection. We will examine these below prior to discussing other terms that may have taken up a place in the worldview of Second Temple Period (2TP) Jews and the problem of evil. The term שטן occurs once in the Aramaic scroll 4Q213a 1 i 10 (Aramaic Levi Document) and five times in the DSS: 1QH^a 22.25 (כול שטן—"every satan," "adversary") and 24.23 (כול שטן—"every satan," "adversary"); 1QSb i 8 (text is very fragmented: [ק . . .] שטן ל[. . .]—it is possible that the reference here is to a human adversary rather than a spiritual being); 4Q504 1_2 iv 12 (ואין שטן—"and there is no satan/adversary"; possibly a human adversary); and 11Q5 19.15 (אל תשלט בי שטן—"do not let a satan rule over me"). There is very little in any of these fragments that would suggest שטן is being used as a proper name. This may affirm what we determined concerning the use of the term in the HB—that it was not a proper name. This begs the question, If "the satan" was the antidivine figure in the HB, as some suggest, why do we not see that clearly depicted in the DSS?

We see a significant number of terms that in some way appear to identify a being along a similar line as "the satan," although, as we will see below, the evidence for this is not conclusive. Some of the other figures in the DSS include Mastema, Belial, Melchiresha (King of Wickedness), and Malach Hahoshek (the Angel/Messenger of Darkness).[1] Each of these suggests

---

1. Paolo Sacchi suggests that as one of the two spirits created to rule over humanity, the Angel of Darkness is "another interpretation of the devil"; see Sacchi, *Jewish Apocalyptic and Its History*, trans. W. J. Short, JSPSup 20 (Sheffield: Sheffield Academic, 1990), 226.

a figure or being that appears to operate at the head of a demonic hierarchy as some have suggested for the HB satan figure.[2] We must be careful, however, in suggesting that these are just other names for the satan figure of the HB—that is, we should not assume the various authors of the DSS equated a figure identified by one name or title with a figure identified with a different name in a different document. In addition, as Loren Stuckenbruck has noted, "We cannot assume that when single figures are referred to, their designations always function as proper names rather than as descriptions."[3]

Scholars are fairly confident that the collection found in the caves at Khirbet Qumran is a "library" of communities that occupied Qumran over a period of decades,[4] although likely not continuously.[5] This is not to say that portions of the DSS were present during each of those occupations but rather that at some point prior to the attack on the community during the period of the Jewish rebellion of 66–70 CE, its members had gathered a collection of writings, some from outside the camp and some authored within the walls of Khirbet Qumran. The corpus includes scrolls containing portions of the Hebrew Scriptures, commentaries on those biblical texts, works of the "Enochic community," and others since categorized as texts of the *Yahad*, or proto-*Yahad*. Other scrolls found in the collection are of unknown provenance, but as has been argued, they held some form of orthodoxy common to the central ethos of the Qumran community or, at worst, were relevant to a common practice of *halakhic* observance in relation to purity and worship, among other issues. In addition, we find ideas that are familiar neither to the sectarian beliefs of the community or to other groups within 2TP Judaism(s). Hence in attempting to offer evidence of the "satan" figure in the DSS, one must approach the material with caution so as to not overly simplify a very complex issue. In particular, one must be careful not to overlay later Christian understandings of the satan figure when those ideas were not present in the 2TP Jewish worldview(s).

---

2. Other possibilities include "Prince of Animosity" (possibly another name for Mastema), "Angel of Mastema" (possibly read as "the angel Mastema," thus identifying Mastema as an angelic being), and the "spirit of Belial."
3. Loren Stuckenbruck, "The Demonic World of the Dead Sea Scrolls," in *Evil and the Devil*, ed. Ida Fröhlich and Erkki Koskenniemi (London: Bloomsbury, 2013), 51–70, here, 61.
4. See Sidnie White Crawford and Cecilia Wassen, eds., *The Dead Sea Scrolls at Qumran and the Concept of a Library*, STDJ 116 (Leiden: Brill, 2015); Carol A. Newsom, "'Sectually Explicit' Literature from Qumran," in *The Hebrew Bible and Its Interpreters*, ed. David Noel Freedman, Baruch Halpern, and William H. C. Propp (Winona Lake, IN: Eisenbrauns, 1990), 167–87; Karl Heinrich Rengstorf, *Hirbet Qumrân and the Problem of the Library of the Dead Sea Caves*, trans. J. R. Wilkie (Leiden: Brill, 1963).
5. See, for example, Norman Golb, *Who Wrote the Dead Sea Scrolls?* (New York: Scribner, 1995); Florentino García Martínez, "Qumran Origins and Early History: A Groningen Hypothesis," *Folio Orientalia* 25 (1988): 113–36; Gabriele Boccaccini, *Beyond the Essene Hypothesis: The Parting of the Ways between Qumran and Enochic Judaism* (Grand Rapids, MI: Eerdmans, 1998).

One of the designations for the primary evil figure in the DSS is *Belial*. The term is found in approximately twenty-four scrolls, with a large portion of those identified as Essene writings.[6] One of the initial efforts at presenting a view of satan in the Qumran literature came from Peter von der Osten-Sacken in *Gott und Belial*. Through focusing on the dualism of Qumran—in particular, the texts of 1QM and the Treatise of the Two Spirits in 1QS 3.13–4.26—*Gott und Belial* presented the developing view of evil within the community, which, according to von der Osten-Sacken, included drawing a parallel between "the satan" and Belial.[7] However, despite the significant dualistic worldview found in the DSS, several manuscripts speak of a strong monotheistic theology (e.g., 1QS 3.15–17). Following Osten-Sacken, Annette Steudel suggests Belial was "the most frequently used name for the power of evil in Qumran," although this was likely a later development as seen in 11QMelchizedek and the Damascus Document. What is unusual, according to Steudel, is the broad range of genres in which Belial appears: rewritten Scripture, midrashic commentaries, wisdom texts, hymns, and community documents. Steudel contends other named figures have a role in evil, such as Mastema, Melchiresha, and the Angel of Darkness, but rightly so, she warns that each text must be examined to determine if the terms are speaking of the same figure. According to Steudel, Belial is the significant manifestation of evil and most often associated with darkness. Belial is a being that was created by God, and he was created for an "evil" purpose (see 1QM 13.11 and 1QS 3.25; cf. Isa 45:7).[8]

Corrado Martone examined the development of the concept of Belial in his role as "a devil," in which he suggests that the Angel of Darkness had Belial as its name.[9] Like Steudel, Martone contends that Belial was the primary moniker for the personification of evil at Qumran. He too suggests that other figures that fell into this category included Mastema, Melchiresha, and the Angel of Darkness.[10]

One might suggest that the concept of a "satan/devil," identified as Belial, was fluid during the 2TP; however, one must keep in mind that it is unclear if in fact Belial and the satan are one and the same being or if Belial is in fact a personification of evil or the abstract concept of wickedness (see chapter 5). In what follows, I will examine the various texts within the DSS that identify these figures and what role they may have played in the texts from Qumran.

---

6. See Annette Steudel, "God and Belial," in *The Dead Sea Scrolls Fifty Years after Their Discovery: Proceedings of the Jerusalem Congress, July 20–25, 1997*, ed. E. Tov, J. C. VanderKam, and G. Marquis (Jerusalem: Israel Exploration Society, 2000), 332–40, here, 333.
7. See Peter von der Osten-Sacken, *Gott und Belial: Traditionsgeschichtliche Untersuchungen zum Dualismus in den Texten aus Qumran*, SUNT 6 (Gottingen: Vandenhoeck & Ruprecht, 1969).
8. Steudel, "God and Belial," 332–34.
9. See Corrado Martone, "Evil or Devil? Belial between the Bible and Qumran," *Henoch* 26, no. 2 (2004): 115–27.
10. Martone, 115.

Dead Sea Scrolls

11QPs^a (11Q5): Plea for Deliverance

Our initial text that we will examine is 11QPs^a col. 19, lines 1–18, identified as the Plea for Deliverance.[11] This psalm was one of eight or nine compositions that were previously unknown prior to the discovery of the Dead Sea Scrolls.[12] The Plea for Deliverance, an apotropaic prayer, has been dated to approximately 30–50 CE. It is part of the largest psalms scroll discovered at Qumran—the Great Psalms Scrolls, 11QPs^a; it contains fifty compositions, of which eleven are not found in the MT Psalter. The Great Psalms Scroll has been organized according to its affirmation of David as the author and includes a clear sanction of the 364-day solar calendar: "And he wrote 3,600 psalms, and songs to sing before the altar over the continual whole-burnt offering every day, for all the days of the year—364" (11QPs^a col. 27, lines 4–6).

Our point of interest in the Plea for Deliverance is found in 11QPs^a col. 19, lines 13b–16a, which reads, "Forgive my sin, O Lord, and cleanse me from my iniquity. Grant me a spirit of faith and knowledge, and let me not dishonor myself in transgression. Let not [a] satan rule over me,[13] nor an unclean spirit; let neither pain nor the evil inclination take possession of my bones."[14] According to David Flusser, the Plea for Deliverance is a petition to God "to avert personal dangers . . . and grant heavenly bliss."[15] Flusser contends the "spirit of impurity" in line 15 (רוח טמאה, *ruah tamah*) was previously unknown in Judean literature but does appear in Zechariah 13:2 and in rabbinic texts *Sotah* 3a and *Numbers Rabba* 9.9.[16] The term becomes

---

11. Plea for Deliverance is also preserved in two of six fragments from 11Q6, most likely a copy of 11Q5; see J. van der Ploeg, "Fragments d'un manuscrit de Psaumes de Qumrân (11QPs^b)," *RB* 74 (1967): 408–13. It is likely that both texts are a product of the Herodian Era. See Stuckenbruck, "Pleas for Deliverance from the Demonic in Early Jewish Texts," in *Studies in Jewish Prayer*, ed. R. Hayward and Brad Embry, JSSup 17 (Oxford: Oxford University Press, 2005), 55–74, here, 57. It is possible the date of the compilation is from the first half of the second century BCE.
12. The other psalm texts include the Apostrophe to Judah, the Apostrophe to Zion, David's Compositions, the Eschatological Hymn, the Hymn to the Creator, and Three Songs (or Incantations) against Demons. See Peter W. Flint, "Psalms and Psalters at Qumran," in *Early Jewish Literature: An Anthology*, ed. Brad Embry, Ron Herms, and Archie Wright, 2 vols. (Grand Rapids, MI: Eerdmans, 2017–19) 1:150–161.
13. Cf. Ps 119:133b, in which the psalmist pleads, "And do not permit any iniquity to rule over me." Similar wording to 11QPs 19.15 is found in the prayer of Levi in the Aramaic Levi Document (4QLevi^b 1.17, third century BCE): "Do not let any satan rule over me." In addition, "every" or "any" satan also appears in 1QH frag. 4, line 6; frag. 45, line 3; and 1QSb 1.8. Flusser contends the satan that appears in the Plea for Deliverance "seems to be only a dangerous spirit . . . and not the cosmic power as in the New Testament." See Flusser, "Qumran and 'Apotropaic' Prayers," in *Judaism and the Origins of Christianity* (Jerusalem: Magnes, 1988), 214–25, here, 217. Stuckenbruck contends satan is functioning here as a proper noun, although not suggesting it is the NT Satan figure. See Loren T. Stuckenbruck, "Satan and Demons," in *Jesus among Friends and Enemies*, ed. Chris Keith and Larry W. Hurtado (Grand Rapids, MI: Baker, 2011), 173–97.
14. For the complete column translation, see J. A. Sanders, *The Psalms Scroll of Qumran Cave 11 (11QPs^a)*, DJD 4 (Oxford: Clarendon, 1965), 76.
15. Flusser, "Qumran and 'Apotropaic' Prayers," 201.
16. Flusser, 205.

synonymous with "evil spirit" in the late 2TP, in particular in the NT; Flusser argues the "unclean spirit" was thought to cause pain and disease. The apotropaic prayers in the Jewish tradition were developed to invoke the protection of God against these spirits. The text of 11Q5 24.12 contains a plea of the author to the Lord, "Cleanse me Oh Lord from a strike (or plague, נגע) of evil," perhaps suggesting a physical attack or affliction by an evil spirit. Likewise, 11Q5 col. 27.10 states that four songs within the psalm were spoken over demon-possessed individuals to bring them protection and deliverance from the evil spirits. Esther Eshel describes apotropaic prayer as a "request [for] God's protection from evil spirits" that appears in the context of exorcism and incantation texts.[17] Eshel considers the Plea for Deliverance (among other apotropaic prayers) to be nonsectarian.[18] Especially important to note is that the effect of an apotropaic prayer is in the here and now in which the petitioner seeks to restrict the destruction that may be brought about by an evil spirit.

Armin Lange has argued that the noun שטן is used here indeterminately and that "satan" and the "spirit of impurity" both designate a demonic being; satan here is describing a "specific type of heavenly being ... as attested, e.g., in Num 22:22, 32; 1 Kgs 5:18; Job 1:6–12; 2:1–10."[19] However, I have noted previously that there is no suggestion that the satan figure in any of the passages noted by Lange functions as a demonic being. Although Lange's focus is on the phrase "spirit of impurity," he states the two terms are in parallel in the Plea for Deliverance, thus suggesting that this is not "the" Satan but rather "a" satan from the world of the HB. However, Lange goes on to argue that in Jubilees 10.11, the term *satan* is being used as a proper name and that it identifies "the ruler of the anti-divine world," although he fails to state exactly what this phrase means. It should be noted that the context of Jubilees 10 suggests that the Mastema/satan figure is not antidivine but very much functioning under the authority of God. In Jubilees 10.11, the lack of a definite or indefinite article in the Ethiopic language leaves open the possibility of translating this as "the satan" or "a satan" rather than in the sense of a proper name, which may unintentionally suggest a parallel to the Christian Satan figure.[20] One should also

---

17. Esther Eshel, "Apotropaic Prayers in the Second Temple Period," in *Liturgical Perspectives: Prayer and Poetry in Light of the Dead Sea Scrolls*, ed. Esther Chazon, STDJ 48 (Leiden: Brill, 2003), 69–88, here, 69.
18. Esther Eshel, "Genres of Magical Texts in the Dead Sea Scrolls," in *Die Dämonen: Die Dämonologie der israelitisch-jüdischen und frühchristlichen Literatur im Kontext ihrer Umwelt*, ed. Armin Lange, Hermann Lichtenberger, and K. F. Diethard Römheld (Tübingen, Germany: Mohr Siebeck, 2003), 395–414, here, 396. Other texts one might consider "nonsectarian apotropaic prayers" include the Prayer of Levi and Jub. 10.1–6 and 12.19–20.
19. See Armin Lange, "Considerations concerning the 'Spirits of Impurity' in Zech 13:2," in Lichtenberger, Lange, and Römheld, *Die Dämonen*, 260–61. Lange suggests other texts in which "satan" is used in a similar fashion: Zech 3:1–2; 1 Chr 21:1; Jub. 23.29; 46.2; 50.5; 4QDibham 1–2 iv 12 (Dibre Hame'orot); 4QLevi^b ar (4Q213a) 1.17 (Aramaic Levi Document).
20. See James Vanderkam, *The Book of Jubilees*, CSCO 511 (Leuven, Belgium: Peeters, 1989), 61.

note the similarity to the phrase found in Jubilees 1.20, in which Moses asks God not to allow the "spirit of Belial" to rule over Israel—again sounding very much like an apotropaic prayer as in 11Q5 (cf. also 4Q213a 1 i 10; also Ps 119:33b). We should not, however, conclude that *satan* and *Belial* are synonymous.

Stuckenbruck argues for the "functional equivalence here between 'satan' and 'unclean spirit'" in the Plea for Deliverance.[21] If one follows the etiology of demons as presented in the Enochic literature, it is possible to equate the unclean spirit here with the spirits of the giants (*mamzerim*) from a portion of the Book of Watchers (1 En. 6–16). The phrase "spirit of uncleanness" also appears in a list of evil spirits in 4Q444 1–4 i + 5.8 that includes the *mamzerim* of the Enoch Watcher tradition. However, the difficulty is that there is no "satan" figure in the Watcher tradition. Stuckenbruck contends that it is difficult to determine if the author here is using "satan" as a particular being—that is, "Satan" in the sense of a proper name. Alternatively, the term may be understood as a kind of being who functions as an adversary.[22] This would suggest that "satan" is not a proper name, while at the same time, it also does not need to indicate an "angelic being subservient to God or as a general designation for one's enemies." Stuckenbruck strongly suggests that this role goes beyond any norm of the satan figure in the HB and should not be understood as one subservient to God.[23]

We can gather little from 11QPs[a] concerning the meaning or identity of the term *satan*. The author seems to be making reference to some sort of spirit as it occurs alongside "spirit of uncleanness." This has been understood to reveal a parallel of function between satan and the spirit of uncleanness.[24] The text 11Q5 col. 19.15 suggests this spirit may lead people to transgress through its evil inclination; this may account for the connection to an "evil spirit." A similar "Plea" is offered by Noah in Jubilees 10.3–6, in which he pleads, "Do not let evil spirits rule over them."[25] Satan may also be responsible for the physical affliction of individuals. Lange has suggested that the term *satan* becomes a proper name in Jubilees 10.8. However, there is no reason to make that leap due to the lack of the definite article in Ethiopic Jubilees 10.8,[26] which allows one to understand the term as a function of the spirit or one of many satans. We

21. Stuckenbruck, "Pleas for Deliverance," 58.
22. Stuckenbruck, 58.
23. Stuckenbruck, 58–59.
24. Stuckenbruck suggests that if the author of 11Q5 was aware of the 4Q213a and Ps 119:133 tradition of satan, then the lack of כול or the negation אין may signal a shift to a "specific malevolent being" named Satan. See Loren T. Stuckenbruck, *Myth of the Rebellious Angels*, WUNT 335 (Tübingen, Germany: Mohr Siebeck, 2014), 95.
25. From this line, one may then move to connect these evil spirits to the "spirits of Mastema" in Jub. 19.28—"May the spirits of Mastema not rule over you and your descendants," which adds to the ever-widening circle of synonyms for *satan* in the DSS: satan, unclean/evil spirit, Belial, Mastema.
26. Unfortunately, no Aramaic fragments are extant of Jub. 1.20 or Jub. 10.8.

also see an attempt to connect the satan figure of 11Q5 to the satan of Jubilees 10, which, in a somewhat strained effort, correlates to the "spirit of Beliar" in Jubilees 1.20.²⁷

Unfortunately, there is nothing in the text that makes it clear that the "spirit" is either subservient or not subservient to God. The term *satan* could simply be understood as having the task of "leading [one] astray" from the path of God as is suggested in the Aramaic Levi Document (4Q213a 1 i 10), which we shall discuss in what follows.

One might argue that there is increasing participation of the figure identified as satan in the "problem of evil" in the mind of the author of the Plea for Deliverance. It might be suggested that a satan, alongside unclean spirits, is becoming one of the tools by which suffering may occur in the life of an individual. It does appear from the prayer that God has the ability to control the satan figure, but it is not clear if the satan is operating under God's authority.

Aramaic Levi Document

The Aramaic Levi Document (hereafter, ALD) is also identified as the Aramaic Testament of Levi, and possibly the Aramaic Testament of Levi from the Cairo Genizah.²⁸ It survives in three fragmentary scrolls from Qumran, 4Q213–14 (4Q213, 213a, 213b, 4Q214, 214a, 214b) and 1Q21, dated to the Hasmonean period around 100 BCE.²⁹ In addition, it survives in a Greek manuscript identified as (Mount) Athos, Koutlousmous, number 39. This text was later used in the reconstruction of the Aramaic text of 4Q213.³⁰

Similar to the Plea for Deliverance discussed above, the prayer located in ALD has been connected to Psalm 119:133b, which Flusser argues was a common Jewish prayer originating perhaps in the second century BCE.³¹ The translation of 4Q213a fragment 1.17 reads, "And do not let *any satan* [כל שטן] rule over me,"³² while, as noted above, Psalm 119:133b reads, "And do not permit *any iniquity* [כל און] to rule over me." Flusser has argued that 4Q213 may be an

---

27. Other connections are between Jubilees and 11Q5 have been made. See Jacques van Ruiten, "Angels and Demons in the Book of Jubilees," in *Angels: The Concept of Celestial Beings: Origins, Development and Reception*, ed. F. V. Reiterer, T. Nicklas, and K. Schöpflin (Berlin: Walter de Gruyter, 2007), 585–609. Van Ruiten offers parallels between 11Q5 col. 16 and Jub. 2.2–3 and the "Hymn of the Creator."
28. Cambridge Genizah frag. T-S 16.94; however, it was later determined this is not the same document. See James Kugel, "How Old Is the Aramaic Levi Document?," *DSS* 14, no. 3 (2007): 291–312.
29. Kugel notes that it is generally believed the author of the Testament of the Twelve Patriarchs used ALD to write the Testament of Levi. He comments that the Aramaic document was translated into Greek and portions were inserted into the manuscript of Mount Athos, Koutloumousiou, no. 39, Testament of the Twelve Patriarchs. See Kugel, 291n3.
30. See M. Stone and J. C. Greenfield, "The Prayer of Levi," *JBL* 112 (1993): 247–66.
31. Flusser, "Qumran and 'Apotropaic' Prayers," 194. Flusser offers a text comparison with the Mishnaic prayers (*Berakhoth* 16b, B. *Baba Bathra* 16a) in which the author of the prayers, perhaps offering his reading of Ps 119.133, inserts "evil inclination" in place of "iniquity" and "satan": "let the evil inclination not rule over us" (198–99). See also E. Eshel, J. C. Greenfield, and M. E. Stone, *The Aramaic Levi Document*, SVTP 9 (Leiden: Brill, 2004), 129–30.
32. See 1 En. 40.7; 65.6, which appear to describe multiple satans.

attempt at a "Midrashic paraphrase" of the Psalm 119 prayer.³³ When comparing the three readings, the prayer of the Plea for Deliverance (19.15) does not include כל preceding the שטן, ALD includes כל ("any," "every") preceding שטן ("satan/adversary") in 4Q213a, and Psalm 119 has כל און instead of כל שטן. This suggests even more firmly that "satan," in each case, is not being used to designate a proper name.³⁴ Henryk Drawnel makes two important points in describing the satan of 4Q213a. He contends this figure is not a spiritual being opposed to God;³⁵ this adversary (spirit being) is a member of the heavenly court. One might argue it is similar to the spiritual being found in Zechariah 3:2 and Job 1–2.

As has been noted by Stuckenbruck and others, the context of the prayer is concerned with a demonic danger that may cause the author to turn from the path of the divine or possibly incur physical or mental affliction by a satan.³⁶ The use of satan in these cases—that is, alongside a spirit of impurity—seems to suggest the term should hold a much broader range of meaning than simply "accuser" or "adversary," thus creating a closer tie to the nature of the evil spirits that emerge during the 2TP.

Similar to the author of the Plea for Deliverance, the author of ALD might be suggesting that a satan, alongside unclean spirits, is becoming one of the tools by which suffering may occur in the life of an individual, thus having a significant role in the problem of evil.

1QHa: HODAYOT

The Hodayot Scroll was published in 1955 by Eleazar Sukenik.³⁷ It is written in Hebrew and dates from the first century BCE. When published, it contained eighteen columns with sixty-six fragments, but the original makeup of the content is difficult to determine definitively due to holes in the physical scroll. The eighteen columns consist of approximately 30–35 hymns of blessing.

The term *satan* appears in 1QHª 22.25 ("for you rebuke every destructive adversary [שטן]"; Suk. 4.6) and 24.23 ("[you rebuked from] them every adversary [שטן] and destroyer"; Suk 45.3). In both cases, שטן is preceded by the term כול, "every/all/any," thus reading "every/all/any adversary." In 1QHª 22.25, there is no indication this is a spiritual adversary; rather, the

---

33. Flusser, "Qumran and 'Apotropaic' Prayers," 197. See also Robert Kugler, *From Patriarch to Priest: The Levi-Priestly Tradition from* Aramaic Levi *to* Testament of Levi, SBLEJL 9 (Atlanta: Scholars Press, 1996), 73. See also Henryk Drawnel, *An Aramaic Wisdom Text from Qumran* (Leiden: Brill, 2004), 216.
34. Stuckenbruck, "Pleas for Deliverance," 61. Cf. Stone and Greenfield ("Prayer of Levi," 262), who contend the same expression (every/any satan) is used in 1QHª frags. 4.6 and 45.3 (Sukenik numbering).
35. Drawnel, *Aramaic Wisdom Text*, 216. Here Drawnel states that satan "seems to be only a dangerous spirit . . . and not the cosmic power as in the New Testament"; the spirit is simply an adversarial spirit. Cf. Flusser, "Qumran and 'Apotropaic' Prayers," 197.
36. Stuckenbruck, "Pleas for Deliverance," 60–61.
37. E. L. Sukenik, ed., *The Dead Sea Scrolls of the Hebrew University* (Jerusalem: Magnes, 1955).

context appears to be speaking of humans, as it follows the term *noble ones* (נדיבים). Similarly, 1QH^a 24.23 indicates more than one adversary, but it is in a context that mentions "the bastards" or "bastard spirits" (הממזרים, 24.16; ממזרים רוחות, 24.26), which could be a reference to the spirits of the giants from the Watcher tradition. However, this does not suggest that the satan figure mentioned here should be understood in the sense that it/he is a leader of the evil spirits. It appears likely these references could be to someone, or something, angelic or human who engages in adversarial activity.

1QS: COMMUNITY RULE

The scroll in question includes three documents, 1QS (Community Rule, or *Serekh HaYahad*), 1QSa (Rule of the Congregation), and 1QSb (Blessings). Each is part of the same scroll written in Hebrew around 100–75 BCE in a Hasmonean script.[38] Other versions of the Community Rule were found in Cave 4 and include 4Q255–64 (likely an early stage of development) and two small fragments, 5Q11, from Cave 5. The Community Rule describes the aesthetic lifestyle of the community members and includes a significant dualistic worldview in which we find the term *satan*.

The Blessings section, 1QSb, contains the only use of the term *satan* in the quite fragmentary line 1.8: [. . .]ק[ודש יר . . .]ל שטן[. . .] ([. . .]*l* satan [. . . h]oly).[39] The term here, although it is difficult to determine context and thus if the author has in mind spiritual or human, is translated "adversary," and it certainly does not appear to be a proper name.[40] Despite the lack of specificity as to the nature of the satan, 1QS introduces what some have argued is a/the leader of the wicked side of this cosmic dualism, the figure of Belial. In 1QS 1.18, the author speaks of events "in the reign of Belial" (בממשלת בליעל), which for reasons that are unclear, suggest a personified evil being, when *Belial* may only indicate an age of unworthiness or wickedness (see chapter 5). Stuckenbruck contends that "Belial becomes a gathering point around which discourse about personified evil is constructed"—that is, a single demonic figure.[41] More will be offered on the "other" names or figures that have been closely identified with the satan figure in chapter 5.

---

38. Elisha Qimron and James H. Charlesworth, *Rule of the Community and Related Documents* (Tübingen, Germany: Mohr Siebeck, 1994), 1.
39. Qimron and Charlesworth, 123.
40. See Stuckenbruck, *Myth of the Rebellious Angels*, 94.
41. Stuckenbruck, "Satan and Demons," 180.

4Q504: Words of the Luminaries

The Words of the Luminaries is a Hebrew work that is extant in three manuscripts among the scrolls—4Q504, 4Q505, and 4Q506. We will focus on 4Q504, which consists of forty-nine fragments that make up nearly the whole text; it has been dated by Maurice Baillet and Esther Chazon to circa 150 BCE.[42] By comparison, 4Q505 consists of only ten fragments, and 4Q506 consists of forty-nine smaller fragments that overlap with 4Q504.[43] Chazon contends this is a nonsectarian text written prior to the settlement of the community. The text served in a liturgical function for weekly prayers that were repeated in the morning and evening with the passing of the moon and sun.

The term *satan* appears in 4Q504 frag 1_2Riv.12–13 in the midst of a prayer of glorification of God, which reads, "Zion, your holy city and the House of your glory. And there is no adversary (שטן) or misfortune," possibly citing 1 Kings 5:4; if this is the case, then the context is that of a military adversary not a spiritual being (cf. 1 Chr 21:1). There is certainly no sense of a proper name, and the context offers little from which to speak to its place in the problem of evil.

Summary

As can be understood from the above discussion, the evidence regarding the term/figure of satan in these sources is quite limited. However, one must keep in mind the fragmentary nature of the scrolls; it may be possible or even likely that the term appeared in other material that is no longer extant. In each identified occurrence, the term suggests some sort of adversary, either a spirit or a human figure, but the extant scrolls offer little context to make a final determination. It is likely, though, that the term is not being used in the sense of a proper name; rather, it appears to describe the function of a figure. It does seem to shift the so-called blame for the problem of evil away from God to some degree, and the use of the term *satan* suggests a figure acting as an adversary that may or may not be operating under the authority of God.

---

42. Maurice Baillet, *Discoveries in the Judean Desert*, vol. 7 (Oxford: Oxford University Press, 1982); Esther Chazon, "A Liturgical Document from Qumran and Its Implications: 'Words of the Luminaries' (4QDibHam)" (PhD diss., Hebrew University, 1991).
43. See Daniel Falk, *Daily, Sabbath, & Festival Prayers in the Dead Sea Scrolls*, STDJ 7 (Leiden: Brill, 1998), 59. There is some disagreement as to whether 4Q505 belongs to *Words of the Luminaries*. Florentino García Martínez argues it belongs to 4Q509, Festival Prayers; see his review of *Qumran grotte 4, III (4Q482–4Q520)*, DJD 7 (Oxford: Clarendon Press, 1982), in *JSJ* 15 (1984): 157–64.

Chapter 4

The Satan Figure in the Second Temple Period Pseudepigrapha and Other Jewish Writings

Introduction

Previously we have examined the term *satan* in the Second Temple Period literature identified as the Dead Sea Scrolls. As noted, there is little extant material that suggests widespread use of the term in the DSS; the occurrences in which we find the term make no suggestion that it is referring to a leader of a group of evil spirits but rather may mean a spiritual or human adversary. However, we discover that the term has been taken up by the authors of the OT Pseudepigrapha and is used in a variety of contexts that will be discussed below.

The Pseudepigrapha is a group of texts, mostly unrelated,[1] of which many are considered deuterocanonical by several branches of Christianity, including the Catholic Church prior to the Reformation. These writings are attributed to various biblical figures who no doubt did not author the writings but held some position of authority within the author's intended audience or community.[2]

There are two corresponding Greek terms used in the Pseudepigrapha that guide our examination: *the satan* (ὁ σατανᾶς) and *the devil* (ὁ διάβολος). In addition, one must take into account the Ge'ez terms used in the Enochic Similitudes and in the book of Jubilees: *satan* (ሰይጣን; *sayāṭān*) and *satans* (ሰያጥን; *səyāṭən*). Several texts from the Pseudepigrapha employ the

---
1. See Matthias Henze and Liv Ingeborg Lied, eds., *The Old Testament Pseudepigrapha: Fifty Years of the Pseudepigrapha Section at the SBL*, SBLEJL 50 (Atlanta: SBL, 2019); also Daniel M. Gurtner, *Introducing the Pseudepigrapha of Second Temple Judaism: Message, Context, and Significance* (Grand Rapids, MI: Baker Academic, 2020).
2. See James H. Charlesworth, ed., *Old Testament Pseudepigrapha*, 2 vols., 2nd ed. (Peabody, MA: Hendrickson, 2010); Richard Bauckham, James Davila, and Alex Panayotov, eds., *Old Testament Pseudepigrapha: More Noncanonical Scriptures* (Grand Rapids, MI: Eerdmans, 2013); portions of the Old Testament Pseudepigrapha appear in Embry, Herms, and Wright, *Early Jewish Literature*.

Greek term σατανᾶς, or a derivative of it: Testament of Dan 3.6; 5.6; 6.1; Testament of Gad 4.7; Testament of Asher 6.4; Testament of Job 3.6; 4.4; 6.4; 7.1, 6, 12; 16.2; 20.1; 23.1, 3, 11; 27.1, 6; 41.5; Ascension of Isaiah (Gk. MS A) 1.9, 11; 2.2; 2.7; 3.2, 8; 5.16; 7.9; 11.23, 41, 43; History of the Rechabites 7.8; 19.1, 2; the Latin Life of Adam and Eve (VITA) 9.1; and the Greek parallel to VITA, Apocalypse of Moses 17.1. Other significant Pseudepigrapha books that translated the Hebrew Helel Ben-Shahar include the suggested synonymous Greek term διάβολος, or a derivative of it: Testament of Naphtali 3.3; 8.4, 6; Testament of Job 3.3; 17.1; 26.6; Testament of Moses 2, 8, 9, 10; Testament of Solomon 15.11; History of the Rechabites 20.1; 21.1, 4; 22.2, Ascension of Isaiah (Gk. MS A) 3.3, 18; Apocalypse of Sedrach 4.5; 5.3; 3 Baruch 4.8; Life of Adam and Eve (VITA) 12.1; and Apocalypse of Moses 15.3; 16.1, 2, 5; 17.4; 21.3; 29.15. We will briefly offer a context for these occurrences.

Testaments of the Twelve Patriarchs

TESTAMENT OF DAN

The Testament of Dan is found among the Testaments of the Twelve Patriarchs (T12 Patr.),[3] a pseudepigraphal work tied to the twelve biblical patriarchs Reuben, Simeon, Levi, Judah, Issachar, Zebulun, Dan, Naphtali, Gad, Asher, Joseph, and Benjamin. Each testament offers the deathbed testimony of each of the twelve sons of Jacob to his children, in which he exhorts them to avoid the sins the patriarch has faced and to embody the virtues of life. The closing portion of each testimony includes prophetic words on the future of Israel and a report of the patriarch's entombment.

Scholars suggest the original collection was composed in Hebrew by a Hellenized Jew post-250 BCE and likely written in the Maccabean Period (ca. 167–163 BCE).[4] Several suggestions of provenance have been offered: Palestine, as an Aramaic or Hebrew original; Egypt, due to the internal evidence; or Syria, the most likely place of origin due to the portrayed power of that kingdom in the T12 Patr. What can be argued is that there are some clear Christian interpolations present in the documents, probably dated from the second century CE.[5]

---

3. Robert Kugler, *Testaments of the Twelve Patriarchs* (Sheffield: Sheffield Academic, 2001); Howard C. Kee, "Testaments of the Twelve Patriarchs," in *The Old Testament Pseudepigrapha*, ed. James H. Charlesworth, 1st ed. (New York: Doubleday, 1983), 1:775–828.
4. Elias J. Bickerman, "The Date of the Testaments of the Twelve Patriarchs," *JBL* 69, no. 3 (September 1950): 245–60.
5. See Robert H. Charles, *The Apocrypha and Pseudepigrapha of the Old Testament*, 2 vols. (Oxford: Clarendon, 1913).

The Testament of Dan describes the patriarch's difficulties with anger and lying. In his testimony, the author explains that during his life, he was under the influence of Beliar (1.7; 4.7; 5.1, 10, 11), who had caused him to turn against Joseph and was the instigator in his plan to kill him. However, one should keep in mind that *Beliar* could be the abstract "wickedness" as previously suggested for Belial in the DSS. Dan's message to his children is that they should avoid anger, as it brings destruction upon all who embrace it. In the Greek version of the Testament of Dan 3, Dan warns that anger is evil, and it is brought on by an evil force. Verse 3.6 states that behind that evil force is the spirit of anger, assisted with the spirit of falsehood that goes out from the "right hand of the satan" (ἐκ δεξιῶν τοῦ σατανᾶ), perhaps suggesting this is not a proper name but rather "the adversary," but a proper name cannot be ruled out. According to Testament of Dan 5.5–6, those who abandon the Lord (ἀποστῆτε τοῦ κυρίου) "will walk among every evil thing," and "with all wickedness, the spirits of error [will be] working in [them]." In 3.6, the author notes that he has read in the book of Enoch (Similitudes?) "that the satan is their ruler" (ὅτι ὁ ἄρχων ὑμῶν ἐστι ὁ σατανᾶς); again, here we have "the satan" likely not signifying a proper name, but the possibility cannot be ruled out. Interestingly, this adversary has working for or with him "spirits of sexual promiscuity" (τὰ πνεύματα τῆς πορνείας) and "spirits of arrogance" (τὰ πνεύματα τῆς ὑπερηφανίας) that cause individuals to sin before the Lord (3.6).

The final satan reference in Testament of Dan is in 6.1. Here Dan exhorts his children to fear the Lord and to be on guard for "the satan and his spirits" (καὶ προσέχετε ἑαυτοῖς τοῦ σατανᾶ τῶν πνευμάτων αὐτοῦ). These spirits may be the same "spirits of wickedness and pride" identified in 5.6. The fact that the author references several spirits working with the satan figure may suggest some connection to the tradition of Jubilees 10, in which Mastema has multiple spirits working with him to test and try humanity with the permission of YHWH.

In Testament of Dan, we see the work of the satan figure is to draw people away from the Lord by testing them, similar to what we see evil spirits attempting throughout the 2TP literature. The figure does not necessarily suggest he/it is autonomous in the sense that he/it is working at his/its own charge. While we do find references to the figure or concept of Belial in Testament of Dan and other T12 Patr. that suggest a spirit working in the realm of evil, under what or whose authority he/it does this work is unclear.

Testament of Gad

The Testament of Gad offers the testimony of the ninth son of Jacob. Gad's difficulties centered on his hatred for Joseph and his desire to kill him. This hatred appears to be brought on by Joseph's dreams (2.2), which made Gad jealous of him and resulted in the plan of Judah and

Gad to sell Joseph to the Ishmaelites. Gad claims in his testimony that the plot to kill Joseph was because of greed (2.4). Gad contends in 3.1 that he was led astray by the spirit of hatred (τῷ πνεύματι τοῦ μίσους), which he describes in 3.3 as an evil that can blind the soul of an individual (ὅτι τὸ μῖσος ἐτύφλωσε τὴν ψυχὴν αὐτοῦ). The term *satan* appears in Testament of Gad only once, in 4.7. Here, Gad warns, "For among all men, the spirit of hatred through discouragement collaborates with the satan (συνεργεῖ τῷ σατανᾷ) in all things to the death of the person." Here again the noun *satan* is used with the definite article, suggesting this is perhaps a title for the being rather than its proper name; at the same time, it could be translated as the "evil one." In the Testament of Gad, the author suggests that the satan figure is working in collaboration with a group of spirits—in this case, the spirit of hatred—to lead astray humanity from the plan of God. The author goes on to suggest that obedience to the Torah is assisted by the spirit of love (τὸ πνεῦμα τῆς ἀγάπης) in collaboration with the Torah, which results in the redemption of the individual. What is revealed here is a cosmological dualism: spirits on two sides attempt to sway the individual to obey or disobey the Torah and to follow or not to follow God. This is similar to what is described in some texts from Qumran (e.g., 1QS).

Testament of Asher

The Testament of Asher stands out among the T12 Patr. in that it does not include the deathbed testimony; rather, the author, as Asher, speaks to his children "while he [is] still healthy" (1.2). The author uses language similar to what we find in the Treatise of the Two Spirits from Qumran: "God has granted two paths to the sons of humanity" (δύο ὁδοὺς ἔδωκεν ὁ θεὸς τοῖς υἱοῖς τῶν ἀνθρώπων; 1.3). In addition to the two paths, God has two mindsets, two ways of practice, two manners of life, and two ends. The "two" are defined as good and evil, which appear to be the choices offered to the two mindsets in the human soul (described in 1.5 as "chest," στέρνοις—the center of the human being).

The author of the Testament of Asher offers one of the clearest views of the problem evil in 2TP literature when he speaks of the ongoing presence of evil in the world and what provokes it. He describes how the individual has two aspects in the soul and that one must be careful to keep the two distinguishable in one's mind (ch. 2). There is clearly an expectation of human responsibility in how evil works in an individual's life and the life of the community. In 1.8–9, the author presents a very clear statement of anthropological dualism. The author writes that if the person follows the counsel of the evil (inclination?) (ἐν πονηρῷ κλίνῃ τὸ διαβούλιον), they accept the evil and are ruled over by "the Beliar" (κυριευθεὶς ὑπὸ τοῦ βελιάρ—here, *Beliar* could be understood as wickedness rather than a personified evil being);

the individual, even in practicing good, turns it to evil (see 2.1–3.2). The author warns his children that this individual has an inclination that is filled with the poison of an evil spirit (ἰοῦ πονηροῦ πνεύματος πεπλήρωται; 1.9). Thus, his children are to avoid the evil choices and pursue only good by fleeing evil and committing only good works. The term *satan* appears only once in the Testament of Asher, in 6.4, and is only extant in the four minor manuscripts (a, β, A, S¹) in the translation of R. H. Charles, while the majority of the manuscripts contain *Beliar*.[6] This does not necessarily equate the two terms but certainly suggests the presence of a "spirit of wickedness" in the author's community, or at least a perceived spirit's presence. The author speaks of the ultimate end of humans and how, in that end, their righteousness is displayed. In the end, the individual is made known to the angels of the Lord and the angels of the satan (τοὺς ἀγγέλους κυρίου καὶ τοῦ σατανᾶ; 6.4). It should be noted that here also, we see the use of the definite article with satan, thus reducing the likelihood of it being a personal name and increasing that of a possible translation being "the adversary." The author goes on to state that upon death, the soul of an evil person will be tormented by "the spirit of wickedness" (τοῦ πονηροῦ πνεύματος) that he served by his wicked deeds (6.5). The soul of the righteous will meet the angel of peace who will comfort them in the eternal life (6.6).

Testament of Naphtali

The Testament of Naphtali presents the deathbed testimony of Naphtali, the eighth son of Jacob. The text, which is quite fragmentary, required reconstruction using a medieval Hebrew manuscript of the text that appeared as part of the Chronicles of Jerehmeel. Additionally, Hebrew fragments of a Testament of Naphtali, 4Q215, were found in the Qumran caves; these offer a parallel to the Bilhah narrative in the T12 Patr. There is no mention of the satan figure in 4Q215. The Testament of Naphtali uses the Greek term ὁ διάβολος (devil, adversary), or a form of it, rather than ὁ σατανᾶς (the satan, the adversary). The theme of cosmological or anthropological dualism runs through the Testament of Naphtali as we saw in the Testament of Gad and the Testament of Asher; in the Testament of Naphtali 3.1, the author seems to be setting the "will of God" (τὸ θέλημα τοῦ θεοῦ) over against "the will of the devil" (τὸ θέλημα τοῦ διαβόλου), which may suggest a cosmological dualism that involves a conflict between God and the devil. The author urges his children to hold fast to the will of God through purity of heart and to cast aside the will of the devil, which is brought on by "corrupt deeds through greediness and empty words that deceive your soul."

6. Robert H. Charles, *The Greek Versions of the Testaments of the Twelve Patriarchs: Edited from Nine Mss., Together with the Variants of the Armenian and Slavonic Versions and Some Hebrew Fragments* (Oxford: Clarendon, 1908), 179n1.

In verse 8.4, the author states that if a person accomplishes good, then God will be glorified through them. At the same time, the devil (ὁ διάβολος) will flee from them and wild animals (τά θηρία) will fear them. The Greek τά θηρία is the same term used in the testing of Christ in the wilderness in Mark 1:13, which suggests the author may have in mind the evil spirits in both Mark and the Testament of Naphtali. Verse 8.6 offers a contrasting situation: if a person does not do good deeds, he will be cursed by men and angels, and God will be dishonored. In addition, the author states that the devil (ὁ διάβολος) will take up residence in that person as his vessel (possession?) and every wild beast (πᾶν θηρίον) will have power over them. Like the other T12 Patr., the term διάβολος appears with a definite article, suggesting this is not a proper name. Like the LXX translation and the Greek NT, the Testament of Naphtali appears to use the term διάβολος synonymously with σατανᾶς.

Other Pseudepigrapha Testaments

TESTAMENT OF JOB

The Testament of Job is similar in form to the T12 Patr., and like the biblical book of Job, it includes as a major character the figure of the satan. The text survives in Greek, Slavonic, and Coptic (incomplete), but some scholars have argued for an Aramaic or Hebrew original. The surviving text dates from the first century BCE or CE and likely came from within an Egyptian Jewish sect, possibly the Therapeutae. However, others suggest a Jewish Christian author from the second century CE translated the surviving Greek version from Hebrew.[7]

The Testament of Job follows the pattern of a Jewish testament that offers ethical wisdom to the dying person's offspring. The story opens with a deathbed scene like those found in most of the T12 Patr.; the testimony offers ethical and moral teachings and ends with the death of the main character. The main character in the Testament of Job went by the name of Jobab until the Lord changed his name to Job, although it is not clear when this occurred. In his testament to his children, he tells them the events of his life concerning his first family, in which he exhorts his current children to live a life of patience.

The term σατανᾶς, or a form of it, appears thirteen times in the Testament of Job: 3.6; 4.4; 6.4; 7.6, 12; 16.2; 20.1; 23.1, 3, 11; 27.1, 6; and 41.5. The first occurrence in 3.6 is used to described a nearby temple of idols known as "the place of the satan" (ὁ τόπος τοῦ σατανᾶ),[8]

---

7. R. P. Spittler, "Testament of Job," in Charlesworth, *Old Testament Pseudepigrapha*, 1st ed., 1:829–68, here, 830–33.
8. Cf. Rev 2:9, 13; 3:9.

which is there for the purpose of deceiving humanity. Jobab asks God to grant him authority to cleanse the temple. The second occurrence of τοῦ σατανᾶ appears in 4.4–5 as a warning to Job should he attempt to cleanse the temple; the light that is speaking to him states that the satan will rise up against Job with wrath—similar to the actions of the satan figure in the biblical Job. The satan is unable to kill Job but can afflict him with plagues and carry off his goods and his children. In a sense, it is a test of the virtue of patience after which, if Job remains faithful, God will restore his goods in double and make his name famous for generations (4.6)—again, much like the biblical Job.

In 5.1–2, after being sealed by the angel (σφραγισθῆναί με ὑπὸ τοῦ ἀγγέλου), Job goes with his children and fifty youths and destroys the temple of the idol (τοῦ εἰδωλίου), which brings about Job's troubles. In 6.4, the satan (ὁ σατανᾶς) comes knocking at Job's door disguised as a beggar, but he is turned away. He appears again in disguise in 7.6 and 7.12, attempting to draw out Job from the house. In chapter 8, the satan figure, following a similar pattern to the biblical book of Job, asks (ὅρκωσεν; "binds by an oath") God for authority over Job's wealth, and it is granted to him. The term appears again in 16.2, which states that the satan came down and unrelentingly killed much of Job's livestock under the authority he had been granted. Other beasts were also taken by Job's countrymen, who had risen up against him, but Job maintained his praise for God (16.7).

In 20.1, ὁ σατανᾶς concedes that he is unable to provoke Job to turn from God and attacks Job with plagues and physical harm. We are told that Job spent forty-eight years on a dung heap outside the city, watching his wife and children be abused by the local noblemen (chs. 21–22). ὁ σατανᾶς appears again in 23.1, 3, and 11, in which the satan disguises himself as a seller of bread to deceive Job's wife, Sitis. He attempts to convince her that she and her family deserve the evil that has befallen them. In 23.11, the author states that the satan "was leading astray (πλαγιάζων) her heart," suggesting his task, one granted to him by God, is to deceive humans. The final two appearances of ὁ σατανᾶς are in chapter 27. In 27.1, Job rebukes him directly for deceiving Sitis. Interestingly, at this rebuke, the satan (identifying Job as a "man of flesh" [ἀνθρώπου σαρκίνου], and himself as a "spirit," [ἐγὼ εἰμι πνεῦμα]), weeping, retreats from any further oppression of Job. In the final occurrence in 27.6, the author states that the satan left Job for three years, with no further explanation as to what that means.

In the Testament of Job, we find the satan (also called "the devil") portrayed in ways that are similar to the satan figure in the biblical book of Job. He is a figure whose task appears to be to test and deceive humanity (in this case, Job), but he can only do this under the authority of God (ch. 7).

Testament of Moses

The Testament of Moses, also known as the Assumption of Moses, offers some evidence for the recognition of the satan/devil figure in the first century CE. The difficulty with the Testament of Moses and the Assumption of Moses in relation to the other "Testaments" discussed here is the lack of a death-and-ascension scene—an event one would expect in an assumption text. However, the surviving Latin manuscript has significant gaps that could explain the missing scene. Some scholars argue for two distinct documents and contend the Assumption of Moses text has been completely lost.[9] It is thought that the Assumption of Moses is cited in Jude 9: "Yet Michael, the Archangel, when contending with the devil and disputing about the body of Moses, did not bring an accusation against him [the devil], but said, 'The Lord rebuke you!'" Clement of Alexandria, in commenting on Jude, states that this verse, Jude 9, confirms the existence of the Assumption of Moses. Origen also affirms this in *On First Principles* 3.2, where he states that Jude is citing the Assumption of Moses. As a result, one can only suggest the actual presence of the terms with which we are concerned—*the satan* and *the devil*.

The only extant text is a Latin palimpsest discovered in Milan in 1861, dated to about the sixth century CE. The content is considered incomplete, with at least one-third to one-half of the text lost (likely where the assumption scene material was situated), and what remains is fragmentary and consists of spelling and grammar "mistakes."[10] It appears the Latin is a translation of Greek with a few transliterations of the Greek, accompanied by obvious Greek syntax, although it likely has Semitic origins. Dating the text is difficult, and scholars have offered several possibilities: (1) first half of the second century CE, (2) following the Maccabean Revolt in 167 BCE,[11] and (3) prior to the fall of Jerusalem in 70 CE.[12] The most likely provenance for the text is a Palestinian location from one of three possible Jewish groups—the Hasidim, a sect of the Pharisees, or the Essenes—but there is no definitive answer as to authorship even in the broadest terms.

The Testament of Moses also differs from the previous testaments discussed in that it does not involve Moses's children; in this testament, the last words of the principal character are addressed to Joshua, his successor. Akin to the biblical account told in Deuteronomy, the

---

9. See Ron Herms, "Testament of Moses," in Embry, Herms, and Wright, *Early Jewish Literature*, 2:639. See also the *Stichometry of Nicephorus* of Patriarch Nicephorus Constantinople from the ninth century, who lists the two as separate texts.
10. J. Priest, "Testament of Moses," in Charlesworth, *Old Testament Pseudepigrapha*, 1st ed., 1:919–34, here, 919–21.
11. See J. Licht, "Taxo, or the Apocalyptic Doctrine of Vengeance," *JJS* 12 (1961): 95–103; George Nickelsburg, "An Antiochan Date for the Testament of Moses," in *Studies on the Testament of Moses* (Cambridge, MA: Society of Biblical Literature, 1973), 33–37.
12. Robert H. Charles, *The Assumption of Moses* (London: A&C Black, 1897).

testimony is made prior to the Israelites passing over into the land. The speech of Moses offers a summation of the history of the nation from the conquest of Canaan to the return from the Babylon exile. The resettlement in Jerusalem and the land is followed by a period of apostasy during the Hellenistic period and the Hasmonean era.

The extant Latin text of Testament of Moses contains no reference to the satan or the devil. One can only suggest the entire testament at one point contained a text similar to that found in Jude 9. Here, the name used is ὁ διάβολος rather than ὁ σατανᾶς. In the Greek text offered by A. M. Denis, a form of the term ὁ διάβολος is used five times—verses 2, 8, 9 (2×), and 10.[13] In verse 2, the archangel Michael is having a conversation with the devil, τῷ διαβόλῳ, concerning the work of the Holy Spirit in the creation account. In verse 8, we find the likely link to Jude 9; here, the author states, "And when Michael, the archangel, considering things with the devil, argued concerning the body of Moses, not daring to bring a judgment of blasphemy, but he said, 'Let the Lord rebuke you'" (cf. Zech 3). In verse 9, the author states why the devil wants the body of Moses: "The devil was blaspheming against Moses, proclaiming [him] a murderer on account of striking the Egyptian." Michael then repeats the statement made in verse 8: "'Let the Lord rebuke you,' he said to the devil." In this context, it appears the devil is only performing a task that has been assigned to him—collecting the dead bodies of sinners. Verse 10 states that on account of the rebuke from the Lord, the devil was not permitted to receive the body of Moses upon his death. An interesting point is brought out in the contrasting of the title "the satan" and "the devil." One might ask why the term *devil* does not receive the same personal name recognition as does *satan*. In the majority of occasions identified in the texts that have been discussed, we do not see ὁ διάβολος being used as a proper name as many have attempted to do with ὁ σατανᾶς. The words both mean "adversary," but only *satan* is suggested to be a proper name.

Testament of Solomon

The Testament of Solomon presents a treatise on how King Solomon, through the power of a magical ring, bound certain demons to assist him in building the temple of YHWH in Jerusalem. The text is extant in various Greek manuscripts that date from the fifteenth to seventeenth century CE; manuscripts in Syriac (Paris BN—fonds syriaque) and Arabic (Vat. Ar. 448) are dated to the sixteenth century and the seventeenth century, respectively. Two main theories have been offered as to the date of the writing of the Testament of Solomon. The first is a date

---

13. Special thanks to Craig Evans for pointing me toward this source. A. M. Denis, ed., *Fragmenta pseudepigrapha quae supersunt graeca*, PVTG 3 (Leiden: Brill, 1970), 63–67.

prior to the fourth century CE based on the presence of a similar demonology in the Divine Institutions of Lactantius, written in Latin between 303 and 311 CE, and also Origen's *Contra Celsum* from 248 CE.[14] F. C. Conybeare suggests that the Testament of Solomon was a revision of a Jewish text from the late first century CE.[15]

Although the Testament of Solomon speaks a great deal on the topic of demonology, it fails to mention the figure of the satan (ὁ σατανᾶς) despite its suggested Christian revisions and a late first century CE date. Surprisingly, it also only mentions the devil (ὁ διάβολος) on one occasion in 15.11. In a conversation that appears to have little in common with the rest of the Testament of Solomon (perhaps suggesting a Christian interpolation), here, in 15.10, the author, or editor, states that Solomon is having a conversation with a spirit that claims that evil spirits "will lead astray all the inhabited world, for a long time, until the Son of God might be stretched upon the wood." Speaking here of the Christ, he adds, "For there has not yet arisen a king like him, one who nullifies all of us [the evil spirits], whose mother shall not have sexual intercourse with a man." Following this, the author describes the test or temptation of the Christ in the wilderness. The spirit again speaks in verse 11: "The one whom the first devil (ὁ πρῶτος διάβολος) shall seek to tempt (πειρᾶσαι) but shall not be able to overcome." The author is drawing an obvious parallel to the satan figure in the Synoptic Gospels' accounts of the trial in the wilderness.[16]

Other Pseudepigrapha

Martyrdom and Ascension of Isaiah (MAI)

The MAI is a composite work that includes the Martyrdom of Isaiah in 1.1–3.12 and 5.1–16. Between these two sections is the portion labeled the Testament of Hezekiah in 3.13–4.22 and is most likely a Christian interpolation. Michael Knibb argues that the martyrdom portion of the text is a "Jewish work which tells in legendary form" the prophet's death at the hands of King Manasseh.[17] Chapters 6–11 are identified as a Christian work, in which Isaiah, when in the

---

14. D. C. Duling, "Testament of Solomon," in Charlesworth, *Old Testament Pseudepigrapha*, 1st ed., 1:935–87, here, 940–41.
15. As cited in Duling, F. C. Conybeare, "The Testament of Solomon," *JQR* 11 (1898): 12; C. C. McCown, "The Christian Tradition as to the Magical Wisdom of Solomon," *JPOS* 2 (1922): 3.
16. Interestingly, the author of the Testament of Solomon describes a numerical value for the Christ similar to the numerical value of the antichrist figure in John's Apocalypse. Here it is 644, which means "Emmanuel" (ἐμμανουήλ).
17. M. A. Knibb, "Martyrdom and Ascension of Isaiah," in Charlesworth, *Old Testament Pseudepigrapha*, 1st ed., 2:143–76, here, 141. Chapter 1 in the martyrdom text is teeming with language that speaks of the satan or devil figure. The author mentions the "prince of this world and his angels"; he notes the "judgment of the angels," a possible allusion to the Watchers from 1 Enoch. We also find the figure Sammael Malkira, who is understood in the Jewish tradition to have tempted Eve and later became the leader of the satans. The figure of Beliar is also present in the ascension section of the text.

court of Hezekiah, was taken up into the heavens and shown a vision during which he sees the seven heavens and the throne room of God. Within the vision, he sees the Lord coming down to earth; his birth, life, death, and resurrection; and his ascension into the heavens.

Knibb contends the MAI was composed in either Greek or Hebrew and later translated in several languages.[18] The entire text of MAI is only extant in the Ethiopic, and within that tradition, it was considered to be a work of the actual prophet Isaiah and was considered part of the Ethiopic Bible and Apocrypha. A small Greek fragment of 2.4–4.4 survives from about the fifth or sixth century CE. Further textual evidence survives in two Latin translations; one is found in two fragments in the Vatican Library (Vat. lat. 5750; pub. 1828), which also date from the fifth or sixth century.[19] The second Latin translation is of a significantly different text tradition and covers only chapters 6–11, which suggests the Vision of Isaiah, chapters 6–11, had an independent existence. It is dated between the fourth and sixth centuries CE. The original text of the MAI was likely written post 68 CE, after the death of Nero and due to the expectation of his return as the antichrist; its origins were possibly established near the end of the first century CE.[20] The dating of these texts is important in attempting to establish some sort of chronology for the reception of the satan tradition and the discussion of the "problem of evil."

The various versions of MAI present difficulties for properly identifying the use of the satan or the devil in the text. Michael Knibb has based his translation on the five main Ethiopic manuscripts with notations concerning the Greek fragment and the Latin and Slavonic translations.[21] One further Greek manuscript is also worthy of note, the Legend of Isaiah (GL), dated to the twelfth century (Paris, Cod, Gr. 1534). MAI contains several other names (e.g., Sammael Malkira, Beliar [GL 1.8]) that have an alleged close affinity to the satan; these will be discussed in the chapter that follows.

The first mention of the satan appears in the Greek Legend 1.9, which states, "For the satan [ὁ σατανᾶς, Eth., በሰይጣን፡ *sayāṭān*] will dwell in the heart of Manasseh." The second mention of the satan (τοῦ σατανᾶ) is also found in the Greek Legend in 1.11; the Ethiopic of the verse reads Sammael (ሰማያል፡ *samāyal*). Ethiopic 2.2 contains the third reference, which reads, "And he served satan (በሰይጣን፡ *sayāṭān*), and his angels, and his powers." This entry suggests that Manasseh was being influenced by an external adversary or perhaps being led by an internal spirit, as is possibly understood in 1.9. Ethiopic MAI 2.7 speaks of Isaiah observing the people

---

18. Knibb, "Martyrdom," 144.
19. Knibb, 144.
20. Knibb, 149.
21. Knibb, 144.

of Jerusalem in "the service of satan" (ወተቀንዮ፡ ለሰይጣን፡), which results in him leaving the city. The Greek fragment of 3.2 contains a further reference to the satan. Here, King Manasseh, at his own desire, makes idols of gold and silver, and he "worships or serves (ἐλάτρευσεν) the satan (τῷ σατανᾷ) and his angels, and his powers." The author of the Greek fragment of 3.2 indicates that Manasseh has turned away from serving YHWH (ὁ δὲ βασιλεὺς μανασσῆς οὐκ ἐμνήσθη τῶν ἐντολῶν τοῦ πατρὸς αὐτοῦ; cf. Eth. 2.2, ወነጸረ፡ ወተቀንዮ፡ ለአግዚአብሔር፡). The Greek fragment of 3.3 includes a very similar context but with a bit more elaboration of the worship: "And they [people of Jerusalem] served the devil (τῷ διαβόλῳ) and his angels with him, and the profane and unclean idols." A further reference to satan in the Greek fragment is found in 3.8. The author notes the people of Jerusalem were falling down in worship and serving the satan (λατρείαν τοῦ σατανᾶ). The final reference to the satan figure in the Greek fragment is found in 3.18; this identifies the devil. It reads, "And to the holy one, Isaiah said to him, 'A curse on you, Melchia, false prophet, devil (διάβολε, vocative)!'" Isaiah is accusing Melchia of being a human adversary to God's people by prophesying falsely to Manasseh. The Ethiopic 7.9 contains a reference to satan (ሰይጣን); Isaiah is on a heavenly journey with a "glorious angel" (Michael?) who shows him the heavens. In this portion of the vision, the angel is showing Isaiah the firmament of the earth; there he sees Sammael (ሰማያል፡, Eth.; *samāyal*, satan in Lat2 [*Satanae*] and Slavonic), and he hears the "words of satan, and they [angels of satan] were envying one another." The Ethiopic chapter 11 offers three instances of the term *satan*. Verse 11.23, speaking of the ascension of the Lord [Jesus] from the firmament to the seventh heaven, states, "And all the angels of the firmament and satan (ሰይጣን፡) saw him and worshipped." Verse 11.41 offers a special notation in which the name Sammael is combined with satan (ሰማያል፡ ሰይጣን፡), who is the one responsible for sawing Isaiah the prophet in half. The final mention in MAI comes in 11.43. Here, the author closes out the story by noting, "But Manasseh did not remember these things [things Hezekiah had told him], he did not place them in his heart, but he became the servant of satan (Lat. *in servitutem redactus Satanae*; Eth. ተቀኒዮ፡ ለሰይጣን፡) and was destroyed." One of the difficulties in the Ethiopic text is the lack of a definite or indefinite article in the language; thus, attempting to determine the nature of the noun is difficult—is it a proper noun? In the case of 11.43, the term could be understood as an adversary of the Lord or as the satan figure who is an adversary to humanity and God's plan for us. Either way one chooses to understand the term—as human adversary or personified evil being—it has a distinct role in the problem of evil the Israelites were facing at the time of the writing of MAI.

History of the Rechabites (H. Rechab)

The Rechabites, also known as the Kenites (1 Chr 2:55), were the descendants of Jethro, the father-in-law of Moses (Judg 4:11). The History of the Rechabites tells the story of Zosimos, a holy man on the Island of the Blessed Ones. Zosimos had lived an apparent monastic lifestyle for about forty years in the wilderness, asking God to show him the Blessed Ones (τῶν μακάρων). The Blessed Ones are the Rechabites, who, according to James Charlesworth, had departed Jerusalem with the aid of angels to their present abode on the island.[22] It is reported in the story that the angels still dwell with the Rechabites (11.1–12.9). The extant Greek version of the H. Rechab may date from the sixth century CE but is likely a translation of an earlier Jewish text possibly dating from the second century CE.[23]

The text is extant in Ethiopic, Greek, and Syriac. Although it is difficult to determine, it is likely that there was a Semitic original, likely Hebrew, that was translated into the Greek version and then Syriac versions.[24] During the process of translation and transmission, it is apparent that Christian interpolations became a part of the story. Charlesworth suggests that the Syriac 12.9a–13.5c and 16.1b–8 are Christian additions to an earlier text.

The Greek version uses *the satan* (ὁ σατανᾶς/ν) three times (7.8 [not in the Syriac], 19.1, and 19.2) and *the devil* (ὁ διάβολος) four times (20.1, 21.1, 21.4, and 22.2); however, according to Charlesworth, the Greek text of chapters 19–23 is likely a Christian expansion.[25] Verses 7.7–8 describe the man's isolation following a meeting with the elders of the Rachabites; in the scene, he is guided by a "man of God." It is suggested to him that he lie so that Zosimos might rest, and the man cries out, "Woe to me that the story of Adam be repeated in me; for that one, through Eve, Satan [ὁ σατανᾶς] deceived." This account, of course, is following the extrabiblical accounts of the Garden scene in which the satan deceives Eve and Adam. The second occurrence of the satan appears in the context of a trial and test of Zosimos by the satan: "But seeing me praised, the satan [ὁ σατανᾶς] desired to test [πειράσαι][26] and hurl me from the place." In verse 19.2, Zosimos is warned by the Angel of the Lord (ἄγγελος τοῦ θεοῦ) that the satan was coming to test him. He is told that God will battle for him and that the "glory of your faith requires you hold off the satan [τὸν σατανᾶν]."

---

22. James H. Charlesworth, "History of the Rechabites," in Charlesworth, *Old Testament Pseudepigrapha*, 1st ed., 2:443–61, here, 443.
23. Charlesworth, 445.
24. Charlesworth, 444.
25. J. H. Charlesworth, *The History of the Rechabites*, vol. 1, *The Greek Recension*, TT 17, PS 10 (Chico, CA: Scholars Press, 1982), 14–107. Cf. M. R. James, *Apocrypha Anecdota: A Collection of Thirteen Apocryphal Books and Fragments Texts and Studies* 2, no. 3 (Cambridge: Cambridge University Press, 1893).
26. This is from the same verb form used in Luke 4 and the trial of Jesus in the wilderness by the satan figure.

For reasons unknown, the author shifts in chapter 20 from using *the satan* to using *the devil*. In verse 20.1, the angels of God are seen ascending to the heavens with the devil alongside (perhaps suggesting he has access to the heavenly realm, cf. Job 1–2) "having an outward form of anger and wildness." The devil then goes into a monologue in which he states that God had enabled the Adam and Eve to be sinless (v. 20.2) and he was going to do the same for Zosimos. For this reason, he states in 20.3, "I brought an evil thought and I entered the vessel of the serpent deceitfully toward a deceitful one." This appears to be one of the primary texts that places the devil in the Garden at the time of the trial of Eve and Adam, although in the disguise of the serpent. He goes on to say in 20.4, "I made Adam the first man [τὸν πρῶτον ἄνθρωπον] to transgress." The suggestion in the text is that if Adam and Eve had not eaten from the Tree of Life, then he would have "remained equal to the glory of God and the holy angels." This is a part of the story not present in the Genesis account but shows the dramatic nature of the failure to heed God's command. Following the speech, the devil departs from him (Zosimos) in 21.1. At that point, things take a turn for the worse for Zosimos; after eight days, the devil returns with 1,360 demons (why such a large number?) and drags him away from the cave; this makes it clear that the devil has evil spirits working for him against humanity. Zosimos is tormented for forty days (similar to the time of Jesus's trial in the wilderness, and apparently, the devil is unable to defeat Zosimos either), after which the devil weeps, saying that he lost the world due to the prayers of this one man. The story then takes an interesting turn in 21.5, in which Zosimos makes the devil take an oath: "You may not escape and flee from me until you swear to me you will no longer test or try a human." In 21.6, the devil swears with great force "upon the firmaments of heaven" that he will no longer approach Zosimos's place of habitation. This seems to suggest the oath is directed to Zosimos and does not necessarily cover all humanity. However, in 21.7, the devil and the demons (δαίμονας) with him are sent to the eternal fire, and in 21.8, Zosimos is escorted by the angel to his cave with much glory, where he then lives for thirty-six years before passing the habitation on to the wilderness fathers (monastics, μοναχοὶ—see 22.4). The final mention of the devil occurs in 22.2, in which the author repeats that the devil is weeping on account of the tablets that tell how the blessed ones came to inhabit their island.

Apocalypse of Sedrach (ApocSedr)

The ApocSedr describes the journey of Sedrach to the heavenly realm to speak to the Lord. The questions asked by Sedrach are focused on the "problem of evil" in the world, and the Lord's answers are centered on humanity's responsibility for evil.[27] It has been suggested that the main

---

27. S. Agourides, "Apocalypse of Sedrach," in Charlesworth, *Old Testament Pseudepigrapha*, 1st ed., 1:605–13.

character, Sedrach, is either Shadrach from Daniel 1–3 or a corruption of the name Esdras from the text 4 Ezra, as there are significant parallels in the dialogue between Esdras and the angel accompanying him on the heavenly journey and between Sedrach and God.

The ApocSedr is extant in only one fifteenth-century Greek manuscript, although it is thought to be from an earlier period (tenth to eleventh century).[28] Other scholars argue the traditions found in the text originate from the early centuries of the first millennium.[29] S. Agourides contends the ApocSedr was originally written in Greek and contains terminology from the Patristic and Byzantine periods. He contends, however, that elements of the text appear more Jewish than Christian; as such, he suggests the apocalypse of the text dates from 150–500 CE.[30]

The text focuses on the idea that humanity was created superior to the heavenly angels, similar to what we know from the Life of Adam and Eve. As such, one might argue that the author of ApocSedr is drawing on LAE or knows of a similar tradition from the second century CE (or earlier). In ApocSedr 5.2, the angels are commanded to bend the knee to Adam and the "first of the angels" (πρῶτος τῶν ἀγγέλων—assumed to be the devil; see 5.3) refuses, which results in him being forced out of heaven. Sedrach asks God why he did not slay the devil. He further asks, "Who is able to fight an invisible spirit? He enters the hearts of men like smoke and teaches them every sin." God then appears to respond that he has given humanity power over all things, including the devil (see 6.1). The ApocSedr mentions the term *the devil* (τοῦ διαβόλου) in verse 4.5 and again in 5.3 (τὸν διάβολον). There is no mention of the satan figure, although the devil is likely synonymous with the satan. In 4.5, the Lord is explaining to Sedrach why he punishes humanity, which is because "he [Adam] refused to listen to my [God's] commandment, and being deceived by the devil [τοῦ διαβόλου], he ate from the Tree [of Life]."[31] A second instance comes in 5.3, which relates the story of the devil not worshipping Adam. Sedrach asks the Lord why he did not kill the devil (τὸν διάβολον) for disobeying him rather than just banishing him from heaven. The author then explains the task of the devil among humanity, a significantly different description than texts from the Second Temple Period. Sedrach states in 5.5, "He enters the hearts of humanity [a reference to Judas Iscariot?] like a smoke and teaches them every sin." In 5.6, the devil wages war against the immortal God; "What then does pitiful humanity have to do to him [the devil]?" The Lord then tells Sedrach that humanity has

---

28. Located in the Bodleian Library, Cod. Misc. gr. 56, fols. 92–100. M. R. James, ed., *Apocrypha Anecdota*, Texts and Studies 2/3 (Cambridge: Cambridge University Press, 1893), 130–37.
29. Cited in Agourides, "Apocalypse of Sedrach," 606: M. E. Stone, "Prophets, Lives of The," *EncyJud*, vol. 13, cols. 1149–50; James H. Charlesworth, *PMR*, 178.
30. See Agourides's argument for the Jewish nature of the text in his "Provenance," in "Apocalypse of Sedrach," 606.
31. Author's translation from the OT Pseudepigrapha Greek text in Accordance: James, *Apocrypha Anecdota*, 130–37.

the ability to resist and make the right choices when approached by the devil (see 6.1). In the ApocSedr, we see that the resolution to the problem of evil has been laid upon the shoulders of humanity, and the ability to reject and defeat it has been granted to humanity through the power of right choice that has been instilled in the human heart by God.

Greek Life of Adam and Eve (GLAE)

GLAE provides a reinterpretation of Genesis 1–5 that, according to Jack Levison, offers hope to the audience "by presenting Adam as a forgiven sinner who endures the pain of existence, faces death with uncertainty, but receives mercy after death."[32]

A wide range of dates can be offered for the text, beginning in 100 BCE and ranging to 600 CE. Scholars who argue for a Jewish origin suggest a date early in this range, while those who contend for a Christian origin propose a date in the second to fourth century CE.[33] Levison plausibly argues that there are features in Paul's portrait of Adam and Eve in Romans 1 that correspond to GLAE, which he suggests allows for presence of the tradition in mid-first century CE.[34]

GLAE uses both *the satan* (only once, 17.1) and *the devil* (six times, 15.3; 16.1; 16.2; 16.5; 17.4; 21.3) in the story. It could be suggested that the author has in mind two different beings—the satan and the devil—due to the sparsity of the term ὁ σατανᾶς in the story. In fact, the satan is said to appear in the form of an angel with other angels and sings hymns to God with them and does not speak to the serpent or to Eve or Adam. There is an odd mix of conversations between the characters in this section. In 17.1, Eve is conversing with the satan figure who then transforms into the form of an angel (17.2); how different that is from his form while talking with Eve is unclear. The occurrence of the satan (ὁ σατανᾶς) in 17.1 describes the event immediately following the devil speaking to the serpent in chapter 16. At this point (17.1), the author makes a sudden shift and states the hour in which the angels ascended to worship God (this seems to suggest they left paradise and *went up* to the place where God resided—along with the satan figure): "Then the satan took on the appearance of an angel and sang songs of praise to God just as the angels." To be clear, the author says "the satan took on the *appearance of an angel*"; it does not say he was an angel. Verse 17.2 presents some contextual difficulties in trying to determine who Eve is speaking of: the serpent, who has hung himself on the wall, or

---

32. See John H. Levison, "The Life of Adam and Eve," in Embry, Herms, and Wright, *Early Jewish Literature*, 1:445–61, here, 445.
33. Levison, 447.
34. See Jack Levison, "Adam and Eve in Romans 1.18–25 and the Greek *Life of Adam and Eve*," *NTS* 50 (2004): 519–34.

the satan figure who has just appeared as an angel.[35] Eve states, "And bending over the wall, I saw him, like an angel," and he asks her (serpent or satan?), "What are you doing in paradise?" But then in 17.4, the author shifts once again, this time focusing on the devil and the serpent; we are told, "The devil [ὁ διάβολος] answered through the mouth of the serpent." Throughout this section, Eve is recounting the story of how she was deceived by the serpent/devil, but the satan figure does not seem to be involved in this deception.[36] It is not clear as to why the author uses *the satan* in this one instance, especially in close proximity to the use of *the devil*.[37] As mentioned, the text suggests that the satan figure has ascended with the other angels and is no longer in the Garden.

The first reference to the devil (ὁ διάβολος) is found in 15.3, in which the devil enters into the portion of the Garden assigned to Adam, the one where the male creatures were kept. The author of GLAE notes that God set apart all male creatures in an area being watched over by Adam and all female creatures were in an area watched over by Eve. It is in Adam's portion of the Garden (so why is Eve there?) that the devil first speaks to the serpent about how it should not fear the Lord but rather listen to him: "Then the serpent went to him, and the devil said to him, 'I hear that you are wiser than all of the living creatures. But I have come to observe you, and I find you greater than all of the living creatures, and they speak to you; nevertheless, you bow down to the lessor one'" (16.2). The devil allegedly convinces the serpent that he need not serve or worship Adam, and if the serpent allows the devil to speak through him, then the serpent might have a greater role in paradise. In 16.5, the devil says to him, "Do not fear! Only be my vessel and I will speak through your mouth a word by which you will be able to deceive him"—interestingly it is "him," not "her." Apparently unaware of the repercussions to come, the serpent allows this to happen (this seems to contradict the statement in Gen 3:1 that the serpent was craftier than all other animals). Because the serpent speaks to Eve, one might suggest the serpent is from the female side of the Garden (although the noun is masculine—ὄφει) and had come over to the dividing wall when the devil called it over to speak to it. However, in 19.1 it appears that the serpent has been talking to her from outside the Garden, as we are told she opened to him the gate to paradise. We are also told in 19.3 that the serpent put upon the fruit of the tree the poison of wickedness, the desire of lust. It seems from this story that Eve

---

35. See John R. Levison, *The Greek Life of Adam and Eve*, Commentary on Early Jewish Literature Series (Berlin: Walter de Gruyter, forthcoming), author's draft of ch. 15, p. 6.
36. Levison describes this section of text as the "Testimony of Eve" and suggests that the devil's role in this section is ambiguous. See Levison, ch. 15, p. 6.
37. Chad Pierce has argued, with others, that "the names 'Satan' and 'Devil' thus appear to be used interchangeably" in the NT. See C. T. Pierce, "Satan and Related Figures," in *Eerdmans Dictionary of Early Judaism*, ed. John C. Collins and Daniel C. Harlow (Grand Rapids, MI: Eerdmans, 2010), 1196–200, here, 1199.

had no chance of avoiding the tree and its fruit, and once she succumbed to the temptation, she was trapped.

The next reference to the devil comes in 17.4; here the devil answers Eve through the serpent concerning her comment in 17.3 about guarding the Garden and eating the food that is in it. We are told in 15.3 that the devil is on the male side of the Garden and he calls the serpent over to speak with him. Interestingly, the devil says to the serpent that he and serpent should have Adam and Eve cast out of paradise just as they both were (already?) cast out (16.3). There is no hint of this prior to the conversation; in fact, the serpent tells the devil that he fears the Lord perhaps of this very thing. As mentioned above, in 16.5 the devil asks the serpent to be his vessel to speak to Eve, and immediately we are told that the serpent hung himself on the wall at the time the angels began worshipping the Lord (17.1).[38] In 17.4, we are told by Eve, "And the devil answered me through the mouth of the serpent: 'You [plu.] are doing well, but you [plu.] are not eating from every plant,'" suggesting the test or temptation is directed at both Adam and Eve. From here, the deception takes place on her side of paradise.

The final mention of the devil in GLAE is found in 21.2–3. In this section, the author describes the incident from the perspective of Eve, recounting the episode with the serpent and Adam in 21.2: "But when your father [Adam] came, I said to him words of lawlessness, which brought us down from great glory." Eve states in 21.3 that when she spoke to Adam the devil was speaking through her: "For at the same time he [Adam] came, I opened my mouth and the devil was speaking, and I began to admonish him [Adam] saying, 'Come, my Lord [κύριε μου] Adam, take heed of me and eat from the fruit of the tree.'" Turning away from blaming Eve for the sin, the author is clearly placing the blame on the devil by having him speak through Eve and having the devil exhort Adam through Eve to eat the fruit of the tree that God had told them not to eat and claiming, "You will be like a god" (only θεός, no definite article). In these passages, the satan/devil is portrayed as a figure intent on deception and bringing down the humans from their place of glory; at the same time, this incident could be understood as a trial of Adam and Eve by the adversary in order to test their faith, which of course they fail miserably. On each occasion, Adam and Eve were given the choice to not commit the sin of eating the fruit but chose to ignore the words God had spoken to them.

---

38. Levison suggests, likely correctly, that there is some sexual innuendo in the phallic image of the serpent along with the language used by Eve in 19.1: "And I opened for him, and he entered inside into paradise" (Ἤνοιξα δὲ αὐτῷ, καὶ εἰσῆλθεν ἔσω εἰς τὸν παράδεισον; translation mine). Levison, *Greek Life of Adam and Eve*, ch. 15, p. 9. This along with the added poison of wickedness, identified as "lust," supports this possible reading.

Latin Life of Adam and Eve (VITA)

The Latin VITA tells a similar story to GLAE with some exclusions (Eve's story of the Garden deception, chs. 15–30) but also with the inclusion of why the satan is exiled from the heavenly court and also the ascension of Adam into the heavenly realm (chs. 25–29). The Latin manuscripts date from the ninth to fifteenth century; those from the fourteenth and fifteenth contain additions to chapters 29 and 51.[39] Johnson contends that it is "most probable that there did exist an original Hebrew document or documents from which the GLAE and VITA were translated."[40] This cannot be definitively concluded, but there are three main sections in VITA that do not appear on most of the Greek manuscripts. Chapters 12–16 is one such section and includes the story of the rebellion of the satan figure. Determining a date for VITA is as difficult as GLAE. Johnson suggests circa 400 CE for the Latin translation, with the original text much earlier—he contends it could have been written between 100 BCE and 200 CE but most likely toward the end of the first century CE.[41]

The only mention of "the satan" in VITA comes in 9.1. Here the author describes how, following their expulsion from paradise, Eve went to the River Tigris to lament and offer penance. In the midst of her lamenting, the satan figure comes to her, attempting to get her to sin again: "Then Satan [*Satanas*] grew angry and transfigured himself into the brilliance of an angel and went off to the Tigris River to Eve." Similar to the author of GLAE, the author of VITA quickly shifts to identifying the figure as "the devil" in 9.2: "He found her weeping, and then, the devil [*diabolus*] himself, as if mourning with her, began to weep and said to her: 'Come out of the water and rest and weep no longer. Cease now from your sadness and lamenting. Why are you uneasy, you and your husband, Adam?'"[42] Interestingly, while attempting to deceive Eve, the devil identifies himself as an angel (*angeli*). The devil is mentioned next in 10.2 (*diabolus*), where he is assisting Eve out of the water as part of the deception, to break her act of repentance. In verse 10.3, "When Adam saw her and the Devil [*diabolum*] with her, he cried out with tears, saying: 'O Eve, O Eve, where is the work of your penitence? How have you again been seduced by our adversary [*adversario nostro*, not the expected *satan* or *devil*], through whom we were alienated from the dwelling of paradise and spiritual happiness?'" The author is making clear the function of the satan/devil in the story; he is one who tests Adam and Eve—that is, humanity.

---

39. See M. D. Johnson, "Life of Adam and Eve," in Charlesworth, *Old Testament Pseudepigrapha*, 1st ed., 2:249–95, here, 250.
40. Johnson, 251.
41. Johnson, 252.
42. W. Meyer, "Vita Adae et Evae," *Abhandlungen der koeniglichen Bayerischen Akademie der Wissenschaften, Philsophisch-philologische Klasse* 14, no. 3 (1861): 185–250.

In verse 11.1, Eve recognizes that it was the devil (*diabolus*) who had deceived her, and in 11.2, she rebukes him for his malice against her and Adam: "Woe to you, devil. For what reason do you fight against us?" She sets up the devil's response with her next question in 11.3: "Did we ever take your glory from you or cause you to be without honor? Why do you persecute us, O enemy [*inimice*]?" The author then describes the so-called fall of the devil in which the term *devil* appears four times.

Beginning in 12.1, the devil recounts his fall from glory in heaven among the angels because of the creation of Adam. Adam responds in 12.3: "Since you have not been harmed nor injured by us, why do you persecute us?" In 13.1, the devil tells Adam that on account of him, he was cast out of heaven. At Adam's creation, God breathed into Adam the breath of life and made him in the image and likeness of God. Because of this, in 14.1, all the angels were told by the archangel Michael to worship the image of God, which was Adam. In 14.2, Michael commands the devil to worship the image of God; in 14.3, the devil refuses because he sees Adam as lower than himself, and the devil declares to Michael and before all the angels, "He ought to worship me." It appears from the text in 15.1 that the devil had angels who were assigned under his authority; these angels also refuse to worship Adam. Here we see a full-on rebellious statement by the devil. In response to Michael's command to worship Adam, the devil states, "If he [God] grows angry with me, I will set my seat above the stars of heaven and I will be like the Most High" (perhaps reflecting Ezek 28). As a result of this rebellion, the devil and the angels with him who refused to worship Adam were expelled from heaven and lost all their glory. Consequently, the devil tricked Eve and caused Adam and Eve to be cast from their glory in the Garden. In 17.1, Adam then cries out to the Lord, asking that he remove the devil ("this adversary," *iste adversrius*) who seeks to destroy his soul. In 17.2, the author writes that the devil no longer appeared to Adam.

One final reference to the devil occurs in 33.2, in which Adam is retelling the story of the fall to his children, including the role the devil had in it. We are told that God gave Adam and Eve two angels to watch over them, and when the hour came for the angels to ascend and worship God, the devil found them in the Garden. In GLAE, we are told that at this point in the story, the satan was an angel who ascended to worship God; one might suggest that the satan was one of the two angels meant to watch over the Garden with Adam and Eve. VITA appears to have had a significant role in the development of the devil character in the Judeo-Christian worldview. He is depicted as a rebellious angel who, to this point in Jewish literature, had been a heavenly figure who operated within the bounds of divine authority and sovereignty. From VITA, it may be suggested that he became a rebellious figure who is out to thwart the divine plan for humanity because of the creation of Adam. The significant question that is left unanswered in the Life of Adam and Eve is, When did the rebellion of the satan/devil figure occur? Was it before or during the creation narrative in Genesis? If during, why did we see him entering into the heavenly court in Job and Zechariah? Why do we see the devil being thrown down from heaven in John's Apocalypse's chapter 12, after Christ's time on earth?[43] These are certainly questions that play a part in the role of the satan figure in the ongoing problem of evil during this period.

BOOK OF JUBILEES

Jubilees contains a retelling of the book of Genesis and the first half of Exodus. Its longer title is "The Book of the Divisions of the Times according to Their Jubilees and Their Weeks" (see CD 16.2–4). The recounting of the two biblical books contains various additions, omissions, and extended versions of the stories. In addition, the author draws upon traditions from biblical texts, including Leviticus, Deuteronomy, Isaiah, Psalms, and 1 Enoch—in particular, the Book of Watchers. The author relates the significant events of these stories while offering an understanding/interpretation for his contemporary audience. As with other apocalyptic pseudepigrapha, the author of Jubilees is unknown.

Jubilees survived in at least fifteen or possibly sixteen fragmentary manuscripts from the caves at Qumran and Masada, which preserve a small segment of the entire book.[44] It is extant in its entirety only in Ethiopic Ge'ez. It is thought the book was copied from the Hebrew original into Greek (possibly Syriac), which was then translated into Ethiopic and Latin.[45] At last count, some twenty-seven Ethiopic Ge'ez manuscripts survive, dating from approximately the fourteenth century CE, which make up the most complete version of Jubilees.[46] The Greek text survives in fragments of quotations in other Greek sources.[47] Only about one quarter of the Latin text of Jubilees is extant; it is dated by Rönsch to the mid-fifth century CE.[48]

---

43. See Archie T. Wright, "The Life of Adam and Eve and Revelation 12:1–17: The Rebellion of the Satan Figure," in *Reading Revelation in Context: John's Apocalypse and Second Temple Judaism*, ed. Ben C. Blackwell et al. (Grand Rapids, MI: Zondervan, 2019), 109–15.
44. 1Q17; 1Q18; 2Q19; 2Q20; 3Q5; 4Q176a; 4Q176b; 4Q216; 4Q217(?); 4Q218; 4Q219; 4Q220; 4Q221; 4Q222; 4Q223; 4Q224; 11Q12.
45. See James C. VanderKam, *Textual and Historical Studies in the Book of Jubilees* (Missoula, MT: Scholars Press, 1977), vi.
46. See Todd R. Hanneken, "The Book of Jubilees," in Embry, Herms, and Wright, *Early Jewish Literature*, 1:510–41, here, 512–13.
47. See Albert-Marie Denis, ed., *Fragmenta pseudepigraphorum quae supersunt graeca una cum historicorum et auctorum Judaeorum hellenistarum fragmentis*, PVTG 3 (Leiden: Brill, 1970), 70–102.
48. H. Rönsch, *Das Buch der Jubiläen oder die kleine Genesis* (Tübingen, Germany: Leipzig, 1874); Robert H. Charles, *The Ethiopic Version of the Hebrew Book of Jubilees* (Oxford: Clarendon, 1895).

The likely date of the writing of Jubilees is between 159 and 152 BCE.[49] Events depicted during the Hellenistic period during the reign of Antiochus IV Epiphanes (175–163 BCE), along with parallels to the history recounted in 1 Maccabees, confirm the approximate date of composition. As a result, Jubilees (should) reflect the contemporaneous view of the satan figure depicted in the DSS and other Jewish literature from the 2TP.

Significant to the satan tradition is the notion in Jubilees 2.2 that God created all the spirits that minister before him. This includes the angels of the presence; the angels of sanctification; the angels of the spirit of fire; the angels of the spirit of the winds; the angels of the spirit of the clouds, darkness, snow, hail, and frost; the angels of the depths and thunder and lightning; the angels of cold and heat and the seasons; and all the spirits of his creatures that are in heaven and on earth.[50] If one is to consider the satan figure as a heavenly spirit, then one must accept that he is a spirit being, good or evil, created by God during the creation account in Genesis.

Jubilees 3.17 offers a brief description of the sin of Adam and Eve in the Garden. During the seventh year from creation, the serpent (no mention of the satan figure) approached Eve and spoke to her concerning the tree in the midst of the Garden. Interestingly, the Greek version of Jubilees 3.23 states that the serpent was the first to take from the tree and eat (presumably the tree in the midst of the Garden—"καὶ διὰ τὸ πρῶτος ἀπὸ τοῦ ξύλου λαβεῖν καὶ φαγεῖν"). In the serpent's efforts to deceive Eve, he states, "It is not true that you will surely die, because the Lord knows that on the day you eat of it your eyes will be opened and you will be like gods, and you will know good and evil." It is clear from the text of Jubilees that the task of the serpent (possibly the devil or the satan figure—see GLAE above) is to test humanity, in this case Eve, as to whether she will obey and follow God.

Jubilees 10.8 describes the event in which Noah has asked God to remove the evil spirits (the disembodied spirits of the giants from the Watcher tradition). God had commanded the archangel Michael to lock up the evil spirits in the Pit with their fathers, the Fallen Watcher angels from the Enochic tradition; the Greek text states, "and the devil (ὁ διάβολος; Eth. መስተማ, Mastema[51]) asked to receive a portion of them [the evil spirits from the Giants] for the purpose of testing humanity." This line follows the command from the Lord to Michael the archangel to throw the evil spirits into the abyss until the day of judgment. Following the request from the devil, God permits 10 percent of the spirits to be given to Mastema in order to test the character of each human concerning their divine inclination.

---

49. Hanneken, "Book of Jubilees," 511.
50. Paraphrased from the Ethiopic text.
51. Mastema is the chief of the spirits; there is no corresponding text from Qumran scrolls.

Integral to the understanding of the satan figure in Jubilees is verse 10.8. The translator/author of the Ethiopic Ge'ez text notes the chief of the spirits, Mastema, asks that he be allowed to keep some of the evil spirits under his rule to help him exercise his authority among humanity. What follows in 10.12 (not in the Greek or Aramaic) draws a nearly direct parallel between the figure Mastema and the figure of satan. The line reads, "All of the evil ones, who are cruel, we bound in the place of judgment, but a tenth of them we let remain so that they might be subject to satan (Eth. ሰይጣን፡, *sayāṭān*)[52] upon the earth." Prince Mastema appears in Ethiopic Jubilees 11.11 (መኩንን፡ መስቴማ፡, no // in Greek or Aramaic) as one who spoils the work of humans on the earth. In 17.15–16, the recounting of the Akkidah from Genesis 22, Prince Mastema comes before God asking if he might be allowed to test Abraham's faith. The author recounts six times God has already tested Abraham and found he was faithful; God then goes ahead with the sacrifice of Isaac to test Abraham's faith again.

Jubilees 23.29 makes reference to the satan figure in relation to the children of Israel. Upon their repentance from rebellion against God, the author notes, "All their days they will be complete and live in peace and rejoicing, and there will be no satan (ሰይጣን; no // in Greek or Aramaic) and no evil one who will destroy." The term *satan* here likely indicates a human adversary (or rather, the lack of one), as they will drive out their enemies. In a similar context, Jubilees 40.9–10 reads, "And there was no satan [ሰይጣን; no // in Greek or Aramaic] and there was no evil." Again, this is likely referring to the lack of a human adversary for Joseph or Pharaoh. The author is describing the kingdom of Pharaoh after he was found upright for treating Joseph favorably. A third instance of the same use of *satan* occurs in 46.2, in which the author describes the years of Joseph: "And there was no satan [ሰይጣን; no // in Greek or Aramaic] or anything evil all the days of the life of Joseph which he lived after his father." Jubilees 50.5 presents the final use of satan in a similar context. The author describes when Israel will enter the land of Canaan: "And then it [Israel] will not have any satan or any evil one."

One final use of *Mastema* occurs in 48.2 and 9. Here the author describes the/a prince of Mastema (መኩንን፡ መስቴማ፡) who desired to kill Moses upon his return to Egypt. Verse 4 states that God delivered Moses from the hand of Mastema in order to bring Israel out of Egypt. In 48.12, Prince Mastema has convinced Egypt to pursue Israel into the wilderness; again, God intervenes for Israel. On all of these occasions, it appears that Mastema is railing against Israel because of its unfaithfulness. Finally, after what appears to be eighteen days of accusing Israel, Prince Mastema is bound up and prevented from further pursuit. But on the nineteenth day,

---

52. It should be noted that there is no article in Ethiopic Ge'ez; this could be read as "a satan" or "the satan."

God releases Mastema and other spirits to help the Egyptians pursue Israel. Several of these episodes suggest that Mastema was operating outside of the authority of God, but the final instance indicates that God continued to be in control of Mastema and his actions against Israel.

1 Enoch

First Enoch is a collection of seven or possible eight writings identified as the Book of Watchers (chs. 1–36), the Similitudes of Enoch (Parables of Enoch, 37–71), the Book of the Luminaries (72–82; also known as the Astronomical Book), the Book of Dreams (83–90; includes the Animal Apocalypse, 85–90), the Epistle of Enoch (91–105; includes the Exhortation of Enoch, 91.1–10, 18, 19), the Book of Noah (106–7), and another book of Enoch (ch. 108). The compilation offers a worldview that identifies the earth as an evil and unjust place in which the Jewish people are awaiting the redemption of God. The figure of Enoch (presented as the author) finds himself in the midst of the dispute between humanity and the offspring of the Fallen Watcher angels, which he attempts to mediate. He also takes several heavenly journeys, during which the Lord, through a mediating angel, reveals to him the coming redemption of the righteous.

It appears that the majority of 1 Enoch was written in Aramaic, as 1 Enoch survives in eleven fragmentary scrolls from the Qumran Dead Sea Scrolls that include chapters 1–36, 85–90, 72–82, and 91–107.[53] The Similitudes (chs. 37–71) and chapter 108 are not extant in Aramaic. Portions of the text survive in several Greek manuscripts from the fourth, fifth/sixth, ninth, and eleventh centuries CE.[54] However, there is no reference to the satan figure or the devil in the Greek manuscripts. The entirety of 1 Enoch only survives in Ethiopic Ge'ez, which appears to be a translation of the Greek, which itself was translated from the Aramaic sometime in the fourth to sixth century CE (best guess). The possible dating of Aramaic 1 Enoch begins in the early third century BCE (4Q201); other portions in various scrolls are dated through the first century BCE or early first century CE (4Q209). First Enoch is an important text from the Second Temple period that reflects a worldview in which the authors reveal a developing demonology that perhaps in some way influenced the evolving view of the satan figure.

The term *satan* only occurs four times in 1 Enoch: at 40.7 (plural, *satans*), 53.3, 54.6, and 65.5 (also plural, *satans*). These instances are in the section described as the Similitudes or the Parables of Enoch, which are extant only in Ethiopic Ge'ez. Nickelsburg and VanderKam suggest

---

53. George W. E. Nickelsburg, *1 Enoch 1* (Minneapolis: Fortress, 2001), 9–11; see also J. T. Milik, *The Books of Enoch: Aramaic Fragments of Qumrân Cave 4* (Oxford: Clarendon, 1976). DSS manuscripts include 4Q201, 202, 204, 205, 206, 207, 212; the scrolls 4Q208, 209, 210, and 4Q211 contain the book of Luminaries.
54. Nickelsburg, 12–14. There are also references to 1 Enoch in Latin and fragments in Coptic and Syriac.

there is a relationship between two early Jewish texts dated in the first century that suggest a similar date for the Enochic Similitudes: 4 Ezra and its parallels to Daniel 7 and the "son of man" language, and Wisdom of Solomon 4.18–5.13 and its eschatological elements and the Davidic king.[55] The date for the Similitudes is circa 40 BCE or possibly the early decades of the Common Era.[56]

The first reference to the satan figure, in this case plural "satans," is found in the first parable in 1 Enoch 40.7. Enoch is in the presence of "thousands of thousands and ten thousand times ten thousand" heavenly beings who are in the presence of the "Lord of the Spirits." In verse 7, he hears the fourth voice of the four Watcher angels (40.9 identifies them as four archangels—Michael, Raphael, Gabriel, Phanuel—who stand on each side of the Lord of the Spirits), who are said to be "driving away the satans" (ሰይጣናት፥, sayəṭānāt) so that they do not come into the presence of the Lord of the Spirits. This is clearly not "the satan" figure of later Christianity but rather a group of adversarial figures whose apparent task is to accuse humans who are on the earth. Verse 40.7 suggests that the "satans" are spiritual beings who are allowed into the heavenly realm but in this case are denied the opportunity to accuse, before the Lord, humans who are on the "dry ground"; this seems to have some semblance to the satan figure in Zechariah 3, who is rebuked by the Angel of the Lord (in the case of 1 Enoch 40, Phanuel) and not allowed to bring accusation concerning Joshua, the high priest.

In 1 Enoch 53.3, the second parable, Enoch is shown a vision in which sinners will perish before the Lord of the Spirits and will be annihilated.[57] In this valley, Enoch sees the angels of punishment, who are "preparing all the [sharp][58] instruments of Satan [መሳዕለት፥ ሰይጣን፥],"[59] which they will use to punish all the kings and the mighty ones of the earth (perhaps an allusion to Isa 24 or Isa 14). According to VanderKam, these instruments are likely the iron chains (see 1 En. 54.3) used to bind these figures until the day of judgment.[60] The term *satan* here could indicate a title or a specific heavenly being, but with the lack of any clear indication, it could also be translated as an "adversary" in that the angels of punishment will use all available

---

55. See George W. E. Nickelsburg and James C. VanderKam, *1 Enoch 2: A Commentary on the Book of 1 Enoch Chapters 37–82* (Minneapolis: Fortress, 2012), 61–62; also Leslie Baynes, "Introduction to the Similitudes of Enoch," in Embry, Herms, and Wright, *Early Jewish Literature*, 2:256–63, here, 259–60.
56. Nickelsburg and VanderKam, *1 Enoch 2*, 62–63.
57. George W. E. Nickelsburg, "A Translation of the Similitudes of Enoch (1 Enoch 37–71)," in Embry, Herms, and Wright, *Early Jewish Literature*, 2:264–96, here, 276.
58. According to VanderKam, the Ethiopic "instruments" suggests a sharp instrument; see Wolf Leslau, *Comparative Dictionary of Ge'ez* (Wiesbaden, Germany: Harrassowitz Verlag, 2006), 95–96; Nickelsburg and VanderKam, *1 Enoch 2*, 196.
59. Nickelsburg and VanderKam, *1 Enoch 2*, 276. Nickelsburg notes that the NT Satan is known as God's "agent of punishment" in 1 Cor 5:5; 2 Cor 12:7.
60. Nickelsburg and VanderKam, 196.

adversarial instruments (angels of destruction?) to punish the kings and mighty. Nickelsburg suggests that the satan figure, having accused the kings and the mighty of their sins, has the angels preparing their punishment.[61]

Chapter 54 offers an account of the punishment of the "rebel angels" from the Enochic Book of Watchers. In 54.5, Enoch is shown the iron chains that will be used to bind the "host of Azazel, that they [angels of punishment?—Michael, Gabriel, Raphael, and Phanuel] might take them and throw them into the abyss of complete judgment, and with jagged rocks they will cover their jaws." According to 54.5, Enoch is told that the Lord of the Spirits will punish them (the host of Azaz'el, ትዕይንተ፡ አዛዚኤል፡;[62] host = Watchers?) for being servants of satan (ላእከ፡ ለሰይጣን፡) "and leading astray those who dwell on the earth." The punishment motif in the Enochic Watcher tradition (see 1 En. 10) continues in chapter 55, in which the author offers further details on the punishment of the Watchers and their offspring. Nickelsburg identifies Azaz'el as a demon, but there is nothing in the 1 Enoch Watcher tradition that suggests this is the case nor is there any evidence in the Similitudes to suggest the figure is anything other than a rebellious heavenly being. According to the Watcher tradition, demons are the spirits of the giant offspring of the Fallen Watchers and human women.

Chapter 65 presents what is described as Noah's vision of the destruction of the earth and Enoch's interpretation of that vision. It appears from the vision that the earth has been thrown off its axis and has tilted causing it "to stagger and shake" (65.3). In 65.6, we see once again a connection to the Enochic Watcher tradition when Enoch states that "they [humanity] have learned all the secrets of the angels"; these secrets are the teachings of Asa'el in the Book of Watchers in 1 Enoch 8.1–3. In addition, humans have also learned "all the violence of the satans [ሰይጣናት፡] and all their powers," among other things. VanderKam suggests that "the secrets of the angels" and "the violence of the satans" are parallel. In addition, he contends that the "satan" of 1 Enoch 53.3 is synonymous with the fallen angel Azazel in 54.5. There is no clarification offered here as to who the satans are; thus, we may perhaps assume they are adversaries as we saw in 40.7. What is clear is that the author is not using "satans" to refer to a single leader of evil forces.

What we have discovered in the Similitudes of Enoch is that there are likely multiple satans / adversaries / heavenly beings operating in the earthly/human realm. That does not eliminate the idea that there may be a single leader of the satans—that is, a Satan, or as VanderKam suggests, Azazel—but the evidence for this is not apparent.

---

61. Nickelsburg and VanderKam, 196, comments on 1 En. 53.3–5.
62. The name appears four times in the Similitudes: 54.5; 55.4; 69:2 (2×).

Other Jewish Texts

Two other Jewish texts employ the terms *satan* and *devil*, Sirach (τὸν σατανᾶν) and Wisdom of Solomon (διαβόλου).

The first occasion is found in Sirach 21.27 in the context in which the author is describing the speech of an unrighteous individual. There is no context by which one can determine whether the satan (τὸν σατανᾶν) is a human or spiritual adversary—the author states, "When an ungodly person curses the adversary [τὸν σατανᾶν], he curses his own soul"—but it is clear that it is an adversary.

The second text in question, Wisdom of Solomon 2.24, speaks of the fall of the satan figure in GLAE and VITA. The author writes, "And by the envy of a devil [διαβόλου], death entered into the world, and the ones whom he tests are of that [his] portion." Most English translations of this verse appear to assume this is "the Devil," when in fact there is no definite article in the Greek nor are there variants that contain one. The text speaks of the devil as one who tests humanity, and because of his own sin, death entered the world. This of course requires that one read into the Genesis Garden pericope that the devil acted on his own, which the biblical text does not mention.

Summary

From the preceding examination, one might suggest that the concept of "the satan/devil" was fluid during the Second Temple Period. As the examination shows, there are a significant number of Pseudepigrapha that employ the term *satan*. Some of the texts examined reveal that the work of the satan figure is to draw people away from the Lord by testing them, similar to what we saw in the DSS (T. Dan). The figure does not necessarily suggest he/it is autonomous in that he is working at his own charge. In the Testament of Gad, the author suggests that the satan figure is working in collaboration with a group of spirits (in this case, the spirit of hatred) to lead astray humanity from the plan of God. The noun *satan* when used with the definite article suggests this is perhaps a title for the being rather than the proper name. The term *satan* and its synonym *devil* are portrayed as functioning in similar ways to the way they are in the biblical book of Job. The satan figure of these texts is one whose task appears to be to test and deceive humanity but can only do this under the authority of God (T. Job).

With several of these texts, one might ask why the term *devil* is not identified as a personal name the way "satan" is. That is, in the majority of occasions that it is used, ὁ διάβολος is not used as a proper name the way many have attempted to do with ὁ σατανᾶς. The words have identical meanings, "adversary," but only *satan* is used in the sense of a proper name.

The author of the Apocalypse of Sedrach explains the task of the devil among humanity in a way that is significantly different from what appears in the other texts from the 2TP. The author suggests the devil "enters the hearts of humanity like a smoke and teaches them every sin." This may suggest the possibility of satanic possession along the lines of the tradition of the satan entering the heart of Judas in the Gospels. The Lord then tells Sedrach that humanity has the ability to resist and make the right choices when approached by the devil; this understanding follows the tradition in the Damascus Document 16 and also in 1 Peter 5:8–9.

GLAE and VITA offer a significantly different story surrounding the satan figure. Here he is depicted as a rebellious angel who draws Eve and Adam into sin against God. However, there is no evidence to suggest he is autonomous; rather, he may simply be doing the same task he performed in Job—that is, performing the function of the heavenly adversary, a function that could also be understood in Jubilees. However, the author relates that the satan fell from heaven due to his refusal to follow God's command and bow down to Adam.

The authors of these texts reveal a satan/devil figure that at times appears to be functioning in a heavenly "office" of adversary or accuser. Some texts also suggest that there were multiple satans functioning within their worldview (see, e.g., Enochic Similitudes). In the following chapter, we will examine other nomenclature that perhaps is related to the satan figure in the Dead Sea Scrolls and Pseudepigrapha.

Chapter 5

Satan and His Other Names?

Introduction

The source(s) of the problem of evil is a prominent topic in the study of 2TP Jewish literature such as the Dead Sea Scrolls, the Pseudepigrapha, and other Jewish texts. Previously, we have examined the figure of the satan/devil in this literature and found he/it is present but is not necessarily aligned with the early Christian understanding of "Satan"; in addition, there is little in the literature examined thus far that offers a great deal of clarity as to who or what is responsible for the problem of evil in the lives of the Jewish people during the 2TP. We noted previously there appeared to be other names by which an adversarial figure, human or spirit, may have been known to the Jewish people. The difficulty one finds in exploring this literature is trying to find direct parallels between the variety of terms found in the DSS, the Pseudepigrapha, and other literature. Some scholars have suggested that these terms are interchangeable with one another, when in fact that may not be the case.[1] In this chapter, we will determine if there are lines that can be drawn to connect figures such as Beliar, Belial, Mastema, or other heavenly beings (or humans) to the satan/devil figure. We will examine the use of these terms in a variety of texts in the corpora of the Dead Sea Scrolls, Pseudepigrapha, and other collections of texts for evidence of a manifestation of evil in these various named figures.

---

1. See arguments on various levels concerning this question in, for example, Stefan Schreiber, "The Great Opponent: The Devil in Early Jewish and Formative Christian Literature," in *Deuterocanonical and Cognate Literature Yearbook, 2007: Angels the Concept of Celestial Beings* (Berlin: Walter de Gruyter, 2007), 437–58, here, 441; Miryam T. Brand, *Evil Within and Without: The Source of Sin and Its Nature as Portrayed in Second Temple Literature*, JAJS 9 (Göttingen, Germany: Vandenhoeck & Ruprecht, 2013), 218–56; Loren T. Stuckenbruck, *The Myth of Rebellious Angels*, WUNT 335 (Tübingen, Germany: Mohr Siebeck, 2014), 98–100; Stuckenbruck, "Demonic Beings and the Dead Sea Scrolls," in *Exploring Evil*, ed. J. Harold Ellens (Denver: Praeger, 2011), 1:121–44; Archie T. Wright, *The Origin of Evil Spirits: The Reception of Genesis 6:1–4 in Early Jewish Literature*, rev. ed. (Minneapolis: Fortress, 2015), 160–63; Thomas J. Farrar, "New Testament Satanology and Leading Opponents in Second Temple Jewish Literature: A Religio-historical Analysis," *JTS* 70, no. 1 (2019): 21–68; Devorah Dimant, "Between Qumran Sectarian and Non-sectarian Texts: The Case of Belial and Mastema," in *The Dead Sea Scrolls and Contemporary Culture*, ed. Adolfo D. Roitman, Lawrence H. Schiffman, and Shani Tzoref, STDJ 93 (Leiden: Brill, 2010), 235–56; Martone, "Evil or Devil?"

Dead Sea Scrolls

Within the Dead Sea Scrolls, the authors offered little in terms of an abstract concept of evil; rather, the concept appears to manifest itself in various figures, spiritual and human, which are there to impact directly the lives and choices of individuals and the Jewish communities. Significant in the scrolls is the idea that the names of heavenly figures are not fixed—the prominent name for the so-called personified evil being is Belial[2] but may be otherwise known as Angel of Darkness, Melchiresha, or Mastema. These figures appear to be the culprits responsible for a variety of problems in the various Jewish communities and the lives of individuals. As mentioned previously, the term שטן, "satan," appears in the scrolls only six times: in 11QPs^a col. 19 lines 13b–16a; 1QH^a 4.6 and 45.3; 1QSb i 8 (possibly a human adversary); 4Q504 1_2 iv 12 (possibly a human adversary); and the Aramaic scroll 4Q213a 1 i 10. Other terminology that designates an apparent principal evil being is widespread among the Qumran scrolls.

A substantial theme that certainly influenced the concept of evil and evil spirits in the scrolls is dualism in the various forms—cosmic, social, and anthropological—that are present in the Qumran worldview. Scholars suggest that this is due to the dualism of Zoroastrianism, which speaks of a cosmic good-versus-evil dichotomy.[3] Chad Pierce contends that the 2TP "development of a celestial enemy was heavily influenced by the Jews' experience under Babylonian ad Persian rule."[4] There is an ongoing battle between light and dark, righteousness and evil, a spirit of truth and a spirit of darkness, and the Prince of Light and the Angel of Darkness. The culmination of this cosmic dualism is the eschatological war between the Sons of Light and the Sons of Darkness, who are led by the Angel of Darkness, possibly the figure identified as Belial. The Sons of Light are led by the Prince of Light, possibly the figure identified as Michael the archangel or Melchizedek.

The most significant text concerning evil and evil spirits in the 2TP is the Book of the Watchers in 1 Enoch. Noteworthy in this material is the fact that there is no figure that can be identified as "the satan," nor any other figures that may be suggested as related to the satan figure. One might suggest that Shemihazah is leading a group of rebellious angels like the satan figure in John's Apocalypse or GLAE. However, there is no identified leader of the evil spirits in Book of Watchers, and although many mistakenly identify the Fallen Watchers as evil spirits, this is not the case. The evil spirits are the hybrid offspring of the Watcher angels and human women;

---

2. See Loren T. Stuckenbruck, "Satan and Demons," in *Jesus among Friends and Enemies*, ed. Chris Keith and Larry W. Hurtado (Grand Rapids, MI: Baker Academic, 2011), 180, where he states, "Belial becomes a gathering point around which discourse about personified evil is constructed."
3. See Pierce, "Satan and Related Figures," 1198.
4. Pierce, 1198.

although the act that resulted in the emergence of the spirits was initiated by Shemihazah, the Watcher angel, he, nor any other of the fallen angels, is identified in 1 Enoch as the leader of the evil spirits. There are four possible leaders of the giant offspring (the evil spirits) prior to their physical destruction by the sword or the Flood in the Enochic book of Giants found at Qumran. These creatures, although not yet evil spirits, are named Mahaway (the one who talks with Enoch), Hahyah and 'Ohyah (each of whom have dreams of the destruction of the giants), and Hobabish. None of these figures have any identifiable relationship with the satan figure or any other figure similar to the satan in the DSS. Only when we find the spirits of the giants in the book of Jubilees do we see them under the leadership of Mastema—but not until after they have been running loose on their own and have been threatened by God with confinement. At a decisive point, Mastema asks for a portion of them to work with him to fulfill his task of testing and trying humanity because he believes humans to be evil by nature (Jub. 10); God grants him 10 percent, and they remain with Mastema.

Stuckenbruck has argued that five main figures can be identified in the scrolls that may be related to the "chief" evil being, the satan, although he is quick to point out that these names do not necessarily designate a proper name but rather may be identifying the function of the being.[5] The five beings include Melchiresha, the Angel of Darkness, S/satan, Belial, and Mastema.[6] The two primary terms that are significant in the scrolls are Belial and Mastema, but first we will examine some of the lesser used, though still significant, terms.

MELCHIRESHA

Melchiresha (מלכי רשע), the king of wickedness or evil, appears in the Visions of Amram (4Q544 2.13) as one of two angelic beings who are in a struggle for control over the biblical patriarch Amram (father of Moses and Aaron; Exod 6:18).[7] The text of 4Q544 is quite fragmentary, but the context appears to present the figure in opposition to its counterpart Melchizedek (2.13–16).[8]

---

5. See Stuckenbruck, "Demonic Beings," 121–44.
6. Devorah Dimant adds the Angel of Mastema or Prince of Mastema, although these are closely connected to the Mastema figure; see Dimant, "Between Qumran," 247.
7. Ryan Stokes suggests a relationship between the satan and Melchiresha due to the allusion to the satan figure bringing judgment against Joshua in Zech 3 and Melchiresha ruling over humankind (4Q543 frags. 5–9; 4Q544 frag. 1; 4Q547 1–2 iii). For Stokes, the satan is associated with wickedness, as is Melchiresha, but there is no correlation established between the two terms or figures. See Ryan Stokes, *The Satan: How God's Executioner Became the Enemy* (Grand Rapids, MI: Eerdmans, 2019), 149–51.
8. Paul J. Kobelski contends that the author of 4QAmram has been under the influence of Zoroastrian dualism and the idea of two angelic opponents, Ahriman and Ahura Mazda. He contends the two angels are now rulers over the world of light and good (Melchizedek/Michael) and darkness and wickedness (Melchiresha/Belial), see Kobelski, *Melchizedek and Melchiresha*, CBQMS 10 (Washington, DC: Catholic Biblical Association of America, 1981), 76.

The story recounts the vision of Amram, who has been separated from his family in Egypt and is struggling to find a way to return. In the vision, he sees two figures who are disputing which of them has authority over Amram. In the midst of the dispute, Amram is told that these two figures have authority over the human race, and he is asked by which one he desires to be ruled. One figure appears dark and hostile in nature, while the other appears pleasant in nature (most of this figure's description is lost from the text). Amram is told the name of the dark figure is Melchiresha, whose dominion is with deeds of darkness. The name of the other, who is speaking to Amram, is lost from the text, but it is suggested he is Melchizedek, King of Righteousness, although we cannot be sure.[9] This figure rules over all light and other things (lost from the text). The outcome of their argument over Amram is left to the patriarch; he is to decide under whose authority Amram will live (suggesting this is not necessarily a predetermined framework as in 1QS, Treatise of the Two Spirits).[10] Much of the conversation between the patriarch and the heavenly being is lost, but it is assumed Amram chose Melchizedek. From this fragmentary text, Melchiresha appears to operate in some degree of authority over humanity in an effort to persuade them to follow the dark path away from YHWH and the Torah. From the confrontation between these two figures, a connection between Melchiresha and Belial may be suggested in light of 11Q13, in which the figure Belial is also seen in opposition to Melchizedek (identified as an *elohim*). Two ideas can be identified from 4Q544 (king and darkness) that may lend to the later NT concept of the "Kingdom of Darkness." This is not to suggest a direct influence of 4Q544 on the NT authors but rather that a tradition concerning this collective concept may have been present in the first century CE.

The Melchiresha figure appears also in 4QCurses (4Q280 2.2–7), in which he is cursed similar to the way those who belong to the "lot of Belial" are in 1QS 2.5–9. The context of 4QCurses suggests that an individual (unclear who) has been set apart from the Sons of Light because of his apostasy (frag. 2.1). Frag. 2.2 then presents a curse upon Melchiresha for all his sinful plans; he is to be an object of terror in the hands of those who seek vengeance. It is unclear if Melchiresha is a human figure or a spirit being in this context. The language seems to indicate that the individual can call out to God for help, but he will be ignored, and the author states that Melchiresha will have no remnant or survivor—indicating he could possibly have previously been capable of having offspring. This suggests he is a human figure, possibly the leader of a group who has turned away from God and the Torah.

---

9. See, for example, Martone, "Evil or Devil?," 125.
10. See Stuckenbruck, *Myth of Rebellious Angels*, 92.

Angel of Darkness

In the Treatise of Two Spirits (1QS 3.13–4.26), the "angel of darkness" is presented in opposition to the "Prince of Lights."[11] The text of 1QS 3.18 states that the God of Knowledge (אל הדעות) created all things, and he created humanity to rule over the world. He also created and appointed two spirits in the world (after the creation of the world but before the creation of humanity)[12]—the spirit of truth (רוח האמת) and the spirit of iniquity (רוח העול)—to walk among humanity until God's visitation.[13] The author states that these two spirits are named Ruler/Prince of Lights (שר אורים, 3.20) and Angel of Darkness (מלאך חושך, 3.20–21). There is a clear cosmological dualism at work in 1QS;[14] at the same time, there is a psychological dualism that reveals a good and evil inclination within the human heart.[15] The Angel of Darkness, 1QS 3.24 notes, has other "spirits" of his lot (רוח גורלו) to assist him in "causing the Sons of Light to stumble." Ryan Stokes contends that the work of the Angel of Darkness in 1QS 3.20–21 does have association with the satan tradition due to the overlap of his activities "with those of Belial and the Prince of Mastema in other literature." He suggests the idea that he has "authority over the wicked, whom he leads astray" (Mastema in Jub. 11.5; Belial in CD 4:12–18). The Angel of Darkness opposes the angel of light in CD 5.17–18, but there is nothing in the satan tradition that suggests this parallel.[16] Maxwell Davidson argues the spirits in 3.24 "are almost certainly evil angels," but there is little evidence in 1QS for this suggestion.[17] These spirits are likely related to the evil spirits that emerge from the Watcher tradition found in the Enochic Book of Watchers.[18] What is interesting, if not alarming, is that

---

11. See Eibert Tigchelaar, "'These Are the Names of the Spirits of . . .': *4QCatalogue of Spirits (4Q230)* and New Manuscript Evidence for the *Two Spirits Treatise*," *RevQ* 84, no. 4 (2004): 543–45.
12. See agreement in Stokes, *Satan*, 171. This "two spirits" concept appears to follow the "two ways" teaching in Prov 4:11–19 and the dualism of Sirach 15:11–20 in which humans are given the choice to choose good or evil.
13. One might question if this "visitation" is the coming of the Messiah (Jesus) or possibly the Day of Judgment.
14. The dualism appears to be related to the Zoroastrian teachings found in the Iranian Gathas (see *Yasna* 30.3–5). See A. Dupont-Sommer, "L'instruction sur les deux Esprits dans le 'Manuel de Discipline,'" *RHR* 142, no. 1 (1952): 296–316. For the argument of the "two spirits" originating in the biblical tradition, see P. Wernberg-Møller, "A Reconsideration of the Two Spirits in the Rule of the Community (1QS III, 13–IV, 26)," *RQ* (1961): 413–41.
15. See Jörg Frey, "Different Patterns of Dualistic Thought in the Qumran Library," in *Legal Texts and Legal Issues*, ed. Moshe Bernstein et al., STDJ 23 (Leiden: Brill, 1997), 275–335.
16. Stokes, *Satan*, 174. Stokes offers further comparative actions between the traditions, such as having a group of evil spirits working with him in 1QS 3.24 as does Mastema in Jub. 10.7–9, which he suggests equates the Angel of Darkness with the Satan figure or at least the tradition circulating in the 2TP.
17. Maxwell J. Davidson, *Angels at Qumran: A Comparative Study of 1 Enoch 1–36, 72–108 and Sectarian Writings from Qumran*, JSPSS 11 (Sheffield: Sheffield Academic, 1992), 152–55. See A. E. Sekki, *The Meaning of Ruah at Qumran*, SBLDS 110 (Atlanta: Scholars Press, 1989).
18. Interestingly, Davidson does not raise the issue of the evil spirits of the giants from the Book of Watchers in his discussion of the use of *ruah* in the DSS, but it should be noted he is examining the sectarian documents among the DSS.

even the righteous can "succumb to the influence of the Angel of Darkness and be led into sin" despite the protection of the Prince of Lights.[19]

Based on the similar oppositional forces in 4Q544, one might suggest a parallel between the Prince of Lights and Melchizedek, and the Angel of Darkness and Melchiresha, although the evidence is not definitive, and this is not a necessary connection to make. As mentioned, there could be multiple spirits of this nature operating in these leadership roles during various times in the 2TP. However, we do see similar tasks for Melchiresha in 4Q544; he has authority over humans, and he leads individuals down paths of darkness and rules over the dark things. By comparison in 1QS, the Angel of Darkness has authority over wicked people (3.21—a slight nuance as to their targets) and leads them down paths of darkness, and he also corrupts the righteous whose "sins, afflictions, every trial, and every rebellious deed are of his prompting" (3.22–23). The text of 1QS 3.24–25 states that the Angel of Darkness is the ruler of the evil spirits who test and try the Sons of Light. This function would suggest a relationship with the figure Mastema in Jubilees 10 who is in a similar role (more on this below). Both 4Q544 and 1QS indicate God's role in this action. It may be assumed in 4Q544 fragment 1.12 that God grants authority to Melchiresha to function in his role, while in 1QS 3.23, "God in his mysteries" appears to grant authority to the Angel of Darkness to function in his (3.15–17: "everything originates with the God of Knowledge").[20] In 3.25, the author states that God "himself created the spirits of light and darkness," thus suggesting he is responsible for their actions. In 4Q544 3.1, we are told that Melchizedek was appointed to rule (given authority) over the light, and it is assumed Melchiresha has similar authority (3.21) over the dominion of darkness (2.13–14). From this evidence, one might suggest there may be a connection between Melchiresha and the Angel of Darkness, while at the same time, it is possible that there are multiple spiritual beings performing similar functions in the cosmos.[21] We now turn to the first of the two major names used to identify the "chief evil being" in the DSS, Belial.

---

19. Stokes, *Satan*, 175.
20. Following Paolo Sacchi (*The History of the Second Temple Period*, JSOTSS 285 [Sheffield: Sheffield Academic, 2000], 252), Martone goes as far as to suggest that the Angel of Darkness in 1QS 3.17 is an interpretation of the devil who has been created by God. Martone, "Evil or Devil?," 126. Cecilia Wassen suggests the Angel of Darkness is the equivalent of Belial in 1QS; see Wassen, "Angels in the Dead Sea Scrolls," in *Angels: The Concept of Celestial Beings: Origins, Development and Reception*, ed. Friedrich V. Reiterer, Pancratiius C. Beentjes, and Nura Calduch-Benages (Berlin: Walter de Gruyter, 2007), 499–523, here, 501.
21. See Dimant, "Between Qumran," 241. Dimant contends the Angel of Darkness is an alias of Belial.

Belial

The term בליעל (*bĕliyaʿal*) appears in the HB twenty-seven times, generally noting wicked behavior; this use appears, in some instances, to be carried over into the 2TP, but it is unclear if it should be understood as a heavenly or spiritual being or simply as a characteristic of individuals.[22] Deuteronomy 13:14 identifies the "sons of belial" (בני בליעל) as those who were acting contrary to the Torah and leading others to worship other gods (cf. Judg 20:13). Multiple references identify the "sons of belial" as simply wicked or perverse men, men of evil, and foolish men (e.g., 1 Sam 10:27; 25:17; 1 Kgs 21:13; 2 Chr 13:7; Job 34:18; Prov 6:12; Nah 1:11).

In several instances בליעל is used to describe things of an ungodly nature (Ps 18:5; 2 Sam 22:5, "torrents"; Ps 101:3, "wicked thing"; Nah 2:1, "wicked opposition to Israel"). Psalm 41:9 indicates a "thing of malice" (דבר בליעל) that is causing a deadly disease to fall upon David. In a single instance, 1 Samuel 1:16, the term is used to describe Hannah as a "wicked woman" or "daughter of pestilence" (בת בליעל) because she appeared drunk to Eli the priest. It is reasonable to suggest that the HB does not employ בליעל as a leader of evil spirits even in texts considered of postexilic origins. However, Maxwell Davidson suggests that the term "does appear to have lent itself to a personified usage, with the idea that behind the worthless actions or thoughts [of individuals] there stands a figure promoting such things."[23] Davidson, in citing P. von der Osten-Sacken, suggests that Nahum 2:1 offers "a possible point of departure" for this understanding.[24] However, Nahum 2:1 is simply identifying בליעל as the "wicked neighbors of Israel" who have been oppressing them; they will be completely cutoff. How, then, do the authors of the Jewish texts of 2TP Judaism personify this term as the leader of the opposition to God and the community? It appears for some that בליעל of the HB came to identify a single individual or a group of individuals with the characteristics identified in the HB texts above. Further developments or traditions appear eventually to have given these men of wickedness a "spiritual leader," perhaps due to the developing dualism in the worldview of the communities.

Determining the function of the term בליעל in the scrolls is difficult due to the fragmentary state of the manuscripts involved, which results, oftentimes, in there being little or no clear textual context for the occurrences of the term. In addition, the theological worldviews within the Dead Sea Scrolls and other literature from the Second Temple Period suggest a complicated collection of traditions or mythemes that lie behind the origins of evil and the various

---

22. Deut 13:14; 15:9; Judg 19:21; 20:13; 1 Sam 1:16; 2:12; 10:27; 25:17; 2 Sam 20:1; 21:13; 2 Chr 13:7; Job 34:18; Pss 18:5; 41:9; 101:3; Prov 6:12; 16:27, 19:28; Nah 1:11; 2:1.
23. Davidson, *Angels at Qumran*, 162–63 (brackets mine).
24. Osten-Sacken, *Gott und Belial*, 74–76.

figures/beings that are a part of it. As a result, the use of בליעל by various authors of the Dead Sea Scrolls, sometimes in the same text, is inconsistent.[25] One must keep in mind that the term's use in one document should not predetermine its use in another. For example, the *Hodyaot* (1QH[a]) use בליעל more in an abstract sense of "wickedness" (see 1QH[a] 10.18, 24; 11.29, 30, 33; 13.28, 41; 14.24; 15.6), whereas in the Community Rule (1QS) it appears, for the most part, to be used as a personal name, "Belial." In the War Scroll (1QM), on the other hand, בליעל can be understood as both an alleged personal name or in an abstract sense, "wickedness" (see 1QM 1.1, 5, 13, 15 [בליעל is reconstructed]; 4.2; 11.8; 13.2 [בליעל is reconstructed], 4, 11; 14.9; 15.3, 17 [בליעל is reconstructed]; 16.11 [בליעל is reconstructed]; 18.1, 3). These texts will be discussed in more detail below.

The term בליעל is the most common word for an evil being in the scrolls; it occurs, as best as can be determined, in fifty of the DSS. The number of occurrences totals approximately 120 throughout the scrolls: 68 times in which the spelling, בליעל, is not in doubt; 52 times in a variety of reconstructed states (in some, the entire word is reconstructed, and in others, one or more letters of the word have been restored). In at least 22 of the total occurrences, there is little or no context from which to determine how בליעל was being used. The term בליעל never occurs with the definite article (e.g., הבליעל) in the Dead Sea Scrolls. However, it does appear with כול, "any" or "every," in 1QH[a] 11.29. Considering the term שטן is used in the same manner (כול שטן) in 1QH[a] 22.25 and 24.23 and is understood to be a human adversary, one may suggest that בליעל is used by the author of 1QH[a] to indicate a human adversary rather than a supernatural spirit being.

The general context of its use is in the continuing conflict between the forces of good and evil. Stephan Schreiber suggests this struggle between good and evil is depicted in the fight between the Teacher of Righteousness at Qumran and the so-called Wicked Priest in Jerusalem. He considers the members of the Jerusalem priesthood to be the "sons of בליעל."[26] This so-called "social dualism" also reflects the cosmic dualism found in the Dead Sea Scrolls that permeated the worldview(s) in the 2TP.[27]

The various ways in which the term בליעל is used among the Dead Sea Scrolls can be summarized as follows:

---

25. Martone, "Evil or Devil?," 120.
26. See Schreiber, "Great Opponent," 443.
27. See Jörg Frey, *Qumran, Early Judaism, and New Testament Interpretation*, ed. Jacob N. Cerone, WUNT 424 (Tübingen, Germany: Mohr Siebeck, 2019); Archie T. Wright, "Social and Economic Injustice: Apocalyptic Themes in the Epistle of Enoch and the Apocalypse of John," in *The Blessings of Enoch: 1 Enoch and Contemporary Theology*, ed. Philip F. Esler (Eugene, OR: Wipf & Stock, 2017), 70–88.

1. It may be used to denote wickedness as an abstract concept, usually used with an adjectival function—that is, "wicked/worthless."
2. It may be used as a personal name, בליעל, to refer to a personified form of evil. This might be either
   a. a sobriquet for a particular evil human being[28] or
   b. the name of a spiritual being, who is sometimes depicted as a heavenly being operating under the authority of God and sometimes as the archdemon who operates autonomously.[29]

The idea that בליעל refers to personified evil had its beginnings in the Dead Sea Scrolls from Cave 1, primarily the War Scroll (1QM), the Hodayot (1QH^a), and the Community Rule (1QS). This idea was put forward by Peter von der Osten-Sacken in his book *Gott und Belial* in 1969 (a revision of his dissertation from 1966), in which he contends that בליעל is the ruler of the demonic realm in the eschatological era.[30] His work revolved around the earliest scrolls, but since then, a significant amount of material has been published. Still, even thirty years on, in 2000, Annette Steudel, in her article "God and Belial," held to the original idea that a single primary figure of evil was found in the Dead Sea Scrolls.[31] Despite the presence of other names for leaders of "demonic" spirits, she and many other scholars argue that the appellations were all speaking of the same figure.[32] Consequently, the notion that the term בליעל was a spiritual being that represented personified evil has become widely acknowledged in 2TP studies.

The title of the alleged "ruler of the demonic realm" does not appear to be fixed in the Dead Sea Scrolls. Besides בליעל, other evil beings who could hold this title are identified, such as Melchiresha (מלכי רשע)—king of wickedness—in 4Q280 2.2. In 4Q544 2.13, although quite fragmentary, the alleged ruler over the Sons of Darkness is given three names in the

---

28. Stephan Schreiber suggests that it could be the Wicked Priest of the Jerusalem temple. Schreiber, "Great Opponent," 444.
29. Devorah Dimant identifies Belial as the "arch-demon" and leader of the forces of darkness. Dimant, "Between Qumran," 236. See also Stuckenbruck, "Satan and Demons," 180. Some scholars contend Belial and Mastema are different names for the same spirit being, a significant point that will be discussed below. See, for example, Steudel, "God and Belial," 332–33; Philip S. Alexander, "Demonology of the Dead Sea Scrolls," in *The Dead Sea Scrolls after Fifty Years*, ed. Peter W. Flint and James C. VanderKam, 2 vols. (Leiden: Brill, 1999), 2:341; Mach, "Demons," 1:191; Martone, "Evil or Devil?," 115.
30. Osten-Sacken, *Gott und Belial*, 74–76.
31. Steudel, "God and Belial," 332.
32. Steudel, 332–33; see Michael Mach, *Entwicklungsstadien des Jüdischen Engelglaubens in Vorrabbinischer Zeit* (Tübingen, Germany: Mohr Siebeck, 1992), 81, 96.

reconstructed text, שר חשוכה, בליעל,³³ and רשע מלכי. These figures are the rulers in opposition to the Sons of Light. In addition, the Angel of Darkness (מלאך חושך) is also portrayed as a leader of the Sons of Darkness who is opposed to the Prince of Lights (שר אורים) in 1QS 3.20–21. In CD 5.18, the Prince of Lights is seen in opposition to בליעל in the retelling of the story from Deuteronomy 32:28 concerning Moses and Aaron against Yannes and his brother. The figure of Mastema is identified as the leader of evil spirits in Jubilees 10.8–11 (identified as Satan in v. 11) and also in Jubilees 17.15–16 and 18.9–12 as a heavenly being performing a similar function of testing the faithful, similar to the satan figure in Job 1–2. Similarly, the leader of the Sons of Light has three possible names—Melchizedek (מלכי צדק in 11Q13 [6×] in opposition to בליעל), Prince of Lights (שר אורים in 1QS 3.20–21), and the archangel Michael. It is possible that over the span of decades during which the scrolls were written, various figures, or various names for the same figure, came and went in the worldview of the members of the community, and this variation is the result. This could also allow for a possible reading of the term בליעל as "wickedness" at various stages and in various scrolls.

Although בליעל appears to be used in some situations for a personified evil being in the Dead Sea Scrolls, it is also employed in a number of other ways, as various scholars, including Devorah Dimant, have pointed out. Dimant questions the long-held view that בליעל should be identified as the "archdemon" and leader of the forces of darkness throughout the Dead Sea Scrolls.³⁴ She contends the HB personified abstract terms such as *Wisdom* and *Zion*, but there is no trace of the personification of בליעל. She argues that several texts from the Dead Sea Scrolls take up biblical idioms in which בליעל designates an abstract quality—for example, "people of wickedness" (בני בליעל), "worthless or wicked thing" (דבר בליעל), "torrents of wickedness" (נחלי בליעל)³⁵—while other scrolls appear to employ it as a proper name.³⁶ On other occasions, בליעל is found in the attributive sense, such as "a congregation of wickedness" (עדת בליעל),³⁷ "a wicked thought" (מחשבת בליעל),³⁸ or "rule of wickedness" (ממשלת בליעל).³⁹

---

33. The Hebrew term שר is generally defined as "leader," "commander," "ruler," or "prince" in the sense of a governing leader. See Ludwig Koehler and Walter Baumgartner, *The Hebrew and Aramaic Lexicon of the Old Testament*, trans. and ed. M. E. J. Richardson (Leiden: Brill, 2001), 2:1350–52.
34. Dimant, "Between Qumran," 236. See also Stuckenbruck, "Satan and Demons," 180; the discussion in Dimant, 238–39, on the process of personification of abstract qualities in the HB and DSS; Stuckenbruck, *Myth of Rebellious Angels*, 98.
35. See 1QHª 11.30, 33; 14.6.24.
36. Dimant, "Between Qumran," 239.
37. See 1QHª 10.2.24.
38. See 4Q174 1–2i.8; 4Q177 12–13i.8.
39. See 1QS 1.18, 24; 2.19; 1QM 14.9; 4Q390 2 i 4; 4Q491 8–10 i 6.

How, then, can one determine if בליעל is being used as a proper name? Some scholars,[40] Dimant included, contend that the use of בליעל as a proper name can be determined with specific syntactic markers such as its appearance as the subject of a verb or with a pronominal suffix.[41] One of the more prominent examples is found in CD 4.12–13,[42] which reads, "But in all these years, בליעל (*Belial*—proper name?) was allowed in Israel"; however, this could equally be read as the abstract "wickedness": "But in all these years, *wickedness* was allowed in Israel." The fragmentary 4Q463 fragment 2.3 is another text that some argue should be read as a proper name, with בליעל as the subject of the verb. Dimant reads it "[. . .] ויגער בליעל [. . .]" ([. . .] and בליעל will rebuke [. . .]),[43] which, in the context of fragment 1, doesn't make sense—although, as mentioned, this is a very fragmentary text.[44] Another reading of the line in the context of God coming to deliver Israel (see 4Q463 frag. 1.1–4) could suggest בליעל as the object of the verb "rebuke." With the lack of a definite direct object marker, which would be needed for a proper name, one can suggest that בליעל in this line should be read as "wickedness."

The second example of a syntactic marker used in identifying Belial as a proper noun is its use in conjunction with a suffixed noun. Our example is found in 11Q13 2.12, which reads, "Its interpretation concerns בליעל and the spirits of *his* lot wh[ich . . .] in [thei]r tu[rning] from the precepts of God to [cause evil]."[45] I suggest this verse could be read with the common phrase "spirits of wickedness" in mind: "Its interpretation concerns wickedness and the spirits of *its* lot." Either way the passage is read raises a larger question of how these presumably evil spirits of his/its lot were following the precepts of God. If these spirits were at one time following God's precepts, this may suggest these spirits are the Fallen Watchers or some other rebellious heavenly spirit.

The process of personification of abstract concepts was prominent in the ancient world, the most well-known example being the personification of Wisdom in Proverbs and Ben Sira.[46]

---

40. See Alexander, "Demonology," 2:341; Martone, "Evil or Devil?," 115; Heinz-Josef Fabry, "'Satan'—Begriff und Wirklichkeit: Untersuchung zur Dämonologie der alttestamentlichen Weisheitsliterture," in Lichtenberger, Lange, and Römheld, *Die Dämonen*, 287.
41. Dimant, "Between Qumran," 240.
42. Cf. 4Q225 2 ii 14: [. . .] וישמע בליעל אל (and בליעל listened to [. . .]). See also 4Q174 frag. 4.3: בליעל היאה [. . .] העת אשר יפתח ([. . .] This is the time when Belial will open [. . .])
43. Dimant, "Between Qumran," 240.
44. See Martone, "Evil or Devil?," 121. Other instances in which Martone contends it appears as the subject of a verb include 4Q225 2 ii.14, "and בליעל listened"; 4Q463 2.3, "and בליעל scolded"; CD 5.18, "and בליעל raised up Johne"; and 4Q174 4.3, "בליעל will open." A similar argument is made for the presence of the Hebrew שטן in 1 Chr 21:1; here, several argue that this should be understood as the proper name Satan rather than simply a human "adversary."
45. פשרו על בליעל ועל רוחי גורלו אש[ר . . .]ים בסו[ר]מה מחוקי אל ל[הדרשיע]
46. Ruth Rosenberg, "The Concept of Biblical 'Belial,'" in *Proceedings of the World Congress of Jewish Studies*, vol. 8/A (Leiden: Brill, 1982), 35–40, here, 38. Rosenberg has suggested that in the HB, Belial is a particular sin related to "the violation of the covenantal relationship between the individual, community and God." So defined, she argues this may have lent to the concept of the evil entity in the Second Temple Period.

Other terms in Second Temple literature, such as Mastema (משטמה), may also reflect this personification process while at the same time it can function as an abstract noun. The text 1QM 13.11 identifies בליעל as an angel/messenger of Mastema (מלאך משטמה)—a phrase in which משטמה could be understood as "hatred" or an evil spirit being called Mastema. This would suggest that בליעל is a messenger of hatred who was made for destruction (עשיתה ... לשחת). The other option is that בליעל is a spiritual being that functions under the leadership of משטמה (see Jub. 10.8). As noted, scholars have argued that personification is a prominent feature in the Dead Sea Scrolls. The personification of abstract concepts is certainly present in ancient Jewish literature, but I would argue that it is not as prevalent in the DSS as is often assumed. We will examine the use of Belial in the relevant DSS below.

Damascus Document (CD)

The Damascus Document[47] includes six occurrences of בליעל (4.12–13, 15; 5.18; 8.2; 12.2; 19.14). Each of these occasions could be understood as the abstract "wickedness," but the personification of evil should not be ruled out. In the first occurrence, 4.12–13, the author notes that "in all these years, בליעל will be allowed in Israel" (GMT and BZW[48] both translate as a proper noun); I would suggest that translating it as "wickedness" fits the context of the passage well alongside what follows in 4.14. The author of CD 4.14 cites Isaiah 24:17, which reads, "Terror and the Pit, and the Snare are upon you who dwell in the Land." The interpretation (פשר, *pesher*) of this is given in 4.14–16, which reads, "The interpretation concerns the three traps of בליעל about which Levi, son of Jacob, spoke, by which בליעל trapped Israel" (GMT and BZW translate בליעל as a proper noun).[49] These three traps of בליעל are identified in 4.17–18 as fornication, wealth, and the unclean temple. Those who are caught in these traps will be subject to "destruction by the hand/power of בליעל" mentioned in CD 8.2. However, the author states that Levi has set before them three kinds of righteousness (in contrast to three traps of wickedness) by which they can be delivered from the traps of בליעל. A translation of "wickedness" in each of the three occurrences, lines 4.13, 15, and 16,[50] would fit well in the context of column 4 in CD, but as in so many of the occasions in the Dead Sea Scrolls, the first interpretation used by the majority of translators is a proper noun. I suggest this is likely due

---

47. For an introduction of the dating and complex makeup of the Damascus Document, see Cecilia Wassen, "The Damascus Document," in Embry, Herms, and Wright, *Early Jewish Literature*, 2:128–34.
48. GMT is Florentino García Martínez and Eibert J. C. Tigchelaar, trans., *The Dead Sea Scrolls Study Edition*, 2 vols. (Leiden: Brill, 1999), here, 557; BZW is Ben Zion Wacholder, trans., "Damascus Document," in Embry, Herms, and Wright, *Early Jewish Literature*, 2:135–59, here, 135.
49. See GMT, 557; BZW, 139.
50. Davidson, *Angels at Qumran*, 180.

to the scholarly focus on the cosmic dualism that is present in the worldview of the Dead Sea Scrolls, while less attention is given to the anthropological and social dualism of the writings of the community. Stuckenbruck contends that "as the statistics indicate, Belial is by far the most frequent designation used for an evil being in the Dead Sea Scrolls";[51] however, these statistics do not suggest that every time בליעל appears, it should be read as a personified evil being, only that when this being is identified, the name most often used is בליעל. As Stuckenbruck suggests, "A number of motifs associated with other malevolent beings found in the Aramaic and Hebrew texts are brought together" under the name of בליעל, but generally, the term is associated with "errant Jews" within the social dualism of Second Temple Period Judaism.[52]

In CD column 5, the author appears to be discussing the actions of the Jerusalem priesthood (or possibly all those outside the author's community).[53] The three traps of בליעל are all connected to the corruption of the priesthood: illegally begotten wealth (stealing from the poor or the temple offerings), marrying foreign women (fornication), and defiling the sanctuary (no separation of the clean and unclean in the temple rituals). This may support the idea that on occasion, בליעל may be used to identify the high priest (i.e., the Wicked Priest). In CD 5.16–20, the author cites Isaiah 27:11 and Deuteronomy 32:28 concerning those in the land who walk about without insight; he contrasts Moses and Aaron, who operated by the power of the Prince of Lights (ביד שר האורים), against Yannes and his brother, who were apparently raised up by בליעל when he hatched a plan to deliver Israel (to evil?) the first time (GMT and BZW both translate as a proper noun).[54] Yannes and his brother were prophesying falsely in an effort to draw Israel away from worshipping YHWH. This might suggest that בליעל, a spirit being (in opposition to the Prince of Lights), is at work behind the scenes through the two brothers, but it is difficult to determine the specific context of CD column 5.16–20 that would make clear how one is to understand the term.

Maxwell Davidson contends that "the *Damascus Document* speaks unambiguously of Belial as a personal figure" in CD 5.18–19.[55] He recognizes a direct contrast between the Prince of Lights and Belial.[56] CD 8.2 and 19.14 suggest that Belial is operating under the authority of God,

---

51. See Stuckenbruck, *Myth of the Rebellious Angels*, 98.
52. See Stuckenbruck, 98.
53. See David Suter, "Fallen Angel, Fallen Priest: The Problem of Family Purity in 1 Enoch," *Hebrew Union College Annual* 50 (1979): 115–35; here, Suter discusses the corruption of the Jerusalem priesthood and the temple.
54. See GMT, 559; BZW, 2:139–40.
55. Davidson, *Angels at Qumran*, 164, 180–82.
56. Davidson draws the parallel between the Angel of Darkness in 1QS 3.20 and Belial in CD due to the similar opposition to the Prince of Lights. This is a possibility, but not a necessity as he suggests: "It seems clear that Belial and the Angel of Darkness represent the same angel." Davidson, *Angels at Qumran*, 183.

and in 12.2, it appears that Belial has spirits working with him to "rule over" individuals in their speech and actions.

In CD 8.2, the author states that the wicked will be condemned to destruction by the power of בליעל on the Day of Judgment.[57] The wicked in this case are the princes of Judah who were all entrapped by the three traps of בליעל; however, there is no mention as to how God will use בליעל to bring destruction; the use of the three traps of "wickedness" might indicate a self-destruction due to the wickedness of the priesthood. As such, this could be understood as destruction by the power/hand of wickedness rather than an evil spiritual being. Ryan Stokes contends that CD 8.2 presents Belial in the role of God's agent of punishment for those who do not hold fast to the Torah (cf. angel of destruction in 2 Sam 24:16).[58] Martone attempts to identify Belial as the "Prince of Darkness," translating what most would render "Angel of Darkness" as "Prince of Darkness." He does this in an attempt to draw a tighter ring around the Prince of Lights and Belial, but of course, this is quite forced and anachronistic—that is, satan is the "Prince of Darkness" in modern parlance.[59]

CD 12.2 makes it clear that all who commit sins that defile the temple or advise apostasy are controlled by the spirits of בליעל (GMT and BZW translate as proper noun[60]). This could be read as external spirits of wickedness or perhaps spirits in the hearts of individuals that are causing the people to defy the Torah and defile the temple. A similar understanding is expressed in CD 19.14, in which all violators of the covenant will face punishment by the power/hand of בליעל (GMT translates as proper noun[61]). There are few clear indicators to help the reader interpret the author's use of the term בליעל in these instances. As with the other scrolls under discussion, the term could be the abstract "wickedness," a human individual who is leading the wicked in Israel, or the "personification of evil" as the leader of a group of evil spirits, "Belial," who is allowed to have temporary dominion over Israel.

The Damascus Document presents Belial as a spirit being that for the most part is understood to be operating under the authority of God at times as a spirit of punishment or destruction. But one should not rule out the concept of wickedness being allowed to influence the people brought into their midst by oppressing nations and individuals.

---

57. See GMT, 561; they translate בליעל as a proper noun: "They shall be visited for destruction at the hand of Belial." See also BZW, 2:141; he translates בליעל as "resulting in them being handed over to Belial for destruction."
58. Ryan Stokes, "Belial," in Collins and Harlow, *Eerdmans Dictionary of Early Judaism*, 436.
59. Martone, "Evil or Devil?," 124–25. Martone wants too quickly to make the jump from "Angel" to "Prince" in relation to Belial in order to justify his "missing link" between the Old and New Testament, the personification of evil.
60. GMT, 571; BZW, 2:155. Both translate as "Belial."
61. See GMT, 577; not included in BZW.

Community Rule (1QS)

The Community Rule, 1QS,[62] contains five occurrences of the term בליעל; all retain the full spelling (1.18, 24; 2.5, 19; 10.21). The first reference in 1QS 1.18 is in the context of addressing those individuals who are entering into the rule of the Yahad—that is, the community. These individuals are commanded not to backslide due to "fear, terror, or test that [occurs[63]] in the dominion/authority of בליעל" (GMT and Frey translate as proper name[64]). The use of the Hebrew ממשלת ("authority") suggests that something or some being is operating with power in/over Israel during this time period. It can be understood that the "dominion of בליעל" is in the eschatological age in which בליעל is given opportunity to test and at times oppress Israel. This could be the supernatural being, "Belial," or a human figure (the Wicked Priest?), but it could also be a time in which "wickedness," in the eyes of the author, is winning out in Israel. This reading fits into the social dualism expressed in 1QS, which contrasts the Yahad community with the wicked of the nation. From this "dominion" of בליעל and the conflation of other terms related to בליעל, one might see how the "Kingdom of Darkness" in the NT could have developed.[65]

The second reference in 1QS 1.24 is found in a similar context in which, beginning in 1QS 1.22, "the Levites recount the iniquities of the children of Israel and all their guilty transgressions and sinful acts in the dominion of בליעל" (GMT and Frey read as a proper noun[66]). All those who are joining the covenant community must confess and repent of these sinful transgressions in order to escape the rule of "wickedness" (בליעל); all those entering the covenant community must confess, "We have been wicked" (1.24).

The third occurrence is found in 1QS 2.5, in a context beginning in 1QS 2.4, in which "the Levites are cursing all men who are of the lot of בליעל" (GMT and Frey read as a proper noun[67]), but again it does not mention the nature of Belial.[68] We only know that those who are part of the lot are wicked and commit guilty deeds for which God will turn them over to ones who will take revenge, possibly angels of destruction in a dark and fiery place (vv. 2.7–8). The idea that "men" now make up this lot of Belial can suggest that בליעל could be read as "wickedness" or that these individuals are following a wicked leader of Israel. This reading is supported in

---

62. See introductory discussion in Jörg Frey, "The Rule of the Community," in Embry, Herms, and Wright, *Early Jewish Literature*, 2:95–115.
63. Possibly a Niphal, masculine plural participle, היה.
64. See GMT, 71; Frey, "Rule of the Community," 2:116.
65. Stuckenbruck, "Satan and Demons," 180.
66. GMT, 71; Frey, "Rule of the Community," 117.
67. GMT 73; Frey, "Rule of the Community," 117.
68. Cf. 4Q174 2.i.8; 4Q177 10–11.4.

2.5 by the curse, which seems to be directed at an individual: "Be you [masculine singular] cursed for all your evil deeds and your guilt."[69] The context may suggest that this person is the leader of the wicked people who are on his side (belonging to his lot), or it may be directed at each individual who is a member of the group of בליעל. If the former is correct, then one can suggest that this curse is directed at the high priest in Jerusalem. Whoever this person is, he has offspring who will face the same consequences as their father, suggesting this wicked figure is human. The text of 2.6–10 continues the priestly curse against the individual(s) in 2.5 with language that describes no path to forgiveness for this person even when he cries out to God for mercy—no atonement is available to him.

The fourth occurrence is found in 1QS 2.19, in the context of an annual ritual to be carried out by the community. In 1QS 2.11, the priests and Levites double down on the curse against anyone who enters the community with an impure heart; this individual too is doomed to eternal destruction and unforgiveness. This ritual is to be performed annually during the days of the dominion of בליעל over Israel (GMT reads as proper noun; Frey excludes 2.19–3.5).

The final occurrence of בליעל is found in 1QS 10.21; here, the author states that Belial will not be given a place in his heart, so it could be understood as wickedness or perhaps a spirit being.[70] The context describes a prayer or confession of the author in which he swears to follow after only the zeal of the Lord. He shall allow no place for a spirit of wickedness to influence him (2.19–10.18; רוח רשעה), and he will not pursue riches gained through violence (one of the three traps of בליעל; 10.19). The language surrounding the verse suggests that wicked or perverse speech and sinful actions are the result of allowing בליעל into one's heart. In 1QS, we find the means of protection for the community against בליעל and the spirits of his lot. During his (בליעל) dominion, the members are to offer petitions through the cursings and blessings of Numbers 6:24–26, which are to be pronounced each year (1QS 2.19).[71]

War Scroll (1QM)

The War Scroll recounts the story of the eschatological battle that will take place between the Sons of Light (the Qumran community) and the Sons of Darkness (all others), in which בליעל has a prominent role. This scroll survives in at least six copies at Qumran and likely was written

---

69. See Wernberg-Møller, "Reconsideration." Wernberg-Møller contends there is no cosmic dualism here but that it reflects the spiritual qualities at work in the individual(s) (433).
70. Davidson suggests that worthlessness or wickedness is an "appropriate" understanding for *Belial* in this case. Davidson, *Angels at Qumran*, 163.
71. Stuckenbruck, *Myth of Rebellious Angels*, 99. Nowhere do we find an attempt at an exorcism of Belial as we do with other evil spirits; the authors only offer curses against him/it.

sometime between the mid-second and mid-first centuries BCE.[72] The War Scroll appears to be the prominent text in which the author (or modern translators) chose to personify בליעל.[73] The text of 1QM offers the largest number of occurrences of בליעל in a single composition among the extant Dead Sea Scrolls—eleven clear references and four reconstructed.[74] Scholars who have examined the role of בליעל in the War Scroll understand the term to be identifying a personified evil being, and in every case of an English translation, the term is capitalized, *Belial*, suggesting a personal name.[75] However, there is no clear context that infers that this is a proper name, although this is the likely scenario; I would argue that some of these occurrences can equally be understood as the abstract noun, "wickedness."[76]

In 1QM 1.1, the "Sons of Darkness," the opponents of the "Sons of Light," are identified as the "army of בליעל"; the author goes on to identify this army as the troops of Edom, Moab, the sons of Ammon, the Amalekites, Philistia, and the Kittim. These armies are also supported by the Israelites, who have violated the covenant of Israel. As this is the opening verse to the War Scroll, there is no previous text to indicate that the term בליעל should be understood as a spiritual leader of these forces. This, of course, does not negate the idea that the concept of a personified figure, Belial, was already in the worldview of the author. Nonetheless, the human forces themselves could be identified as "armies of wickedness" rather than the armies of the "leader of the evil spirits." The Sons of Light include the sons of Levi, the sons of Judah, the sons of Benjamin, and those exiled to the wilderness. The inclusion of "the congregation of the *Elim*" (עדת אלים) in 1.10 seems to indicate that heavenly beings are taking part in the war alongside the "assembly of people" (קהלת אנשים).[77]

---

72. See Maurice Baillet, *Qumrân Grotte 4, III*, DJD 7 (Oxford: Clarendon, 1982). See also 1QM; 1Q33; 4Q491–97; 11Q14(?).
73. See the introductory discussion in Brian Schultz, "The War Scroll," in Embry, Herms, and Wright, *Early Jewish Literature*, 2:349–58.
74. See 1QM 1.1, 5, 13, 15 (RC); 4.2; 11.8; 13.2 (RC), 4, 11; 14.9; 15.3, 17 (RC); 16.11 (RC); 18.1, 3.
75. See, for example, Osten-Sacken, *Gott und Belial*; Philip Davies, *1QM, The War Scroll from Qumran: Its Structure and History*, BibOr 32 (Rome: Pontifical Biblical Institute, 1977), 113–23; Jean Duhaime, "War Scroll (1QM; 1Q33; 4Q491–496 = 4QM 1–6; 4Q497)," in *The Dead Scrolls: Hebrew, Aramaic, and Greek Texts with English Translations*, vol. 2, *Damascus Document, War Scroll, and Related Documents*, ed. James H. Charlesworth (Tübingen, Germany: Mohr Siebeck, 1995), 80–203; Brand, *Evil Within and Without*, 232–38; Stuckenbruck, "Demonic Beings," 121–44; Martone, "Evil or Devil?," 115–27; Stokes, *Satan*, 181–89; Ida Fröhlich, "Evil in Second Temple Texts," in *Evil and the Devil*, ed. Ida Fröhlich and Erkki Koskenniemi, LNTS 481 (London: Bloomsbury, 2013), 23–50; Dimant, "Between Qumran," 237–46.
76. The term רוח (*ruah*, "spirit") occurs a number of times in relation to Belial: for example, CD 7.2//4Q271 5i.18, "spirits of Belial"; 1QS 3.18, 24, "spirits of the lot of the Angel of Darkness"; 1QM 13.2, 4, "spirits of the lot of Belial"; 1QM 13.11, "spirits of his [Belial] lot"; the angel of destruction"; 1QM 15.14, "spirit of wickedness"; 1QHᵃ 25.6, "spirits of wickedness"; 1QHᵃ 25.8, "spirits of iniquity"; 4Q177 1–4.7 and 12–13i.9, "spirits of Belial"; 4Q449 1.3, "spirits of his [Belial] lot"; 4Q491 14–15i.10, "spirits of [his] lot"; 11Q13 2.12, "against Belial and the spirits of his lot."
77. Davidson, *Angels at Qumran*, 217.

The next occurrence of בליעל is in 1QM 1.5, which speaks of the "everlasting destruction for all the lot of בליעל" (וכלת עולמים גורל בליעל). The "lot" could be speaking of everyone who is currently under the influence of Belial (see CD 4.12–18). However, there has been no mention of a leader of evil spirits up to this point in the scroll, and the passage could equally be speaking of the end of the forces of wickedness in general—that is, the armies mentioned in 1QM 1.1.

The text of 1QM 1.6 could offer support for the author's personification of בליעל in other occurrences in the War Scroll. In this line, the author uses the term רשעה (*rasha*) to speak of "wickedness" rather than בליעל, which has the abstract meaning "wickedness." A portion of the line reads, "להכניע רשעה לאין שארית" (to cause the end of *wickedness*, there will be no remnant; see also 1QM 3.9, "לשחת רשעה" [to destroy wickedness]). Further support for the author's use of בליעל as a proper name is found in a similar use of רשעה in 1QM 1.13, which reads, "three lots of the Sons of Light will be strong against רשעה. And the three armies of בליעל will gird themselves." Although the author has used two different terms for wickedness in one line, the armies of בליעל could be a reference to the human armies of the enemies of Israel mentioned in 1QM 1.1—that is, "the wicked armies of the nations."

A possible further example of a personified being is found in 1QM 1.14–15. Although בליעל is completely reconstructed, the figure is mentioned with the "all the angels/messengers of his dominion" ([בליעל ובו]ל מלאבי ממשלתו)[78] "and all the men of [his lot]" (ולכול אנשי[גורלו]). The text that follows the reconstructed "[his lot]" is also reconstructed. The suggested reading is "[his lot shall be destroyed forever]," but the reconstructed "[his lot]" could be referring to the lot of God—that is, the "Sons of Light" from lines 13–14. This may permit בליעל to be read as "wickedness": "God shall overcome wickedness and all the messengers of its dominion." However, the possibility of a figure of personified evil in this case should not be overlooked. A further option is that בליעל is a sobriquet for the human leader of the evil forces working against the community.[79] These are the ones who are fighting against the Sons of Light and the congregation of the *Elim*.

---

78. In 1.15, the author identifies the "angels of his dominion" (מלאבי ממשלתו) as those who will be overcome by the "hand of God"; the "his" of "his dominion" has been reconstructed in the text as Belial. Cf. 1QM 4.1–2, which states that Belial and all the men of his lot will be destroyed, without a remnant, by the anger of God (אף אל). A similar phrase (אף יהוה) is used in 2 Sam 24:1, which is often understood to be the satan figure in the HB due to the corresponding story in 1 Chr 21:1.

79. See Matthew A. Collins, *The Use of Sobriquets in the Qumran Dead Sea Scrolls*, LSTS (London: T&T Clark, 2009), 197–98. Collins argues that "the minority status of the Qumran group suggests that those who became members could well be considered by others or have considered themselves as deviating from normative Jewish behavior in certain ways." In addition, he contends that the scrolls suggest that the community "viewed the rest of Israel as deviant or in error (cf. CD 1.1–8a)." I concur that the term בליעל may be used to refer to a personified spirit on some occasions, but it is also being used as a sobriquet to address the human enemies of the community.

In 1QM 11.8–9, the "troops of Belial" (גדודי בליעל)⁸⁰ are described as the "seven arrogant nations" (cf. 15.2), which may be referring to the nations mentioned in 1QM 1.1; again, it is difficult to determine the nature of בליעל in this context; although it is likely that of a spirit being, it could be a human leader of the armies arrayed against Israel.

In 1QM 13.1–5, the term בליעל is used twice in the context of Belial and those with him being cursed for his actions. The first occurrence in 13.1 speaks of Belial and all the "spirits of his lot" (רוחי גורלו) who are cursed by the chief priest (reconstructed [RC] in 12.20), the Levites, and the elders of the [Qumran priestly?] order (זקני הסרך) with him. In 1QM 13.4–5, we find בליעל in the context of being cursed: "And בליעל is being cursed for the 'plan of hatred/ *mastema*' [משטמה במחשבת] and he is being rebuked for his sinful plan. And all the spirits of his lot are being cursed for their evil plan [במחשבה רשעם]. And they are being cursed for all the work of their ritual impurity, for they are a lot of darkness, but the lot of God is eternal light." The language used against the spirits of בליעל's lot may suggest that the service they are performing is an unclean ritual, which could be referring to priestly functions in the Jerusalem temple. This may suggest that there are evil spirits at work behind the priesthood in the Jerusalem temple or that the high priest and the priesthood itself are wicked. If one assumes these are spirits working behind the scene, then it could be understood that בליעל (sobriquet for the high priest) has a group of spirits working with him (knowingly or unknowingly) that are assisting in bringing about his plan of hatred (משטמה, *mastema*) against the Qumran community.

Davidson argues that the use of בליעל in 1QM 13.10–11 "clearly means a personal being and an evil angel, the leader of the lot of darkness, and enemy of the Prince of Light";⁸¹ however, it is possible that this might be read quite differently. One could possibly read it as "You made wickedness (בליעל) for destruction, a *messenger* of enmity,"⁸² thus raising the question of whether the text is identifying so "clearly . . . an evil angel." In 1QM 13.11, in establishing a contrast between the Prince (Ruler) of Light (13.10) and Belial, we are told that Belial was created by God (אל) for the place of destruction (שחת) and is an angel/messenger (מלאך) of *mastema* (hatred).⁸³ Davidson argues that the author of 1QM is revealing an etiology of sin as a result of God creating Belial to corrupt humanity and cause them to stray from God. But in the end, the author reveals that God is in control of all things, including the role of Belial and his lot. In 1QM 13.11–12, Belial

---

80. Compare, for example, to its use in 1QM 1.2, 3; 11.8; 1QHᵃ 11.40; and 14.31, where it is used to describe the physical armies of the nations.
81. Davidson, *Angels at Qumran*, 163.
82. We may be too quick to assign the heavenly angelic title to the Hebrew מלאך rather than a more simplistic "messenger," in this case, a messenger of malevolence.
83. It is possible that Belial is understood here as a heavenly being subordinate to the figure Mastema. See discussion in Davidson, *Angels at Qumran*, 217–19.

has under his control "the spirits of his lot, the angels/messengers of destruction," suggesting that he is a spirit being. These appear to be two distinct groups— גורלו רוחי and מלאכי חבל; as Philip Alexander contends, it is not clear if Belial has evil spirits (demons) working with him or angelic beings—two very distinct groups in 2TP that should not be conflated.[84] One must keep in mind the מלאכי חבל could also be human messengers of destruction.

In 1QM 15.2–3, we find the army of בליעל alongside the king of the Kittim on the day of vengeance(?) by the sword of God. בליעל could represent the one who leads the army, or it could be a characteristic of the armies—"armies of wickedness." The other instances of בליעל in 1QM offer little other information: 14.9, Belial rules; 15.17, Belial is reconstructed with little discernable context; 16.11, Belial is reconstructed and paired with the Sons of Darkness, possibly leading to his identification as the Angel of Darkness;[85] 18.1–3, Belial (2×) is mentioned with the forces of his rule that will be slaughtered by the hand of God.

One final note should be addressed regarding 1QM 17.4–6. The author adjures the people of the community not to fear the nations of the wicked (17.1), for they will be judged by God. In 17.5, a unique phrase occurs, "prince of the dominion of wickedness" (שר ממשלת רשעה). This is the leader who will be "subdued and humiliated" in God's appointed time. Some have suggested that this phrase is identifying בליעל in an exalted status due to the use of "prince" of a dominion and is connected to the figure Melchiresha in 4QAmram 2.3.[86] This comparison is due in part to the presence of Michael the archangel in 17.6, who is understood to be the angel contrasted with Melchiresha in 4QAmram. This may be a possibility, but the evidence is not definitive. Michael is also connected to the "Light" in 17.6, and this may also lend to the idea that he is the Prince of Light and Melchizedek in various other documents (e.g., 1QM 13.10–11; CD 5.17–19; 4.12–18; 1QS 3.20–21), but again, we need to be careful not to read these terms or ideas the same way across all DSS texts.[87]

It is difficult to come away from 1QM with a clear understanding of who or what בליעל is to the author. As noted, there are instances in which the term could be understood as the abstract noun "wickedness," or a human adversary of the community (the high priest?), or a spiritual adversary of the community or individuals. The primary reading of בליעל by scholars of 1QM

---

84. Alexander, "Demonology," 2:334.
85. See Dimant, "Between Qumran," 242. Dimant contends that in CD 5.18, Belial is in opposition to the Angel of Light and, in 1QS 3.20–22, the Angel of Light is opposed by the Angel of Darkness, thus drawing the parallel. Martone contends that Belial and the Angel of Darkness are one entity, "the personification of evil." Martone, "Evil or Devil?," 123–24.
86. J. T. Milik, "Milkî-ṣedeq et Milkî-rešaʿ dans les anciens écrits juifs et chrétiens," *JJS* 23 (1972): 95–144, here, 142; Davidson, *Angels at Qumran*, 219.
87. Davidson, *Angels at Qumran*, 263–64.

has been that the figure is the demonic leader of a group of evil spirits.[88] But this is not the only way this term can be interpreted as noted above. The term בליעל could be read as a human leader of the Sons of Darkness, who are people outside of the community: it is clear that there were evil spirits operating in the worldview of Second Temple Period Judaism, and it has been shown that these spirits of destruction (1QM 14.10, רוחי חבל) are on his (בליעל) side assisting him and those individuals (Sons of Darkness) who are members of his lot during his temporary dominion. In addition, there are people who play a role in the dominion of בליעל (14.10) who are in direct opposition to the righteous (Sons of Light) and YHWH. A third reading of בליעל is that it is the abstract noun "wickedness," as seen in the discussion above of 1QM 1.13–15.

Thanksgiving Hymns (Hodayot, 1QH^a)

The Hodayot (1QH^a)[89] offer several instances in which בליעל certainly signifies an abstract quality rather than personified evil. The term appears twelve times (nine complete, three partial reconstructions).[90] The Hodayot are very fragmentary and determining a firm context for the occurrences of בליעל is difficult. The beginning of this section includes the author's pleas against those afflicting him, whom he describes as the "wicked" (רשעים). He speaks of the assembly of the wicked (קהלת רשעים), who have come against him violently in 1QH^a 10.14. All those coming against him appear to be human. In 1QH^a 10.18 (line 16 in GMT), he speaks of the "men of deceit" (אנשי רמיה) who roar against him; it is here that we find the first reference to בליעל. The author speaks of the plots of בליעל (מזמות בליעל) that the men of deceit are devising. Of course, בליעל could be referring to a spiritual being, or perhaps the Wicked Priest, but it is likely referring to the plots of wickedness the men of deceit are carrying out (GMT and Schuller and Newsom translate, "devilish schemes"[91]; Turnage, "schemes of Belial"[92]—that is, as a proper noun).

What is interesting is how some translators of the Dead Sea Scrolls seem to switch randomly between identifying the term בליעל as a proper noun and translating it as an abstract noun. In 1QH^a 10.24 (line 22 in GMT), these ruthless men are the council of worthlessness or deception (סוד שוא) and the "congregation of Belial" (עדת בליעל). Here, בליעל could be

---

88. Dimant, "Between Qumran," 246. Dimant contends that בליעל is the personification of all evil in the world during the eschaton—the dominion of בליעל.
89. See the introductory discussion in Angela Kim Harkins, "Hodayot," in Embry, Herms, and Wright, *Early Jewish Literature*, 2:450–58.
90. See 1QH^a 10.18, 24 (RC); 11.29, 30, 33; 12.11, 14; 13.28 (RC), 41 (RC); 14.24; 15.6.
91. See Eileen M. Schuller and Carol A. Newsom, *The Hodayot (Thanksgiving Psalms): A Study Edition of 1QH^a*, SBLEJL 36 (Atlanta: SBL, 2012), 34.
92. See Marc Turnage's "Hodayot (1QH^a)," a translation of the Sukenik Hebrew text, in Embry, Herms, and Wright, *Early Jewish Literature*, 2:470.

referring to an individual (perhaps the Wicked Priest?) who is in opposition to the author of 1QH[a], but this does not rule out that it may simply be the "congregation of the wicked," those who are outside of the community and aligned with a human leader of the wicked. There is nothing that suggests בליעל is referring to an evil spirit in the context of 10.24.

In 1QH[a] 11.19, following a description of the Gates of Sheol and the Pit of Abaddon, the author suggests the presence of "spirits of wickedness" (רוחי אפעה)[93] that have been at work in the midst of Israel and are now being shut up in Abaddon. These spirits have caused the people to follow wickedness and abandon the covenant (11.29; line 28 in GMT): "But a time of fury will come against all wickedness" (וקץ חרון לכול בליעל; GMT translates as proper name "Belial"; Turnage as "wickedness," Schuller and Newsom as "devilishness"). Beginning in 11.27, the author speaks of all the "traps of the pit" (פחי שחת), the wicked snares (מצודות רשעה), and the net of the wretched ones (מכמרת צלכאים) that will be set against the righteous. He then shifts, in 11.28, to what seems to be a coming judgment against the unrighteous; within this judgment, the author speaks of wrath upon the ones being forsaken, upon all the ones being deceived, and against all that belongs to בליעל. The text of 11QH[a] 11.29 affirms that the time of anger/fury will come against all who belong to בליעל and they will be surrounded by the snares of death.

In 11.30 (line 29 in GMT; GMT and Turnage translate as "Belial," Schuller and Newsom as "devilishness"), a familiar term from the HB, "the torrents of Belial" (נחלי בליעל), appears from 2 Samuel 22:5 and Psalm 18:5 (Hebrew) that speak of the wickedness that is overrunning the nation(s) and will be the destruction of these people. In the 1QH[a] and the two HB texts, a context of fast-approaching snares of death (11.29) is expressed along with the torrents of בליעל that will devour with fire all that comes in their path. In 11.33 ([line 32 in GMT]; GMT, Turnage, Schuller and Newsom all translate as "Belial"), these same torrents burst into Abaddon—the pit—which results in the outcry of the ones who were plotting evil from the deep. In 11.35–37, the author describes, in very apocalyptic terms, the wrath of God being poured out and how the Hosts of Heaven will overcome evil and destroy it completely. The author in 1QH[a] 11 undoubtedly is using the term בליעל to refer to the abstract noun "wickedness" rather than a personified evil spirit being. As argued above, he is certainly informed by the nonuse of the term as a personified evil being in the Hebrew Bible.

There does not appear to be any sense of a chief evil being in the 1QH[a] context; rather, it may indicate ongoing attacks of wicked individuals (or nations) or the overpowering force of

---

93. The term אפעה is used in the DSS eight times to designate an abstract "wickedness": in 1QH[a] 10.30; 11.13; 4Q428 frag. 4.1 (// to 1QH[a] 11.13); 11QH[a] 11.19 ("spirits of wickedness"); reconstructed in 4Q432 frag. 5.6 ("works of wickedness"); 5.7 (// 1QH[a] 11.19, "spirits of wickedness"); and 11Q11 6.12 ("serpent").

wickedness over the land. In 1QH^a 12.7–9, the author speaks of how the people of Israel will go astray (although reconstructed), for they flatter themselves with words, and the mediators of deceit cause them to err, and they are cast down without knowledge, and their works are deceitful, and they reject good works. In 12.10, the author speaks of all his friends who have been driven away from him because they see him as a ruined vessel. In 1QH^a 12.11, the author writes, "They plotted בליעל against me[94] to exchange your Torah, which you impressed [שננתה] upon my heart, for false teachings [בחלקות][95] for your people." In this line, בליעל should certainly be identified as "wickedness" rather than a supernatural being; the wickedness is that which is used by those outside the community to try to draw the author away from the covenant in exchange for falsehoods/flattering words (Turnage and Schuller and Newsom translate as "devilry"; GMT [12.13] "devilish things"[96]).

In 1QH^a 12.13–14, God rejects these plans of wickedness (בליעל; GMT and Turnage[97] translate as "Belial"; Schuller and Newsom as "devilish [plans]") that are hatched by the deceivers who are operating with a "double heart" (ולב בלב), which may be hinting at the presence of the "spirit of falsehood" (see 1QS 3.19) in the human heart; in this case, the author could simply be referring to every plan of wickedness of those who are coming against him. In 1QH^a 13.28 (Sukenik, not in GMT[98]), the wicked people plan the destruction of their heart "and with wor[ds] of Belial" (ודב]רי[בליעל)—they exhibited a lying tongue (Turnage translates as "Belial";[99] Schuller and Newsom as "devilish words"[100]); this could be understood as words of wickedness from the evil inclination. Colossians 13 contains significant discussion of the heart and the thoughts of the heart; in 13:33, the heart is tormented, perhaps by the battle going on between the "spirit of truth" and the "spirit of falsehood" over the thoughts of the author.

In 1QH^a 13.41 (13.39 in GMT, ונחלי ב]ל[י]על]), the biblical phrase ונחלי[בליעל is reconstructed and בליעל is identified as a proper noun, "torrents of Belial," by GMT, Turnage, and Schuller and Newsom. But as we have previously mentioned this phrase is not read this way in the HB.

In 14.24 (14.21 in GMT), GMT, Turnage, and Schuller and Newsom identify בליעל as the proper noun in the phrase "like a counselor, בליעל is with/in their heart,"[101] perhaps hinting

---

94. "בליעל [. . .] זממו עלי"; the content of the *vacat* has not been determined.
95. The term here, בחלקות, can also be interpreted as "smooth things/words"; as such, the author may be offering an allusion to the "seekers of smooth things (interpretations)," a well-known sobriquet in the Second Temple Period for those who are attempting to turn people from God's path.
96. GMT, 169.
97. GMT, 169; Turnage, "Hodayot (1QH^a)," 474; Schuller and Newsom, *Hodayot*, 42.
98. GMT includes a reconstructed "ואנ]שי ב[ליעל" (and m[en of B]elial) in 13.26.
99. Turnage, "Hodayot (1QH^a)," 477.
100. Schuller and Newsom, *Hodayot*, 42.
101. Schuller and Newsom, 47; GMT, 177; Turnage, "Hodayot (1QH^a)," 479.

at the *yetser ra* (יצר רע). In 14.25, we are told they (those plotting against the author) have a plan of wickedness (מחשבת רשעה), which may be paralleled with the words "like a counselor, בליעל is in their heart" (14.24). בליעל here could be understood as "wickedness in their hearts" rather than interpreting בליעל as a spirit that offers counsel to their hearts; the context is not clear. Finally, in 15.6 (15.3 in GMT), GMT, Turnage, and Schuller and Newsom identify בליעל as the proper noun in the phrase "for בליעל causes their destructive inclination [*yetser*, יצר] to be revealed" (הוחם הופע יצר).[102]

In 1QH^a 15.6, the author describes those who are plotting against him with evil. In rather vivid, destructive language (see 15.5–6), he describes the effects of the evil around him on his physical body. In all three cases, בליעל could equally be read as "wickedness" (e.g., "for wickedness causes . . ."). It does not seem necessary, in this instance, for *Belial* to equate to an evil spiritual being, but it is not something that can easily be ruled out. The other instance of Belial found in 1QH^a 13.41 is reconstructed, and the text does not offer a clear context for understanding the term.

Cave 4 Documents

The collection of scrolls from Cave 4 contains eighty references to בליעל: thirty-seven times, it appears as the complete word, and forty-four times, it appears in various stages of reconstruction.[103] In what follows, we examine those somewhat helpful in understanding the nature and use of בליעל.

The text of 4Q171 fragment 1 2ii.9–10 speaks of how the righteous who endure the time of error will be delivered from the snares of בליעל—perhaps the three traps of בליעל mentioned in CD 4.13–18. בליעל could simply mean "wickedness" in this context, although the CD 4.13–18 context may be referencing a spirit being, but as mentioned in the discussion of the Damascus Document, it is also unclear as to the intention of the author. The text 4Q174, which is concerned with the captivity of Israel and her future restoration, contains four occurrences, one of which (frag. 1 2i.8) is a reconstruction. The context of the first occurrence in fragment 1 2i.8–9 suggests that the "children of בליעל" (בני בליעל)[104] may be human adversaries similar to the enemies of David in 2 Samuel 7:11. The children of בליעל are determined to destroy the righteous with their

---

102. Schuller and Newsom, *Hodayot*, 49; GMT, 177; Turnage, "Hodayot (1QH^a)," 2:480.
103. The following is a comprehensive list of documents from Caves 1, 4, 5, and 6 that contain בליעל. The discussion will cover only those that have a relevant and understandable context and will omit those in which the term *Belial* is reconstructed in some manner. See 1Q40; 4Q88; 4Q171; 4Q174; 4Q175; 4Q176; 4Q177; 4Q178; 4Q225; 4Q226; 4Q253; 4Q256; 4Q257; 4Q260; 4Q266; 4Q267; 4Q271; 4Q286; 4Q287; 4Q290; 4Q299; 4Q300; 4Q379; 4Q386; 4Q390; 4Q398; 4Q425; 4Q428; 4Q429; 4Q430; 4Q432; 4Q433; 4Q463; 4Q471; 4Q495; 4Q496; 4Q511; 4Q525; 4Q544; 5Q13; 6Q15; 6Q18.
104. The "בני בליעל" are identified as those who opposed the religious cult of Israel and attempt to persuade others to worship other gods in Deut 13.14.

plans in order that they might fall prey to בליעל (wickedness?) through their errors. Fragment 1 3ii.1–2 contains בליעל, possibly in reference to the "children of בליעל," but both lines of the text are quite fragmentary: "That will be a time of testing that is to co[me upon the House of J]udah, to the end of sealing up [the wicked in consuming fire and destroying all the children of] בליעל." The reconstructed text speaks in contrasting terms with the chosen ones who keep the entire Torah (frag. 1 3ii.2). בליעל here could be understood as simply wickedness but could be speaking of a group of people who are following after a wicked human leader or a wicked spirit. The final mention in 4Q174 fragment 4.3 offers little context to determine the meaning of בליעל—"[. . .] this is the time when בליעל will open [. . .]."

The text 4Q177 offers ten occasions of בליעל, six of which are reconstructed and offer little context. In 4Q177 fragment 1 4.8, the Lot of the Light (ו[ג]ורל אור) will mourn under the rule of בליעל (בממשלת בליעל), likely in the last days (frag. 1 4.7—[. . . הימים] באחרית), but little more can be determined due to the fragmentary nature of the text. Similarly, 4Q177 fragment 1 4.10 is too fragmentary to determine a context, and ב[ליעל . . .] is partially reconstructed. Fragment 10 11.4 identifies "men of בליעל and all the discontented mob," but there is no other context. אנשי בליעל could possibly indicate "men of wickedness" or a "wicked group" opposed to Israel; considering it is followed by "the discontented mob" (האספסוף), this is a plausible meaning. Fragment 12 13i.6–7 speaks of the plans of בליעל in a broader context in which the angel of (God's) truth helps free the children of the Light from the hand of בליעל (מיד בליעל), a phrase often used to designate "power of בליעל." This use could be understood as a human adversary, the power of wickedness, or a spiritual being, but the context does not offer anything definitive. Fragment 12 13i.11 identifies the men of the lot of בליעל (ב[ל]י[ע]ל . . .]) over against what has been reconstructed as all the children of Light (. . . בני א]ור) who will be gathered; although there is little context to determine the nature of בליעל, it likely falls under the same identification as fragment 12 13i.6–7: a human adversary, a spiritual being, or the power of wickedness. The general usage for בליעל in 4Q177 may be understood as wickedness, a human adversary, or possibly a spiritual being, but in general, the context suggests the power of wickedness.

The text of 4Q225 fragment 2ii.13–14 includes two interesting notes concerning בליעל. In line 13, we find the phrase "the ruler of Mastema was bound" (שר המשטמה—"the leader/chief of malevolence");[105] however, there is very little context to determine its meaning. Line 14

---

105. The Hebrew term שר is most often translated in the scrolls as "prince," but based on its use in the HB, it seems a better translation would be "chief," as in "the chief/commander of the armies," in various contexts; see, for example, Gen 21:22; Exod 18:25; Judg 4:2; Dan 1:7; 10:13 (the chief spirit over the kingdom of Persia); even in the oft-cited 12:1, Michael could be understood as the great chief (angel) over Israel.

appears to personify both the chief of (the) Mastema שר המשטמה and בליעל; we are told that בליעל "listened to" or "obeyed" (וישמע) שר המשטמה (שר המ[ש]טמה is reconstructed), and בליעל could be understood as a human adversary who is operating with the authority of a foreign power that is oppressing Israel, although a spirit being should not be ruled out.

A parallel to 1QS 10.21 is 4Q260 5.2, in which the narrator states that he will give no room for בליעל in his heart—"And I will not keep בליעל in my heart." From this passage, it appears the fruit of בליעל is speaking foolishness, sinful deceit, and lies (5.3). Here, בליעל could be understood as acts of wickedness: "I will not keep wickedness in my heart," which would be the cause of these "fruits of wickedness." These characteristics are contrasted with the fruits of holiness in 4Q260 5.4. Speaking of God's righteousness, not abominations, these "fruits" are nurtured by the person who has "thanksgiving" in his heart: "For thanksgiving will open my mouth." On this occasion, the term בליעל is certainly not referring to a personified evil being but rather to an attitude of the heart toward things righteous—either rejections by a wicked heart or acceptance by a thankful heart.

Similarly, 4Q271 fragment 5i.18 parallels CD 12.3, in which all wicked people are ruled over by the spirits of בליעל, speak falsehood, and attempt to get others to turn away from YHWH and the Torah. It clearly speaks of wicked spirits that could be operating under the authority of בליעל, which could be identified as a personified evil spirit or a wicked human.

In 4Q286 fragment 7ii.1–5, the author states that the members of the Yahad will curse בליעל and his lot because of the plans of Mastema (משטמה). בליעל and the spirits of his lot (RC—רוּחֵי גוֹרלו) are of darkness and to be punished in the eternal pit (שחת). Frag. 7ii.6 offers an interesting reading that perhaps suggests that the sons of בליעל (בלי[על]) are "cursed for all the iniquities of *their office* (מעמדמה)." This may indicate the office of the priesthood in Jerusalem, thus lending credence to the idea that בליעל is the Wicked Priest in Jerusalem. However, in 4Q286 fragment 7ii.7, although the text is reconstructed, the author refers to בליעל as the "spirit of Abaddon" (האב[דון רוח), who is the "angel/messenger of the Pit (or destruction)" (מלא[ך שחת . . .). These phrases seem to indicate a heavenly being, but the author may be indicating that the Wicked Priest represents both these images with his actions. He offers wicked counsel, holds an unjust dominion, and operates as a wicked authority—again, keeping in mind the reconstruction of the text. As mentioned, the author could have in mind a spirit being, perhaps a heavenly angel; this spirit being has rule over all those who listen to him and turn away from the Torah.

A retelling of Ezekiel 37, 4Q386 fragment 1ii.3–4 gives the impression that בליעל might be a human figure, as the author identifies an enemy with the reference to "a son of בליעל" who will plan to oppress Israel. This could imply a wicked person or one identified with the lot of

בליעל or the lot of wickedness. Along a similar line, in 4Q387 fragment 1.3–10 (although quite fragmentary), the author appears to address an individual or individuals who have defiled the temple, ignored the festivals, profaned holy things (likely in the temple), and offered sacrifices to "goat demons" (לשעירים). All of these offenses would suggest a connection to the priesthood or possibly a foreign ruler who has taken over Jerusalem such as Antiochus IV Epiphanes. Torleif Elgvin contends that the angels/messengers of Mastemot (מלאכי המשטמות, "messengers of malevolence") mentioned in 4Q387 fragment 2iii.4 are symbolic of the Diadochian kings and the ungodly priests Jason Menelaus and Alcimus who reigned circa 174–160 BCE.[106]

In 4Q390 fragment 2i.4, a group of people who have turned away from God and the Torah are suggested to be under the dominion of בליעל (ממשלת בליעל, "dominion of wickedness") in order to hand the wicked people over to the violence of the sword for a period of seven years. They had forsaken God for their own pleasure and illegal financial gain by oppressing their neighbors and one another. They had defiled the temple (frag. 2i.2—מקדש הקד[ש) and failed to keep the proper feasts. These sins committed by this group fit the description of the three traps of בליעל described in CD 16, suggesting that they may be part of the Jerusalem priesthood. In fragment 2i.7, we are told that this group will be given "into the hand the angels/messengers of mastema" ([ביד מל]אכי המשטמות), who will rule over them (ומשלו בהם). This parallel(?) may suggest that the rule of בליעל (frag. 2i.4) and the rule of the angels/messengers of Mastema (2i.7) are one and the same or at least similar in nature. The text indicates or suggests that the "angels of Mastema" are operating at the behest of YHWH; if so, then that would indicate that בליעל is also operating under the sovereignty of YHWH.

In 4Q398 fragment 14 17ii.5, the author recounts the counsel concerning the works of the Torah (מעשי התורה) given to those who are seeking the Lord; they are to ask God to keep them from evil thoughts (מחשב [ו]ת רעה) and the counsel of בליעל (עצת בליעל). There is little in the text that might define the nature of עצת בליעל; it could be understood as simply wicked counsel, the counsel of a wicked person, or the counsel of an evil spirit. Due to the author's references to the biblical text, it seems likely that he is using בליעל in the same sense as it is used in the HB—"wicked."

In our final reference of the Cave 4 texts, 4Q511 fragment 18ii.5, בליעל is used in the sense of wicked words—that is, the author speaks of the utterance of his lips, in which there can be found no wickedness (בליעל). There is little context that would help determine its use beyond what is noted here.

---

106. Torleif Elgvin, "Belial/Beliar/Devil/Satan," in *Dictionary of New Testament Backgrounds* (Downers Grove, IL: InterVarsity, 2000), 154.

From this discussion of the Cave 4 texts, we can see that there is no single meaning for the term בליעל. The most common contextual translation used by the authors describes בליעל as the abstract "wicked" or "wickedness," or a human adversary of Israel or the author's community. However, there are a few occasions in which one can suggest that the authors are referring to some sort of evil spiritual entity.

Cave 11 Documents

In 11QMelchizedek (11Q13),[107] dated in the first century BCE,[108] there are six occurrences of בליעל (2.12, 13, 22, 25; 3.7; 5.3). As is the case with other scrolls, 11Q13 is very fragmentary; as a result, it is difficult to draw any definitive conclusions about author's use of the term בליעל. The text of 11Q13 2.10–12 offers a *pesher* on Psalm 82:1–2 and Psalm 7:7–9. The 11Q13 text first cites Psalm 82:1–2, in which Elohim (אלוהים) stands in the Council of God (בע[דת אל]) and, "in the midst of divine beings [אלוהים], will judge."[109] The author of 11Q13 2.11 then cites Psalm 7:7–8 (MT) but makes a change in terminology by using *El* (אל) in place of YHWH (יהוה). This change creates some confusion as to who this "divine being" (אל) is in the 11Q13 text. The texts of Psalm 7 and Psalm 82 make it clear that it is YHWH who is doing the judging; however, the one(s) judging is less clear in 11Q13. The author of 11Q13 2.11 cites Psalm 82:2, in which the author of the biblical text has asked, "How long will you judge [second masculine plural verb] unjustly and show partiality to [second masculine plural] the wicked?" So to whom is the author of the biblical Psalm speaking, YHWH or the divine council? The plural verbs suggest he is speaking to the members of the divine council, which is made up of the members of the hierarchy of heavenly beings, as portrayed in Job 1–2 (בני האלוהים). The author of 11Q13 2.12 then offers his interpretation (*pesher*) in which the "wicked" (הרשעים) is interpreted as a reference to בליעל and "the spirits of his lot" (רוחי גורלו)—that is, those spiritual beings (or humans) that are operating on the side of בליעל.[110] This interpretation would line up with the cosmological (spiritual beings in conflict) and social (social groups in conflict) dualisms that are prevalent in the writings of the Qumran community. Some scholars contend that בליעל, due

---

107. A reconstructed "Sons of Belial" (בל[י]על) appears in 11Q11 6.3, but there is little context to determine a meaning for the phrase.
108. R. Steven Notley suggests that the paleography of 11Q13 "is indicative of late Hasmonean or early Herodian book hand (50–25 BCE)"; J. T. Milik suggests a slightly earlier date of 75–50 BCE. See R. Steven Notley, "The Melchizedek Scroll," in Embry, Herms, and Wright, *Early Jewish Literature*, 1:490–97, here, 490.
109. See the Elohim tradition concerning "angels" in 2TP in Wright, *Origin of Evil Spirits*, 97–104.
110. About half of this line is reconstructed text. Although there is no room to thoroughly examine the idea in this essay, one might ask if the author is using the phrase רוחי גורלו to refer to humans due to the fact that these "spirits" have departed from God's statutes (חוקי אל G) and now serve on the side of wickedness. See, for example, Stuckenbruck, "Demonic Beings," 137.

to its close proximity to רוחי גורלו, is being identified as an evil spirit being, thus the use of the proper noun;[111] however, one could equally suggest that בליעל is a sobriquet for the high priest, who, knowingly or unknowingly, has a group of spirits working with him or behind him. The author states that בליעל and these spirits "have rebelled, departing from God's statutes, [and are being wicked]." This appears to be speaking of a group of spirits that were previously serving YHWH but now are not. One might wonder if this is an allusion to the Fallen Watchers in 1 Enoch. The terms בליעל and רוחי גורלו occur again in 11Q13 2.13: "And Melchizedek will carry out the vengeance of God's judgments, [and on that day, he (Melchizedek?) will de]li[ver them (the righteous) from the power of] בליעל and from the power of all the sp[irits of his lot]."[112] Here we see the figure of מלכי צדק (Melchizedek) carrying out the judgment against the leader of the wicked and the spirits that are with him, for which the author of 11Q13 2.11 is crying out. This would suggest that Melchizedek is a member of the divine council, one of the בני האלוהים (*bene ha'elohim*). But again, it is unclear if the term בליעל is the personified evil spirit, a wicked human leader who opposes the Qumran community, or "wickedness." The first part of the line can be read "[and on that day he will de]li[ver them from the power of wickedness"; however, "the sp[irits of his lot]" would need to be read "the spirits of its lot"—that is, "those who have cast their lot with wickedness." There are two other occurrences of בליעל in 11Q13; neither offers any significant context with which to determine the term's usage. The first is 11Q13 2.22, which speaks of "[the end of something belonging to] בליעל," which will be "re[turned to ... (the object of the verb is unknown)]." The final occurrence is in 11Q13 2.24–25, but the text can only be reconstructed to read "and your di[vi]ne being [ואל[ו]היך] [Melchizedek, who will deliver them from the ha]nd of בליעל."[113]

As mentioned previously the very fragmentary nature of 11Q13 makes it difficult to determine a clear reading of the text; however, in lines 2.12, 13, 22, and 25, בליעל could be read as "wickedness" or possibly as an allusion to the high priest—that is, the Wicked Priest. The identity of Melchizedek may be the key to understanding the identity of בליעל. In several Dead Sea Scrolls, it is the case that the hope of atonement and deliverance will come through a "divinely appointed human figure—most often portrayed as an exalted priest"[114]—in this case, the leader of the Qumran community. However, the author's contrast of Melchizedek as

---

111. See GMT, 1207; they translate as a proper noun. See, similarly, Notley, "Melchizedek Scroll," 1:499. See also Dimant, "Between Qumran," 240; Martone, "Evil or Devil?," 125–26.
112. See Florentino García Martínez, Eibert J. C. Tigchelaar, and Adam S. Van Der Woude, *Qumran Cave 11*, DJD 23 (Oxford: Clarendon, 1998).
113. Cf. Jub. 50.5; T. Moses 10.1; T. Levi 18.12.
114. Notley, "Melchizedek," 1:493. See the Greek T. Levi 17.1–2; 4Q175 11–13; T. Moses 10.1.

the "divine being" commanding the Sons of Light and בליעל as a possible "divine being" with power over those outside of the covenant community leaves open the possibility that the author is alluding to the leader of the evil spirits.[115]

The final instance of note of בליעל in this examination is found in the Temple Scroll, 11Q19 55.3. Here, the term appears to be used to describe a group of men (although reconstructed), in this case "worthless" men (אנש[י]ם [ב]ני [בלי[על), who have gone out from the midst of the community to speak evil and wickedness to incite others to worship and serve other gods. Here, בליעל is being used in a similar sense as in the HB—"worthlessness" or "wickedness."

We have seen a variety of occasions and uses for the term בליעל in the DSS. It can be understood as a characteristic of an individual or a group of people, which can be translated as "worthless" or "wicked." It can be understood as a wicked ruler of one of the nations oppressing Israel. On several occasions, we have seen it used to designate an influential spirit that seeks to turn individuals or groups from God and the Torah. It is difficult to determine based on the evidence presented; it appears the most likely understanding falls in the realm of the unknown. Various authors used the term to speak of wickedness, whether it was a human characteristic or a human influence, and at the same time, it was presented as part of the cosmological dualism of Qumran, in which בליעל is the/a leader of a group of spirits, his lot, whose purpose was to test, try, and influence people to choose a path contrary to God's plan.

Mastema

The term משטמה (Mastema) gained its notoriety in the book of Jubilees, where it represents a figure that has been granted dominion over a group of evil spirits that have their origin in the Enochic Book of Watchers (1 En. 1–36)—the spirits of the dead giants. However, how Mastema is being used specifically by the authors of various scrolls is unclear. It is also ambiguous as to its relationship to the satan figure or even the figure of Belial. As mentioned previously, one should not assume that Mastema is just another name for the figure of personified evil; nor should one assume that Mastema, the satan, and Belial are one and the same.[116] Mastema or a form of it occurs twenty-two times in the DSS; twelve of those are in full, משטמה (also with the definite article—המשטמה), and ten times in a reconstructed state with the complete word supplied or

---

115. There is no context in 5.2 from which to determine the meaning of "בליעל: [. . .] בליעל ימרו [. . .]." Notley argues (probably correctly) that the author is not identifying Melchizedek as a divine being but rather that he is speaking of the period of righteous judgment in which the eschatological priest will act; see Notley, "Melchizedek," 495.
116. Stuckenbruck, *Myth of Rebellious Angels*, 96.

partial reconstructions.[117] It appears in a variety of contexts, including as "an angel" (מלאך), "the angel" (המלאך), "angels of" (מלאכי), "prince/chief/ruler of" (שר), or with the third masculine singular suffix in relation to a plan, purpose, or thought (מחשבת). The term can be defined as "enmity," "animosity," "malevolent," or "malevolence." The noun form that appears in the DSS only appears in Hosea 9:7 and 8. According to Koehler and Baumgartner, משטמה is derived from the root שטם, "to be at enmity with" or "to be hostile toward"; it appears in the form of a finite verb six times in the HB (Gen 27:41; 49:23; 50:15; Ps 55:4; Job 16:9; 30:21).[118]

Angel of Mastema

Mastema appears in construct with angel/messenger (מלאך המשטמה) in CD 16.5 and has the definite article attached—"the Angel/Messenger of Mastema." It is set in the context of obedience to the Torah: "On the day a man takes on himself the oath to return to the Law of Moses, the Angel of Mastema will leave him." Here, Mastema is translated as an angel of hatred or possibly obstruction whose task is to keep an individual away from God and his Torah.[119] This phrase may be understood as an angel operating under the authority of the heavenly being Mastema, or it perhaps should be read as "the Angel Mastema," thus identifying the proper name of the angel.[120] It is possible the definite article attached to Mastema in this case indicates a *nomen rectum* of the construct phrase, which could indicate a proper name, but this is not necessarily the case (cf. 4Q225 2ii.6—[. . .]מלאכי המ[שטמה—the Angels of Mastema). This same use is identified in 4Q270 fragment 6ii.18 (partial RC—מלאך המשט]מה; also 4Q271 frag. 4ii.6), in which the Angel of Mastema will leave a person alone when that individual returns to the Torah. In 1QM 13.11, Mastema is again used with angel (מלאך משטמה, "an angel of malevolence/hatred"—in this case no definite article) to describe בליעל as "an angel of mastema" whose task is to condemn and convict those under his dominion (see also 4Q495 frag. 2.3, complete reconstruction based on 1QM 13.11: "You made [בליעל for the pit, an angel of malevolence . . .]"). It might be argued that בליעל here is a subordinate of the figure Mastema or as mentioned it could be describing one of the characteristics of the role or purpose of בליעל.

---

117. Other instances preserve the term but with no context: CD 16.5; 1QS 3.23; 1QM 13.4, 11; 4Q177 frag. 9.5; 4Q225 frag. 1.8; frag. 2i.9; frag. 2ii.6, 7, 13, 14 (2×); 4Q270 frag. 6ii.18; 4Q271 frag. 4ii.6; 4Q286 frag. 7ii.2; 4Q287 frag. 6.2; 4Q387 frag. 2iii.4; 4Q390 frag. 1.11; frag. 2i.7; 4Q495 frag. 2.3; 4Q525 frag. 19.4; 6Q18 frag. 9.1; 11Q11 2.4. 4Q525 frag. 19.4; 6Q18 frag. 9.1.
118. See Koehler and Baumgartner, *Hebrew and Aramaic Lexicon*, 1316.
119. It might be plausible to suggest this was the action of the satan figure in the wilderness test of Jesus. When tested, Christ turned to the Torah/Scriptures in order to reject the attempts of the satan figure to turn him away from God's plan.
120. See Stuckenbruck, *Myth of Rebellious Angels*, 97.

However, what is clear in this context is that the author does not equate בליעל and משטמה but suggests that בליעל is a heavenly being with the characteristic of malevolence.[121]

Angels of Mastema

In 4Q387 fragment 2iii.4 (Pseudo-Ezekiel), Mastema appears in construct with angels (מלאכי המשטמות); it reads "the Angels of Malevolencies" (pl.). The context suggests that God will abandon the Land of Israel to the Angels of Mastema due to the people rejecting the Torah (frag. 2ii.12). Thus, as we saw in CD 16.5, when the people return to God and his Torah, the Angels of Mastema will depart the land. Another text related to Ezekiel, 4Q390 fragment 1.11, states that the Angels of Mastema (מלאכי המש[ט]מות) will rule over the people of the land because they have "forgotten the Law, festivals, Sabbath, and Covenant . . . and commit evil before the Lord" (frag. 1.8–9; see also frag. 2i.7, although a partial reconstruction). In its retelling of Genesis 22, 4Q225 fragment 2ii.6–7 (Pseudo-Jubilees) suggest two occurrences of Mastema in the context of (the) Angels of Mastema, but both are reconstructed; the first occurrence is a partial reconstruction, the second a full reconstruction, reading "the Chief/ Leader of Mastema" (שר המשטמה). The author relates how the Angels of Mastema were watching over Abraham while he was being tested with the sacrifice of Isaac. These occurrences of *Mastema* in construct with *angels* suggest a specific group of angels / heavenly beings who have been given authority over people who turn from God and disobey the Torah or, in the case of 4Q225, are testing the faithful. It is difficult, however, to determine if they are operating under the authority of a single figure named Mastema or if the task is to bring malevolence to sinners—like the "angels of destruction."[122]

Prince of Mastema

Mastema appears with the term שר (*sar*, "prince, chief, ruler") five times, which may suggest the leader of a group of malevolent beings. Four of those occasions are in 4Q225 (Pseudo-Jubilees).[123] The first episode in 4Q225 fragment 2i.9–10 recounts the story of the sacrifice of Isaac in Genesis 22, in which the Chief of Mastema (שר המשטמה, "chief of malevolence") approached God about Abraham and his son Isaac, similar to the approach the satan figure made in Job 1–2 concerning the faith of Job. We are told in fragment 2i.10 that the Chief of

---

121. See Stuckenbruck, 96.
122. See Stuckenbruck, "Demonic Beings," in Ellens, *Exploring Evil*, 1:136.
123. Stuckenbruck contends that any reference to "Prince Mastema" (שר המשטמה) should be equated with the Mastema in Jub. 10. Stuckenbruck, *Myth of Rebellious Angels*, 97.

Mastema (שר המשטמה) was angry with Abraham on account of Isaac, but no details as to why are given. The name given to this being may suggest that it holds the function of bringing enmity against those it feels are unworthy of God's faithfulness; in this case, שר indicates it is the leader of a group of beings that carry out this role.

Three occurrences are found in fragment 2ii.13–14, which, unfortunately, is quite fragmentary. The first in line 13 suggests that the Chief of Mastema (שר המשטמה) is bound (can also carry the meaning of "forbidden to"), perhaps suggesting he is forbidden to act on account of Abraham, Isaac, Jacob, and Levi; why this occurs is unclear due to the fragmentary text. We also see "the holy angels" (מלאכי הקדש) present, who are perhaps there in opposition to שר המשטמה, as was the Angel of the Lord in the Zechariah 3 text in which the satan figure accuses Joshua, but there is no indication of their purpose due to the missing text. The reconstructed phrase שר המשטמה occurs twice in line 14; the second occurrence is a complete reconstruction. There is little context for the first occasion, simply a partially reconstructed שר המ[ש]טמה that appears to end the sentence. The second reference in line 14 implies some sort of relationship with the figure בליעל: "And Belial listened to [the Chief of Mastema . . .]" ([. . . שר המשטמה אל] וישמע בליעל); however, there is no discernible context to determine its meaning. Each of these occurrences suggests Mastema is a chief or leader of malevolence or malevolent beings.[124]

In 11Q11 (*ApocPs*) 2.4, Mastema is identified within a reconstruction of the name alongside שר (וש]ר המשט[מה). It is in the context of a story of Solomon (2.2; related to the Testament of Solomon?) that identifies spirits (הרו]חות), demons (שדים), and the Chief of Mastema (וש]ר המשט[מה); perhaps, as in 4Q225, the reference here is suggesting the/a leader of malevolent beings—evil spirits and demons.

Mastema occurs in 4Q286 fragment 7ii.1–3 and its parallel text, 4Q287 fragment 6.2; the latter is a full reconstruction. Here *Mastema* (w/3ms suffix—משטמתו) is used to speak of the actions and purposes of Belial and those spirits in the lot of Belial. In 4Q286, the author describes the plan/purpose of Belial as "Mastema" and the plan/purpose of the spirits of his lot as "wicked" (רשע), thus drawing a parallel between Mastema and wicked. It appears in a similar form in 1QS 3.23: "בממשלת משטמתו" ("in his malevolent rule"; the "his" in this case is the Angel of Darkness). A similar occurrence of Mastema is offered by 1QM 13.4 in relation to his plan of malevolence—on this occasion without the 3ms suffix. Belial is cursed by the righteous for his role: "ארור בליעל במחשבת משטמה" (Cursed is Belial in the plan of malevolence). In these

---

124. Esther Eshel suggests שר המשטמה, found in another Pseudo-Jubilees text found at Masada, Mas 1 j: 1276–786 (also identified MasJub, MaspsJub), is sent to kill Moses on his journey from Midian back to Egypt. See Eshel, "Mastema's Attempt on Moses' Life in the 'Pseudo-Jubilees' Text from Masada," *DSD* 10, no. 3 (2003): 359–64.

few instances, there is no mention of Mastema being the "chief" evil character; rather, the term refers to the nature of the plans and purposes of Belial and the wicked spirits of his lot.

Beliar in the Pseudepigrapha and Other Early Jewish Literature

The primary figure of evil in the Pseudepigrapha and other early Jewish literature again is not the satan figure; rather, Beliar (βελιάρ), apparently synonymous with Belial, and Mastema (particularly in Jubilees) share the distinction. The book of Jubilees appears to draw a parallel between the two figures (more on this below). Beliar features significantly in the Testaments of the Twelve Patriarchs as an instigator and a leader of a group of evil spirits whose task is to afflict humanity and draw them away from the Lord.[125] Beliar also appears twice in the Sibylline Oracles and also in the Lives of the Prophets on three occasions and in the Martyrdom and Ascension of Isaiah. We will examine each of these texts and how they present the figures of evil and how they relate to the Satan figure in the Judeo-Christian tradition.

Testaments of the 12 Patriarchs

The T12 Patr. represent the deathbed testimonies of each of the twelve sons of Jacob. The texts likely date from the late second century BCE (some argue in Hebrew), written by a Hellenized Jew, but contain Christian interpolations dated to the second century CE.[126] The texts survive in Greek, Armenian, Slavonic, Hebrew(?), and the Aramaic Testament of Levi (ATL) from Cairo Genizah, as well as what are likely fragments of it at Qumran.[127] As mentioned, the chief evil figure in T12 Patr. is Beliar (βελιάρ), which is likely synonymous with Belial in certain contexts in the DSS. The term occurs twenty-eight times in the Greek T12 Patr.[128]

---

125. See Graham H. Twelftree, "Exorcism and the Defeat of Beliar in the Testaments of the Twelve Patriarchs," *Vigiliae Christianae* 65 (2011): 170–88, here, 175.
126. See H. C. Kee, "Testaments of the Twelve Patriarchs," in Charlesworth, *Old Testament Pseudepigrapha*, 1st ed., 1:775–828, here, 778. See Piero Capelli, "The Outer and Inner Devil on Representing the Evil One in Second Temple Judaism," in *The Words of a Wise Man's Mouth Are Gracious (Qoh 10:12)*, ed. Mauro Perani (Berlin: Walter de Gruyter, 2005), 139–52, here, 144.
127. See the discussion of manuscript evidence in chapter 3.
128. See T. Reub. 2.2; 4.7, 11; 6.3; T. Sim. 5.3; T. Levi 3.3; 18.12; 19.1; T. Jud. 25.3; T. Issa. 7.7; 6.1; T. Zeb. 9.8; T. Dan 1.7; 4.7; 5.1, 10, 11; T. Naph. 2.6; T. Ash. 1.8; 3.2; T. Jos. 7.4; 20.2; T. Benj. 3.3, 4, 8; 6.1, 7; 7.1, 2. Capelli ("Outer and Inner," 144) contends that Beliar is a "reformulation of *belior*, 'the Lightless One,'" because of a false popular etymology or as an intended allusion to his capacity as Prince of Darkness." See also S. D. Sperling, "Beliar," in *The Dictionary of Deities and Demons in the Bible*, ed. K. van der Toorn, B. Becking, and P. van der Horst (Leiden: Brill, 1999), 169–71.

The author of the Testament of Reuben identifies seven "spirits of error" (τὰ πνεύματα τῆς πλάνης) that appear to operate under the dominion of (the) Beliar (see 2.2); these include the spirits of sexual immorality, greed, fighting, deception, arrogance, lying, and unrighteousness, as well as a "spirit of sleep" (πνεῦμα τοῦ ὕπνου) that seems to rule over these seven others and grants individuals visions of nature and images of death (see T. Reub. 3.1–7); what is not clear is if this is synonymous with the "spirit of Beliar." These spirits appear to operate against the individual and the spirit of truth that is available as a guide for each person to follow (see T. Jud. 20.1). In the majority of occasions in which Beliar appears in T12 Patr., it is with the definite article, and the term does not decline to reflect the various Greek cases (see, e.g., τοῦ βελιὰρ in 2.2). This evidence, along with the presence of the other proper names of the patriarchs with the definite article, suggests that Beliar is being used as a proper name. However, this does not suggest that Beliar used as the name of the chief evil figure equates to the satan figure or any other chief figure, and it does not completely rule out that this is the title of an office holder in the heavenly realm. This figure may in the various instances be different beings operating in the world of 2TP Judaism. Below, we will examine how the term *Beliar* is used in each of the testaments.

Testament of Reuben

The Testament of Reuben 2.2 states that there are seven "spirits of error" that were appointed by Beliar (τοῦ βελιὰρ) against humanity;[129] these spirits are identified as the heads of works of rebellion (αἱ κεφαλαὶ τῶν ἔργων τοῦ νεωτερισμοῦ). One can assume that "rebellion" here implies rebellion against God, as there are no other indicators as to its meaning. Verse 2.3 identifies seven other spirits (ἕτερα ἑπτὰ πνεύματα) that were given to him at creation (implies given by God).[130] Apparently these spirits are good spirits to assist humanity in every work—a spirit of life (nature of man), spirit of sight (seed of desire), spirit of hearing (teaching), spirit of smell (inhalation of air), spirit of speech (knowledge), spirit of taste (strength), spirit of procreation (sins of pleasure). But over all these spirits is an eighth spirit, one of sleep, which, strangely, grants an image of death. Mingled within these seven spirits are the spirits of error (τὰ πνεύματα τῆς πλάνης; 3.2). These are the spirits of sexual immorality, lust/greed, battle/fighting, flattery/deception, pride/arrogance, and lying; each of these six spirits works in tandem with the spirit of unrighteousness to bring destruction to the individual (3.3–6). These lists of spirits seem to

---

129. Paolo Sacchi contends that the term *Beliar* is a later Jewish interpolation to the text in order to keep separate the list of evil spirits from the other seven spirits that were given by God. See Sacchi, ed., *Apocrifi dell'Antico Testamento* (Turin, Italy: Unione tipografico-editrice torinese, 1981), 1:725–948.
130. Capelli, "Outer and Inner," 145.

have been influenced by the dualism of the 2TP, in particular that of the Qumran DSS. These spirits operate under the authority of Beliar in what appears to be a plan of affliction and temptation against individuals in an effort to turn them away from God (2.2).

The Testament of Reuben 4.6–7 speaks of the sin of fornication, which is brought about by the spirit of fornication. This sin brings destruction to the soul, separating it from God and enticing the person to draw near to idols. The individual then becomes a reproach and is a stumbling block for (i.e., on behalf of) Beliar (τῷ βελιάρ). Verse 4.11 offers hope to the individual that if "fornication does not overcome your mind, neither is Beliar (ὁ βελιάρ)[131] able to overcome you." In 5.1, the author paints a very negative picture of women: "For women are evil" (πονηραὶ γάρ εἰσιν αἱ γυναῖκες) and they entice men with their outward appearance in order to draw the man to themselves. In 5.6–7, the author draws on the 1 Enoch Watcher tradition, but in this case, perhaps drawing on the Jubilees version of the story, the author blames the women for enchanting (suggesting some kind of witchcraft?) the Watcher angels who lusted after the women, and the women, in their minds, lusted after the heavenly appearance of the angels and gave birth to the giants in the Book of Watchers. Reuben then warns his children to guard themselves and their minds from fornication and be pure in mind (διανοία). What the author does not do is connect Beliar to the Watcher tradition. From Testament of Reuben 5.6–7 and other references, the human struggle with these spirits and Beliar appears to be an internal one within the individual soul and mind rather than an external affliction. This could reflect the idea of the *Yetser Ra* (יצר רע) and the *Yetser Tov* (יצר טוב), which are significant themes in the 2TP literature.[132] Kee contends this is a clear ethical battle for the soul of the individual. He maintains, "If the human will is strong, Beliar is unable to gain control; if the will is weak, Beliar dominates."[133] The usage of Beliar in the Testament of Reuben suggests that the figure has a specific task to perform under the authority of God, who has given him the spiritual forces to accomplish this task.

Testament of Simeon

The Testament of Simeon follows a similar line to that found in the Testament of Reuben of guarding oneself from fornication. The one use of Beliar appears in 5.3, in which Simeon warns his children not to commit fornication, for it will separate them from God and push

---

131. The continued use of the definite article with Beliar and a lack of declension of the noun, certainly seems to suggest that the term is being used as the title of an officeholder, "the wicked one" or "the one who causes wickedness," or a proper name, "Beliar."
132. Capelli, "Outer and Inner," 145.
133. Kee, "Testaments," 784n4d.

them toward Beliar (τῷ βελιάρ); he calls fornication (ἡ πορνεία) "the mother of every evil."[134] The author again emphasizes the power of πορνεία, which he contends is a spirit operating against humanity under the authority of Beliar. In 2.7, the author appears to identify Beliar (or some other figure) as the ruler/chief of error or deceit (ὁ ἄρχων τῆς πλάνης; also T. Jud. 19.4; T. Dan 5.5–6), who sent a spirit of jealousy (τὸ πνεῦμα τοῦ ζήλου) to afflict Simeon, "to blind [his] mind," which may suggest an internal struggle for Simeon rather than an external affliction. In line with this internal struggle, the author of the Testament of Judah 20.1 depicts two spirits that are "devoted/available to" humanity, the spirit of truth and the spirit of deceit. The use of σχολάζουσι ("devoted to," "available to") may suggest that the individual has a choice in which spirit to follow or by which to be influenced. The Testament of Judah 20.2 supports this idea by introducing the guiding principle of the understanding/intelligence (συνέσεως) of the mind, which inclines itself as it wishes (cf. T. Reub. 3.3–4). Perhaps once again we see the concept of the Qumran "two spirits" in the worldview of this author.

Testament of Levi

Beliar appears three times in the Testament of Levi (3.3; 18.12; 19.1). While describing the seven levels of heaven, the author states in 3.3 that the third heaven contains the "powers of the barracks" (likely using the language of armies) who are appointed to take vengeance on Judgment Day against the spirits of error and Beliar (τοῖς πνεύμασι τῆς πλάνης κα τοῦ βελιάρ), which suggests the two are working together against humanity and will be defeated on the Day of Judgment. The second usage of Beliar appears in the midst of what could be a Christian interpolation identifying a messianic figure that reflects Christ. In 18.12, the author states that Beliar (ὁ βελιάρ) will be bound by this messianic figure and the messiah's children shall trample on the wicked spirits that are with Beliar. Beliar appears to be the chief evil figure in this case, with evil spirits working with him, but the messianic figure will overcome him and the spirits. In 19.1, Levi tells his children to consider wisely the light or the darkness, the "Law of the Lord" (νόμον κυρίου) or the "works of Beliar" (ἢ ἔργα βελιάρ—no definite article!). The author is clearly drawing the distinction between the light and dark forces by using much the same language as is found in some of the DSS. This occasion in 19.1 could be one occasion in which Beliar, without the definite article, is best translated as "wickedness" rather than as a proper name.

---

134. Simeon also mentions in T. Sim. 5.4 the "writing of Enoch," although this particular story does not survive in the present collection of Enochic texts. Kee suggests that this theme may be found in 2 En. 34.2; see Kee, "Testaments," 786n5b.

Testament of Judah

The term βελιάρ appears once in the Testament of Judah 25.3 in the context of the coming of a messianic figure who will bring redemption to Israel. Chapter 24 and verses 25.1–2 incorporate eschatological and messianic passages from the HB (e.g., Isa 11:2; 61:11 Joel 2:28–29; Jer 23:5; 33:15; Zech 3:8; 6:12).[135] Similar messianic language is found in CD 1.7 and 7.19–20. The term is used to identify a deceitful spirit of (the) Beliar (καὶ οὐκ ἔσται ἔτι πνεῦμα πλάνης τοῦ βελιάρ—again, with the definite article) that has been afflicting the people but will be thrown into the fire for eternity and beyond (NT language connected to the satan figure). The author does not speak specifically of the destruction of Beliar but of one of the spirits working with him (if Beliar is understood as a figure and not wickedness) to deceive humanity/Israel. However, the term *Beliar* here could be understood as "(a spirit of) wickedness" rather than the proper name of a "chief evil being." The closing lines in chapters 25 and 26 speak of a period in which the resurrection of the righteous will take place following the destruction of all evil and all people shall glorify the Lord (25.5).

Testament of Issachar

The term βελιάρ appears twice in the Testament of Issachar, at 6.1 and 7.7. In 6.1, the author warns the children of Issachar that their children will forsake generosity and will cling to greediness and draw near to wickedness while forsaking the commandments of the Lord and joining together with (the) Beliar. Interestingly, in 7.1, Issachar professes not to have known any sin (mortal sin?) unto death and suspects that his children and their children can do the same. In 7.2–4, he notes the sins he did not commit—fornication, adultery, drunkenness, coveting of others' things, allowing deceit in his heart, and lying. In 7.5, he notes how he has helped the poor and kept the truth all the days of his life. In 7.6–7, he states that, following his example, his children need only love the Lord with all their strength and their neighbors (πάντα ἄνθρωπον), and every spirit of Beliar (καὶ πᾶν πνεῦμα τοῦ βελιάρ) will flee from them; perhaps this may suggest a connection to a similar concept in CD 16, in which Mastema must flee from those who "repent and remember the Lord" (cf. T. Zeb. 9.7; T. Dan 5.9–10; 6.5).[136] Similar to previous instances, the term *Beliar*, with the inclusion of the article, likely suggests a title or perhaps proper name. However, it could also be understood here as "every spirit of wickedness," although the use of the definite article may limit this understanding, and perhaps

---

135. See Kee, 801n24b–c.
136. Cf. T. Ash. 3.1–2; T. Naph. 8.4, 6, which contend that the children should join together with the spirit of goodness and turn from evil to destroy Beliar. See Twelftree, "Exorcism," 178.

ὁ βελιάρ should be translated as "the wicked one" much the same as "the satan" could be understood as "the adversary."

Testament of Zebulon

βελιάρ occurs once in the Testament of Zebulon 9.8, in the context of deliverance of the people by the Lord himself after they have repented and turned back to the Lord. He will come to "redeem all the captive children from Beliar (τοῦ βελιάρ) and every spirit of deceit (πᾶν πνεῦμα πλάνης) will be trampled." As a result, all the nations will be zealous for the Lord. The author reveals the influence of Beliar and the spirit of deceit have had upon the people likely through the spirits that have been operating under Beliar's authority. In 9.7, he states that the spirits of deceit (τὰ πνεύματα τῆς πλάνης) deceived the people in all their deeds/actions, thus causing them to turn away from the Lord. But when they repent for their evil actions, the Lord will return to them. As in the previous occasions, Beliar may be understood as a title or a proper name or the wicked one, but what is clear is there are evil spirits at work among all the nations, including Israel.

Testament of Dan

The Testament of Dan contains five references to βελιάρ—1.7; 4.7; 5.1, 10, and 11. The first instance in 1.7 offers an intriguing insight into the work of the spirits associated with Beliar. Dan confesses that he was under the influence of a spirit of jealousy (τὸ πνεῦμα τοῦ ζήλου), which instigated the sale of Joseph to the slave traders. Dan states that the spirit spoke to him saying that he too was a son of Jacob. In 1.7, Dan reveals that one of the spirits of Beliar (the spirit of anger, ὁ πνεῦμα τοῦ θυμοῦ) worked within him saying, "take this sword and kill Joseph with it." This is quite an elaborate story in which a spirit, identified in 1.8 as "the spirit of anger," is said to speak to an individual and "assist" him to commit an evil deed that appears to have been inspired by another spirit, the spirit of jealousy; all of the spirits seem to be a part of Beliar's lot. In 1.9, Dan speaks of God's authority over the situation in that the "God of Jacob, our father, did not allow him into my hands," thus preventing him from committing an act of lawlessness (τὸ ἀνόμημα).

The Testament of Dan 4.7 notes that the spirit of anger and the spirit of lying are a two-faced evil. They join together to disturb the senses (ὁ διαβούλιον) and trouble the soul (τῆς ψυχῆς), which causes the Lord to depart from that soul, and Beliar then rules over it. However, in 5.1, Dan states that if one guards himself and departs from anger and lying and keeps the Law of God, then the Lord may dwell with them and Beliar may flee (cf. CD 16). Interesting is the use of the aorist subjunctive verb form for both "dwell" (κατοικήσῃ) and "flee" (φύγῃ), which suggests conditions are set for Beliar to flee, but it is not a guarantee.

In the Testament of Dan 5.5–6, the author speaks of those who depart from the Lord and go about doing evil. These people have the spirits of Beliar working in them causing them to commit the abominations attributed to the nations and engaging in sexual sin with women from other nations. In 5.6, the author makes note of 1 Enoch, in which the satan figure (ὁ σατανᾶς) is the leader/ruler (ὁ ἄρχων) of those who depart from the Lord. He states that the satan and the spirits of fornication and pride are attacking the Levites in an attempt to get them to sin before the Lord. Unfortunately, there is no Enochic text that contains such a story, but one might surmise that it is speaking of the corrupt priesthood in Jerusalem (see T. Dan 5.7).[137] Within this passage, one might suggest that the author is drawing a parallel between the figure of Beliar and the satan figure; both act as the ruler of evil spirits that are at work among the people.

The Testament of Dan 5.10 and 11 offer a context in which a messianic figure will rise up out of the tribe of Judah and Levi (king and priest), one who will bring (or be) the salvation of the Lord. This figure will make war against Beliar and give victory to the righteous. He will free all the holy ones who are held captive by Beliar and turn back the hearts of those disobedient to the Lord, which as we have seen previously, removes Beliar from their midst. In 6.2, although the term *Beliar* is not found (6.1 does mention the satan and his spirits: "τοῦ σατανᾶ καὶ τῶν πνευμάτων αὐτοῦ"), the author states that the angel of God (perhaps Michael the archangel) who intercedes for Israel will stand against the "kingdom of the enemy" (τῆς βασιλείας τοῦ ἐχθροῦ). *Ekhthrou* can mean "enemy" or "hostile one," which may suggest a connection to Mastema, or it may be speaking of the satan figure in 6.1; if so, this may be a Christian interpolation. The task of the "hostile one" in 6.3 is to try to destroy all those who call upon the Lord. We are told in 6.4 that the enemy knows that this kingdom will be brought to an end.

The language in the Testament of Dan seems to point to Beliar as the figure who is the/a chief of the wicked spirits and his task is to draw individuals away from the Lord and the Torah. The author of the Testament of Dan or a later editor appears to be trying to connect the satan figure to the Beliar figure and perhaps also to Mastema, which does not necessarily reflect a correct understanding of how Beliar was perceived in the Testaments.

---

137. See an argument for an interpretation of the Book of Watchers along these lines in Suter, "Fallen Angel, Fallen Priest," 115–35.

Testament of Naphtali

The term βελιάρ occurs in the Testament of Naphtali only once in 2.6. The author presents a dualistic world in which individuals have to make choices based on their inclinations and thoughts. In 2.6, Naphtali speaks of parallels between human characteristics and their outcomes. He states, "As is his strength, so also his work; and as his mind, so also his craft/skill; and as his choice, so also his actions; as his heart, so also his mouth; as his eye, so also his sleep; as his soul, so also his word; [he shall be guided by] either the Law of the Lord or by the law of Beliar." This is followed in 2.7 by the contrast between light and darkness; the language here is very much part of an anthropological dualism present in a 2TP worldview. What is interesting in this particular occurrence of Beliar is its connection to its own law (ἐν νόμῳ βελιάρ—note there is no article with Beliar), the same term used with the "Law of the Lord." This may suggest a set of principles set out for the wicked to follow and laid out in the identities of each of the spirits under Beliar's authority: sexual immorality, lust, fighting, flattery, deception, wicked pride, and lying.

The Testament of Naphtali 3.1 sets the "will of God" (θέλημα τοῦ θεοῦ) over against the "will of Beliar" (θέλημα τοῦ βελιάρ)[138] in an admonition to complete one's deeds for right purposes, not greed or flattery; only then will a person understand how to take hold of God's will and cast aside the will of Beliar. Verse 3.3 suggests that the nations have been influenced by the spirits of Beliar; here the author states that "the nations were deceived (πλανηθέντα) and abandoned the Lord, altering their order, and following after stones and trees [idols], following spirits of error." This "spirit of error" is one we have previously identified as operating under the authority of Beliar. In 3.5, the author notes that the Watchers, in a similar manner to the nations, "changed the order of their nature" and were cursed by the Lord. In 4.1, he makes note of "the writing of Enoch," which states the children of Naphtali will also depart from the Lord and the Lord will send them into captivity.

The Testament of Naphtali presents Beliar in a dualistic context in direct contrast to God's will and God's Law. In this dualistic setting, Beliar is be set up as a figure who has corrupted the nations by leading them astray through spirits of error, leading the nations to idolatry. One might suggest the author sees Beliar as an anti-God figure, although there are hints that his position is not one of complete autonomy.

---

138. Two manuscript recensions offer different names for the figure in opposition to God's will. MS A^{ab} contains διαβόλου, "devil," and MS A^{b*cde} contains Σατανᾶ, "Satan." It should be noted that the Greek text has uppercase sigma in the Greek, *Satan*, which might suggest a later Christian interpolation. See Charles, *Greek Versions*, 149n11.

Testament of Asher

The term βελιάρ occurs in the Testament of Asher twice, at 1.8 and 3.2. The author of the Testament of Asher offers a further depiction of the dualism in the 2TP worldview, in which, in this case, God has given two paths (δύο ὁδοὺς) for humanity to choose from (1.3). Apparently within these two paths are the two counsels/inclinations (διαβούλια, or a form of it, appears twenty times in the T12 Patr.[139]—possibly best defined as "internal counsel"), two kinds of action, two ways of doing things, and two goals. According to the Testament of Asher 1.5, the internal counsel (good or evil) evaluates the two types and chooses which to follow. Verse 1.8 reports what will happen to the soul if it should incline toward evil, by which all its deeds are wicked: the soul drives away all that is good and holds onto the evil (this could be understood as "the evil one," τὸ κακὸν). As a result, Beliar rules over this individual and all they do turns to evil, even if their intention was for good. Beliar will turn those things that began as good works toward evil because the treasure of the inclination of this individual is poisoned and "filled with an evil spirit." This passage displays the suggested power that Beliar has in the life of an individual who has turned from the Law of the Lord and allows the evil inclination to drive them to wickedness.

The Testament of Asher 3.2 admonishes the children of Asher to run away from evil and destroy the inclination (toward evil) with their good works/deeds: "For those people who are two-faced are not of God, but serve as slaves to their own lusts in order to please Beliar and those like themselves." This verse certainly sets Beliar in a position of opposition to God, but from this verse, it is clear that his purpose is to deceive and afflict humanity in order to persuade them to turn from the Lord.

The Testament of Asher 6.4 reveals a possible connection between Beliar and Satan.[140] Upon one's death, the person will meet the angels of the Lord and the angels of the satan. If a soul passes from life in a troubled state, it will be tormented (6.5; presumably by a spirit from satan); if it departs in a calm state, then the person will meet the Angel of Peace (6.6; presumably sent by the Lord). One difficulty with trying to connect Beliar and Satan here (if that is even possible based on the manuscript issues) is that the spirits operating under Beliar's authority are acting among the living; this spirit of the satan is active in the afterlife, as is the Angel of Peace.

The Testament of Asher presents Beliar within an anthropological dualistic context that reflects the two inclinations or two spirits in Qumran dualism. There are external spirits

---

139. See T. Reub. 4.9; T. Sim. 4.8; T. Jud. 11.1; 13.2, 8; 18.3; T. Issa. 4.5; 6.2; T. Dan. 4.2, 7; T. Gad. 5.3, 7; 7.3; T. Ash. 1.3, 5, 8, 9; T. Jos. 2.6; T. Benj. 6.1, 4.
140. A problem arises here in the translated version of T. Ash. Kee in his translation in Old Testament Pseudepigrapha uses *Beliar* in 6.4 based on the majority manuscripts, while a second recension based on four minority manuscripts (α, β, A, S¹) contains the Greek ὁ σατανᾶ; this may be a later Christian interpolation.

that attempt to influence humans in the choices they make within their souls. Beliar is depicted as the chief of these spirits, and the children of Asher are told to flee from their influence and follow the good inclination.

Testament of Joseph

The term βελιάρ occurs in the Testament of Joseph twice, in 7.4 and 20.2. One of the main focal points of the Testament of Joseph is his ongoing dilemma with Pharaoh's wife. Chapter 7 states that "her heart was inclined toward immorality," and she continued to pursue Joseph. In 7.4, Joseph states that he "understood the spirit of Beliar [τὸ πνεῦμα τοῦ βελιάρ] was troubling her." The spirit appears to be one of sexual immorality that causes evil lust (ἐπιθυμίας πονηρᾶς), which is one of the seven spirits operating under Beliar throughout the T12 Patr. Joseph attempts to turn her from her sin (caused by the spirit), as she has threatened to commit suicide should Joseph not sleep with her. In 7.7, Joseph suggests that the Lord spoke words through him that convinced her to accept that he will not sleep with her. The author is drawing a contrast between the spirit of the Lord speaking to and guiding Joseph and the spirit of Beliar that is troubling and seducing Pharaoh's wife.

Verse 20.2 offers a contrast between the Lord and Beliar as well as between the Israelites and the Egyptians. When the Lord comes to redeem Israel while she is in bondage in Egypt, the verse states, "The Lord by light will be with the people and Beliar [no definite article!] in darkness will be with the Egyptians." In this example without the definite article, one might suggest this is understood as "wickedness" rather than a personified evil, but it is difficult to offer a definitive answer.

The Testament of Joseph presents Beliar as a concept or figure who has spirits working with him to cause individuals to sin. In addition, the author presents a contrast between the Lord and Beliar, light and darkness, and the spirit of the Lord and a spirit of Beliar.

Testament of Benjamin

The term βελιάρ occurs in the Testament of Benjamin six times—in 3.3, 8; 6.1, 7; and 7.1, 2. The first occurrence is in 3.3, in which Benjamin tells his children that they need to "fear the Lord and love [their] neighbor"—both verbs are in the imperative. They are told that if they do this, then "the spirits of Beliar, [who] desire to persecute you with every wicked oppression, will not have power over you." The verse describes the purpose and task of the spirits operating under Beliar—to oppress and persecute humanity. Verse 3.8 seems to reflect a Christian interpolation with the inclusion of "the Lamb of God, and Savior of the world . . . the spotless one who was delivered up for the lawless ones, and a sinless one who will die for the ungodly by the blood of the covenant." By fearing the Lord and loving one's neighbor, the person "will neutralize Beliar and the ones serving under him." This seems to suggest Beliar will not yet be destroyed, but his power will be neutralized. If this is a Christian interpolation, then one might suggest that early Christianity understood Beliar as Satan or that they recognized two distinct figures with similar functions—that is, multiple satan figures. What does not fit this scenario is Beliar as a human leader who is oppressing Israel.

The Testament of Benjamin 6.1 returns to the idea of inclination or internal counsel that is in the good man. This person is not in the hand (under the power) of a deceitful spirit of Beliar (τὸ διαβούλιον τοῦ ἀγαθοῦ οὐκ ἔστιν ἐν χειρὶ πλάνης πνεύατος βελιάρ), but his soul is guided by the Angel of Peace. Here again is one of the few times in which Beliar appears without the definite article, lessening the likelihood of a proper name in this case in the Testament of Benjamin. Thus it could be translated as a "deceitful spirit of wickedness," but again, it is difficult to offer a definitive conclusion. The good person described here is not inclined to look upon things that corrupt or gather up lustful riches, nor lust by the lifting up of his eyes (6.3), nor is he double-minded (6.5–6). Verse 6.7 contrasts the works of the good intention/inclination (τὴν διάνοιαν) in an individual with the evil kind that is guided by Beliar. The man with a good inclination is of a single mind that is sincere and pure concerning every choice (6.5) and knows that the Lord looks after his soul (6.6). In verse 6.7, the works of Beliar are double-minded, having no generosity. In 7.1, Benjamin tells his children to flee the evil of Beliar (φεύγετε τὴν κακίαν τοῦ βελιάρ), "for he gives the sword to those who are persuaded by [trusting] him." In 7.2, he states that the "sword" is the "mother of seven evils," which are conceived in the mind through Beliar: envy, destruction, oppression, captivity (exile?), wanting/lacking, turmoil, and desolation. "Sword" in some instances in the Pseudepigrapha may represent war in the land (e.g., Sib Or. 3.751; 3 Bar. 16.3; 1 En. 14.6), which would certainly result in an opportunity for these evils to occur.

Summary of Testaments of the 12 Patriarchs

The T12 Patr. present βελιάρ as the/a chief being responsible for the evil that comes upon the people as a nation or as individuals. However, we should note here that Charles argues "that Beliar was never regarded as aught else that a satanic spirit, until the Beliar myth was amalgamated with that of the Antichrist," thus becoming a personified evil being.[141] The primary task is to afflict individuals and persuade them to turn from the Law of the Lord. There are

---

141. Robert H. Charles, *The Ascension of Isaiah: Translated from the Ethiopic Version, Which, Together with the New Greek Fragment, the Latin Versions and the Latin Translation of the Slavonic* (London: A&C Black, 1900), lvii.

strong dualistic components in the testaments (ethical, anthropological, cosmological) that are reflected in the concepts of (1) the two spirits, truth and deceit (T. Jud., T. Sim.); (2) the two inclinations/intentions (throughout the T12 Patr.); (3) the two sets of seven spirits, one good and one evil (T. Reub.); (4) a messianic figure over against Beliar (T. Levi); (5) the Law of the Lord and the law of Beliar (T. Naph.); (6) the Angel of the Lord and the spirit of Beliar (T. Dan); (7) the Angel of Peace and the spirit of Beliar (T. Benj.); (8) light and darkness (T. Naph.); and (9) the will of God and the will of Beliar (T. Naph.).[142] There is also a sense of the spirits of Beliar having possession of individuals in mind or soul. If it is not a physical possession, it is certainly a strong external oppression that influences the mental choices of individuals who are under their influence (T. Ash., T. Reub.). This takes on the form of an internal struggle in the Testament of Reuben and the Testament of Simeon. The evidence revealed in T12 Patr. points to the strong possibility of a belief in the existence of a spirit being that influences the evil activities that take place in the human realm under the sovereignty and authority of God. However, the T12 Patr. reminds the audience that a Messiah figure will neutralize Beliar and the spirits with him and will dispatch them into the fire for eternity (see T. Levi 3.2–3; 18.12; T. Dan 5.10–11; T. Jud. 25.3).

LIVES OF THE PROPHETS

The Lives of the Prophets is a collection of texts that gives "the names of the prophets, and where they are from, how and where they died, and where they lie."[143] It is extant in several languages, including Syriac, Ethiopic, Latin, and Armenian, which have been translated from Greek.[144] Scholars suggest that Lives was originally written in a Semitic language, likely Syriac,[145] while others have suggested Hebrew or Aramaic.[146] According to D. R. A. Hare, the dating of Lives of the Prophets is very difficult due to the lack of contemporary historical markers. The document survives only in Christian manuscripts, with no evidence from Qumran or any reference in 2TP Jewish literature. It is the consensus that the author was Jewish and likely wrote the original document in the early first century CE in Palestine.[147]

---

142. Capelli goes as far as to suggest that Beliar is an anti-God figure, "God's counterpart in past, present, and future." See Capelli, "Outer and Inner," 147.
143. See D. R. A. Hare, "The Lives of the Prophets," in Charlesworth, *Old Testament Pseudepigrapha*, 1st ed., 2:379–99, here, 379.
144. See Hare, "Lives," 379, for a list of major Greek manuscripts dated from the sixth through thirteenth centuries.
145. See Isaac. H. Hall, "The Lives of the Prophets," *JBL* 7 (1887): 28–40.
146. See C. C. Torrey, *The Lives of the Prophets*, JBLMS 1 (Philadelphia: SBL, 1946), 7; S. Klein, "Al ha-seper Vitae Prophetarum," in *Sefer Klozner*, ed. H. Torczyner (Tel Aviv: Vaad Ha-yovel, 1937), 189–208.
147. Hare, "Lives," 380–81.

βελιάρ appears in the Lives three times—4.7, 21; and 17.2. Chapter 4 is describing the life of Daniel, the prophet who was taken to Babylon during the exile. He is depicted as a eunuch in the eyes of the Judeans. In describing King Nebuchadnezzar—who, in his youth, was a lover of pleasure and stubbornness (4.6)—the author notes he *has come under the yoke of Beliar* (ὑπὸ ζυγὸν γίνονται τοῦ βελιάρ) and as an adult has become a beast who is inclined to seize and destroy everything (4.7). It is not clear from the passage what the nature of Beliar is, but one might suggest, due to the presence of the article, it is similar to what we saw in the T12 Patr.; in this case, Beliar is responsible for Nebuchadnezzar taking on animal characteristics, perhaps due to mental affliction or illness. The activity of Beliar here does not seem to reflect the same internal ethical struggle of choosing right or wrong but rather more of a spiritual affliction or even possession, similar to what is revealed in Mark 5 and the story of the demoniac. The author states in the text that Nebuchadnezzar was restored to his human self through the hand of God, although it is not clear exactly how this takes place, only that Daniel knows it will happen.

In Lives 4.21, the author relates a prophetic word/vision given by Daniel in which he speaks of the end of Babylon, devoured in a burning fire, along with the end of all the earth. The final lines of the passage, although not particularly clear in their message, state that the Israelites will return to their land should water flow from the mountain in the south, but if it should flow blood, then the slaughter of Beliar will take place over all the earth. The Greek text could be understood in two ways: (1) Beliar will be slaughtered over all the earth, meaning an end to evil, or (2) the most likely reading due to the contrast with the "good" event of the water flowing from the mountain in the first part of the line (a return from exile), Beliar will bring about a slaughter over all the earth.

The third occurrence of Beliar is found in 17.2 and the story of the prophet Nathan. Presented in the manner of rewritten Scripture, Nathan is given a vision of David committing the transgression with Bathsheba before it occurs. While on his way to warn David, the author states that Nathan was thwarted by Beliar (ἐνεπόδισεν ὁ βελίαρ), who apparently set a dead man in his path to prevent him from approaching David (17.2). We are not told why, but Nathan remains with the body, and that night David commits adultery with Bathsheba (17.3). Here, Beliar seems to function in opposition to that which is good, thus allowing the sin of David to occur. This action could be understood as an episode allowed by God to test David, but the text is not clear. Verse 17.4 recounts the biblical version of the story in which Nathan approaches David to admonish him.

Beliar in the Lives of the Prophets is presented as a seemingly lone figure, with no mention of any spirits working with him, who seems to be working to bring about God's plan that we see in the biblical accounts of the prophets.

Martyrdom and Ascension of Isaiah

Due to the composite nature of the text of the Martyrdom and Ascension of Isaiah,[148] it is difficult to identify the exact number of occurrences of Beliar in the original text.[149] In the Ascension of Isaiah, Beliar is found thirteen times, in 1.8–9; 2.4; 3.11, 13; 4.2, 4, 14, 16, 18; 5.1, 4, and 15. The entire text of MAI only survives in Ethiopic Ge'ez with small portions of it surviving in Greek and Latin. According to Michael A. Knibb, Beliar is variant of Belial and is used synonymously in MAI with Satan and Sammael[150] and also is identified as the "angel of lawlessness," "ruler of this world," and Matanbukus, which Charles suggests is derived from the Hebrew מתן בוקא (*matan buka*, "worthless gift").[151]

The first occurrence of Beliar (ὁ σατανᾶς in the Greek Legend)[152] is found in 1.8–9. Here Isaiah is describing to King Hezekiah how his son Manasseh will turn away from God and become a follower of Beliar. In verse 1.8, the author notes that Manasseh will be served by Sammael Malkira.[153] He will cause Judah and Israel to desert the faith and follow Beliar (cf. 2.3), and he notes in 1.9 that Beliar will dwell in (ἐν) Manasseh.[154] The author states in 1.11 that Sammael[155] has a plan against Manasseh, but it is not clear what his plan is; we only know that Hezekiah is prevented from killing Manasseh by "the Beloved," likely a designation for Jesus.[156] In this brief pericope, one might suggest that Beliar and Sammael are one and the same being or that one is working for or alongside the other; the author has not made this relationship clear. At the same time, it appears the authors/translators have substituted the satan figure for both these terms on several occasions.

In MAI 2.1–4 (a retelling of the 1.8–9?), the author tells of how Sammael will dwell with/in Manasseh (note that in 1.9, Beliar/satan is the one who dwells with/in Manasseh) and Manasseh will turn the house of his father (Judah and Israel; 2.3; cf. 1.9) and his own heart from the Lord and serve satan (2.2).[157] In 2.4, the author has noted that Manasseh turned the people of

---

148. See discussion on the MAI in chapter 4.
149. See Knibb, "Martyrdom," 2:143–76.
150. Knibb suggests Satan, Beliar, and Sammael are used synonymously; see Knibb, 158.
151. Charles, *Ascension of Isaiah*, 11n4; Knibb suggests "gift of desolation"; see his "Martyrdom," 158ne.
152. The Greek Pseudepigrapha Ascen. Isa. (MS A) 1.9 indicates ὁ σατανᾶς, not ὁ βελιάρ. See the discussion of the Greek Legend manuscripts in Knibb, "Martyrdom," 146.
153. Knibb notes that "according to Jewish tradition Sammael was originally one of the chief archangels, but after inciting the serpent to tempt Eve, he became the leader of the satans." Knibb, 157nu. *Malkira* is translated "king of evil." Sammael also appears in 1.11; 2.1; 3.13; 5.1; 7.9; 11.41; here, he is identified as Sammael Satan.
154. With the dative ἐν can mean "in, with, by, to" and does not necessarily indicate possession of Manasseh by Beliar/Satan.
155. Greek Legend 1.11 has ὁ σατανᾶς.
156. Knibb, "Martyrdom," 156nk.
157. Satan appears approximately seven times in MAI 2.7; 5.16; 7.9; 11.23, 41, 4; see Knibb, "Martyrdom," 158.

Hezekiah's house away from God, and they served Beliar, "the angel of lawlessness and the ruler of this world whose name is Matanbukus."[158] In 2.7, we are told that it came to the point that the people of Jerusalem began to worship the satan. From this passage, one might propose that Beliar and Sammael are the same being (both dwell with/in the heart of Manasseh) or that both represent wickedness (Sammael is identified as the "king of wickedness" in 1.8—an equivalent of Melchiresha from the DSS?).

The next occurrence of Beliar is found in 3.11, in which that author states that "Beliar dwelt with/in the heart of Manasseh and the hearts of the princes of Judah and Benjamin"[159] and the court of the king. It seems unlikely that a single spiritual being such as Beliar could possess all these individuals at the same time, and the author likely intends to speak of the presence or oppression by Beliar of the leading figures in Jerusalem. As has been the case in the previous examples in MAI, this use of the term *Beliar* could be understood as a spirit or as wickedness, but with the synonymous use of Sammael and the satan, it is likely, at least in the mind of the translators, that a chief evil figure is intended. One should keep in mind there is a great deal of later Christian influence present in MAI, which may account for some of the language being used.

MAI 3.13 begins a Christian interpolation that extends to 4.22 and is called the Vision of Hezekiah. The focus of the actions of Beliar now shifts to the oppression or attack against the prophet Isaiah. Verse 3.13 states that Beliar is angry with Isaiah because of the prophecy/vision he has given against Jerusalem and Judah that they will be laid waste, which apparently exposed the plan of Sammael. This verse seems to hint that Beliar and Sammael are two different beings, but there is nothing in the Ethiopic or Greek texts that clarifies their identities. The exposing of Sammael's plan results in the coming of "the Beloved (Jesus/Messianic figure) from the seventh heaven." The language of 3.13 clearly indicates a Christian influence in the text, describing the "coming of the twelve disciples" and that the Beloved "must be crucified upon a cross" and would be raised from the dead on the third day.

The next reference, found in verse 4.2, states that Beliar will descend to the earth as the image of an antichrist, the Great Ruler (ἄρχων), the Ruler of This World (ὁ ἄρχων τοῦ κόσμου) (cf. 2.4; 10.29) since its beginning; this seems to reflect some of the language of the gnostic groups that would emerge in the first century CE (more on this in chapter 7). He has ruled over the world since it came into existence, which may suggest that he is the "evil" Demiurge who created the physical world, which in the worldview of the Gnostics is evil. We are told that Beliar will enter the world in the form of a king, which may, as some suggest, identify him as a stand-in for

---

158. Charles, "Ascension," 11.
159. Charles, 18.

the Roman emperor Nero in this context.[160] This reference appears to be the root of the false rumors of Nero's resurrection; he is the "king of iniquity" who murdered his mother and will persecute the Church (4.3). MAI 4.4 perhaps suggests that this ruler (some manuscripts insert Beliar) will come in the form of Nero with all the powers of the world (it's unclear if these are spiritual powers or kings of the earth). The language clearly identifies him as the/an antichrist and includes language that suggests a Christian interpolation ("twelve apostles of the Beloved" in 4.3).[161] Verse 4.14 speaks of the Lord (Christ) coming with his angels and the armies of the holy ones[162] to drag Beliar and his armies into Gehenna.[163] The author here, although clearly Christian, is connecting Beliar to the Satan figure of the NT.

Verse 5.1 returns to the Jewish "ascension" with a restatement of Beliar's anger with Isaiah over the visions. Here, he reiterates that Beliar dwells in the heart of Manasseh (1.9; 3.11) and he has Isaiah sawn in half. In 5.15–16, again we find a possible Christian interpolation with the use of "Beloved." The context of these verses suggests Beliar and Sammael are two different beings.[164] The author states that Beliar killed Isaiah through the false prophets Balkira and Manasseh because Sammael was angry with Isaiah, a grudge from the days of Hezekiah, in particular, because of the vision of the destruction of Sammael. As a result, Manasseh did as the satan wished, which seems to suggest Sammael and this Satan are one in the same in the author's worldview. As mentioned previously, it is difficult to offer a clear understanding of the relationship among these three beings—Beliar, Sammael, and Satan—due to the complex nature of the extant Ascension of Isaiah. But generally speaking, one might suggest that the three names represent a personified evil figure; the question is if it is one or two or three separate figures.

Sibylline Oracles

The Sibylline Oracles are a collection of texts that predict the problems and disasters that humanity will face that fall in line with the message of the biblical prophets.[165] Collins identifies fourteen books and eight fragments within the group of texts. He argues the oracles "functioned widely as political propaganda,"[166] but all were religious in that all issues relate to the gods. The dates of the Sibylline Oracles range from the mid-second century BCE through the seventh

---

160. See Charles, 24–25.
161. See Knibb, "Martyrdom," 161nf.
162. Charles notes 2 Thess 1:7; 1 En 1.4, 9; Jude 14; 1 Thess 3:13. See Charles, "Ascension," 33.
163. Charles notes Rev 19:20; 17:8, 11. See Charles, 33.
164. Charles suggests 5.15–16 are editorial additions to the text. See Charles, 42.
165. See John J. Collins, "Sibylline Oracles," in Charlesworth, *Old Testament Pseudepigrapha*, 1st ed., 1:317–472, here, 318.
166. Collins, 320.

century CE. The provenance of the individual books varies: books 3, 5, and 11–14: Egypt; books 4, 6, and 7: Syria; books 1–2: Asia Minor; book 8: provenance undetermined.[167] This examination will focus on the two books that contain references to Beliar—books 2 and 3.

Book 2 is found in conjunction with book 1 as a single unit. It is thought to be a Jewish oracle that contains significant Christian redaction. Book 2 offers "an account of eschatological crises and the last judgment."[168] The books' combined Jewish and Christian content makes dating the book difficult; Collins suggests a date or dates from no earlier than 30 BCE until 150 CE.[169] The only occurrence of βελιάρ in book 2 appears in a section in which the author is describing "signs of the end"; the term appears in line 167. He begins the description in 165, which speaks of the end days, "when lying deceivers appear instead of the prophets, speaking upon the earth. And Beliar will be present and many signs he will do for people." The description suggests an antichrist or false-prophet role for Beliar, which is a role we have seen assigned to the figure previously in the Ascension of Isaiah. These roles have not been taken up by the other figures that have been introduced, in particular the satan figure.

The next occurrence in the Sibylline Oracles occurs in book 3.63. Book 3 was most likely written sometime between 163 and 145 BCE in Egypt, possibly within the circle of the Jewish temple priesthood in Leontopolis.[170] The context for the appearance of Beliar is eschatological, predicting the demise of Rome by the armies of God. Beliar emerges as a powerful figure in lines 63–69, which state, "Beliar[171] will come from the *Sebastenon* [probably a city in central region of modern Turkey]. He will raise the height of mountains and he will raise the sea, the great fiery sun, and shinning moon, and he will raise the dead and he will do many signs for people; but they will not be effective in him. But he deceives and indeed he will deceive many of the faithful and elect ones, the Hebrews, and other lawless men, those who have never listened to the word of God." This passage certainly portrays Beliar as an anti-Messiah figure, like we saw in book 2.167.

The final occurrence of βελιάρ is located in line 3.73, in the midst of the recounting of the coming vengeance of the Great God who sends a wave of power to the earth and burns up Beliar and those with him; the language suggests Beliar is a human figure with human followers. Sebastenon is the name given to the region of Samaria by King Herod in 25 BCE. Collins

---

167. Collins, 322.
168. Collins, 330.
169. Collins, 332.
170. Collins, 355. However, it should be noted the first 96 verses of book 3 are thought to have circulated separately but still have their origins in the same date and provenance.
171. Ryan Stokes in this context contends that Beliar is a "human opponent" to Israel. Stokes, "Belial," 436.

suggests the figure is Simon Magus (see Acts 8:9–23) or another anti-Messiah figure. The other possible option for the identity of Beliar is Nero, who we have seen previously in relation to Beliar in the discussion of Ascension of Isaiah 4.1. This would suggest that this section of book 3, likely added post-70 CE, speaks to the ongoing eschatological expectations of the author and his community.[172]

The Sibylline Oracles' books 2 and 3 present the Beliar figure as an anti-Messiah figure, generally representing a human who is oppressing the people of God. This is different from what we see in other texts from the same period, in which Beliar is understood to be a spirit being who is the leader or director of the evil spirits that are operating against humanity. Therefore, one must use caution when suggesting connecting this Beliar figure to the satan figure in the Judeo-Christian tradition.

Beliar, Mastema, and Spirits in the Book of Jubilees

The book of Jubilees is one the most significant texts that present the issues of the problem of evil and a detailed angelology in the 2TP.[173] Not the least significant is its inclusion of the Watcher tradition found in 1 Enoch. Jubilees portrays angels and evil spirits as having specific tasks to complete in the world. There are good angels who help control the forces of nature, assist humanity, and act as intermediaries between humans and God. The evil spirits in Jubilees are the author's way of dealing with the problem of evil in his worldview. For the author, evil "affirm[s] both the omnipotence and goodness of God."[174] It is understood to be a heavenly spiritual force that has emerged out of the angelic realm, but the question is, Was it created by God? Significant to this discussion is Jubilees' presentation of what appears to be a chief spiritual being that has the evil spirits produced in the Watcher tradition working with it. This figure is primarily identified as Mastema, which will be discussed below, but it also includes the figure of Beliar and the satan.

Jubilees can be described as "rewritten Scripture," as it presents a "retelling" of the book of Genesis and the beginning chapters of Exodus. It recounts in chapter 1 the giving of the Law to Moses at Sinai, in which God tells Moses of the coming apostasy of Israel (cf. Exod 24:12–18).

---

172. Collins, "Sibylline," 360.
173. See Michael Segal, *The Book of Jubilees: Rewritten Bible, Redaction, Ideology and Theology* (Leiden: Brill, 2007), 9–10.
174. O. S. Wintermute, "Jubilees: A New Translation and Introduction," in Charlesworth, *Old Testament Pseudepigrapha*, 1st ed., 1:47–48.

In addition, the Lord commands the Angel of the Presence to recount to Moses the history of the people from creation until the building of the temple (1.27).

Most scholars of Jubilees suggest a date of composition in the second century BCE, around 161–152 BCE.[175] The book survives in fifteen or sixteen quite fragmentary Hebrew scrolls from Qumran.[176] The only complete copy of Jubilees extant is in Ethiopic Ge'ez, but portions survive in Latin and Greek.[177]

Beliar

The first suggested occurrence of Beliar is found in 1.20 but only in Ethiopic, which reads ቤልሐርᎄ; that is likely the translation of the Greek Beliar or possibly Belior (beli/ar/beli/or). Here, Moses asks of the Lord, "Do not let the spirit of Beliar rule over them [Israel] to accuse them before you and ensnare them from every path of righteousness," which suggests the role of Beliar here is one of an accuser, similar to that of the satan figure in Job 1–2 and elsewhere. The translation reads, "the spirit of Beliar," but this could also be read as "a spirit of Beliar" (መንፈሰ፡ ቤልሐርᎄ), since Ge'ez lacks the definite article. If so, this might be a similar situation as in the T12 Patr., in which Beliar has an army of spirits working with him to perform his task. Interestingly, in the midst of the explanation of the cultic practices (e.g., keeping the Sabbath), there is no mention of any of the spirits of Beliar attempting to persuade the Israelites to disobey the commandments, particularly in the warning given against fornication in 7.20. In 7.27, the suggestion is that there are spirits working to mislead the children of Noah (which still involves human choice!). Here the spirits are አጋንንት፡ (*agānnət*),[178] but there is no connection to Beliar; in fact, these are the evil spirits that have emerged from the giants in the Watcher tradition but are not yet placed under the authority of Mastema, although one might suggest that Beliar may be exploiting the spirits for his own purposes. If this is the case, then the author may be indicating that Beliar (as a spirit being) and Mastema are two different beings functioning in similar roles in the 2TP—or perhaps Beliar is a subordinate of Mastema in the hierarchy of spirits.

---

175. See James C. VanderKam, "The Origins and Purposes of the *Book of Jubilees*," in *Studies in the Book of Jubilees*, ed. M. Albani, J. Frey, and A. Lange, TSAJ 65 (Tübingen, Germany: Mohr Siebeck, 1997), 3–24, here, 19–20. See also Segal, *Jubilees*, 36–40.
176. 1Q17; 1Q18; 2Q19; 2Q20; 3Q5; 4Q176a; 4Q176b; 4Q216; 4Q217; 4Q218; 4Q219; 4Q220; 4Q221; 4Q222; 4Q223–24; 11Q12. See James C. VanderKam et al., *Qumran Cave 4: Parabiblical Texts Part 1*, ed. Emanuel Tov, DJD 13 (Oxford: Clarendon, 1994), 2.
177. James C. VanderKam, *The Book of Jubilees*, 2 vols., CSCO 510–11 (Leuven, Belgium: Peeters, 1989), 1:ix; 2:xi–xiv; Wintermute, "Jubilees," 41–42.
178. Wintermute, "Jubilees," 70, translates it as "demons." See also Segal, *Jubilees*, 149; Segal contends that the demons caused the people to sin, which "points to a specific view regarding the source of evil in the world"; it is not God or the choices of people but an external force that leads people down the path of disobedience toward God.

In 10.1–2, these same spirits (spirits of the giants), this time though identified as "unclean spirits" (አጋንንት፡ ርኩሳን፥ *agānnət rəkusān*), begin to lead the children of Noah's children astray, to folly and destruction. This function of the spirit parallels that of those in T12 Patr., in which the spirits of Beliar mislead the Israelites and draw them away from the Lord, which will lead to their destruction. In 10.3, Noah's prayer concerns these spirits, following a similar petition spoken by Moses in Jubilees 1.20; in this case, Noah prays, "Do not let the evil spirits [መናፍስት፡ አኩያን፥ *manāfəst 'akuyān*] rule over them." This may present a connection between these spirits and the/a spirit of Beliar (መንፈሱ፡ ቢልሖር፥ *manfasa bēlḥor*) in 1.20. Within Jubilees, we have various types of evil spirits at work: the *manāfəst 'akuyān* (unclean spirits), the *'agananet* (demons, in the sense of *ginn*), the/a *manfasa bēlḥor* (spirit of Belior).

In Jubilees 15.33, Beliar is mentioned in the context of the children of Israel who refuse to circumcise their sons—these are called the children of Beliar (ውሉደ፡ ቢልአር፥ *wəluda bēlə'ar*).[179] This reading could be following the meaning in the HB of "sons of worthlessness" or "sons of wickedness" rather than relating them to the chief evil being, Beliar. Due to the various spirits present in Ethiopic Jubilees, it is difficult to determine if the term *Beliar* is representing a chief evil being or simply one of the several evil spirits operating under the authority of Mastema, which we will now discuss.

Mastema

In Jubilees 10.8, one encounters the ruler of the spirits (መልአከ፡ መናፍስት፥ *mal'aka manāfāst*), Mastema (መስቴማ፥ *mastēmā*). Several scholars have suggested a close relationship between Mastema and Beliar in Jubilees, to the point that they maintain the two may be one in the same spirit being. Interestingly, in 10.8, he is not identified as ruler of the "evil spirits," just "ruler of the spirits"; in fact, there is no sense that Mastema has a close affinity with this group of spirits: he speaks of "them" rather than "my spirits."[180] This may suggest that these spirits are operating with Beliar, who is operating under the leadership of Mastema. Though this may be the case of audience knowledge of the history of the figure in their tradition—that is, they know Mastema as the ruler of the evil spirits—there is nothing in Jubilees or any other 2TP literature that identifies his origins. Mastema is able to come before God on multiple occasions in Jubilees, which reflects a similar narrative framework of the satan figure in Job 1–2. As we have seen, figures in the role or position of the hierarchy of spirits like Mastema are in opposition to humanity; as understood here, Mastema sees humans in need of testing, for "the evil of humanity is great." In

---

179. Other manuscripts have "Belehor," but it could also read "Beloar." See Charles, *Jubilees*, 55.
180. See Segal, *Jubilees*, 176.

10.9, Mastema asks God to allow a tenth of the spirits that have been afflicting Noah's children (he doesn't designate which of the spirits—see the various spirits listed earlier in this chapter) to remain with him under his authority to fulfill his task to lead astray the already corrupt (in his opinion!) humanity, thus ending the evil spirits' free run at afflicting humanity. There is no sense here that he has taken up this task on his own; rather, by his asking permission, one might suggest he is operating under God's authority. The author also states through the words of Mastema in 10.8 that his dominion is only temporary ("before my punishment"); the day will come when he will be judged.[181]

In 10.11, we find a clear connection, or as clear as we have seen so far, between a spirit being of another name and the satan figure. One might assume Mastema is an angel in Jubilees due to his comparison to the satan figure. If so, then he was likely a part of the angelic creation that took place in Jubilees 2.2, although there is no specific mention of the names, including either Mastema or the satan, in the list presented. This may suggest that God created Mastema and the satan to "serve before him: the angels of the presence . . . and all of the spirits [πνεύματα; መናፍስት፡, manāfəsət] of his creatures which are in heaven and on earth." One may posit that the task and purpose of Mastema and the satan figure were originally sanctioned by God.

In 10.11, one of the archangels, in describing the scene, states that they were instructed to bind up the evil ones (አኩያን፡, 'akuyān) and allow a tenth of them to be under the authority of the/a satan (ሰይጣን፡, sayəṭān) upon the earth, which is the same action described in 10.7–8 that identifies Mastema as the one to whom the spirits are being allotted. From this parallel, we can see the possible connection between Mastema and the satan figure. Following the release of the spirits, the archangels instruct Noah and his offspring in how to heal the afflictions and avoid the seduction of the evil spirits, and we are told that the spirits were restrained from following after the children of Noah.

Jubilees 11 marks an interesting period in the history of the children of Noah, as they appear to fulfill the fears of Noah's prayer found in chapter 7. We are told of the first establishment of kingdoms of the children of Noah that will war against each other, shedding blood and killing one another. In addition, we are told that they are guilty of many sins against the Lord, in particular the sin of idolatry, thanks to the assistance of the evil spirits (11.4). In verse 11.5, the author notes the prince/ruler/chief Mastema (መኩንን፡ መስቴማ፡, makunen mastēmā)[182] acted

---

181. See van Ruiten, "Angels and Demons in the Book of Jubilees."
182. The term *makunen* in Ge'ez means "to rule over something"—a region, people, or similar—thus, "ruler" or "chief" may be the better translation here rather than Charles's and Wintermute's "Prince"—there is no connotation of royalty here.

forcefully to do these things. He is the one who sent out the other spirits to cause the people to transgress—certainly identifying him as the possible leader of the evil spirits. In Jubilees 11.11, Mastema meddles with the natural order (or shows his authority over it) by sending crows and other birds to eat the seed being planted for crops in order to spoil the works of the people. This appears to grant him power over the minds of creatures of the earth, which may suggest, if he wishes, he can have power over the minds of individuals, as may be understood in 11.2–5. Segal has argued correctly that this portion of Jubilees 11.11 reveals "the human suffering caused by the birds is part of the problem of evil" in the worldview of the author and audience: Can God be "omnipotent and good" if human suffering, such as the poverty suggested here, exists? The author's answer to the problem of human suffering in the world is the "interference of another heavenly character, Mastema."[183] What is not expressed in the text is under whose authority Mastema is acting; in the worldview of 2TP Judaism, one would assume God's authority.

Jubilees 17.15–16 may offer some insight to this issue of authority. In a retelling of Genesis 22 and the sacrifice of Isaac, the author shares that Mastema[184] came before God and questioned him about the faith of Abraham. Considering Mastema's view of humanity as capable of every evil, this might suggest that he sees Abraham as one who would turn from God if pushed in certain situations. He turns to God and suggests that to test the love of Abraham, he should tell Abraham to sacrifice his son Isaac in order to test his faith (ch. 18); this scenario is very similar to the actions of the satan figure in Job 1–2.[185] What does the entrance of Mastema into the Akedah suggest about his authority and God's sovereignty over all that takes place on the earth? Does this speak to the omniscience of God (Jub. 17.17)? In the midst of the testing of Abraham and Isaac, the angel who is telling the story states that he stands before the Lord and Mastema (who is watching the events), and the Lord tells him to prevent Abraham from harming Isaac (by showing him the ram) after Abraham has raised the knife to sacrifice Isaac. Mastema, seeing the events and the presentation of the ram in the thicket, is disgraced (18.12).

The next occurrence of *Mastema* takes place in chapter 48, in which the term occurs three times. In 48.2–4, the author reveals that while Moses was on his way back to Egypt, Mastema desired to kill him in order to save the Egyptians from God's judgment.[186] Why would Mastema want to kill Moses or protect the Egyptians? The Exodus passage in 4:24 states that God wanted to kill Moses. Does the rewriting of the story to include Mastema suggest an effort to remove any apparently

---

183. Segal, *Jubilees*, 186.
184. "Ruler of the demons" (ὁ ἄρχων τῶν δαιμονίων) is absent from the Ethiopic.
185. Ida Fröhlich, "Invoke at Anytime," *Biblische Notizen* 137 (2008): 41–74, here, 63.
186. See discussion in Eshel, "Mastema's Attempt."

unwarranted evil actions by God—such as to kill Moses! There is a sense in the Jubilees account that Mastema is acting on his own without permission from God.[187] In 48.4 the author states that "I [God] delivered you [Moses] from his [Mastema's] hand and you did the signs and wonders"; if this is the case, then we see another failure of Mastema to fulfill his will among the people as he failed in the retelling of the Akedah. However, this does not necessarily rule out any involvement of the authority of God in the events. The author may be affirming the ultimate sovereignty of God over events on the earth while at the same time separating God and the problem of evil—that is, Mastema is responsible for it. The author goes on to describe the great plagues that the Lord brought upon Egypt on account of Israel in Jubilees 48.5–8.

The second occurrence of Mastema is found in 48.9, in which the author relates how Mastema helped the Egyptian magicians. Interestingly, in verse 10, the angel states that he and others helped the magicians do evil but did not empower them to heal. This description suggests the struggle is between Mastema and the angel and not with God directly, but the result of Mastema's actions—failure—suggests his powers are limited, whereas the angel stands in for the Deity—that is, it is the Angel of the Lord. In 48.12, Mastema is *not* (Charles omits the negation from the text) disgraced, perhaps because the magicians were also assisted by other angels. However, the omission of the *not* makes sense in what follows: "until he had become strong and called to the Egyptians so that they might pursue after you [Moses] with all the army of the Egyptians." In 48.15, the author states that on the eighteenth day into the exodus from Egypt, "Mastema was bound and shut up from (pursuing) the children of Israel so that he might not accuse them." Here again we find a similar task, accusing humanity, to those of the satan figure being performed, though in this case prevented, by Mastema. On the nineteenth day, Mastema is released to assist the Egyptians in their pursuit of Israel. The author states that he (presumably Mastema) hardened their hearts and strengthened them to pursue Israel, a task that God performed in the biblical Exodus account ("I will harden Pharaoh's heart and he will pursue them"). This might suggest that God is using Mastema, who is unaware of God's plan to destroy the Egyptian armies. Segal argues that the insertion of Mastema into the biblical account removes the theological difficulty of God hardening Pharaoh's heart and at the same time encouraging him to pursue Israel.[188] In 48.18, the author relates that Mastema had been previously bound on the fourteenth day to prevent him from accusing them while the Israelites were collecting vessels of silver and gold. Twice in chapter 48, Mastema is identified as the accuser, a task also attributed to the satan figure in the HB and elsewhere.

187. See discussion in Segal, *Jubilees*, 203–6.
188. Segal, 216.

Jubilees 49.1–8 presents the final occurrence of Mastema. Here, the author is recounting the story of the Passover in Egypt and the killing of the firstborn (Exod 12:21–23). We are told in the biblical account that the Lord, by the work of the "destroyer," will pass through and strike down the Egyptians; this destroyer could be understood as an angel of destruction, but it has been given permission for its mission. In Jubilees 49.2, the destroyer is identified as "all the powers of Mastema" (ኀይላቲሁ፡ ለመስቴማ፡, *xayelātihu lamastēmā*) who were sent to kill all the firstborn of Egypt; they apparently did not go on their own. This would suggest that Mastema and his spirits, or at least just his spirits, were being used by God against Egypt at the beginning of the Exodus.

Jubilees presents the Mastema figure as one who operates in the same office as the satan figure in the HB, but this does not necessarily identify him as the same satan figure mentioned elsewhere. It may be that Mastema and the satan figure operate in the same office of "the accuser." At the same time, Mastema is portrayed as a figure who attempts to come against the will of God in an individual's life, whether with permission of God or at times when it appears he is acting semiautonomously.

Summary

We have seen in the scrolls that the idea of the names of heavenly figures are not fixed; we discovered though that the prominent name for the so-called personified evil being is Belial but may be otherwise known as the Angel of Darkness, Melchiresha, or Mastema. These figures are responsible for a variety of problems in the 2TP Jewish worldview. We identified various dualisms in the Qumran worldview that influenced the concept of evil in the 2TP. Scholars suggest this is due to the dualism of Zoroastrianism, which speaks of a cosmic good-versus-evil dichotomy. This resulted in an ongoing battle between light and dark, righteousness and evil, and a spirit of truth and a spirit of darkness, as well as the eschatological war between the sons of light led by Michael and the Sons of Darkness who are led by the Angel of Darkness. Five main figures can be identified in the scrolls that may be related to the "chief" evil being, the satan: Melchiresha, the Angel of Darkness, S/satan, Mastema, and Belial.

We identified the primary figure of evil in the Pseudepigrapha and other 2TP Jewish literature as Beliar (βελιὰρ), apparently synonymous with Belial and, to some degree, Mastema. As we saw, the book of Jubilees draws a parallel between the two figures. The T12 Patr. identifies Beliar as an instigator and a leader of a group of evil spirits under his authority, whose task is to afflict humanity and draw them away from the Lord. Similar to the scrolls, there are strong dualistic components in the T12 Patr. (ethical, anthropological, cosmological) that are reflected in various concepts: (1) the two spirits, (2) the two inclinations, (3) the two sets of seven spirits, (4) a messianic figure over against Beliar, (5) the Law of the Lord and the law of Beliar, (6) the Angel of the Lord and the spirit of Beliar, (7) the Angel of Peace and the spirit of Beliar, (8) light and darkness, and (9) the will of God and the will of Beliar. The evidence revealed in T12 Patr. points to strong possibility of the belief in the existence of a spirit being that influences the evil activities that take place in the human realm, but under the sovereignty and authority of God.

The book of Jubilees is one the most significant texts that present the issues of the problem of evil and a detailed angelology in the 2TP. Not the least significant is its inclusion of the Watcher tradition found in 1 Enoch. Jubilees portrays angels and evil spirits as having specific tasks to complete in the world. There are good angels who help control the forces of nature, assist humanity, and act as intermediaries between humans and God. The evil spirits in Jubilees are the author's way of dealing with the problem of evil in his worldview. For the author, evil "affirm(s) both the omnipotence and goodness of God." It is understood to be a heavenly spiritual force that has emerged out of the angelic realm, but the question is, Was it created by God? Significant to this discussion is Jubilees' presentation of what appears to be a chief spiritual being that has the evil spirits produced in the Watcher tradition working with it, the figure of Mastema.

We will now move into the New Testament and other Early Christian literature in an effort to see what if any relationship the figures highlighted in 2TP Jewish literature have with the satan figure in early Christianity.

Chapter 6

Satan in the New Testament

Introduction

We have previously examined the satan figure and other possibly related figures in the 2TP literature outside of the NT. Authors of the various texts we examined suggest only a few roles for the satan figure such as a leader or chief over a group of evil spirits, an accuser of humanity, and one who tests the faith of individuals. However, other names emerged that many scholars have suggested are related to if not the same as the satan figure. Such monikers include Belial, Beliar, Mastema, Prince Mastema, Melchiresha, the Angel of Darkness, the Angel of Mastema, and the Wicked or Evil One. What is particularly interesting concerning these other names is how they apparently fell out of use in the writings of the New Testament, with one or two exceptions. One might ask what caused the shift of the prominent use of the terms *the satan* and *the devil* in the HB/LXX and its seemingly less pronounced role in the 2TP. The authors of the NT offer a new set of names and characterizations for the satan/devil figures, although none have the same level of distinction as the Belial, Beliar, or Mastema we discovered in, for example, the DSS, T12 Patr., or Jubilees. Some of the characterizations of the figure in the NT echo a few depictions from the 2TP Jewish literature such as ruler (שר) of the demons/evil spirits, Ruler (ἄρχων) of This Age, Ruler of This World, the Great Dragon, and the Angel of the Pit. In addition, a variety of other NT figures or titles may be closely tied with the satan in his role as the adversary, although not clearly identified as the same figure. These include the "lawless one" in 2 Thessalonians, the two beasts in Revelation 13, and the antichrist figure in 1 John 2:18 (one of many).

The reader is told in 2 Thessalonians 2:9–10 that the satan figure uses "all capability, signs, false wonders, and every wicked deception against the ones who are perishing because they refused to love the truth that would save them"—in other words, the satan figure turns them from God and his Messiah. First Corinthians 2:12 perhaps suggests that there is a spirit of deception in the world that prevents people from hearing and understanding the spirit of God (2:11). Ephesians 6:11

warns that the devil (τοῦ διαβόλου) has plans or schemes that are established by and function through spirits in the unseen realm (ἐπουρανίοις) to deceive individuals. Ephesians 4:27 makes the reader aware that the devil is continually looking for individuals to turn away from following God (cf. 1 Pet 5:8). James 4:7 warns that a person must submit themselves to God's plan and in doing so, the devil must leave them alone (cf. CD 16). As we further examine the satan figure in the NT, we will highlight the possible functions he performs and under whose authority he is operating—his or God's—while comparing these functions to those of the various figures in the 2TP literature. Susan Garrett offers several premises that likely were understood by Jews concerning the function of the satan figure in the period leading up to the writing of the NT Gospels. First, an individual's "righteousness and service to God" may provoke the satan figure or the spirits operating with him to oppress or afflict the person (much like Job). Second, God has given the satan authority over the physical life of the individual, and only they themselves can surrender authority over their soul by cursing God. Third, the authors of the NT Gospels present the satan figure as one who is "authorized by God but seeking nonetheless to lead God's faithful astray."[1] In what follows, we will identify the various roles in which the satan figure is portrayed.

The Satan Figure in the Gospels

The Greek term ὁ σατανᾶς, or a form of it, appears in the Synoptic Gospels fifteen times and once in John's Gospel.[2] The generally accepted synonymous term ὁ διαβόλος, or a form of it, appears in the Synoptic Gospels thirteen times and once in John's Gospel.[3] The question to be raised in each of these occurrences is whether or not ὁ σατανᾶς is the personification of evil, the ruler of the evil spirits, and the anti-God figure that has been part of the Judeo-Christian tradition for two thousand years. In addition, one might ask why the Gospel authors, with the exception of Mark, use both terms, ὁ σατανᾶς and ὁ διαβόλος, to refer to the same figure. Is this simply a linguistic difference due to the terminology of the source the author was using?[4]

---

1. Susan R. Garrett, *The Temptations of Jesus in Mark's Gospel* (Grand Rapids, MI: Eerdmans, 1998), 42.
2. Voc. m.s., Matt 4:10; 16:23; Mark 8:33; Nom. m.s. + def. art., Matt 12:26; Mark 3:26; 4:15; Luke 11:18; 13:16; John 13:27; Nom. m.s., no def. art., Mark 3:23; Luke 22:3; Acc. m.s., + def. art., Matt 12:26; Luke 10:18; Acc. m.s., no def. art., Mark 3:23; Gen. m.s. + def. art., Mark 1:13.
3. Nom. m.s. + def. art., Matt 4:5, 8, 11; 13:39; Luke 4:3, 6, 13; 8:12; Gen. m.s. + def. art., Matt 4:1; Luke 4:2; John 8:44; 13:2; Nom. m.s., no def. art., John 6:70. Interestingly, διαβόλος does not appear in the Gospel of Mark.
4. The Gospels in the Aramaic Peshitta use the term ܣܛܢܐ to translate σατανᾶς and also for διαβόλος in Matt 13:39; Luke 8:12; John 6:70; and 13:2. In the ten other occurrences of διαβόλος the translator uses the Aramaic term אכלקרצא, which is usually translated "accuser," or "slanderer." The term appears to be a compound word that could mean "feeder of accusations," "eater of flies," but its limited use makes it difficult to make a definitive determination.

This does not appear the case in Matthew 4 and John 13, as the authors used both, but in the other references, one or the other is used, either ὁ σατανᾶς or ὁ διάβολος. Is there a difference between the functions of each of the figures? Or are they identical? Again, as we suggested with the identities of the various figures in the 2TP Jewish literature, we must use caution when making such immediate connections; this applies to all of the other terms used to identify some kind of personified evil being.[5] In what follows, we will examine each use of each term in its individual context.

Gospel of Matthew
The Satan and the Devil in Matthew 4

The first encounter with the satan/devil figure in the Gospel of Matthew is found in Matthew 4:1; the section is identified as the Trial of Jesus in the Wilderness.[6] Commentators propose the passage represents a testing to determine if Jesus exhibits the characteristics of the "Son of God."[7] This point is supported by the satan comments found in Matthew 4:3 and 6: "Since you are the Son of God," in which he may be attempting to get Jesus to use his "powers" as the Son of God to work things out on his own without God.[8] Each of the tests that Jesus is offered questions whether he will be obedient to the Father or take an opportunity to display his Messianic powers.

In Matthew 4:1, the author states that Jesus was led up (ἀνήχθη) by the Holy Spirit into the wilderness to be tested (πειρασθῆναι, aor. pass. inf.) by the devil (τοῦ διαβόλου).[9] This portrayal of the devil as the one who tests individuals follows the primary function of the being in the HB (see esp. Job 1–2—we see here that God through the Spirit has established the opportunity

---

5. The LXX uses ὁ διάβολος to translate שׂטן or השׂטן, "enemy" or "adversary"; it also translates צרר, "affliction" or "enemy," as διάβολος in Esth 7:4 and 8:1. It also translates שׂטן in the sense of a human enemy or adversary, which is paralleled with רשׁע, as in "wicked person" in Ps 109:6.
6. This pericope likely originates from the Q source, as it is also found in Luke, although there are some differences in content. One significant difference is the inclusion of the statement by satan that the kingdoms of the world are his to give to whomever he wishes in Luke but excluded from Matthew. This is of course a profound theological issue that suggests the satan figure has rule over the world; if this is the case, why would Matthew omit such a statement? This could also be explained by different recensions of Q that each author was working with; see A. H. McNeile, *The Gospel according to St. Matthew* (London: Macmillan, 1915).
7. Donald Hagner identifies these characteristics as "trust, obedience, faithfulness." Donald A. Hagner, *Word Biblical Commentary: Matthew 1–13*, WBC 33a (Dallas: Word Books, 1993), 61. Hagner suggests the story line here and that portrayed in the Exodus wilderness narrative are similar, the difference being that Israel failed its test, whereas Jesus did not (62–63).
8. Daniel J. Harrington argues that the three tests are instigated to determine "what kind of Son of God Jesus is." Daniel J. Harrington, *The Gospel of Matthew*, Sacra Pagina (Collegeville, MN: Liturgical Press, 2007), 1:66.
9. Sirach 2:1 reveals a common theme of testing of the faithful in 2TP Judaism: "Child, if you come to serve the Lord, prepare your soul for testing."

for testing but the actual tests are accomplished by his agent, in Job's case the satan figure).[10] Perhaps this might suggest the satan figure made a similar approach to God concerning Jesus, perhaps testing his willingness to be the Messiah of God. In Matthew 4:3, he is called the one who tests or tries individuals (πειράζων, pres. act. part.), further supporting one of his functions or roles in the NT. This may be a deliberate shift for Matthew to establish the reason Jesus is led out into the wilderness (Luke uses ὁ διαβόλος). The literature of the 2TP reveal a shift in the idea of theodicy, in which actions previously attributed to God are now ascribed to the satan figure or some other heavenly being.[11] The satan tests Jesus with Scripture, perhaps in an effort to persuade him from turning from God and a proper understanding of the Torah and the Scriptures. As we saw in the Damascus Document, CD 16, if one follows Scripture properly and turns to God for their sanctuary, the Angel of Mastema must leave him. In Matthew 4:3–10, one might suggest the connection between the satan and Mastema as previously suggested in Jubilees. In 4:5, the author identifies the tester from 4:3 with ὁ διαβόλος, the one who takes Jesus to Jerusalem to test his willingness to be the Messiah of God; again, Jesus answers with Scripture: "Do not put the Lord your God to the test!" One might ask if here Jesus is making a declaration of his divinity or simply responding with Scripture. Is he declaring to the devil, "Stop testing your God; you cannot defeat him!"? Perhaps even more intriguing is the fact that he says his Father is the devil's God!

Matthew 4:8–9 offer a clear picture of the satan's task to turn people away from God and worship another—in this case, worship the devil himself. Upon stating his resolute intention to follow God and not turn away from his Torah, we are told the devil left Jesus, perhaps again echoing the theme of CD 16 noted above. In the midst of this testing, the first instance of the term *the satan* appears in Matthew 4:10. In the context of Jesus rebuking him, he states, "Be gone, satan!" (voc. m.s.), and he leaves. The author then notes that the angels come and serve Jesus, thus ending the pericope. We can see in this story that the task of the devil/satan is to test Jesus to see whether he is willing and able to pass the test as the Messiah of God—the satan obviously must have doubts, since he questions if he is the "Son of God," a title used for the Messiah in the 2TP. The term *satan* in this context could be best understood as "adversary" or, as the text makes clear, "one who tests," πειράζων.

---

10. See Robert H. Mounce, *Matthew* (Peabody, MA: Hendrickson, 1991).
11. See Gen 22:1 and Jub. 17.15–18; Exod 4:24–26 and Jub. 48.2–3; 2 Sam 24:1 and 1 Chr 21:1. Here, in Matt 1, God is still involved through the spirit leading Jesus into the testing, as we saw God directly testing Israel in the wilderness in Exod 16:4 and 20:20. See Harrington, *Matthew*, 66; Harrington contends that in preexilic Israel, God is the one who does the testing of the nation and individuals, whereas in 2TP, this function has been turned over to the satan and his namesakes (see Job 1–2; Zech 3; 1 Chr 21). The satan figure does, however, still operate under God's authority.

The Satan in Matthew 12

Matthew 12:26 (para. Mark 3:22–26; Luke 11:15, 17–18) presents the term ὁ σατανᾶς in an interesting context, in which the author relates how Jesus healed a man who was blind and mute and, according to the reaction of the crowd, was thought to be possessed by or afflicted by a demonic spirit (δαιμονιζόμενος, pres. mid. part.). After Jesus heals the man, the Pharisees claim that it is by the "ruler of the demons" (ἄρχοντι τῶν δαιμονίων),[12] Beelzeboul (βεελζεβούλ)[13] that Jesus was able to cast out the wicked spirit. Based on Jesus's words in 12:26, "If the satan casts out the satan" (καὶ εἰ ὁ σατανᾶς τὸν σατανᾶν ἐκβάλλει), many scholars have argued that the Pharisees are speaking of the satan figure;[14] however, if that is the case, why would the Pharisees not name the figure satan, or perhaps Belial, if this is the connection they are trying to make?[15] If one can draw a line between Beelzeboul and Belial of the 2TP Jewish literature, then the claim of the Pharisees that Jesus is being used by the "ruler of the demons" might make sense.

Unfortunately, the term *Beelzeboul*, or *Beelzebub*, does not appear in other 2TP Jewish literature, thus making any connection difficult.[16] A similar name, Baal Zebub (זבוב בעל), appears in 2 Kings 1:2–16 as the god of Ekron, to whom Ahaziah inquires whether he will die from his injuries. The LXX translates the term as "Lord of the Flies," as does Josephus in *Antiquities* 9.2.1. Beelzeboul appears in the Testament of Solomon 3–16 and is identified as the "ruler of demons," but the dating is likely post-first century CE.[17]

The language surrounding Beelzeboul is in the context of the crowd asking, "Can this be the Son of David?" (12:23), which suggests they think Jesus could be the Messiah of God. The

---

12. Cf. the similar story in Matt 9:32–34, in which the Pharisees accuse Jesus of casting out demons by the power of the "ruler of the demons," but there is no mention of Beelzeboul. Jesus indicates in Matt 10:25 that some of his opponents have already called him Beelzeboul and warns his disciples that they should expect the same when they go out into the towns.
13. *Beelzeboul* occurs three times in Matthew: 10:25, Jesus suggests that he has already been accused of being Beelzeboul, the Master of the House; in 12:24 and 27, he is accused of being used by Beelzeboul to cast a demon out of the demoniac. See discussion Hagner, *Matthew*, 282.
14. See Harrington, *Matthew*, 183; Harrington suggests the term *satan* here is a proper name equated to Beelzeboul. Harrington also implies that the kingdom language used by Jesus grants a kingdom to satan: "If satan was acting through Jesus, he would be destroying his own kingdom and thus acting at cross-purposes with it."
15. Hagner argues that satan "is clearly an alternate way of referring to Beelzeboul" based on the "kingdom" language used by Jesus in his response to the Pharisees. However, there is no clear evidence that Jesus intends to connect the kingdom he mentions to satan; this is the only occasion (besides the Synoptic parallels) in which commentators connect satan to a kingdom. See Hagner, *Matthew*, 342.
16. Wolfgang Herrmann suggests that Beelzeboul is perhaps derived from the Latin, in which the Greek *dia-* is often replaced with the Latin *za-*, creating *zaboul* from *diabolos*. See W. Herrmann, "Baal Zebub," in *Dictionary of Deities and Demons in the Bible*, ed. Karel van der Toorn, Bob Becking, and Pieter W. van der Horst (Leiden: Brill, 1999), 154–56, here, 154.
17. The dating of T. Sol., though, is a matter of much debate; some suggest as early as the second century CE, but the text reflects characteristics of first-century Judaism or early Christian traditions. D. C. Duling suggests the best evidence places it in third-century CE Alexandria. See D. C. Duling, "Testament of Solomon," in Charlesworth, *Old Testament Pseudepigrapha*, 1st ed., 1:935–87.

Pharisees' accusation is likely a response that mocks the crowd for thinking such a thing. Jesus responds to them with some commonsense wisdom in 12:25: "Every kingdom divided against itself is laid waste, and no city or house divided against itself will stand." The contemporary understanding of this response is that he is speaking of the kingdom of satan—the archenemy of God, when, in fact, there is little evidence of such a figure having such a kingdom in 2TP Judaism. One might argue a connection between two terms that have been suggested as synonyms for the satan in the DSS. The first term is *Melchiresha*, "king of wickedness or evil," in 4Q544 (Visions of Amram), but there are no clear lines drawn between the satan and Melchiresha. The second term or phrase, *Angel of Darkness*, is found in 1QS 3.20–21, the Treatise of Two Spirits, in which this angel/messenger is put in opposition to the Prince of Lights. Thus, the combination of these two names might imply a "kingdom of darkness," but the suggestion is tenuous at best. The second part of his response in 12:26 has been interpreted as the figurehead of evil, the satan of the Judeo-Christian tradition. However, if one interprets ὁ σατανᾶς as "the adversary"—that is, if the adversary in a situation casts out the adversary, he is divided in his own interests and his kingdom will not stand. The issue at play with the comparisons drawn by Jesus is that the exorcism of the evil spirit would be in direct conflict with the interests of the "ruler of the demons"; thus, he cannot be casting out the spirits via the power of Beelzeboul. Then in responding to the Beelzeboul accusation in 12:27, he asks how the exorcists of the Pharisees cast out demons,[18] implying then they too must be casting them out by Beelzeboul. He then states how he is actually casting out the demons: "It is by the Spirit of God that I myself cast out the demons, then the Kingdom of God has been presented to you" (12:28).

It appears, however, that Jesus intended to suggest that the spirits were working under the authority of the satan figure regardless of whether or not he is identifying the figure in 12:26 as simply an adversary or the Chief of Evil. If this is the case, then one might suggest a connection between the satan figure of the NT and the Mastema figure of Jubilees, the Belial figure in select DSS, or the Beliar figure in, for example, the T12 Patr. If this is the case, then one would have to maintain the satan is working under the authority of God and has these evil spirits working with/for him to accomplish his task of testing the faith of individuals through trial or affliction.

The Satan and the Devil in Matthew 13

The next occurrence of the satan/devil figure occurs in Jesus's explanation to his disciples of the Parable of the Sower in Matthew 13:36–43, in particular in 13:39. Jesus explains that it is

---

18. For example, Acts 19:13–20 notes that the seven sons of the Jewish high priest were exorcists; Josephus also mentions in *Jewish Wars* 7.178–89 how Jewish exorcists travel about the land expelling evil and unclean spirits.

the "Son of Man" (ὁ υἱὸς τοῦ ἀνθρώπου) who sows the good seed in the world, and the weeds are from the seeds of the "enemy" (ἐχθρός), who is the devil (ὁ διάβολος). One may immediately draw a parallel between the devil and the satan figure in this context. However, the term ἐχθρὸς the "enemy," is used to describe a human enemy or adversary in its seven occurrences in the NT, with the possible exception of here in 13:39. In 13:38, Jesus uses the term along with ἄνθρωπος, making it clear it is a human enemy who has sown the seeds of the weeds in the parable. But when it comes time to explain the parable to the disciples, he uses what might be described as the language of a cosmological dualism—the field is the world, the good seed are the children of the Kingdom sown by the Son of Man (Messiah), the weeds are the children of the Evil [One] (possibly making a connection to the sons of Belial in 2TP literature), sown by the enemy who is no longer a human enemy but ὁ διάβολος, the adversary of the children of the kingdom. Jesus has drawn a contrasting image of the children of the Kingdom and the children of the Evil [One],[19] and the Son of Man and the adversary (cf. language of 1QS 2.4; 4.17).

The Satan in Matthew 16

The reference to the satan figure in Matthew 16:23 has been understood in a context in which Peter, the apostle, has been influenced by the satan figure to the point of opposing Jesus and his mission. The pericope begins in 16:21, in which Jesus tells the disciples what lays ahead for him in Jerusalem. Peter takes Jesus aside and begins to rebuke him, "saying, 'Mercy to you O Lord, never will this happen to you!'" Jesus responds, "Get behind me O satan! You are an offense to me; for you are not wise to the things of God but [to] the things of men." The traditional interpretation of this verse is, as mentioned, that the satan has taken hold of Peter and is using him to try to stop Jesus, but if one understands "satan" here as simply "an adversary," then Jesus may simply be calling Peter an adversary or hindrance to God's plan and wants to get him on the same page. The Greek used here, ὕπαγε ὀπίσω μου, suggests that Peter needs to physically get away from Jesus—"go to the back of me." Peter is acting as a stumbling block to Jesus (see the language of the temptation in Matt 4:11), perhaps tempting him to turn from the mission of the Father.[20] Of course, one can argue this is the role of the satan, to influence

---

19. Interestingly, we find an opportune moment for the author to identify the devil with a "kingdom" in order to contrast it with the Kingdom of the Son of Man, but he fails to do so. One should also note the use of apocalyptic language by Matthew to describe an eschatological event: final judgment, Son of Man and his angels, fiery furnace (Dan 3:6); weeping and grinding of teeth, Kingdom of the Son (Dan 7:13–14); the righteous shining like the sun (Dan 12:3; 2 Esd 7:97); Kingdom of the Father; and so on, which suggests an eschatological dualism present in other 2TP literature.
20. See John Nolland, *The Gospel of Matthew*, NIGTC (Grand Rapids, MI: Eerdmans, 2005), 688–89; Hagner, *Matthew*, 480; Harrington, *Matthew*, 248–49.

individuals to turn from God and his will; if so, then the satan figure here would certainly fit into the Jewish understanding of the satan—that is, he is working under the authority of God.

The Devil in Matthew 25

The final occurrence of the satan figure in Matthew, in this case ὁ διάβολος, is found in 25:41, in the context of the coming of the Son of Man in the eschaton. The King (Christ) is separating the righteous from the wicked in what can be described as the final judgment in heaven. He describes the righteous as those who have fed the hungry, welcomed strangers, clothed the naked, taken care of the sick, and visited those in prison (which may suggest a period of persecution of Christians). As for the wicked, they are those who have failed to do any of these acts of righteousness. They are to be cursed and sent to the eternal fire (τὸ πῦρ τὸ αἰώνιον), the one being prepared for the devil and his angels (τῷ διαβόλῳ καὶ τοῖς ἀγγέλοις αὐτοῦ). The inclusion of the devil's angels in this verse suggests some connection to early Jewish understandings of the chief evil figure who, at times, is identified with a group of angels; see, for example, the Life of Adam and Eve, although the LAE is from the late first or early second century CE (also Rev 12:7–9; 20:10; 2 Cor 12:7), though the LAE could be from an early period. This could also be a later addition to the Gospel that postdates the ideas presented in John's Apocalypse, which speaks of the satan figure and the angels who allegedly fell with him.

Summary of Gospel of Matthew

The author of the Gospel of Matthew suggests the satan figure and the devil are synonymous terms. This is quite different from the variety of terms used for what appears to be a chief or at least a leading figure in the realm of evil in the 2TP. However, one should still be cautious in definitively drawing the conclusion that they are one in the same figure. The Gospel of Matthew presents the satan/devil figure in roles similar to those assigned to various satan-like figures from 2TP Jewish literature. In Matthew 4, this figure is identified as the "tester of the faithful ones," a role occupied by figures such as Belial and Mastema in the 2TP. If one concludes that Beelzeboul and the satan are the same figure, although this seems doubtful, then he could be identified as the "ruler of the demons."

In Matthew 12, it has been suggested that this is the ruler of the "Kingdom of Darkness," but this can only be concluded with some creative drawing of parallels between Melchiresha and the Angel of Darkness, two prominent figures in the DSS view of the problem of evil; there is little evidence in the Gospel to make this determination. The satan is presented as an adversary in Matthew 13, in which he is seen as persuading the sons of the evil one (the sons of

Belial?) to disrupt the lives of the righteous, and in Matthew 16, he is depicted as an adversary (Peter) who is opposed to God's plan for Jesus as he approaches Jerusalem.

Finally, as the devil figure, he is characterized as an evil adversary who has a group of angels working with him to oppose humanity and God's will for them. One might suggest that with the distinct roles presented for the satan figure and the devil figure, they are two heavenly beings that are functioning in distinct offices or roles under the authority of God.

Gospel of Mark

The term *satan* (ὁ σατανᾶς or a form of it) occurs six times in Mark's Gospel (1:13; 3:23 [2×]; 3:26; 4:15; 8:33).[21] Interestingly, the Gospel of Mark does not include the term ὁ διάβολος, "devil."

The Satan in Mark 1

The first instance of the satan (τοῦ σατανᾶ) occurs in the Markan parallel of the Trial of Jesus in the Wilderness pericope, beginning in 1:12 (Matt 4:1 and Luke 4:2 use τοῦ διαβόλου).[22] Differing significantly from the Matthean version, the author of Mark states that the Spirit (presumed the Holy Spirit), taking an active role, drove out (ἐκβάλλει)[23] Jesus into the wilderness, suggesting that this is in the plan and purpose of God.[24] R. T. France contends the focus of the Markan pericope is what goes on behind the scenes in the entire ministry of Jesus on the earth (the battle in the spirit realm) with the mention of the wild beasts and the satan (Mark 1:13) over against the Holy Spirit and the angels (Mark 1:12, 13).[25]

Susan Garrett suggests there are similarities in the Markan trial pericope to the Job episode in terms of the satan figure carrying out the act of divine testing, although we do not hear any

---

21. John R. Donahue and Daniel J. Harrington contend that *satan* is synonymous with *devil* and "clearly identified as 'the prince of demons' in Mark 3:23, 26; he opposes the word in 4:15 and leads people astray in 8:33." See their *The Gospel of Mark*, Sacra Pagina 2 (Collegeville, MN: Liturgical Press, 2002), 66.
22. As mentioned, the "testing in the wilderness" theme likely carries theological significance tied to the wilderness testing of Israel as God's son in Exodus. The later Apocalypse of Abraham (extant in Slavonic) offers a similar forty-day trial in which, in chapter 13, Abraham, accompanied by an angel (Jaoel), encounters the spirit figure of Azazel (see 1 En. 6.7: Gk. Ἀζαλζήλ, Ἀσεάλ; Eth. አዛዝኤል፡ አዛዝኤል፡) speaking through a bird, whose task is to tempt Abraham and lead him astray. The angel tells Abraham in chapter 15 that God has given Azazel power over those who speak with him. See the translation by Alexander Kulik, *Retroverting Slavonic Pseudepigrapha* (Atlanta: SBL, 2004; Leiden: Brill, 2005).
23. This is the same term used by the Gospel writers elsewhere for the exorcisms performed by Jesus. Mark uses it in the sense of "historic present" throughout his Gospel. Robert A. Guelich contends that one is left with the impression that the Spirit took control of Jesus, "impelling Jesus to go into the wilderness." See Guelich, *Mark 1–8:26*, WBC 34A (Nashville: Thomas Nelson, 1989), 37–38.
24. Wis 2:12–20 and 5:1–23 states that God tests the suffering just person and if they remain faithful and do not sin, then they will be called a child of God.
25. R. T. France, *The Gospel of Mark*, NIGTC (Grand Rapids, MI: Eerdmans, 2002), 85. See discussion of the "wild beasts" and demons in H. A. Kelly, "The Devil in the Desert," *CBQ* 26 (1964): 190–220.

words of request by the satan in Mark.[26] We see a Jobian role for Mastema in Jubilees 17, in which he is granted authority to execute the test of Abraham with the sacrifice of Isaac. We are told that Jesus is in the wilderness for forty days being tested (πειραζόμενος) by the satan (τοῦ σατανᾶ)—perhaps, as Garrett suggests, to see if he is able to fulfill the task of the Son of God.[27] However, the author does not share the details of the testing process as in Matthew and Luke (the Q material); we are only told that he was in the wilderness for forty days[28] with wild beasts (θηρίων) and that the angels ministered to him.[29] Some argue the wild beasts in this instance may be referring to demons,[30] perhaps an allusion to the demonic figures in Psalm 91 (also Ps 22:11–21; Ezek 34:5, 8, 25; Deut 32:17; Isa 34:14),[31] which is cited by the satan figure in Matthew 4:6 and Luke 4:10–11. But there is no prior evidence of this usage of the term in the LXX with the possible exception of Job 40:15, which translates Behemoth (בהמות) with θηρίων, though this does not suggest an evil spirit. The audience may be reminded of Isaiah 34:14, which mentions the wild beasts in a context of demonic beings, terminology that the LXX translates as δαιμόνια, "demons." Morna Hooker suggests that the presence of the wild beasts may represent Jesus's defeat of the demonic realm, while the angels are there to wait on him during the forty days, as they were with Elijah in 1 Kings 19; however, Mark does not openly suggest that either is the case.[32] As noted in the discussion of Matthew 4, this usage of the satan figure in Mark 1 suggests that he is a tester of individuals and their faithfulness to God's will and plan.

---

26. Garrett, *Temptations of Jesus*, 56; see Job 1:8–12; 2:3–6.
27. Garrett, 56, 59. The question of whether the wilderness experience for Jesus was a real test of his mission to be the Messiah / Son of God or just an example of obedience to God's call should be raised. The test, in light of the dialogue in Matthew's account, suggests this test was real and that Jesus is proven to be worthy of the call.
28. The number forty could be significant in relation to the wilderness wandering of Israel or two other figures who were also ministered to by angels in the wilderness: Moses and Elijah in Mark 9:2–8. If compared to the forty days of Moses in the wilderness, perhaps the focus of the forty days should be on the revelation given to Jesus or on the testing by satan. François Bovon, in discussing Luke 4, suggests that forty days was the "standard length of time for receiving divine revelation" in Jewish tradition. See François Bovon, *Luke 1: A Commentary on the Gospel of Luke 1:1–9:50*, Hermeneia (Minneapolis: Fortress, 2002), 141.
29. If the pericope is original to Mark, did he omit the details of the testing or did Matthew and Luke have additional sources to the event (possibly Q—which, of course, could only have come secondhand from Jesus)?
30. See discussion of wild beasts as demons in Adela Yarbro Collins, *Mark: A Commentary on the Gospel of Mark*, Hermeneia (Minneapolis: Fortress, 2007), 151–53.
31. Psalm 91 is a prayer that is cited for protection against evil spirits in 11Q11, 11Q5 (Great Psalms Scroll), and also in the Psalms Targum. See Craig A. Evans, "Jesus and Psalm 91 in Light of the Exorcism Scrolls," in *Celebrating the Scrolls: A Canadian Contribution*, ed. Peter W. Flint, Jean Duhaime, and Kyung S. Baek (Atlanta: SBL, 2011), 541–55. Cf. T. Naph. 8.4. See also Alexander, "Demonology."
32. Morna D. Hooker, *The Gospel according to Saint Mark*, BNTC 2 (London: A&C Black, 1991), 50–51.

The Satan in Mark 3

The next occurrence of the satan figure is found in Mark 3:20–27, which presents the incident of Beelzeboul, but in a different context to that of Matthew 12. The Markan Beelzeboul account may represent another testing of Jesus, but this time by those who are blinded by their own self-righteousness or lack of divine knowledge of Christ's identity.[33] In Mark 3:19, Jesus has met with his disciples, but a crowd has gathered; for some unspoken reason, people are saying he is out of his mind (a common characteristic of demon possession),[34] which causes his family to go and restrain him. It is at this point that the author states that the scribes accused Jesus of having Beelzeboul (βεελζεβοὺλ ἔχει—similar terminology used when a person is possessed by a demon: "he has a demon") and that by the ruler of demons (ἄρχοντι τῶν δαιμονίων), he cast out demons (ἐκβάλλει τὰ δαιμόνια). What is intriguing is that if the satan figure has such a strong presence in the demonic realm, why did the scribes not accuse Jesus of "having satan"? It is likely that Beelzeboul is a demon and not the satan figure, although this is a rare naming of a demon in the NT, whereas it is often present in 2TP Jewish literature (see, e.g., T. Sol., although the date is uncertain).[35] The author of Mark does not make the clear connection between Beelzeboul and the "ruler of demons," although it could possibly be implied.[36] In addition, in 3:23, he states that Jesus "spoke to them in [five] parables," which suggests he is not being literal. He states, "How can satan cast out satan?" Interestingly, in Mark 3:23 there is no definite article present with the terms σατανᾶς or σατανᾶν, unlike in Matthew 12, which includes the article in both cases. This may suggest that Mark understands the term *satan* to mean simply an "adversary" and not the proper name of the so-called "chief of the evil spirits." Syriac Peshitta does not include a definite article here in either reference to satan, which

---

33. The testing of the righteous is a feature of Jewish wisdom texts in the 2TP: for example, book of Job, Testament of Job, Wisdom of Solomon. Wis 2:13–20 reveals the actions of the wicked in trapping the righteous person: "He [the righteous one] professes to have knowledge of God and calls himself a servant of the Lord . . . the very sight of him is a burden to us, because his manner of life is unlike that of others . . . and he boasts that God is his father. Let us test him with insult and torture that we may find out how gentle he is and make trial of his patience." The passage goes on to say that those who would test the righteous "were led astray, for their wickedness blinded them"; this may indicate that those testing the individual, in the case of Jews in Mark 3, were being led astray by the chief of the evil spirits, in this case Beelzeboul. Cf. Luke 11:16; Matt 16:1; 19:3; 22:18 in which the Pharisees and Sadducees test Jesus in his calling as Messiah (πειράζοντες, or a form of it—same term used with the testing of Jesus by satan in the wilderness). This may suggest that the satan figure is behind their actions and reflect the "more opportune time" mentioned in Luke 4:13.
34. Archie T. Wright, "The Book of Watchers: 1 Enoch 1–36 as a Background for the Demonic Pericopes in the Gospels," *Henoch* 28 (2006): 189–207.
35. In the Testament of Solomon, Beelzeboul confesses that he was "a holy angel among those of the first rank," likely an archangel or one of the Fallen Watchers of the Enoch tradition, although the name is not among those of the Watchers listed in 1 Enoch.
36. See notes on Beelzeboul in the section on Matt 12 above. The term may be related to the Semitic deity Baal Zebul (בעל זבל), "Baal the Prince," although the deity in first-century Palestine has been demoted to a demon in the Synoptics. See Collins, *Mark*, 229–30.

infers no proper name and may suggest simply "adversary" in both instances. As in Matthew, this could be understood as "How can an adversary cast out an adversary?" Why would an adversary fight against himself? The comparable examples he continues with suggest a similar use—"kingdom against kingdom," "house against house"—until verse 3:26, which reads, "εἰ ὁ σατανᾶς ἀνέστη ἐφ' ἑαυτὸν," translated as "if the satan rises up against himself," "being divided, he is not able to stand, but has an end." Jesus is not suggesting that satan is actually doing this, as the scribes suggest; rather, if he was, it would be counterproductive to his task. There is an implied notion in verses 24–26 that the satan figure has a kingdom, but this is a result of the rhetorical language Jesus uses in describing the illogic of the scribes' statements. However, if one sets the satan alongside Belial from the DSS, then one could compare the language of "kingdom of satan" with the "dominion of Belial" in 1QS and 1QM. *Dominion* does only mean rule or authority not necessarily as a kingdom in the sense of the Kingdom of God. One might ask why the author of Mark chooses not to use the definite article with σατανᾶς in 3:23 but does in 3:26, ὁ σατανᾶς; as is the case in Matthew 12, the satan figure here could be understood as "the adversary" or "an adversary" or both—an adversary in verse 23 and "the Adversary" in verse 26.[37]

In verse 27, Jesus returns to figurative language, speaking of a strong man and his house. Jesus states that the adversary can only be overcome when he is first bound (spiritually?); only then can those in his captivity be set free. He is making clear that he has come to bind the spirits in the demonic realm, the house of the strong man / the satan; *binding* is a common term used in taking control of creatures or beings in the demonic world (see 1 En. 10.4; Jub. 10.5–11; 48.15–19; Tob 8:3). The question is, When did Jesus actually bind the satan figure if the exorcisms are considered taking the strongman's goods? This may not have occurred yet; the author may be speaking of a future event in which satan is bound by the actions of Jesus, perhaps at the resurrection and ascension.

The Satan in Mark 4

In Mark 4:15, the satan figure appears in the Parable of the Sower, which, as in Matthew, Jesus is asked to explain to his disciples. Jesus seems appalled that the disciples do not know the meaning of the parable, but he does explain it to them even though they are supposed to

---

37. Mark does not include Jesus's question about how the exorcists among the Pharisees cast out demons, nor does he tell the Pharisees how he casts out demons as in Matthew: "But if it is by the Spirit of God that I cast out demons, then the Kingdom of God has come to you." This could also be expressed in a contrasting statement: "If it is by Beelzeboul that I cast out demons, then the kingdom of Beelzeboul has come to you"; if stated this way, one might infer there is a kingdom of the ruler of demons.

know the "mystery of the kingdom of God." In 4:15, Jesus identifies "these ones" (οὗτοι)³⁸ as those who are outside of the kingdom (4:11)—they hear the word sown but once heard, the satan (ὁ σατανᾶς) comes and takes away the word sown in them (here the satan is still active in his task, unlike 3:27).

When Jesus is telling the parable to the crowd in 4:4, he states, "And as he sowed, some seed fell on the path, and the birds came and ate it up." In explaining the parable to the disciples, the birds are replaced by the satan figure. In Jewish apocalyptic literature, it was a common motif that birds represented evil or possibly evil spirits.³⁹ In Jubilees 11.11–14, Mastema, who is paralleled with satan, sends birds to eat the seed that is being planted on the earth in order to spoil the work of humanity; this may suggest the birds in the parable are sent by the satan. Each result of the "sowing" represents ways in which people, by persecution and the cares/pleasures of this world, could be distracted by the Adversary from following God's will and purpose. This may be accomplished by persuading them to change their commitment to following the Lord through the actions of others. Those who avoid the distractions of the satan figure are successful (v. 20). If this is the case, then one might argue this being is similar to the Mastema figure in Jubilees, who is working under God's authority to test individuals.

The Satan in Mark 8

Mark 8:33 presents the pericope of Jesus's teaching concerning the suffering the Son of Man *must* undertake: be rejected by the elders, the chief priests, and the scribes; be killed, and arise from the dead after three days. The term δεῖ ("must," "it is necessary") indicates the emphatic nature of the events, suggesting they are part of the divine will for Christ.⁴⁰ From what follows, one might deduce that Peter understands that Jesus is the Son of Man, which, according to 8:29, can be understood to mean he is the Messiah. Immediately after hearing what will happen to the Son of Man, Peter makes an effort to stop Jesus from going on this path.⁴¹ He takes Jesus aside and rebukes him for suggesting such a plan. It appears that Peter is not able to comprehend how the Messiah, or the Son of Man, would have to suffer death at the hands of some of the Jewish leadership and the Romans. Adela Collins suggests that

---

38. The use of demonstrative pronouns is common in 2TP apocalyptic literature, interpretations of dreams, Daniel, and the DSS. See Collins, *Mark*, 252.
39. See, for example, 1 En. 90.6–13. In Apoc. Abr. 13.2–8, an unclean bird speaks to Abraham, trying to persuade him to leave the side of the angel Iaoel; see also Rev 18:2.
40. See Hooker, *Saint Mark*, 206.
41. Garrett, *Temptations of Jesus*, 70, contends the disciples in Mark's Gospel are not the most cooperative of "friends" to Jesus, continually "trying his patience": "Judas betrays him; Peter denies him; in Gethsemane the disciples fall asleep; at Jesus' arrest they all flee." Garrett suggests that Peter, among others, is an "agent of trial" for the ministry of Jesus; whether the "agency" is diabolical in nature is not clear.

Peter has the messianic expectation of a Davidic Messiah in mind, one who would defeat the Romans and others in order to reinstate the kingdom of Israel, but Jesus is not interested in reinstating that kingdom; rather, he is bringing about the Kingdom of God/Heaven.[42] However, despite Peter's motives for denouncing these plans, Jesus turns the table on Peter and rebukes him with the famous words, "Get behind me, satan." This is a fairly strong rebuke made in front of the other disciples, perhaps suggesting it is directed to them also. The phrase "ὕπαγε ὀπίσω μου" (get behind me!) suggests that Peter needs to get back in line and follow after Jesus. The phrase "after me" (ὀπίσω μου) is used in verse 34, in this case for those who wish to be disciples of Christ (see 8:34–9:1). In verse 33, again, Mark omits the definite article with the term *satan*, σατανᾶ, which may allow this to be read simply as "adversary," as in a human adversary,[43] for Peter has his mind on the human concepts of the Messiah and not on those of God—his own expectations of the Messiah and not God's.[44]

Summary of Gospel of Mark

The author of Mark appears to use the term *satan* as an adversary, both human and perhaps heavenly. He also presents the satan as the one who tests individuals with the authority of God as in the case of Jesus in the Wilderness. In Mark 3, he may be making a connection between the satan and the ruler of the demons, Beelzeboul, but it is not clear if that is the case.

GOSPEL OF LUKE

The term σατανᾶς occurs five times in the Gospel of Luke, while διάβολος or a form of it also occurs five times (once as διαβόλου).[45]

The Devil in Luke 4

The first occurrence of διάβολος is found in 4:2, the "Trial in the Wilderness" in which Jesus is being tested (πειραζόμενος)[46] by the devil (ὑπὸ τοῦ διαβόλου) in the wilderness

---

42. Collins, *Mark*, 402–7.
43. See Craig A. Evans, *Mark 8:27–16:20*, WBC 3B (Nashville: Thomas Nelson, 2001), 19.
44. The wife of Job in the Testament of Job is said to be influenced by the satan figure to persuade Job to turn from the path God has for him. We are told in T. Job 23.11 that satan followed her along the path and was leading her astray. When she addresses Job, she tries to convince him to "speak some word against the Lord and die." This does not necessarily suggest that Peter is acting as the proxy of satan, as in the case of Job's wife; rather, he may simply be acting as an adversary to God's plan.
45. Satan: Luke 10:18, accu. m. s. w/ DA; 11:18; 13:16; 22:31, nom. m. s. w/ DA; 22:3, nom. m. s. w/o DA; devil: Luke 4:2, gen. m. s. w/ DA; 4:3, 6, 13; 8:12 w/ DA.
46. Joseph Fitzmyer contends that the verb for "test" can be used in the sense of "sinister intention," as in Acts 5:9 and 15:10. The devil is attempting to "frustrate the divine plan of salvation" rather than simply testing the faith of the Son of God; see Joseph A. Fitzmyer, *The Gospel according to Luke (I–IX)*, ABC 28 (New York: Doubleday, 1970), 514.

trial.⁴⁷ The figure here could fit very well with the satan figure found in Job and other occurrences we have discussed previously.⁴⁸ The Lucan wilderness pericope states that during the forty days⁴⁹ of the "trial," Jesus fasted from food, and during the fast, he was approached by the devil, who with various questions was testing Jesus's faith to complete his task as Messiah and obedience to God. François Bovon suggests that forty days was the "standard length of time for receiving divine revelation" in the Jewish tradition. In addition, he notes that the forty days should be linked with the "was led" (by the spirit) rather than the "was tested/tempted" participle. Thus, the forty days is connected to receiving the revelation from God (of his task?) rather than the length of the testing by the devil.

The next two occurrences of the term, in 4:3 and 6, offer tests from ὁ διάβολος, the first perhaps challenging Jesus's obedience in the role as the Son of God: "Since (or if) you are the Son of God, speak to this stone, in order that it may become bread." It appears that the devil is not questioning "if" Jesus is the "Son of God"; rather, the issues appear to be related to the power that the Messiah can demonstrate—"since you are."⁵⁰ This may suggest the devil expects some sort of "magical" power to be put on display by Jesus, but Jesus replies citing Scripture: "It has been written, 'One will not live by bread alone.'" Jesus does not appear interested in putting that power on display; he demonstrates his obedience to and reliance on the Torah as his defense. His reliance on Scripture may be an echo of the account in CD 16 from Qumran, which states that if a man turns to the Torah, then Belial must flee.

The second test concerns what may be understood as a challenge to the power and authority of God over all creation. After showing Jesus all the kingdoms of the inhabited world, the devil offers glory and authority over these kingdoms to him; all Jesus has to do is worship the devil. This statement by the devil likely reflects Luke's view of the figure as the "ruler of this world," that is the inhabited world (τῆς οἰκουμένης).⁵¹ However, within the context of the passage, these appear to be human kingdoms and not a "Kingdom of Darkness" belonging specifically to the

---

47. There is no use of "the tester" as in Matt 4. Luke also uses the preposition that could be read as "brought in" (ἤγετο ἐν) the spirit rather than "taken up . . . by" (ἀνήχθη . . . ὑπὸ) the spirit in Matthew. However, with both verbs, "passive" suggests a translation of "by" or "by means of" in both cases; see John Nolland, *Luke 1–9:20*, WBC 35A (Dallas: Word Books, 1989), 178.
48. Some have compared the temptations of Jesus with the temptations of Belial in the Damascus Document 4.12–19, in which he attempts to trap Israel in the "three nets of Belial"; see A. Dupont-Sommer, *The Essene Writings from Qumran*, trans. G. Vermes (Oxford: Blackwell, 1961), 128.
49. See Bovon, *Luke 1*, 142–43.
50. See Bovon, 143.
51. Matt 4:8 identifies them as "kingdoms of the Cosmos" (τὰς βασιλείας τοῦ κόσμου), perhaps suggesting also kingdoms other than the inhabited world—for example, spirit realms. Some scholars suggest an allusion may be found in Rev 13:7, which states that the "Beast" (not satan) is given authority over every nation; see Susan R. Garrett, *The Demise of the Devil: Magic and the Demonic in Luke's Writings* (Minneapolis: Fortress, 1989), 38.

devil. He likely wields authority over the rulers of these earthly kingdoms through the king's choice to reject God's authority and allow the devil's authority. The enticement offered to Jesus cannot be these human kingdoms; rather, the temptation is to be king by compromising with the forces that currently are in control without the authority of God.[52] The devil in Luke 4 has somehow been given authority in the human realm, which reflects a similar authority granted to the satan figure in the HB in Job 1–2; Zechariah 3:1; and 1 Chronicles 21:1 to test and try the will of humanity, or in the case of Luke, the kings of the nations. The task of the devil in Luke 4 falls into one of his primary functions understood thus far in our examination: he tests individuals, he accuses individuals of not being true to YHWH, and he attempts to lead various individuals astray from the path YHWH has set for them.[53] But Christ again responds with Scripture in 4:8: "It has been written, you will worship the Lord your God and serve him only."[54] Both responses from Jesus suggested the Torah of God was and is firmly established, cannot be moved, and certainly should not be rejected.

It is implied in Luke 4:9 that the devil then takes Jesus to Jerusalem, although the term for *devil* (ὁ διάβολος) is not in the text. He once again challenges Jesus concerning his role as the Son of God. In this test it is the devil who cites Scripture in 4:10–11; interestingly, he uses the perfect passive verb form, "It has been written," when citing Psalm 91:11–12 rather than trying to "trick" Jesus. Jesus responds quite differently in 4:12 than he did in the previous attempts. He states, "It has been said, 'You will not test the Lord your God,'" perhaps suggesting this is an oral tradition rather than written Scripture, although it is a portion of Deuteronomy 6:16. One might ask if this significant change in response is an allusion to the divinity of Jesus. Jesus's responses in each of the tests reveal one weakness in the work of the devil: he cannot force individuals to make poor choices.

Luke 4:13 has been regularly translated, "When the devil finished every test, he departed," but in the context of verse 4:12, it may be suggested that Jesus is the subject of the participle συντελέσας, an aorist active participle, "after finishing." If so, then 4:13 may be better translated, "After [Jesus] finished every test, the devil departed from *him* [Jesus] until an[other] opportunity." If this is considered a plausible translation, then one might suggest this was a permitted testing that had been "prearranged" for Jesus. The results of the testing of Jesus in the

---

52. See Nolland, *Luke 1–9:20*, 180.
53. See Garrett, *Demise*, 39n12. See, for example, "testing": T. Job 4.4–9; Jub. 10.7–9; 17.16; 1 Cor 7:5; "accusing": Jub. 1.20; 48.15; MartyrIsa 3.6; 5.2–3; "leading astray": Jub. 11.4–5; 22.16–17; MartyrIsa 1.9; 2.4; T. Job 2.2–3.5; CD 12.2b–3; LAE 9.1–11.3; T. Job 23.11; 26.6. Several instances suggest that the/a satan figure takes this authority too far in his attempts to fulfill his task: Apoc. Abr. 13.9–13; 23.11–13; T. Job 8.1–3; 16.2, 4; 20.1–3.
54. The Greek *Textus Receptus* inserts a familiar phrase preceding "It has been written" that reflects Mark 8:33, "ὕπαγε ὀπίσω μου σατανᾶ"—"get behind me satan," which certainly appears to be a gloss.

wilderness reveal the beginning of the end of the authority of the satan figure over humanity and the earth: Jesus serves as the example of how one should react to a test or trial. Luke's account offers hope to the righteous concerning the problem of evil: through the adherence to the Torah by the guidance and empowerment of the Holy Spirit one can overcome the tests of satan.[55]

The Devil in Luke 8

The final occurrence of ὁ διάβολος appears in Luke 8:12. Jesus is explaining the Parable of the Sower to his disciples, and in doing so, he explains that some have heard the word (the seed), the message of the Kingdom, but once hearing it, the devil comes and takes up the word from their hearts. This action by the devil is certainly in line with other chief evil figures attempting to turn people away from God and the Torah. If so, one might suggest the devil here may be acting in that role; whether he is the same figure is questionable, but it certainly could be considered the same function or role performed by other "evil figures." What follows with the rest of the individuals in the parable suggests similar actions being done by this figure. In 8:13, the people are falling away (ἀφίστανται) in the time of "testing" (πειρασμοῦ); the next group in 8:14 fall away after being overcome by the pleasures of this world; both of these causes could be linked to the function of the chief evil character in 2TP Judaism and the "three traps of Belial." However, Luke 8:15 suggests a realm of protection for those who hold fast to the word, Torah; there is no place for the devil to attack them.

The Satan in Luke 10

The satan figure first appears in Luke 10:18 in one of the more troublesome verses concerning his position in the heavenly and earthly realms.[56] Many interpret this verse as the "fall of satan from Heaven," but this understanding of the satan figure, which is derived from an interpretation of Isaiah 14 and Ezekiel 28 (and possibly the tradition behind John's Apocalypse 12), does not appear a prominent concept previous to or during the time of Jesus ministry.[57] This may mean that imparting the story of the immediate fall of the satan figure is not Jesus's intention; rather, he is emphasizing the disciples' power over evil spirits to afflict and oppress humanity,

---

55. Cf. T. Job 27:2–6; *Hermas Mandate* 12.5.2; 1 Pet 5:9; Jas 4:7.
56. See Simon Gathercole, "Jesus' Eschatological Vision of the Fall of Satan: Luke 10, 18 Reconsidered," *ZNW* 94, nos. 3–4 (2003): 143–63.
57. In François Bovon, *Luke 2: A Commentary on the Gospel of Luke 9:51–19:27*, Hermeneia (Minneapolis: Fortress, 2013), 31, Bovon contends that Isa 14:12–14 was understood to speak of the fall of satan, citing the work of Armand Puig Tàrrech, "LC 10, 18: La Visió de la Caiguda de satanàs," *Revista Caralana de Teologia* 3 (1978): 217–43 (in Catalanese). Puig Tàrrech attempts to make connections between the satan and the Fallen Watchers of Enochic traditions, though, as mentioned previously, the Book of Watchers does not make that connection—there is no satan mentioned in the Enoch texts that would precede the Gospel of Luke.

which suggests the beginning of the end of the influence of the satan and his minions (cf. Rev 12:7–18). We know from Jubilees that the satan figure (Mastema) had evil spirits, presumably the same evil spirits we see in the Gospels,[58] operating under his authority; thus, their defeat signals the beginning of the end of the power or task of the satan.

In 10:2, Jesus dispatches the disciples in the region to spread the news of the Kingdom, but in doing so, he warns them of the pitfalls that they may face: "You will be as lambs among wolves" (10:3). In verse 9, he suggests they will heal the sick (through prayer?), but there is no mention of the casting out of evil spirits that the disciples proclaim in verse 17, although the issue of healing may be connected to exorcism.[59] He then proclaims doom upon those locales that do not accept the message of the Kingdom (10:11) and draws parallels to other cities (Chorazin, Bethsaida, Capernaum) that have refused to accept God's message with Sodom, Tyre, and Sidon. In what is a decidedly apocalyptic scene, verse 10:17 may be the key to understanding 10:18. The disciples proclaim in verse 17 that the demons (τὰ δαιμόνια) submit to the authority of the name of Christ (ὑποτάσσεται),[60] suggesting perhaps the notion of Christ's divinity or at least the use of the divine name over them.

In 10:18, Christ states, "I was watching[61] the satan (τὸν σατανᾶν) while (he was) falling from heaven like a bolt of lightning."[62] Fitzmyer suggests a reading of the Greek that clears up some of the ambiguity of the verse. There are several variant readings of the Greek, but the majority reading, "I was watching satan like lightning falling from heaven" (ἐθεώρουν τὸν σατανᾶν ὡς ἀστραπὴν ἐκ τοῦ οὐρανοῦ πεσόντα), offers a clearer picture to the action that is occurring. In this Greek version, it is the lightning that "is falling from heaven" rather than the satan figure.[63] This removes the question of the chronology of the "fall of satan" and puts the focus on the beginning of his loss of power with the emergence of the ministry of Jesus and the disciples.

---

58. Archie T. Wright, "Evil Spirits in Second Temple Judaism: The *Watcher Tradition* as a Background to the Demonic Pericopes in the Gospels," *Henoch* 28, no. 1 (2006): 189–207.
59. Graham H. Twelftree, *Jesus the Exorcist: A Contribution to the Study of the Historical Jesus* (Eugene, OR: Wipf & Stock, 2011).
60. The verb is a present passive indicative third singular, "being submissive," but the subject is nominative neuter plural, which may suggest this is considered a collective subject: the demonic realm.
61. The reading of this verb has resulted in several proposals: (1) Jesus saw the fall of satan in his own preexistent state, prior to the incarnation; (2) the subject of the verb is actually the demons from 10:17; or (3) Jesus is giving a prophetic vision of the fall of the satan in the eschaton. See, for example, Ulrich B. Müller, "Vision und Botschaft: Erwägungen zur prophetischen Struktur der Verkündigung Jesu," *ZThK* 74 (1977): 416–48; Joseph A. Fitzmyer, *Luke the Theologian: Aspects of His Teaching* (London: Paulist, 1989), 164–69.
62. Garrett, *Demise*, 51; Garrett contends that the vision of the satan's fall "will be fulfilled between this point in Jesus' earthly ministry and the time of the birth of the church as depicted in Acts." She suggests a further option for the satan's demise is the resurrection and ascension of Jesus, at which time his divine sonship is made manifest (Acts 13:32–33).
63. Joseph A. Fitzmyer, *The Gospel according to Luke X–XXIV*, ABC 28A (New Haven, CT: Yale University Press, 1985), 861n18.

The imperfect active indicative verb for "watching" (ἐθεώρουν)[64] suggests a vision of the ongoing action of the figure falling (losing his authority),[65] perhaps as the disciples are out declaring the coming of the Kingdom of God and casting out demons.[66] Fitzmyer argues this should not be understood as an ecstatic vision of the fall of satan but as a symbolic image of the work accomplished by the disciples.[67] With the use of the aorist active participle ("falling," but as a punctiliar action), the author is likely referring to the final action (or authority to act) of the satan figure.[68] However, the author may be suggesting this is the beginning of the end of the authority granted to the satan figure in his role as tester and oppressor of the people; as such, he continues to work until his authority to act comes to an end in the eschaton.[69] Samuel Vollenweider contends that the threatening rule of the satan figure is coming to an end with the arrival of the Kingdom of God.[70]

However, it does not make sense to suggest this is the ultimate end of the satan figure and his role as adversary, as we are told he still functions in this role in Luke 22.[71] Mark 13:19–22 further maintains that leading up to the final end of evil, "a time of oppression will take place that has not happened since the beginning of creation" (cf. Luke 21:25–27).[72] In addition, Revelation 12:12 states, "The devil [ὁ διάβολος] came down to you having great wrath, while knowing that he has little time."[73] The Luke 10 text and the Revelation 12 text should be understood as a present happening and a future happening concerning the fall of satan, perhaps suggesting his power is weakening over time until the end.[74] One must keep in mind the possible apocalyptic

---

64. The verb ἐθεώρουν or a form of it is used in the LXX OT to speak of visionary experiences describing events that will take place in the future, such as in Dan 4:13; 7:2, 4, 6, 7, 9, 11, 13, 21; cf. 1 En. 1.2.
65. Kelley suggests this "falling from heaven" should be understood as "diminution in his power; and at His [Christ's] second coming Christ will completely subdue him." Kelley, "Devil in the Desert," 205–6.
66. Cf. William Manson, *The Gospel of Luke* (London: Hodder & Stoughton, 1930), 126. T. Levi 18.12 provides a possible parallel that supports the ability of the disciples to cast out evil spirits: "And Belial will be bound by him [Messiah], and he will give authority to his children to trample upon evil spirits." This would suggest that Christ has at some point in his ministry bound up the satan.
67. Fitzmyer, *Luke X–XXIV*, 860.
68. John Nolland, *Luke 9:21–18:34*, WBC 35B (Nashville: Thomas Nelson, 1993), 563.
69. Edward Langton argues that 10:18 is not referring to the direct fall of the satan but to the casting out of demons as the beginning of the end of his powers; see his *Essentials of Demonology* (London: Epworth, 1949), 170. See also Gathercole, "Jesus' Eschatological Vision," 2.
70. Samuel Vollenweider, *Ich sah den satan wie einen Blitz vom Himmel fallen (Lk 10:18)*, WUNT 144 (Tübingen, Germany: Mohr Siebeck, 2002), 190–200.
71. See Gathercole, "Jesus' Eschatological Vision," 10.
72. Echoes of the Jewish tradition of the final conflict between God and the primary figure of evil, in this case the satan, are reflected in the passage: for example, 1QM 15–17; 11Q13 13–14; T. Levi 18.12; T. Dan 5.10; T. Jud. 25:3.
73. Gathercole, "Jesus' Eschatological Vision," 13, notes a possible parallel in T. Sol 20.16–17, in which the demon Ornias states that demons are "dropped like flashes of lightning to the earth" and they appear like "stars falling from heaven." Gathercole rightly notes the difficulty of heavy Christian redaction in T. Sol, which could have knowledge of the Luke 10 and Rev 12 passages.
74. See Alfred Wikenhauser, *Die Offenbarung des Johannes*, RegensNT 9 (Regensburg, Germany: Pustet, 1959), 96.

nature of 10:17–20 as a visionary report and tread carefully in its interpretation. As Fitzmyer notes, it could be symbolic of the work of the disciples, or it could be understood as an event in the immediate future, but certainly an event that God has planned.[75]

The Satan in Luke 11

The second reference to the satan is in 11:18 (cf. Matt 12:22–30; Mark 3:22–27) in the context of the Beelzeboul incident in which the scribes accuse Jesus of casting out evil spirits under the authority of Beelzeboul, who may be identified as one of the "chief" evil beings in 2TP Judaism. In Luke 11:14, Jesus is casting out a demon from a deaf person, which amazes the crowds of people. The pericope suggests three groups emerge out of the crowd of those watching: some marvel at the exorcism, recognizing the power of God, and others test Jesus (a satanic task) by asking him to perform a sign from heaven, while a third group (in Matt 12:23, Pharisees) accuses him of casting out the demon through Beelzeboul, the ruler of demons (τῷ ἄρχοντι τῶν δαιμονίων), who apparently is a member of the demonic hierarchy that is present in 2TP Jewish demonology (see T. Sol.). No one doubts the reality of the exorcism of the demon; under whose authority Jesus is operating is the question.

The chronology of the passage implies that his response in 11:17 is directed at those who are asking for a sign from heaven in verse 16; Jesus responds stating that division within a kingdom will cause that kingdom to become desolate. In 11:18, he states if ὁ σατανᾶς is divided against himself, how will his kingdom stand (this does not require ὁ σατανᾶς to be "*the* satan")? As suggested earlier, in this context ὁ σατανᾶς could be understood to be an adversary of the kingdom or the Adversary, the chief of the evil spirits (e.g., Belial), which would make sense with the previous mention of Beelzeboul. He then questions if Beelzeboul is working against himself if Jesus is casting out demons with his power, by whom are your sons casting out (demons).[76] He suggests in verse 20 that he is casting out evil spirits by the finger of God (by the power and authority of God—the sign from heaven?). Although the Luke 11 passage does not indicate the scale to which the satan is able to take over people's lives through possession, illness, or oppression, Luke, like some of his contemporaries, indicates that the introduction of the Messiah marked the beginning of the end of this figure's authority to function on the earth (Luke 11:22; 4:31–37).

---

75. Cf. Amos 8:1–2; Isa 6; Jer 1:13–19; Ezek 2:9–10. See Nolland, *Luke 1–9:20*, 563–64.
76. See, for example, 1 Sam 16:14–23; Luke 9:49–50; Acts 19:13–17; Josephus, *Ant.* 8.2.5.46; *Bell.* 7.6.3.185; 1QapGen 20.29.

The Satan in Luke 13

The next reference to ὁ σατανᾶς occurs in Luke 13:16, in the story of the woman who has been bent over for eighteen years, whom Jesus heals on the Sabbath, an event reported only by Luke. The focus of the pericope is on keeping the Sabbath and not on who or what has bound the daughter of Abraham for eighteen years. The leader of the synagogue and others complain about his actions. Jesus responds calling them hypocrites and explains that the woman who has been bound by ὁ σατανᾶς deserves to be set free, even on the Sabbath. The action by the satan figure portrays something not often seen in the NT; the affliction of a person is usually accomplished through the actions of an evil or unclean spirit, but here it presumes direct affliction by the satan. The description here may be implying that it is ultimately the satan who is responsible for her affliction, but it was likely caused by one of the spirits under his authority.[77] Setting aside the issue of responsibility, the pericope reveals the power and authority that Jesus is operating under—the authority of God by the laying on of hands. The author suggests that with each encounter with the satan figure or the devil, the authority of the ruler of the evil spirits is being reduced and will ultimately come to an end.

The Satan in Luke 22

Luke 22:3 presents a quite different episode than previously encountered with ὁ σατανᾶς. The term occurs here without the definite article (σατανᾶς). The pericope concerns the betrayal of Jesus by Judas Iscariot. We are told in 22:3 that a σατανᾶς entered (εἰσῆλθεν) Judas, perhaps suggesting some kind of spiritual possession,[78] which apparently caused Judas to go the chief priests and betray Jesus. Bovon suggests that the argument has moved beyond the leaders of Israel and Jesus to a conflict between the satan and God.[79] However, the Gospel to this point has shown the attempts of the Sanhedrin to remove Jesus from the scene, perhaps under the influence of the satan; in this story, they now have an insider to assist them. According to the various passages that describe "demonic possession," Judas does not present any of the usual symptoms. The language used in Luke 4:33 indicates the individual "has a spirit of an unclean demon,"[80] language that is absent in the Luke 22:3 passage. A "possessed" individual would exhibit several characteristics such as crying out with a loud voice, some sort of physical affliction, or an

---

77. Langton suggests the language of being bound, ἣν ἔδησεν, may indicate "possession," but the question would remain by what spirit; see Langton, *Essentials*, 169.
78. We see this with the Beliar figure, a possible equivalent to a satan, in the Martyrdom of Isaiah 3.11, in which he "dwelt in the heart of Manasseh and in the heart of the princes of Judah."
79. François Bovon, *Luke 3: A Commentary on the Gospel of Luke 19:28–24:53*, Hermeneia (Minneapolis: Fortress, 2012), 135–36.
80. Also Luke 6:18: "troubled by an unclean spirit."

inability to socially function with others.[81] If one is to accept that this is the satan figure previously identified in the NT, then this is the only incident in which the figure takes possession of a human being. Nolland argues that the language here "should not be confused with demon possession."[82] He suggests the possession is likely related to the concept of the "two spirits" from 1QS 3:13–4:25; however, the Luke passage reflects no such language. One might argue the circumstances of the task required no less than the chief of the evil spirits to carry out the possession of Judas—no lower-level spirit could be trusted—but the lack of the definite article leaves the door open for some other explanation. Perhaps this is only an adversarial spirit that has taken possession of Judas's thoughts, which stirs up in him his messianic expectations of a warrior figure who will rise up against the Romans; by betraying Jesus, he might believe this will cause Jesus to make that move.

The final reference to ὁ σατανᾶς in Luke 22:31 offers support for the satan figure functioning like the satan in the book of Job and as the heavenly prosecutor in Zechariah 3.[83] While listening to a discussion among the disciples about who shall be the greatest among them (perhaps part of the sifting), Jesus tells them that each must humble himself as a servant in order to sit at the table in the Lord's Kingdom. In 22:31, Jesus tells Peter (calling him, "*Simon, Simon*," but the warning is directed at all the disciples—ὑμᾶς) that the satan figure desires to sift them like wheat; this is a request from the satan to the Lord. As such, it establishes a place for him in the hierarchy of God's governmental system in the cosmos. The satan's hope, as in Job, is to uncover the lack of true devotion of the disciples to God. Jesus also tells him that he has prayed for him so that he might not completely fail the test (22:32). Peter responds that he is ready to die alongside Jesus, but Jesus tells him that in the test, he will deny Jesus three times. This pericope reflects the actions of the Mastema figure in Jubilees 17 when he suggests to God that he needs to test the love and faith of Abraham with the sacrifice of Isaac. From this story, one might suggest there are multiple traditions at work in the writings of Luke concerning the satan figure. One in particular that stands out is the apparent possession of Judas Iscariot by a satan, something not previously seen in extant literature.

---

81. Signs of possession include convulsions, foaming at the mouth, raving, grinding teeth, and abnormal strength. See Archie T. Wright, "The Demonology of 1 Enoch and the New Testament Gospels," in *Enoch and the Synoptic Gospels: Reminiscences, Allusions, Intertextuality*, ed. Loren T. Stuckenbruck and Gabriele Boccaccini (Atlanta: SBL, 2016), 215–44.
82. John Nolland, *Luke 18:35–24:53*, WBC 35C (Nashville: Thomas Nelson, 1993), 1029.
83. See Langton, *Essentials*, 169.

Summary of Gospel of Luke

The Gospel of Luke appears to use the terms *satan* and *devil* synonymously. The devil is identified as the one who tests the faith of individuals beginning with the testing of Jesus in the Wilderness. This appears to be one of the primary purposes of the satan/devil figure in the Gospels, which follows the model set out in significant texts from the 2TP. The Synoptic accounts of this trial suggest that this was a prearranged episode that was instigated by the Holy Spirit in driving Jesus into the wilderness to meet the satan/devil figure (see Luke 4:13). Similar functions or roles for the figure are seen in Luke 8 and the Parable of the Sower, which indicates the key to overcoming the trials set before us is holding fast to the Torah. Luke 10 contains one of the more enigmatic passages concerning the satan figure, which describes Jesus's vision of the satan falling from the heavens like lightning. As we read, Fitzmyer suggested this vision describes the beginning of the end of the power and authority granted to the satan figure on the earth. In Luke 11, we saw the introduction of another name for what appears to be a supernatural evil being who is thought to be a ruler of evil spirits on the earth—Beelzeboul. Jesus is accused of operating under the authority of this being when he is casting out demons, but of course he is able to turn the tables on those questioning his authority from God as the Messiah, which a portion of the crowd apparently thought was his role. In Luke 13, we are offered an example, probably one of many that took place but were not recorded, of Jesus having authority over the power of the evil spirits at work in the lives of individuals: in this case, the woman who was healed on the Sabbath. Other pericopes in Luke 22 reveal the role of the satan figure as the tester of humanity in an attempt to move them off or even against the plan of God—for example, the treachery of Judas and the story of the satan requesting permission to sift or test the disciples concerning their faith.

GOSPEL OF JOHN

The satan/devil figure is somewhat aloof in John's Gospel. ὁ σατανᾶς appears only once, in John 13:27, and διάβολος appears once without the definite article in 6:70 and as τοῦ διαβόλου in 8:44 and 13:2.

The Devil in John 6

The pericope in which we find διάβολος, John 6:70, concerns Jesus being the bread of life (6:48) that came down from heaven, which some of the Jews found offensive. We are told that the Jews interpret this as Jesus giving his flesh to eat (6:52); Jesus appears to affirm this in 6:53–56. At this point, many of his disciples have difficulty with this teaching and depart from him; recognizing this, Jesus asks the twelve if they wished to leave him also. In 6:68–69, Peter responds that Jesus has the "words of eternal life" and that he is ὁ ἅγιος τοῦ θεοῦ, the "Holy One of God"; this suggests his messianic role. In 6:70, Jesus states that he chose them, but one of them is a διάβολος, with no definite article. This reference could be understood as "the devil," but as an anarthrous noun, it likely indicates simply an adversary who is going to betray him, whom Jesus identifies as Judas (6:71). This may be similar to Jesus's rebuke of Peter in Mark 8:33, in which he calls Peter an adversary (σατανᾶ); in this case, Judas also has the plans of man in mind; he sees Jesus as a militaristic Messiah rather than the Messiah within the plans of God.

The Devil in John 8

The next occurrence of "devil" appears in 8:44 as τοῦ διαβόλου.[84] The pericope, filled with deep theological issues not previously spoken by Jesus in the other Gospels, describes the discussion Jesus is having with the Jewish people concerning who their father is; they insist they are the children of Abraham, but Jesus says they are not acting like his children because they are trying to kill a man who is telling them the truth that comes from God (8:42). He then suggests they have a father other than Abraham; they respond that they are not born out of adultery (πορνείας), but they have one father, God (v. 41). In 8:44, Jesus then makes the accusation that "ὑμεῖς ἐκ πατρὸς τοῦ διαβόλου ἐστέ"[85] (you [yourselves] are from the father [who is] the devil); most translations read this as "your father the devil," but this can only be implied using the next phrase in the passage, "and the desires of *your* father you wish to do" (καὶ τάς ἐπιθυμίας τοῦ πατρὸς ὑμῶν θέλετε ποιεῖν). However, the contrast between "God the Father" and the "truth of God" makes it clear "your father the devil" is correct.

This parental language could be alluding to the "sons of Belial" ("sons of wickedness") discussed previously in various DSS. What follows is a description of the devil, which contains notions not previously assigned to him: "He was a murderer from the beginning" (John 8:44). Raymond Brown proposes that this phrase may be a reference to the murder of Abel by Cain (see the discussion that follows in chapter 7). The Targum of Genesis 5:3 claims that the father of Cain was the evil angel Samael who fathered Cain with Eve.[86] It is here in 8:44 that another well-known title is attributed to the satan figure—"because he is a liar and the father of it" (ὅτι ψεύστης ἐστὶν καὶ ὁ πατὴρ αὐτοῦ). What exactly the "it" is is unclear; perhaps it

---

84. The Peshitta uses the term ܐܟܠܩܪܨܐ (*ochelkartso*, "slanderer or liar"), not the expected ܣܛܢܐ, *satana*.
85. The United Bible Society Greek text reads, "ὑμεῖς ἐκ τοῦ πατρὸς τοῦ διαβόλου ἐστέ" (You are from your father the devil).
86. Raymond E. Brown, *The Gospel according to John (I–XII)*, ABC 29 (Garden City, NY: Doubleday, 1966), 358.

is the concept of lying in general or something specifically related to the countermessage of the Kingdom of God.

The satan certainly has been understood as a deceiver in multiple descriptions of the Chief of Evil in other literature; however, this deception was used primarily to test the faith of individuals or groups of people. This could be the understanding of the Jews accusing Jesus of lying—he is doing it to persuade the people to follow him rather than God. Throughout Jewish literature, in the role of tester or adversary, the satan figure has used deception to try to lead the faithful off the path God has set for them. Jesus accuses them of being part of the "lot of deception"; thus, they are followers of the satan. The Jews then respond with the accusation that Jesus is a Samaritan and he has a demon (8:48), perhaps trying to make the connection to the chief of evil spirits, Beelzeboul; he answers that he does not have a demon—he is not demon possessed. All of the accusations against him are a result of his teaching, which they apparently assume are all lies.

The Devil and the Satan in John 13

The final occurrence of τοῦ διαβόλου is found in John 13:2, which presents the Passover meal Jesus has with the disciples. The verse appears to be a side note to set up what will occur in due time in verse 13:27, which contains the only reference to ὁ σατανᾶς. Here, the author of John presents the notion that the devil had already placed deception in the heart of Judas—that is, the idea that he might hand over Jesus to the authorities.[87] This deception may be Judas's understanding of Jesus's messianic role as a militaristic Messiah. In a sense, we see the deceptive work of the devil preparing Judas to be an adversary to Jesus, following his own plan rather than God's plan for Jesus, which follows the primary role of the satan figure in the 2TP and portions of the NT. This reference to the deception of Judas by the devil perhaps suggests a spiritual influence upon Judas that will open the door for the satan figure to enter into him in 13:27.

The language of spiritual possession (εἰσῆλθεν εἰς ἐκεῖον ὁ σατανᾶς—the only use of the satan in John) occurs here in 13:27 as in Luke 22:3. The same phrase, εἰσῆλθεν εἰς ἐκεῖον, "entered into him," is found in the case of an evil spirit entering an individual in Mark 5:12 and Luke 8:30. As mentioned previously, there is limited evidence of the concept of the satan/devil figure possessing a human; however, the Martyrdom of Isaiah 3.11 suggests Beliar (a possible synonymous figure to the satan) "dwelt in the heart of Manasseh and in the heart of the princes of Judah," but this does not necessitate "possession" in the sense of demonic possession. As mentioned in the previous chapter, the preposition ἐν can mean "with" or "in." The John

---

87. C. K. Barrett suggests 13:2 should be read "The devil had already made up his mind that Judas should betray him [Jesus]." See C. K. Barrett, *The Gospel according to St John*, 2nd ed. (London: SPCK, 1978), 439.

13:27 text includes the definite article ὁ with σατανᾶς, unlike the occurrence in Luke 22:3, but it is difficult to determine what difference this makes to the interpretation of the verse and the concept of possession.

Summary of Gospel of John

The Gospel of John offers relatively little information concerning the satan/devil figure compared to what we see in the Synoptic Gospels. The term διάβολος is used to describe the role of humans as adversaries against Jesus's mission, as well as the apparent supernatural being. The other occurrences of διάβολος in the Gospel of John seem to identify the chief of the evil realm, who can afflict or influence individuals, similar to other instances of his appearance with one new feature: the possible possession by the satan figure of an individual (although the language may be read as "oppression" rather than "possession") in the story of the betrayal of Jesus by Judas.

Acts of the Apostles

Like Luke's Gospel, the author of the Acts of the Apostles refers to both ὁ σατανᾶς and τοῦ διαβόλου. The text contains two references to the satan, 5:3 (ὁ σατανᾶς) and 26:18 (τοῦ σατανᾶ), and two references to the devil, 10:38 (τοῦ διαβόλου) and 13:10 (υἱὲ διαβόλου, "son of an adversary/enemy/devil").

THE SATAN IN ACTS 5

The first instance of ὁ σατανᾶς in 5:3 recounts the story of Ananias and Sapphira, who have chosen to sell a property (apparently there is a commune lifestyle already at play in the first century; 4:34) but to keep some of the proceeds as a "nest egg." The apostle Peter, seemingly with spiritual discernment, accuses Ananias of lying to the Holy Spirit by withholding (ἐνουφίσατο, "to steal") part of the sale price. This deception has been instigated by the satan figure, who has filled their hearts to lie to the Holy Spirit and the community ("διατί ἐπλήρωσεν ὁ σατανᾶς τὴν καρδίαν σου, ψεύσασθαί σε τὸ πνεῦμα τὸ ἅγιον" [Why did the satan fill your heart (that caused) you to lie to the Holy Spirit?]). Luke emphasizes the role of satan as a deceiver who tests Ananias and Sapphira with the things of the world (cf. Luke 8:12—here, Luke uses the term *the devil*; cf. the "three traps of Belial").

THE SATAN IN ACTS 26

The second reference to ὁ σατανᾶς comes in Acts 26:18 when Paul is recounting the story of his conversion to become a follower of Christ while defending himself against the accusations of the Jews before King Agrippa. Jesus announces to Saul (Paul) the call God has put upon his life: he is to go to the Gentiles, from whom he is being rescued, in order "to open their eyes to turn from darkness to light and from the authority of the satan to God" (ἀνοῖξαι ὀφθαλμοὺς αὐτῶν, τοῦ καὶ ἐπιστρέψαι ἀπὸ σκότους εἰς φῶς καὶ τῆς ἐξουσίας τοῦ σατανᾶ ἐπὶ τὸν θεόν). Luke makes it clear that the satan figure has authority over the nations (Luke 4), and if they chose to turn to God, then they will be forgiven and will no longer be under the authority of satan (cf. CD 16).

THE DEVIL IN ACTS 10

The first mention of *devil* is found in 10:38, in which Peter recounts the story of the early days of Jesus's ministry following his baptism by John (interestingly, there is no mention of the Trial of Jesus in the Wilderness). Jesus has been anointed with the/a Holy Spirit and power (δυνάμει), by which "he went about doing good and healing all *who were under the power of the devil*" (τοὺς καταδυναστευομένους ὑπὸ τοῦ διαβόλου) There is no characterization of the devil's power present in the passage, other than that it required healing for those who were oppressed by it. This does suggest this power may have been used to keep people from God or to turn them away from God (see, e.g., Mark 5).[88]

THE DEVIL IN ACTS 13

The final reference to the devil occurs in 13:10, which describes the encounter Paul and Barnabas had with the magician Elymas. They are called before the Roman proconsul Sergius Paulus, who wanted to hear about the message of God (λόγου τοῦ θεοῦ). Elymas opposed them and tried to turn the proconsul from the faith. Paul called Elymas "a son of a devil" (υἱὲ διαβόλου), one who was full of deceit and wickedness. According to Paul, Elymas was attempting to pervert the ways of the Lord. The use of "son of a devil" may be a reference to those who are "sons of Belial" ("sons of wickedness") or members of the "lot of Belial" ("lot of wickedness") prominent in the DSS. They are used as adversaries to oppose those who wish to follow God's straight path

---

88. See, regarding demonic possession and exorcism in the NT context, Twelftree, "Exorcism"; Twelftree, *In the Name of Jesus: Exorcism among Early Christians* (Grand Rapids, MI: Baker, 2007); Amanda Witmer, *Jesus the Galilean Exorcist* (New York: T&T Clark, 2012).

(τὰς ὁδοὺς τοῦ κυρίου τὰς εὐθείας)—here, the very thing Elymas was attempting to pervert. From this encounter, one might suggest Paul is familiar with the tradition of Belial in 2TP texts.

Summary of Acts of the Apostles

As we have seen, there is limited use of the figure of satan/devil by Luke in the Acts of the Apostles. The Gospel accounts suggest a more prominent role for the figure in opposition to Jesus and his mission while on the earth, but beyond the resurrection of Christ, we see the Holy Spirit taking a central role in the lives of the apostles and disciples of Christ, perhaps signaling the slow demise of the authority of the satan/devil on the earth (see Luke 10 above).

New Testament Epistles

The goal of this section is to identify the role of the satan/devil figure in the early Church through the evidence of the epistles during the apostolic age and the Church's understanding of the problem of evil.[89] The NT epistles vary in which term they use for the Chief of Evil; however, the authors are not always clear as to the role of this figure and at times are not clear if the figure is an otherworldly figure or a human adversary. Notably, there is no mention of the devil or satan in Galatians, Philippians, Colossians, or Philemon.

Letter to the Romans

The term τὸν σατανᾶν occurs only once in Romans 16:20, in the context of Paul warning the community to be wary of those who cause dissension and oppose the teaching of the Kingdom of God. This could signal that the satan here is a human adversary who is opposing the work of Christ in the Church. Paul alludes to the idea that such individuals are doing the work of the satan, as their task is to "cause dissensions and offenses in opposition to the teaching you have learned" by "deceiving the hearts of the innocent" through "smooth talk and flattery" (language used in the DSS to refer to the enemies of the communities). Paul encourages the community with the news that "the God of Peace will crush the satan/adversary" (συντρίψει τὸν σατανᾶν—notice it is something yet to come in the future) and they will have the grace of

---

89. Here is not the place to discuss the Pauline authorship of the NT epistles. For discussions on the authorship of the NT epistles see, for example, N. T. Wright, *Paul and the Faithfulness of God* (Grand Rapids, MI: Fortress, 2013); Kurt Aland, "The Problem of Anonymity and Pseudonymity in Christian Literature of the First Two Centuries," *JTS* 12 (1961): 39–49; Gordon J. Bahr, "The Subscriptions in the Pauline Letters," *JBL* 2 (1968): 27–41; Richard J. Bauckham, "Pseudo-Apostolic Letters," *JBL* 107 (1988): 469–94; Jerome Murphy-O'Connor, *Paul the Letter-Writer: His World, His Options, His Skills* (Collegeville, MN: Liturgical Press, 1995); E. Randolph Richards, *The Secretary in the Letters of Paul* (Tübingen, Germany: Mohr Siebeck, 1991).

the Lord to withstand the test; the concept of "obedience" suggests they are under some sort of test. Paul's words suggest that the satan figure is working through nonbelievers in an effort to dissuade the faithful ones from seeking the Kingdom of God.

First and Second Letters to the Corinthians

The figure of ὁ σατανᾶς occurs in the letters to the Corinthians five times—twice in 1 Corinthians (5:5; 7:5) and three times in 2 Corinthians (2:11; 11:14; 12:7).

The Satan in 1 Corinthians 5 and 7

The first reference in 1 Corinthians 5:5 presents the satan in a role that suggests he is subservient to the Lord in the punishment of the disobedient. This may suggest he is functioning in the role of an angel of destruction. The story discusses the individual who has committed sexual immorality (πορνεία) by living with his father's wife (not necessarily his mother). The man is to be handed over to the satan for the destruction of the flesh in order that his spirit might be saved on the Day of the Lord. Paul's warning is against those within the community who are corrupt and wicked; each one is to be dealt with accordingly. What exactly will happen to the man in the hands of the satan is not made clear other than the flesh will be destroyed. There is no sense whether this is the actual physical body of the man or if Paul is using flesh metaphorically in the sense of "wicked desire." Either way, it appears the satan figure is doing the work of correcting the man under the judgment of the Lord. From this context, one might suggest that the idea of "evil" lurks within the individual and the community, and people must be on guard and take steps to confront it through choice. It must be noted that the apparent task of the satan figure is to save the individual from the eternal destruction of their soul.

A similar idea of human choice emerges in 1 Corinthians 7:5, which references the satan figure. The passage discusses the sexual relationship of a husband and wife, in which Paul suggests that depravation by either party, through lack of self-control, can bring on tempting or testing by the satan. The testing appears to involve sexual relations outside of marriage, as seems to be the case in 1 Corinthians 7:8–9, which describes individuals who do not have self-control over their sexual desires should marry. The testing by the satan is apparently brought on by the weakness of an individual, in this case regarding sex, and the individual will apparently have opportunities to commit sexual immorality with someone other than their spouse. Again, we see a clear connection here to the issue of choice in the midst of a testing or temptation by the satan.

The Satan in 2 Corinthians 2, 11, and 12

Second Corinthians 2:11 presents an instance of testing, but in this case by Paul. It appears someone within the community has caused disunity among the members and Paul wants to see if they are able to forgive the individual. He warns them that if they do not forgive, then they open the door for the plans (the mind) of the satan ("plots of Belial"?) to take advantage of their weakness. This concept suggests that individuals must forgive, as God forgives, or risk the hand of the satan, who awaits to take advantage of such occasions in an effort to test the person's faith.

Second Corinthians 11:12–15 presents the clearest case that suggests the satan uses people in his plans to disrupt God's work in the life of Paul. Paul warns the community that there are those among them who are false apostles and deceitful workers, who wish to boast of their position. Paul compares these individuals to the satan who transforms himself into a messenger/angel of light (11:14: μετασχηματίζεται εἰς ἄγγελον φωτός). This has often been understood to be descriptive of the satan's physical appearance, but in the context of the false apostles, it may be describing his work in discrediting the message of the Gospel through the false apostles. In verse 15, Paul states that these individuals are working for the satan, as they are "his servants" (οἱ διάκονοι αὐτοῦ), who, like him, transform themselves into servants of a pseudorighteousness (διάκονοι δικαιοσύνης) in order to deceive the righteous in the community.

The final reference to the satan in 2 Corinthians is the famously troublesome passage in 2 Corinthians 12:7. In the midst of discussing his heavenly journey/vision, Paul considers the problem of boasting and what can happen to an individual who decides to boast—in particular, concerning issues of the divine. Paul states that he can be tormented by "a thorn in the flesh" (σκόλοψ τῇ σαρκί)—that is, "a messenger of satan" (ἄγγελος σατανᾶ, "messenger of an adversary") in order to keep him from being overzealous. The two phrases, "a thorn in the flesh" and "a messenger of satan," are understood by most commentators to be synonymous, which may suggest the "messenger of satan" is a physical malady, or perhaps they both indicate a human adversary that is in opposition to the work of Paul for the Kingdom. The lack of the definite article with σατανᾶ suggests this may simply mean *an* adversary or adversarial messenger ("super apostles" in 12:11?). In 12:9, Paul appeals to the Lord for the removal of this "affliction," which may suggest that the Lord has a hand in it (permitting it), but if Paul maintains his reliance on the Lord, then he will be given the grace to overcome whatever the thorn or messenger might be.

Letter to the Ephesians

The Letter to the Ephesians contains two references to the devil—4:26–27 ("neither give a place to the devil") and 6:11 ("wear the complete armor of God, so that you are able to stand up to the crafty schemes of the devil"). The first occurrences appear in a context of individuals forgiving others—a possible parallel to 2 Corinthians 2:11. There appears to be lying going on in the midst of the community, and so the author calls for all members to speak the truth. This lying appears to have caused anger among some of the people, which the author warns, if left unchecked (as with any sin—lying, anger, stealing), will allow opportunity for the devil ("enemy, adversary"—"μηδὲ δίδοτε τόπον τῷ διαβόλῳ" [neither give a place for/to the devil]) to sow seeds of disunity in the community. The author does not identify who or what the "devil" is in this case; it could simply be understood as a human adversary who likes to cause trouble—a "false teacher." The lack of clarification regarding his actions leaves open to interpretation as to who or what the adversary is.

Ephesians 6:11 warns the community against "the crafty schemes or plans of the devil/ adversary" (τὰς μεθοδείας τοῦ διαβόλου). The language that follows in verse 12 indicates that this devil or adversary is one that operates in the supernatural realm (ἐν τοῖς ἐπουρανίοις, "in the heavenlies"). The community is told to stand strong against the "crafty plans" of the devil. These plans emerge through the actions of the rulers, authorities, and world rulers of this darkness, which could be understood as human figures (Caesars) or nations (Rome) that are under the control of the evil forces that operate in the spiritual realm. These rulers or authorities may be referring to the kingdoms of the earth that the devil was offering to Jesus in the wilderness testing in the Gospels. The author warns that all temptation to submit to these authorities and all oppression upon the people will come through these forces, which can only be overcome by standing firm in the spirit. In each of these descriptions, we can see the role of human choice at work. First, the rulers of these nations who choose not to follow YHWH open the door for these evil spirits to direct their decision-making (4:26–27). Second, each person in the Church at Ephesus has the choice to stand against the adversaries by putting on the armor of God, his Torah, which will cause the adversary to flee during those days of evil (cf. CD 16).

First and Second Letters to the Thessalonians

The two letters to the Thessalonians include only two references to ὁ σατανᾶς—one in 1 Thessalonians 2:18 and one in 2 Thessalonians 2:9. The first instance is found in Paul's explanation as to why he was delayed time and again in coming to the city (cf. Rom 15:22;

Gal 5:7);[90] it was due to the fact that the satan hindered them (ἐνέκοψεν ἡμᾶς ὁ σατανᾶς). The context clearly reveals the function of the satan—to hinder the spread of the Gospel.[91] In addition, it appears unlikely that this is a human adversary, although the adversary could be the authorities in Athens who were holding and persecuting Paul and others in jail, which is why Timothy was sent to Thessalonica with Paul's message.[92] Also interesting with the issue of Paul being prevented from traveling is why he immediately blames the satan figure and not God; after all, God has guided him in other directions on other occasions such as Acts 16:6–10 and Romans 1:13. This may lend some credence to the idea that he is using the term *satan* to represent the government authorities. However, further support for a superhuman figure appears in 3:5 when Paul reveals his fear that the tempter/tester had tempted them (ἐπείρασεν ὑμᾶς ὁ πειράζων) and had convinced them, the people of Thessalonica, to turn from the Gospel. Here again, we see the function of the satan figure/tester (ὁ πειράζων) is to turn people from God's plan.

The second occurrence of the satan in 2 Thessalonians 2:9 is found in what might be described as an apocalyptic eschatological passage concerning the second coming of Christ, which describes the appearance (ἡ παρουσία—the same term used for the second advent of Christ)[93] of the antichrist in the last days (2:3) as a result of the activity (ἐνέργεια) of the satan figure. As is typical with apocalyptic passages, the reader must use care in interpreting the language used by the author and its literal meaning. Prior to the coming of Christ, a rebellion must take place in which the antichrist, the man of lawlessness (ὁ ἄνθρωπος τῆς ἀνομίας), "the son of destruction" (ὁ υἱὸς τῆς ἀπωλείας), will appear. This figure reflects the king identified in Isaiah 14 and Ezekiel 28 who chooses to exalt himself to be worshipped and takes his seat in the Jerusalem temple, declaring he is God. Many commentators have attempted to identify this king of Isaiah 14 as the satan, but as can be understood here, this figure is a human who is being manipulated by the satan (2:9). During this rebellion, the author warns that the satan will be allowed to use every false wonder, sign, power, and every wicked deception through a

---

90. F. F. Bruce argued that the Greek suggests he tried on numerous occasions to come to Thessalonica. See Bruce, *1 & 2 Thessalonians*, WBC 45 (Nashville: Thomas Nelson, 1982), 55.
91. Bruce suggests that the Greek rendition of the Hebrew indicates the satan in the NT is "the adversary *par excellence*; his main activity is putting obstacles in the path of the people of God, to prevent the will of God from being accomplished in and through them." Bruce, 55.
92. W. M. Ramsay contends that the "interpretation of the term 'Satan,' as denoting action taken by the governing power against the message from God, is keeping with the figurative use of the word throughout the New Testament"; see Ramsay, *St. Paul the Traveller and the Roman Citizen* (London: Hodder & Stoughton, 1920), 231.
93. *Parousia* is being used in a similar fashion to the term ἐπιφάνεια, "epiphany" (as in Antiochus IV Epiphanes). In the Roman period, following the time of Caligula, "epiphany" was generally used to indicate the coming of the emperor—that is, the "manifestation of divinity"; see Bruce, *1 & 2 Thessalonians*, 175.

delusion *sent by God* against those who do not believe (2:9–11; this seems to affirm he is working under the authority of God). Similar language is used in Acts 2:22 by Peter to describe the works of Christ and may be used here in contrasting the man of lawlessness's activity with that of Christ.[94] However, in this moment, the deceiver is deceived, and his end has come. Here and only here are we told that the work of the satan figure is finished through the coming of Christ. The warning from the author is this: do not grow weary, as there will be trials and temptations by the adversary that will try to draw you away from God.

FIRST AND SECOND LETTERS TO TIMOTHY
The Satan and Devil in 1 Timothy

The two letters to Timothy use both terms, ὁ σατανᾶς and ὁ διάβολος, in varying contexts. The satan occurs first in 1 Timothy 1:20, in which Paul hands over Hymenaeus and Alexander to the satan (a context similar to 1 Cor 5:5) in order that they might learn not to blaspheme. These two individuals were likely leaders of the opposition in the Church at Ephesus. According to William Mounce, one of the teachings may have been about the already passed resurrection (2 Tim 2:17) and another charge that these individuals were possibly Judaizers.[95] First Timothy 1:19 speaks of how one must make good decisions by maintaining their faith and acting on a good conscience. If one rejects these, then they will eventually turn from faith and God. The role of the satan in this passage appears to be as an instructor or, perhaps in this context, punisher. We are only told that the two individuals will be taught not to blaspheme, but we are not told what this instruction entails. We are also not told exactly what it means to "turn them over to Satan." Did the satan figure physically appear, and Paul handed them over to him? Or is this metaphorical for excommunication and pushing them out into the world, which was allegedly the devil's realm?[96] A similar phrase appears in 1 Corinthians 5:5, in which a man is handed over to Satan for the destruction of his flesh, which appears to suggest physical punishment, but who is going to inflict the punishment? The Church? In neither case are we told the outcome of the lives of these two individuals or the man in 1 Corinthians, but it is clear that the satan figure here in 1 Timothy works under the sovereign rule of God in order to turn the two people back to God's ways.

In 1 Timothy 3:6, 7, and 11, the author switches to the term ὁ διάβολος. In verses 6 and 7, the author is describing the expectations of a bishop in the first-century Church. Two particular

---

94. See Bruce, 175.
95. See William D. Mounce, *Pastoral Epistles*, WBC 46 (Nashville: Thomas Nelson, 2000), 67–68.
96. Mounce, 69.

sins are identified that may result in "contact" with the devil. The first in 3:6 is pride/conceit, of which, if one is guilty, will result in the individual falling into disgrace by a snare or trap of the devil (παγίδα τοῦ διαβόλου—the traps of Belial?). This does not appear to be a concept assigned to the devil in any previous contexts, although it is possible this may reflect the bishop being handed over to the devil for correction. First Timothy 3:7 requires the bishop be thought well of by those outside the Church—that is, he must not allow disgrace to fall on him; if so, he will be ensnared by the devil. But again, there is no explanation as to what this ensnarement may include (perhaps the author is alluding to the three traps of Belial in CD 4.17–18: fornication, avarice [see 1 Tim 3:8], and defiling the sanctuary).

The second sin is found in 1 Timothy 3:11, which uses the term διαβόλους (no article) in reference to the behavior of women—they must not be adversaries ("slanderers"); it is not clear to whom, but it might be suggested it is in reference to their husbands.[97] (It is possible the ὁ διαβόλος in 3:6 is the leader of the slanderous group rather than the evil being the devil.)[98] Here, it is clear that it is not a superhuman devil the author has in mind but the slandering person. From the occurrences in 1 Timothy 3, one can assume that the author is focused on the choices people can make and that if they make poor choices, then the devil is there to correct the person on his own or by God's permission; by whose authority the author does not make clear.

The author of 1 Timothy 5:15 returns to the term σατανᾶς in a discussion concerning the behavior of young widows. Timothy is warned of the idleness of young widows and the problems that idleness can create (5:13). Young widows are encouraged to remarry and raise a family in order that there is no occasion for "the adversary" to slander the Christians. Here (v. 14), the term translated "the adversary" is not ὁ σατανᾶς or διαβόλος but τῷ ἀντικειμένῳ, usually indicating a human adversary. The author then states in 5:15 that some widows have already turned away from God to follow after the satan (τοῦ σατανᾶ). There is no indication in the text what "following after the satan" would mean; as such, one might suggest this is referring to a human adversary who is opposed to the Church, perhaps one of the false teachers. It seems that the author sees the adversary's opposition to the Church and individuals behind the decisions and lifestyles of individuals.

The Devil in 2 Timothy

Second Timothy includes two occurrences of *the devil*, in 2:26 and 3:3. The reference in 2:26 follows the concept in 1 Timothy 3:7, in which an unbelieving person, upon learning the truth,

---

97. See also Titus 2:3, which uses the same term in a similar context concerning the behavior of widows.
98. Mounce, *Pastoral Epistles*, 181.

will repent, and they may escape the "snare of the devil" (τῆς τοῦ διαβόλου παγῖδος). Here, the author claims the person had been held captive and did the will of the devil. These individuals are identified in 2 Timothy 3:2 as lovers of themselves and money, boasters, arrogant, blasphemers, unholy, and slanderers (διάβολοι in 3:3); apparently all who fall into these categories are being held in the trap of the devil and being used for his purposes. Those who reject these "lusts" and return to the truth of the Lord will be freed from the snare of the devil.

LETTER TO THE HEBREWS

The Letter to the Hebrews contains one reference to a chief evil being, in Hebrews 2:14. The context speaks of the flesh and blood of Christ and his shared humanity, by which through his death he might destroy the one who has power over death, the devil (τὸν διάβολον—cf. Wis 2:23–24; 1 Cor 15:26, 55; Rev 20:14).[99] It seems clear here that the author is speaking of a supernatural being and not an earthly adversary, although the author could be alluding to the Roman Empire, which certainly held the power of death in the Mediterranean world. Christ came to free those who lived their lives enslaved to the fear of death (through persecution?). What is not clear in the passage is how the adversary/devil had this power over death; does this suggest he was in some way responsible for death among humanity? If so, then this would suggest this is a human adversary, as there is no apparent spiritual being that has power over death in the heavenly realm except God. Another possibility is that the power of death is brought on by the devil in that he turns people away from God and his Torah, which in the end results in their death and final destruction.

THE LETTER OF JAMES

The reference to the devil in James 4:7 offers one of the clearest allusions to the CD 16 concept of how turning to the Torah and God causes Belial to flee. The author states in the imperative (ὑποτάγητε, "submit!") that the community must submit themselves to God, and if they resist the temptations or tests of the devil, the devil will flee (but the context certainly appears conditional on the person "resisting"). The concept concerns the issue of purity in which the individual, through the cleansing of sin, is able to draw near to God. The function of the "adversary" in James is that of a tempter who awaits individuals who choose a path other than the one God has for them by being double-minded—of two souls (δίψυχοι). This is perhaps an allusion to the two-spirits concept in 1QS, which suggests individuals must make correct choices during times of testing by the adversarial spirits. Like the two spirits in 1QS, a person can choose to follow the "good spirit."

---

99. See Alan C. Mitchell, *Hebrews*, Sacra Pagina Series 13 (Collegeville, MN: Liturgical Press, 2009), 75.

First Letter of Peter

First Peter 5:8 has the devil play a role similar to that of the satan figure in the book of Job. The author warns the community to be alert and under self-control because "your [legal] opposer, an adversary [ὁ ἀντίδικος ὑμῶν διάβολος; interesting that we do not have the definite article here with διάβολος—read: 'an adversary'], goes about like a roaring lion seeking someone to swallow." He goes on to warn in 5:9 that each person must resist him ("him" could be the ἀντίδικος or an adversary) in the midst of suffering—perhaps as Job had to resist cursing God. It seems likely the author of 1 Peter was drawing on the Job tradition of the satan figure in his exhortation to the community concerning the works of the adversary.

First Letter of John

The author of the First Letter of John identifies the figure διάβολος four times in his brief letter. The figure appears three times in 3:8, which uses familial language to describe sinners in the world. He states that the one who practices sin (of a habitual nature) is from the devil "because the devil is sinning from the beginning" (ὅτι ἀπ' ἀρχῆς ὁ διάβολος ἁμαρτάνει); what we are not told is "since the beginning" of what—the beginning of creation? This will become a major point of argument in the period of the early Church apologists and the Gnostics (see chapter 7). The author then states that the Son of God was revealed (ἐφανερώθη ὁ υἱὸς τοῦ θεοῦ) in order that he might destroy the works of the devil (ἵνα λύσῃ τὰ ἔργα τοῦ διαβόλου).

Two interesting points to raise in this verse: The first is that the verb used "to destroy" is in the subjunctive, which suggests the potential for an action to take place, but likely not immediately; something that is not generally noted in the English translations. The second point is about the term *works*; we are not told what these "works" are. There is a hint they involve the deception of the people in order to have them turn away from the Torah (see 3:4, they are lawless people—ἡ ἁμαρτία ἐστὶν ἡ ἀνομία) and commit all manner of sin, but it is not made clear in the letter. In 1 John 3:10, the author suggests that the sin of these individuals is the failure to do acts of righteousness and failure to love a brother or sister, thus not living out the Torah. In 1 John 3:12, we may find a clarification for this dichotomy in a possible allusion to the devil as a murderer from the beginning (again, the beginning of what?). The author states that "Cain was from the evil one (ἐκ τοῦ πονηροῦ)[100] and murdered his brother." Cain's deeds were evil; thus, he was a child of the devil. Abel's deeds were righteous; thus, he was a child of God.

---

100. The term *evil one* is used in the Lord's Prayer to allegedly identify the satan figure.

Letter of Jude

In the Letter of Jude 9, the author presents the alleged citation from the Assumption of Moses, in which the archangel Michael contended with the devil over the body of Moses.[101] The author uses the event as an example to the community of how not to slander or rebuke those who oppose them. At the same time, the role of the devil in the first century is one not to be taken lightly. Even Michael, the apparent highest-ranking archangel, refused to rebuke the devil in their argument over the body of Moses. One can see a common theme of 2TP literature: battles between angelic beings (see previously mentioned Zech 3:1; CD 5; T. Ash. 6; 1QS 3). Michael refuses to bring a judgment of blasphemy against the devil and pronounced the Lord's rebuke against him.

The dispute reflects a similar discussion between the Angel of the Lord and the satan figure in Zechariah 3 and the court scene involving Joshua.[102] In Zechariah 3:2, the satan figure apparently will bring evidence against Joshua, but the Angel of the Lord proclaims, "Let the Lord rebuke you" (imperfect jussive). A similar form is used in the Jude text, an aorist optative, which would render the translation "May the Lord rebuke you," suggesting a similar scenario with that found in Zechariah 3. This may suggest the author of Jude has a similar understanding of the role of the devil figure and the function of the satan figure as that of Zechariah. In Zechariah, the satan figure is finding fault with Joshua, and here in Jude, he is blaspheming the "glorious ones" (v. 8; although it is not clear who these "glorious ones" are—possibly angels or individuals held in high esteem in the community). As in other 2TP literature, the satan/devil is one whose task involves finding the faults of the righteous and brings them to the attention of the Lord. It seems clear the author of Jude is drawing on various Jewish folklore traditions in his telling of this battle in Jude 9.

Summary of New Testament Epistles

The NT epistles vary in which term they use for the Chief of Evil—the satan or the devil; however, the authors are not always clear as to the role of this figure and at times are not clear regarding whether the figure is an otherworldly or a human adversary. Interestingly, despite the volume of writing in the NT epistles, there is limited discussion of the presence or role of a supernatural personified evil being. The Letter to the Romans only mentions the figure once, and that is in the context of his pending doom in the eschaton. The letters

---

101. See Jerome H. Neyrey, *2 Peter, Jude: A New Translation with Introduction and Commentary*, ABC 37C (New Haven, CT: Yale University Press, 1993), 65. Its presence is noted by Clement of Alexandria; see his *Die Griechische christliche Schriftsteller* 3.207; Origen, *De Prin.* 3.2.1.

102. Neyrey, *2 Peter, Jude*, 65.

to the Corinthian church identify the satan figure as one who punishes the disobedient with apparent approval from God (see 1 Cor 5:5). The satan figure also tests individuals for various reasons, including for self-control (1 Cor 7: 8–9). Paul becomes a target of testing through individuals who are apparently working knowingly or unknowingly for the satan (2 Cor 11:12–15; 12:7–9). The author of Ephesians uses *the devil* rather than *the satan* in the context of human behavior toward one another: the devil has plans in which he will use individuals or governments to get in the way of people on the right path of God. In the letters to the Thessalonians, we see that the role of the satan is to thwart the plans of the Gospel; however, it is not clear if this is a spiritual adversary or a human/governmental adversary. The letters to Timothy use both *the satan* and *the devil*—satan as a disciplinary figure for blasphemers and the traps of devil in a context of trials of one's faith and, in the case of 1 Timothy 3, the faith of church leadership. The author of 1 Timothy 3 also uses the term *devil* to describe human adversaries or slanderers, which of course could be under the influence of an evil spirit, but the author does not make that clear. The Letter to the Hebrews identifies the devil as the one who has power over death, but the author does not make it clear who this is or how the devil has this power. The letters of James, 1 Peter, and 1 John identify the satan or the devil as one who is an adversary that is out to thwart the plans of God for an individual's life. The final epistle to note, Jude, describes the work of the devil in a context similar to the presence and action of the satan figure in Zechariah 3—he is functioning in a position of a prosecutor in the court of YHWH but is rebuked by the archangel Michael.

We can see a variety of roles for the satan or devil figures in the NT epistles, but all of them are directed at testing or rebuking various individuals in the letters. All of this appears for the most part to be carried out under the authority of God in an effort to keep his people on the straight path and bring back those who have turned away from the Torah.

John's Apocalypse

The author of John's Apocalypse uses both terms, σατανᾶς and διάβολος, among others, when referring to the apparent chief evil being in the NT. The Apocalypse offers no simple solutions as to the satan's identity, however; in fact, his position, function, and the chronology of his presence are quite complicated in relation to the other NT texts. The term σατανᾶς or a form of it is used eight times, in Revelation 2:9, 13 (2×), 24; 3:9; 12:9; 20:2, 7. The author uses διάβολος or a form of it five times, in 2:10; 12:9, 12; 20:2, 10; as can be seen, on occasion, he uses both terms in the same verse or in near proximity of one another. In addition, the author uses the term *dragon* (δράκων) thirteen times—as many as *satan* and *devil* combined—in a context in which the term appears synonymous with satan and devil (12:3 [2×], 4, 7 [2×], 9, 13, 16, 17; 13:2, 4, 11; 16:13; 20:2). He also uses the term ὄφις, "serpent/snake," in parallel with *satan*, *devil*, and *dragon* in 12:9, 14, 15; and 20:2.[103] The serpent of the Apocalypse may be connected to the python (πυθών) of Acts 16:16, which empowers the slave girl to give oracles for her master.

The Satan and the Devil in Revelation 2

The first references to the satan (ὁ σατανᾶς) are found in the letters to the seven churches in chapter 2. The church involved in the first mention of the satan is the city of Smyrna. Smyrna was a center for many Greco-Roman gods, including Meter, the Nemeses, Zeus (Polieus), Akraios, and Soter, among others.[104] There were likely many sociopolitical pressures on the Christians in the city, including issues related to the imperial cult of the Roman emperor. There was a well-established Jewish community in Smyrna that appears to be significant in the warnings of the author of the Apocalypse, although some scholars suggest these are apostate Jews.[105] Verse 2:9 identifies a group who are creating difficulties for the Church at Smyrna through affliction and what appears to be financial injustice, but that is unclear.[106] The author states that he is aware of the affliction and poverty of the Christians, which may have occurred due to the Roman trade guilds connected to the Roman deities, but specific reasons are not presented.[107] The opposing group is made up of individuals who say "they are Jews and are not" and are denouncing (blaspheming in the sense of "slandering" with false rumors)[108] the church (likely before Roman authorities—cf. Acts 14:2); the group may have included Jewish Christians. For this action, John accuses them of blasphemy for showing disloyalty to the God of Israel.[109] The author identifies the group as "a synagogue of the satan" (συναγωγὴ τοῦ σατανᾶ); this may be

---

103. Note that in 2 Cor 11:3, the author identifies ὄφις as the creature that deceived Eve in the Garden, but he makes no connection to satan or the devil.
104. See Craig R. Koester, *Revelation*, ABC 38A (New Haven, CT: Yale University Press, 2014), 272.
105. Koester, 273.
106. Aune suggests a parallel to this community's situation in 4QpPs^a 1–10 ii 10–11, which reads, "The congregation of the poor ones who will accept the appointed time of affliction, and they will be delivered from all the traps of Belial." See David E. Aune, *Revelation 1–5*, WBC 52A (Dallas: Word Books, 1997), 161.
107. Aune, 161; Aune offers four reasons as to why the group might be suffering in poverty, suggesting it is likely due to the trade guild restriction they faced.
108. See discussion in Aune, 162.
109. Adela Yarbro Collins, "Insiders and Outsiders in the Book of Revelation and Its Social Context," in *To See Ourselves as Others See Us: Christians, Jews, "Others" in Late Antiquity*, ed. Jacob Neusner and Ernest S. Frerichs (Chico, CA: Scholars Press, 1985), 187–218, here, 203–10. See also discussion in Koester, *Revelation*, 275–76. It seems the most likely scenario is these are Jews who were participating in the imperial cult in the city, thus denying their faith. Aune, *Revelation 1–5*, 162, argues that "Jews" is being used in a positive sense as those who are loyal to God's will. Those who are opposed to it are part of the "synagogue of the satan."

a parallel to the "congregation of Belial" (עדת בליעל)[110] in the 1QH 2.22 and 1QM 4.9[111] and could indicate a synagogue community or simply a gathering of individuals who are apparently doing the work of the satan (see also 3:9 below). This suggests that the work of the satan is the affliction and oppression of those who are trying to follow God.

The author then switches to the term ὁ διάβολος in verse 2:10, in what he describes as a test of the community in which they will be cast into prison (suggesting Roman participation in the action) and tested (πειρασθῆτε) with tribulation/oppression (θλῖψιν) for ten days. There is an apparent possibility of death (see v. 13, which notes the death of Antipas in Smyrna) for these people, as they are asked to be faithful to the point of death while under this testing because he (the angel of the community?) will not abandon them (cf. 1 Cor 10:13; 1 Pet 1:6–7; James 1:2, 12) and they will be granted an eternal award ("the wreath of life," τὸν στέφανον τῆς ζωῆς).[112] It is highly unlikely that members of the Jewish community would have the authority to imprison the Christians in Smyrna and punish them to the point of death; this suggests they were collaborating with the Romans.[113]

In Revelation 2:13, part of the letter to the church at Pergamon, the author returns to the use of the term *the satan* twice. The first identifies the city of Pergamum as the "throne of the satan" (ὁ θρόνος τοῦ σατανᾶ) but offers little more as to the activity of the satan figure in the city. The author's use of the article (ὁ) with "throne" may suggest a specific place of governing or power. Aune suggests that from the presence of "the throne," the audience would have known what he was describing.[114] Pergamum was a center for the pagan worship of the Greek gods Zeus, Athena, Hermes, Heracles, and Dionysus, among others. In 29 BCE, the city built the first temple to Augustus and the goddess of Rome, which may be why it is "the throne of the satan." We find in Revelation 13:2 that the Dragon, who is occupying the throne, hands it over to the Beast of the Sea, which suggests this is the seat of the imperial cult. Helmut Koester contends that coin images from the temple may have informed the portrayal of the beast in

---

110. The LXX translates the Hebrew עדה with the Greek συναγωγή over one hundred times—for example, Num 16:3; 20:4; 26:9; 31:16; see also 1QS 5.1–2: עדת אנשי העול, "congregation of wicked men"; 1QM 15.9: עדת רשעה, "congregation of wickedness"; the Epistle of Barnabas 5.13 and 6.6 includes the phrase πονηρευομένων συναγωγαί—"synagogues of evil people." See discussion in Aune, *Revelation 1–5*, 165.
111. Koester, *Revelation*, 274.
112. See excursus 2C in Aune, *Revelation 1–5*, 172–75, which discusses the history of the "Ancient Wreath and Crown Imagery."
113. Koester, *Revelation*, 277; Aune, 163. See the argument that these are not apostate Jews but Jews opposed to Christianity in Adele Yarbro Collins, "Vilification and Self-Definition in the Book of Revelation," *HTR* 79 (1986): 308–20.
114. Aune, *Revelation 1–5*, 182. We find a second throne in Rev 13:2, this one belonging to the dragon, a likely synonym for the satan.

Revelation 13:4, 7.[115] From the Letter to Pergamum, it appears there was significant resistance to the Roman rule and the emperor cult.[116] The oppression of the Church appears quite significant, as the person named Antipas is martyred in the city, but no person is assigned responsibility for his death. Koester argues that the death of Antipas in the city is the most likely reason for Pergamum being identified as the "throne of satan";[117] however, this is likely not the only city in the region in which a Christian was executed. If he was officially executed, this would have meant Roman involvement in the action and may suggest that the Romans in the region were operating under the authority of the satan, knowingly or unknowingly. It could also have been a stoning or some other ritual execution by a Jewish group opposed to the Christians. One of the more promising theories for the meaning of the title "throne of satan" is the fact that Pergamum was the site of the "healing sanctuary of Asclepius," who was the god of healing in the Roman world. Asclepius is called "the savior" and is symbolized with a snake, which of course appears in Revelation 12 as an image or name for satan.[118] However, as Aune mentions, it is difficult to determine what exactly the author meant by "the throne of the satan." The most likely theory identifies it with the Temple of Augustus and Roma (cf. T. Job 3.5b and 4.4c, which identifies a pagan temple as "the place of the satan" [ὁ τόπος τοῦ σατανᾶ]).[119]

The next reference to the satan is found in 2:24, which is found in the Letter to Thyatira, beginning in 2:18. This section of John's Apocalypse contains the only occurrence of the phrase "Son of God," in verse 18a, which may depict a contrast with the Roman emperor. The Christians in Thyatira are apparently allowing a false prophet named Jezebel who is teaching and deceiving the Church to eat the food sacrificed to idols and to practice fornication (πορνείας), which likely refers to having sex with temple prostitutes who are participating in the emperor cult (v. 20). Jezebel is also accused of fornicating, suggesting she may be one of the prostitutes who are deceiving the Christians. However, the name likely is used to identify the false teachings of a cult within the community and to argue that those participating in that cult are subject to the punishment of the Lord (2:23). If those participating fail to repent from their works in the cult, they shall all be struck down as a sign to the other churches (ἐὰν μὴ μετανοήσωσιν ἐκ τῶν ἔργων αὐτῶν).[120] Those following the cult teaching of Jezebel are committing metaphorical

---

115. Koester, *Revelation*, 284.
116. Adela Yarbro-Collins, "Pergamon in Early Christian Literature," in *Pergamon: Citadel of the Gods*, ed. Helmut Koester (Harrisburg, PA: Trinity, 1998), 163–84, here, 163–66.
117. Koester, *Revelation*, 286. See here his rebuttal and for other possible theories for the title.
118. Aelius Aristides, *Orations* 42.4; Justin Martyr, *1 Apol.* 54.10.
119. See Heinrich Schlier, *Principalities and Powers in the New Testament* (New York: Herder & Herder, 1961), 29; see also the discussion in Aune, *Revelation 1–5*, 182–84.
120. Several manuscripts read, "τῶν ἔργων αὐτῆς" (her works), but the idea that those participating in the cultic practices of Jezebel must repent of "their works," supported by multiple manuscripts, makes more sense contextually.

adultery (worshipping idols) in breaking the covenant with God. The teachings of this cult are identified as the "deep things of the satan" (τὰ βάθη τοῦ σατανᾶ)[121] in verse 24, which may suggest, in light of 2:13, a connection to the temple cult of Rome, thus idolatry, or all things contrary to the gospel of the Kingdom. This phrase is likely being used by the author in contrast to the "deep things of God" (see 1 Cor 2:10; Dan 2:22; Rom 11:33), just as we saw the "synagogue of God" contrasted with the "synagogue of the satan."

The Satan and the Devil in Revelation 3

In a letter to the Church at Philadelphia beginning in 3:7, a second group is identified as "the synagogue of satan, who say that they are Jews and are not"; this follows a similar accusation against the group attacking the Church at Smyrna in 2:9. From Revelation 3:9, it appears some members of the Christian community were Jewish, which seems to have caused some conflict in the community. Ignatius (*Epis. Phila.* 6:1; 8:2) states that some of the Christians were continuing to follow Jewish teachings, some of which were contradictory to the Christian faith.[122] However, it is conceivable these individuals were following pagan rituals related to the temple cult of the Romans while at the same time continuing to go to synagogue. The Church at Philadelphia appears to have been oppressed in a similar manner to those in Smyrna, but the passage lacks any details other than the people of the Church maintained their faith and love of God in the midst of the trials (τῆς ὥρας τοῦ πειρασμοῦ; see 3:10). The author of the Apocalypse suggests that at some point, the ones who are oppressing the Church will bow down to them; he does not hint that this will take place in their present situation, which may suggest an event in the eschaton when God reveals to the "Jews" that the Christians were following the Messiah.

The Satan and the Devil in Revelation 12

The next set of references to the satan and the devil appears in the enigmatic chapter 12,[123] which is full of apocalyptic imagery, although lacking the language of a visionary report ("and I

---

121. Aune contends the phrase ὡς λέγουσιν, "as they say," reflects a concern of the Nicolaitans, who may have followed the teachings of the satan figure in second-century Gnostic groups—perhaps reflecting secret knowledge of the "things of the satan." See Aune, *Revelation 1–5*, 207–8.
122. Koester, *Revelation*, 323.
123. According to Aune, Rev 12 is thought to be a combination of "two or more sources with the possible addition of several redactional glosses." David E. Aune, *Revelation 6–16*, WBC 52B (Nashville: Thomas Nelson, 1998), 666–74. One suggested source is a Jewish myth depicting the battle between Michael and the Dragon that may have been inserted into the Greek myth concerning Leto and Python the Dragon (see Hyginus, *Fabulae* 140). One Jewish version of this myth is reflected in chapter 12, in which the satan becomes the lead antagonist, identified with several names in 2TP literature; these include Belial, Beliar, Beelzeboul, the devil, Mastema, Sammael, the Dragon, the Great Serpent of Old, and the deceiver, among others. Another possible source, although a distant analogy, is the Egyptian Isis-Osiris-Horus-Typhon myth found in Plutarch's *De Iside* 355D–58F.

saw"),[124] in connection to the persecution of the Church in John's Apocalypse. The story begins in 12:1–2 with a description of a woman who appears in a heavenly sign "clothed with the sun" and wearing a crown of twelve stars who is giving birth to a male child.[125] In a second heavenly sign in 12:3, a "great red dragon" (δράκων μέγας πυρρός—notice there is no article with the "dragon") appeared that had seven heads and ten horns and seven crowns upon his heads. A dragon often reflects a mythical creature such as Leviathan in Psalm 74:13–14 or represents "chaotic forces that needed divine control."[126]

This is no less true of the satan figure in the world of John's Apocalypse. The powers of God battle with the figure in chapters 12 and 20 in an effort to end this figure's activity on the earth. In verse 12:3, he is identified as the great red dragon who becomes the opponent of the woman and the child.[127] The seven crowns upon his seven heads suggest he has great authority over significant portions or kingdoms of the earth (cf. Luke 4:5–6); how he gets that authority is not made clear by the author. The author is likely drawing on Daniel 7, which identifies the ten horns as ten kings (cf. Sib. Or. 3.396–400). Verse 12:3 has been understood to depict the fall of the satan figure, but the image of him with seven heads is quite different from any previous visions of the figure. Aune suggests this is likely an interpolation taken from 17:3, as there is no interpretation given in 12:3, and the removal of the phrase does not interrupt the narrative.[128] As a result, there is not a clear explanation as to its meaning here in chapter 12 (see the interpretation in 17:9–14).

In 12:4, the author depicts the dragon sweeping his tail across the heavens and throwing a third of the stars down to the earth. Again, the author may be drawing on Daniel, in this case 8:10, which states that one of the horns cast down "some of the host and some of the stars fell to the ground and it trampled upon them." The host here may represent angelic beings of some sort, but if that is the case, what then are the stars? The Apocalypse text in 12:4 does not include the term *host* but does designate a "third of the stars of heaven." This type of language presumes some kind of assault on the heavens by the dragon; in the case of Daniel 8, it is likely being used to describe Antiochus IV Epiphanes in the second century BCE. Perhaps the author

---

124. See Aune, *Revelation 6–16*, 665.
125. The identity of the woman is open to much debate. She is the "people of God"; the Christian church; Jesus's mother, Mary; or the Jewish people. See discussion Koester, *Revelation*, 542–43.
126. Koester, 544.
127. *Dragon* is used in the NT only in John's Apocalypse and appears thirteen times—12:3, 4, 7 (2×), 9, 13, 16, 17; 13:2, 4, 11; 16:13; 20:2. It is one of the names of the satan figure in other 2TP Jewish texts, such as 3 Bar 4:3–5. It is used in the LXX to translate the Hebrew *Leviathan* in Job 40:25; Pss 73:14; 103:26; and Isa 27:1; and also for "sea monster" (תנין) fifteen times. In T. Abr 17.14; 19.6–7, "death sometimes appears as seven fiery red heads of dragons." Aune, *Revelation 6–16*, 683.
128. Aune, 683–84.

of the Apocalypse is depicting an assault on the authority of Christ by the Roman emperor (Dan 8:10). The stars could represent the angels that fall to earth with satan as seen in LAE 12–16 and 1 Enoch (18:14; 21:3–6; 86:1–3; 88:3),[129] but why then has the author omitted the "host"? The language used in 12:4 depicts a violent act by the Dragon against the stars, which suggests they are not angels on his side but some other heavenly body.

In 12:4b, the dragon then approaches the woman in order to devour the child when it is born.[130] Following the birth and rescue of the child by God and his enthronement in heaven, we are told in 12:7 that a war began in the heavenly realm in which the archangel Michael and his angels fought against this same dragon and his angels (although the angels were supposedly thrown down to the earth in 12:4—this may suggest the "stars" in 12:4 are not his angels after all), and they are defeated (cf. Sib. Or. 5.512–13). The author states that there was no longer a place for the dragon in the heavenly realm (see Job 1, 2; Zech 3; Rev 12:8), which will create chaos on the earth.[131] The battle between Michael and the dragon/satan is reminiscent of the struggle between Michael/Melchizedek and Melchiresha and Belial (see 1QM 17.5–9; 11Q13 9–15; T. Levi 3:3; Ps 82:1) or the Prince of Light and the Angel of Darkness.[132]

In verse 12:9, the great red dragon is thrown down from the heavens, and he is further identified as "that ancient serpent, the one called devil and the satan, the one who led astray the whole world; he was thrown down to the earth and his angels were cast down with him" (cf. Isa 14:12–15; 2 En. 29.4–5; LAE 16). The image of the "ancient serpent" hints at Genesis and the Garden,[133] but that connection is not made in Genesis 3:1; there is no mention of satan or the devil as the serpent in the Garden. Possible connections may be hinted at in 2TP literature such as 1 Enoch 69:6; 2 Enoch 31.6; Apocalypse of Moses 17.1; LAE 16.3; and Wisdom of Solomon 2:24. As will be seen below, the further the satan figure is removed from the HB and 2TP Jewish texts, the longer the list of his aliases. Verse 12:9 also offers one of the clear

---

129. See Wright, "Life of Adam and Eve," 109–15.
130. Jer 28:34 (LXX) identifies Nebuchadnezzar as a dragon (MT uses the term *tannin*, "monster") who devoured the prophet. This may suggest that the author of the Apocalypse is referring to a political leader at the time of the writing of the text. The child is most likely symbolic of the birth of Christ, although some suggest it is his resurrection (12:5). See discussion Koester, *Revelation*, 546–47. The Greco-Roman myth of Leto offers a similar story; Leto is the mother of Apollo and Artemis (the twins' father is Zeus). Leto is pursued by Python the Dragon, who attempts to kill her, but she is rescued by the wind (Hyginus, *Fabulae* 140; Lucan, *Pharsalia* 5.79–81); see the discussion in Koester, 555–56.
131. Aune, *Revelation 6–16*, contends that verses 7–9 are an interruption to the narrative between the woman being protected in the wilderness by God and the proclamation of the Kingdom of God in 12:10.
132. See Aune, 691–93, for a discussion of other heavenly battles that offer parallels to the battle here in 12:7.
133. Aune contends that Rev 12:9 "provides the only explicit biblical identification of satan with the serpent who tempted Eve in Gen 3:1–7." He suggests two other possible connections in Rom 16:20, which may allude to Gen 3:15 with "crush satan under your feet," and Luke 10:19 and the ability of the disciples to tread on serpents. Cf. 2 Cor 11:3, in which Paul claims the serpent deceived Eve; see also Aune, 696–97.

functions of the satan figure in the HB and 2TP literature: he is "the one who deceives." He is identified as ὁ πλανῶν, "the deceiver," in reference to his task of leading the whole world astray. Several other figures function in this role in the Apocalypse; Jezebel in 2:20; the devil in 20:3, 8, 10; the beast in 13:14; and the false prophet in 19:20 all act as deceivers.

The satan figure here is depicted as having authority on the earth, in the human realm, similar to such 2TP figures as Belial (see 1QS 1, 3; T12 Patr.). He is identified as the "ruler of this world" in John 12:31 and 16:11 and ruler of the power of the air in Ephesians 2:2. Interestingly, in Revelation 2:13, he is given a throne in the city of Pergamum, which would denote a position of authority in and over the human realm. His status in the world is certainly elevated when we reach the close of the 2TP from one in which he is working under the authority and restrictions of God to one that appears to be moving toward a semiautonomous position. He carries on his role as the deceiver, in which he tests people and the nations (Rev 20:7–8), often causing them to turn away from God (1 Chr 21; Matt 4; 1 Cor 7:5; T. Job 3:3, 6; T12 Patr.; 1QS).

The final defeat or throwing out of the satan figure seems to be triggered by the rescue and the taking up of the male child born to the woman, which likely signals the resurrection and ascension of Christ (12:5). We are also told in 12:11 that the defeat of the devil is brought about through the blood of the Lamb—this event seems to be the blockade of the heavenly realm for the satan who had been previously allowed to enter to accuse individuals before the divine court and God (12:10–11; cf. John 12:31–32).[134]

The author states in 12:10 that one of the functions of this figure is to accuse the "brothers" (ὁ κατήγωρ τῶν ἀδελφῶν ἡμῶν)—it's not clear who these brothers are, as the voice who makes the proclamation comes from heaven. It is also stated that he accuses these people before God, suggesting a similar role to the satan in Job 1–2 and Zechariah 3. However, in the case of Revelation 12:10, he is identified as "the one who accuses" (ὁ κατήγωρ or ὁ κατηγορῶν), not "the satan."[135] The author then gives a warning to all who are on the earth and the sea that the devil has come down to the earth "having great anger knowing that he has a short time"

---

134. Other theories suggest 12:9 depicts an event in the primeval period through interpretations of Isa 14; Ezek 28; LAE 12–16; and 2 En. 29 and 31. This idea was later heightened by Milton in *Paradise Lost* 1.34–39. Of course, the chronology of this interpretation doesn't work if the rescuing of the male child is the exaltation of Christ in Rev 12, as the battle takes place after this occurs. Others try to connect this fall to the Watcher tradition in 1 En. 6–16, but the angels in the Enochic tradition are operating in the role for God's purposes on the earth when they fall rather than in a battle in the heavens. One further option is that this battle is yet to come in the eschaton, but again this doesn't quite fit in the story line presented in Rev 12 and the woman and the child.
135. The satan figure under the name of Mastema is involved in accusing Abraham of loving Isaac more than God, which results in the testing of Abraham in the sacrifice of Isaac in Jub. 17.15–16. The Apocalypse of Zephaniah (ca. 100 BCE–pre-70 CE) describes an angel (no name is given) with the body of a serpent who would accuse individuals of their sins before the Lord (3:8–9; 6:8, 17). Cf. 1 En. 40.7, in which the "satans" come before the "Lord of the Spirits" to accuse those on the earth.

(12:12). Those on the earth will have the choice of falling into the trap of idolatry through the beasts and the whore of the devil or resisting the devil with repentance and following after God (see 6:17; 13:10).

The author continues to refer to the satan figure using the other terms he first introduced in 12:9. In 12:13, the dragon, once upon the earth, pursued the woman who had given birth to the male child. In 12:14, he is identified as the serpent and has been given wings to fly to safety at least for a short time ("a time, times, and a half time"; cf. Dan 7:25; 12:7). Verse 12:15 describes how the serpent pours out water from his mouth to try to capture the woman; in 12:16, he is once again referred to as the dragon who had poured the water out of its mouth. Here, the Lord opens up the earth to swallow up the river (interestingly, the dragon is not swallowed up but is permitted to continue persecuting people, perhaps suggesting God's allowance of the satan's actions in the Apocalypse); in 12:17, the dragon goes off to make war with the other offspring of the woman—"the ones keeping the commandments of God and having the testimony of Jesus." The dragon is identified once again in 12:18 as one who stands upon the sand of the sea.

THE SATAN AND THE DEVIL IN REVELATION 13

In Revelation 13:1, the author announces the appearance of a beast coming up from the sea.[136] This beast appears to be one of the proxies for the satan who would lead many on the earth to worship false gods. Aune and others contend the "beast of the sea" represents the Roman Empire and not one particular antichrist figure.[137] The author of John's Apocalypse uses such beasts to represent political powers and those who lead them (cf. Dan 7:2–8; Pss 74:14; 87:4; Jer 51:34; Ezek 32:2–3).[138] The beast has ten horns adorned with ten crowns, indicating political and military authority upon the earth (see Dan 7; cf. 1QM 15, in which the nations are aligned with the satan).[139] The beast is also covered with "blasphemous names," which could indicate the epithets by which the Roman emperors used in the imperial cult such as "lord," "savior," and "son of god." In 13:2, the author states that the dragon gives its power, authority, and

---

136. There is a strong likelihood that the beasts mentioned in 12:18–13:18 are tied to the Jewish myths of the Leviathan and Behemoth found in the HB (e.g., Gen 1:21; Job 40–41), but also in 1 En 60.7–11 and in 2 Bar 29.4 and 4 Ezra 6.49–52, two Jewish texts that originated around the time of John's Apocalypse.
137. See Aune, *Revelation 6–16*, 729. The lack of the definite article with θηρίον, "beast," suggests this is something unfamiliar to the audience (732), whereas the articular form in 11:7 is likely a gloss or suggests the audience was familiar with the beast: "the beast who came out of the Abyss."
138. Other Jewish texts identify the Romans as forces rising out of the sea—cf. 1QpHab 3.9–11; 4 Ezra 11.1; here they are identified as an eagle. See also CD 8:10, which uses the term *dragons* (תנינים) to identify the "kings of the nations"; see also Pss. Sol. 2:25. See Steven J. Friesen, "The Beast from the Land: Revelation 13:11–18 and Social Setting," in *Reading the Book of Revelation*, ed. David L. Barr (Atlanta: SBL, 2003), 49–64.
139. See the discussion of possible earthly representations in Koester, *Revelation*, 570–74.

throne to the beast, described with the "four beasts" (empires) language similar to that found in Daniel 7:1–8. The "throne of the dragon" is likely synonymous with the "throne of satan" at Pergamum in Revelation 2:13 (cf. 2 En. 29.4; LAE 47.3; Apoc. Moses 39.2).

In 13:4, this same dragon is worshipped by the new monsters that have appeared on the scene; as a result, the whole earth follows after the beast and they worship the dragon. In 13:11, a second beast appears from the earth and its purpose, on behalf of the first beast, is to deceive the ones dwelling upon the earth and tell them to make an image of the first beast, who had been wounded (13:14). Aune suggests this beast represents the "Koinon of Asia" rather than an individual,[140] but the imagery in 13:11–18 suggests a single antagonist, which is identified as the false prophet.

The final appearances of the devil and the satan occur in chapter 20 of John's Apocalypse, which describes the binding of the figure(s). In verse 1, we are told that an angel came down from heaven holding a key to the abyss and a great chain. In verse 2, the angel "seized the dragon, that ancient serpent who is a devil and the satan, and he bound him for a thousand years"; this is reminiscent of the binding of the Watchers in 1 Enoch 10.4–13 (cf. Jude 6; 2 Pet 2:4, alluding to the Enochic Watcher tradition; 1 En. 54.1–5; also Jub. 10.11, in which evil spirits are bound in the abyss with the Watchers). The dragon is thrown into the abyss, and it is locked and sealed over him in order that he would not lead astray the nations for a thousand years (v. 3). One significant difference with this event is that it takes place at the end of the age, whereas in the Watcher tradition the binding of the angels and spirits occurs in the age of the Flood. The satan appears again in 20:7 after the thousand years have passed and he is released,[141] and he will resume his task of leading the nations astray and the beginning of the great war between Gog and Magog (cf. Ezek 38:2–3, 8; see also 4Q161, in which the Davidic Messiah defeats the nations and rules over Magog). The release of the satan from the abyss may indicate judicial clemency by God, but this would have required a show of repentance on the part of satan (see Josephus, *Antiquities* 10.40), which of course does not occur. The Great War occurs in 20:8–9, when all the nations come together to battle the armies of the Lord (cf. 1QM 11.16); the defeat of the nations is accomplished by the hand of God when "fire came down from heaven and devoured them." The author describes the end of the devil in 20:10, in which, after he has deceived the nations (20:8), he is thrown into the lake of fire and sulfur where the beast and the false prophet were thrown (cf. 11Q13 3.7, in which Beliar is destroyed by fire; also T. Jud. 25.3). Here, we are told, is where he will be tormented day and night forever.

140. See Aune, *Revelation 6–16*, 729.
141. For the significance of the one thousand years, see the discussion in Koester, *Revelation*, 773–74.

Summary of John's Apocalypse

As we have read, the Apocalypse of John offers no simple solutions as to the identity of the satan or the devil figures; in fact, his position, function, and the chronology of his presence are quite complicated in relation to the other NT texts. The author uses other terms that some suggest are synonymous with the satan—dragon, serpent—but making the connection is no easy task, similar to attempting to connect the various names used for evil figures in earlier 2TP literature. The figure of the satan has a variety of roles and possible functions in the Apocalypse, including functioning through the Roman rulers who are testing the church through tribulation. The temple of Roman deities is thought to be called the "throne of the satan," likely referring to the adversarial role of the government that controls the membership in the workers' guilds in the various provinces. The author also suggests that the false teachings of groups or individuals in the church are operating under the influence of the satan figure and causing some of those under their spell to turn away from God. Those who participate in the prophetic groups are identified as "the synagogue of the satan," indicating their adversarial role against the gospel.

Some of the more troubling references to the satan and devil are found in Revelation 12. Here we see the author allegedly drawing parallels between the satan, the great red dragon, and other mythical beasts. Some argue this is where we discover the "fall" of the satan figure and his angels, but as we have seen, there are other possible interpretations for this enigmatic chapter. We can suggest that the primary role of the satan figure and the other possible monikers for him is to test and try individuals and promote a plan of interference for the fulfillment of the gospel of the Kingdom, but in the end, we see he is unsuccessful and he faces the end of his mission.

Summary

Authors of the various texts of the NT suggest a few roles for the satan figure: as a leader or chief over a group of evil spirits, an accuser of humanity, and one who tests the faith of individuals. However, other names emerged that many have suggested are related to if not in fact other names for the satan. Such titles used in the NT include Beliar (although only once), Ruler of This World, Angel of Darkness, the Evil One, the Serpent, and the great red dragon, but similar to the variety of names in the Jewish literature of the 2TP previously discussed, although not quite as murky, it is unclear if all these names relate to the same single figure. What is particularly interesting concerning these other names is how they were not part of the nomenclature of the alleged personified evil being of the previous literature (except perhaps Angel of Darkness in the DSS) and how the nomenclature of the previous literature dropped out of use in the NT. One might ask what caused the shift of the use of the term *the satan* in the HB and the devil in the LXX, their less pronounced role in the 2TP, and then return to prominent use in the NT in relation to the problem of evil. Some of the characterizations of the figure in the NT echo a few of the figures from the 2TP Jewish literature such as chief of the demons/evil spirits, Ruler of This Age (dominion of Belial), and as mentioned, the Angel of Darkness. In addition, a variety of other figures in the NT may be closely tied with the satan figure in his role as adversary, although they are not clearly identified as the same figure. These include the "lawless one" in 2 Thessalonians, the two beasts in Revelation 13, and the antichrist figure in 1 John 2:18 (one of many). One of the most significant similarities between the names of the evil figures in the earlier 2TP literature and those in the NT is their use in identifying religious human or governmental figures of the periods. It seems the various authors saw spirits at work behind and within various groups that were in opposition to God's plan and his people.

We will now shift our discussion to the period of the early Church in the late first century through the fourth century CE. During this time, we find ongoing disputes between the various gnostic groups and the theologians/apologists of the "orthodox" Church concerning the satan figure and his function in creation, the origin of sin, and the problem of evil.

Chapter 7

Satan and the Devil in the Early Church

Introduction

Christianity owes a deep debt of gratitude to the group of scholars/theologians known as the Apostolic Fathers (AF) and the Early Church Fathers (ECF). Much of what the Church believes today as doctrine and dogma is due to the study and interpretation (or misinterpretation) of Scripture by these people. One might call the exegesis of these individuals an early "Reader Response Hermeneutic," in which the modern interpreter reads their current circumstances into the text rather than applying the contextual understanding of the text intended by the original author. This understanding does not negate the interpretations of Scripture by these early theologians, but certainly we should keep their contextual view in mind when we read their interpretations of the texts relevant to our discussion on the satan/devil figure(s).

Christian literature in the mid- to late second century reveals some noteworthy developments concerning the problem of evil and the figures involved in it. During the first century CE, we have seen the disappearance of such 2TP terms as *Belial/Beliar* (depending on the dating of Christian interpolations in the T12 Patr.), *Mastema*, or *King of Wickedness*, among others; now the theological views being considered concerning the origin of evil identify ὁ σατανᾶς (the satan) or ὁ διάβολος (the devil) as the "leader" of the forces of evil. The question that is the center of the debate among these theologians and the Gnostics concerns the nature of this figure at his/its creation—good or evil.

The satan figure is identified with his own characteristics in the NT and other Jewish literature from the 2TP. One of the more common titles for the satan is "the ruler of this age" (ὁ ἄρχων τοῦ αἰῶνος τούτου).[1] It is unclear how he earned this title, but the idea of "this age" likely

---

1. Thomas Farrar suggests that ἄρχων reflects the Hebrew term שר in Dan 10:13; see his "The Intimate and Ultimate Adversary: Satanology in Early Second-Century Christian Literature," *JECS* 26, no. 4 (2018): 517–46.

reflects a similar phrase, "dominion of Belial," in various Dead Sea Scrolls in which Belial is at times referred to as the שר, "prince," "chief," or "ruler," as in "the ruler of this age." The satan figure is linked to the crucifixion of Jesus in Luke 22:3, 53; and John 13:2, 27. It is argued that he is also behind the persecution of Christians in 1 Thessalonians 2:18; 1 Peter 5:8; and Revelation 2:10 and 12:17. One of the more significant ideas, and important to this study, is the idea that Satan is a fallen angel and the angels that fell with him are demons.[2]

Justin Martyr is considered one of the primary apologists among the AF who used the idea of fallen angels to argue against the Greco-Roman religions that promoted idolatrous worship and polytheism.[3] Justin's Fallen Watcher interpretation of Genesis 6:1–4 represents the "first known Christian author to rework this myth subsequent to the New Testament."[4] In his *2 Apology* 5 (ca. 155–60 CE), Justin identifies the offspring of the "sons of God" and the daughters of humanity in Genesis 6:1–4 as demons incorporating the Enochic Book of Watchers as the basis of his interpretation.[5] Thus for Justin, evil and sin did not begin with human disobedience but by the rebellion of the Watchers in 1 Enoch. If this is the case, then how does one categorize the fall in the Garden, if not as sin. Unfortunately, as Justin notes, the Watchers did not take care of the things under the heavens that were appointed to them by God, including humanity (Jub. 7). He suggests the reason for the breach of the cosmic order was their attraction to human women, with whom they had intercourse and begat offspring called demons (οἱ λεγόμενοι δαίμονες, "the ones called demons"; *2 Apol.* 5.3). In verse 5.4, Justin states that "they enslaved the human race to themselves, partly by magic writings and partly by the fears and punishments they brought upon them and partly by the teachings regarding sacrifices." Justin does not identify who the "they" is in the passage—but the closest antecedent is the δαίμονες—but the actions described in the verse are those of the Fallen Watchers of 1 Enoch.

In his explanation of Genesis 6, Justin implies that the Fallen Watchers subjugated humanity and taught them to offer sacrifices, incense, and libations to the gods of the pagans (see LXX

---

2. See, for example, Tertullian's discussion concerning renouncing the satan prior to Christian baptism in *De Corona* 3:387: "When we are going to enter the water, but a short time before, in the presence of the congregation and under the hand of the authority, we solemnly profess that we reject the devil, and his pomp, and his angels." The Fourth Lateran Council in 1215 established the official Church doctrine of the devil in Canon 1: "The devil and the other demons were indeed created by God good by nature, but they became bad through themselves; [hu]man[ity], however, sinned at the suggestion of the devil."
3. See Annette Yoshiko Reed, "The Trickery of the Fallen Angels and the Demonic Mimesis of the Divine: Aetiology, Demonology, and Polemics in the Writings of Justin Martyr," *JECS* 12, no. 2 (2004): 141–71.
4. Yoshiko Reed, 144. Other Christian authors such as Tatian, Athenagoras, Irenaeus, Clement of Alexandria, and Tertullian would follow Justin's view on the Watcher tradition.
5. Yoshiko Reed, 146.

Ps 95:5), perhaps drawing on 1 Enoch 19.1.[6] According to Justin, the Watchers are the ones who caused the existence of the demons, which are posing as the gods/idols of the nations. He then makes it clear in 5.5 that the angels and the offspring δαίμονες are two distinct spiritual beings. It appears though that Justin (and the author of 1 En. 19) ignores the point in 1 Enoch 10.11 that the Fallen Watchers have been thrown into the pit until Judgment Day and are not free to do anything upon the earth. He does, however, blame the Fallen Watchers for the ultimate destruction of the world (in *2 Apology* 7.1), saying that their demonic progeny will continue to afflict humanity until the end. As Annette Yoshiko Reed rightly points out, Justin ignores other Enochic or the Enoch-like accounts in the Epistle of Enoch, the Animal Apocalypse, and the book of Jubilees, which offer distinct origins of evil in the 2TP literature that do not lay blame on the fallen angels.[7] In addition, not only does Justin ignore these other accounts in *2 Apology* 5; he makes no mention of the fall of Adam and Eve in the Garden as to the origin of evil in the world; he instead, lays the blame squarely on the Watcher angels who rebelled against God. The most significant point of Justin's account in *2 Apology* 5 is his failure to mention the satan figure (he does just once in *1 Apol.* 28.1—see below); this suggests, and rightly so, that Justin did not recognize that the satan figure had a role in the Fallen Watcher tradition in the Book of Watchers.

This view of the "fallen angel tradition" as being responsible for the demons of the world is the most substantial concept in the further development and understanding of the satan/devil figure in the early Church and ultimately in the modern Church. However, prior to the late first and early second centuries CE, the lack of language related to a supernatural demonology among the AF led to an etiology of evil and evil spirits that was not attributed to heavenly beings but derived from human activity.[8] The AF do acknowledge the existence of a satan/devil figure; however, close scrutiny of these early Church theologians reveals that they did not have a consistent understanding of it. They generally acknowledged the satan figure during the numerous occasions they were in dialogue with heretics and their teachings, which they ultimately blamed on the satan (e.g., Ignatius, *Eph.* 17; *Trall.* 10).

---

6. See discussion in Stokes, *Satan*, 69–73; Stokes contends that the imprisoned angels in 1 En. 19 are the demons that are worshipped by idolaters; thus, he connects the Fallen Watchers with demons, something I am not convinced the Book of Watchers permits. Stokes draws support for this reading from Isa 24:21–22, which mentions the "host of heaven" but does not mention anything about idol-worshipping or angels being demons. See also Nickelsburg, *1 Enoch 1*, 287.
7. Yoshiko Reed, "Trickery," 151–53.
8. See Jonathan Burke, "Satan and Demons in the Apostolic Fathers: A Minority Report," *Svensk Exegetisk Årsbok* 81 (2016): 127–68.

One should also keep in mind the near disappearance of the satan figure from some Jewish apocalyptic texts at the end of the first century CE (see, e.g., 2 Bar, 4 Ezra). The author of 2 Baruch 55:10–12 retells the story of the Garden without mentioning the satan figure. However, in the apocalyptic text of 2 Enoch 7, a figure identified as the "prince" of the Fallen Watchers from the Enochic tradition in 1 Enoch is identified as "Satanail." This same figure is later identified in chapter 18, which, according to Andrei Orlov, "exhibits familiarity with the Adamic mythology of evil by recalling some of features of the story of Satan's fall."[9] In addition, there is a lack of a distinct satanology in the NT;[10] both these issues are reflected in the lack of a singular satanology among the AF and the ECF. It should be noted that these theologians of the early Church serve as the modern Church's interpretive lens to read or understand the satan/devil figure found in the NT and the OT. The AF blamed much of the theology of the early heretical groups on the influence of a devil figure, but as we will see, this figure is not necessarily the modern Church's "Satan" figure.

We will next examine the prominent Gnostic groups from the early Church period whose heresies these early theologians were attempting to refute.

Gnostic Groups

Heretical teachers and groups were a growing threat to early Christianity, as is apparent in various NT texts.[11] Minor distinctions in beliefs were becoming major differences. The author of 1 Timothy 6:20 warns the community, "Avoid the profane, foolish talk and the contradictions of the false knowledge." This is a clear warning against heretical teaching. In addition, Rome was beginning a programmatic denunciation of various forms of Christianity, which appears to have forced the Church toward an orthodox system of beliefs in some form, but this would take considerable time with the wide range of theological communities that were emerging in the late first and early second centuries CE. In the midst of this struggle for an orthodox identity against what were identified as heretical groups, the devil or satan figure became a central theological issue and weapon the church leadership used to battle the teachings of these heretics. The devil became identified as the "arch-heretic" due to the NT terminology associated with him such

---

9. See Andrei A. Orlov, *Dark Mirrors: Azazel and Satanael in Early Jewish Demonology* (Albany, NY: SUNY Press, 2011), 90–91.
10. See Sacchi, *Jewish Apocalyptic*, 231, where Sacchi notes the "various forms, from the tempter of Jesus to Peter's roaring lion, prowling around us (1 Pet. 5.8), and the first sinner of John (1 Jn 3.8), the cause of the terrifying cosmic drama."
11. See Neil Forsyth, *The Old Enemy: Satan and the Combat Myth* (Princeton, NJ: Princeton University Press, 1987), 309–10.

as the "ruler of this world" (John 16:11) or "father of lies" (John 8:44). It may be suggested that these various monikers came about solely for the purpose of denouncing the Gnostics and other groups rather than being actual characteristics of the satan figure. By applying these titles, those seeking an orthodoxy for the Church were placing the heretical teachers in a camp that was opposed to God, at least in their eyes. Forsyth suggests, "The enormous diversity of sects and beliefs with which one disagreed could be comprehensively labeled 'error' and collectively damned as 'firstborn of Satan.'"[12]

The early Christian leaders were doing all they could to defend "their" view of Christianity and the sovereignty and authority of God. Significant to this discussion is that there does not appear to be a single view of a satan figure (or demons) among these early groups or the early Church leadership. The struggle with heresy in the early Church appears to have been the driving force behind the emerging story of the devil's/satan's original apostasy and rebellion within the developing Christian mythos, one that is quite different from that of the figure prior to the NT. The ongoing opposition to Christ as the "divine/human son of God" was retrofitted back into the story of the devil's rebellious beginnings. But his origins were reinforced with various prooftexts from the NT. The author of 2 Corinthians 4:4 calls him "the god [ὁ θεὸς] of this world who blinded the minds of the nonbelievers so that they will not see the light of the Gospel." In Ephesians 2:2, the author speaks of those who previously "followed the course of this world, following the prince of the power of the air (τὸν ἄρχοντα τῆς ἐξουσίας τοῦ ἀέρος), the spirit now working in the children of unbelief." A form of ἄρχων is used in four other titles that the NT authors use, allegedly, to speak of the devil/satan figures. These include the *"ruler* of this world" (John 16:11; 14:30; 12:31); *"ruler* of the kingdom of the earth" (Rev 1:5); and *"ruler* of the demons" (Luke 11:15; Mark 3:22; Matt 12:24; 9:34). Often, the text of 1 Corinthians 2:6 and 8 have been used to identify the devil or satan, but it should be noted the Greek reads *"rulers* of this age" (τῶν ἀρχόντων τοῦ αἰῶνος τούτου), plural, which is most likely referring to the human authorities (and their human wisdom) rather than spiritual beings such as the devil. All of these titles refer (except the 1 Cor reference), in some way, to the origins story of the devil/satan, which was at the heart of the debate between the heretics and the Church leadership and later apologists.

There is clear evidence in the NT that heretical teachers were attempting to infiltrate the various Christian communities. Second Thessalonians 2:7–12 speaks of "the mystery of lawlessness" (τὸ μυστήριον . . . ὁ ἄνομος) and "the lawless one" (ὁ ἄνομος) who comes to deceive those

---

12. Forsyth, 310, 419.

who do not believe the truth. Verse 11 states that God has sent a "work of delusion" (ἐνέργειαν[13] πλάνης) to those who believe the lie. This "lawless one" is sent as part of "the working of the satan" (ἐνέργειαν τοῦ σατανᾶ); this may suggest that the satan is working on behalf of God—that is, God has sent the "lawless one." Second Peter 2:1 warns against the teachings of "false prophets" who are among the community who will secretly bring in "destructive heresies" (αἱρέσεις ἀπωλείας). The author of 1 John 2:18–19 warns that the false teachers, although identified as "antichrists," are coming, ones who were previously believers in the community but now deny the truth of the Christ. In 1 John 3:8, we are told that these people are there to do the works of the devil to deceive the people. It appears that the "lawless one" may be the leader of these heretical teachers who are coming against the gospel of Christ. There appears to be a growing interest or necessity among the NT authors to link the heresies of these teachers with the satan figure, but exactly why is unclear.

Gnostic View of the Cosmos

The AF and later ECF were responding to a variety of groups that fell under the umbrella term of Gnostics; one of the key issues of conflict was the gnostic view of theodicy.[14] The Gnostics promoted a dualistic worldview in which God (YHWH) was not responsible for evil; rather, an autonomous, evil being, the Demiurge (the satan), was the cause of evil in the cosmos. This dualistic concept of evil forced the AF and ECF to react to the various Gnostic and other heretical groups and develop a clear understanding of the power and authority of the satan figure. One difficulty with this particular Gnostic view of evil was that it was not coherent among the various groups that embraced Gnosticism.[15]

One of the prominent Gnostic groups that came into conflict with the Church was the late third-century CE Manichaeans. This group's namesake was Mani, "the Apostle of God," a prophet born around 216 CE in Babylon. Legend has it that he had a religious experience with the "twin spirit" at an early age, declared himself a prophet, and went about proclaiming the visions he had been given.[16] Having grown up under the influence of Persian culture, he had been influenced by Zoroastrianism, and it is easy to see this in his understanding of the dual

---

13. This term, ἐνέργειαν, is only used in relation to the work of a superhuman being—that is, God or the satan figure.
14. Gnosticism is not a singular belief system; rather, it is, broadly speaking and with some variations, a belief system (to some degree Christian) that differentiates the evil god of this world (e.g., Marcion's god of the Old Testament) from a more abstract God of the NT who was revealed by Jesus Christ. Its primary pillar of belief regards the material world as the creation of the Demiurge. Its adherents promoted a hidden wisdom or knowledge that permitted only a select group to find salvation and escape from the evil material world.
15. See Jeffery Burton Russell, *Satan: The Early Christian Tradition* (Ithaca, NY: Cornell University Press, 1981), 53.
16. See the various legendary stories in Cologne Mani Codex (CMC): L. Koenen and C. Römer, eds., *Der Kölner Mani-Kodex. Über das Werden seines Leibes*, Kritische Edition (Opladen, Germany: Westdeutscher Verlag, 1988).

nature of the cosmos that included the contrasting forces of light and darkness, good and evil, spirit and material. His teachings, however, caused problems for him with the magi of the Zoroastrian religion. As a result, he was allegedly banished from Persia. He traveled to many different regions and assimilated some of the ideas from other religions that he encountered into his own; at the same time, he called himself an apostle of Jesus. Following a long absence, he returned to Persia but was arrested and executed circa 275 CE. One of the most influential of the ECF, Augustine was a Manichaean (ca. 373–82) prior to his conversion to Christianity.[17]

As mentioned above, the Gnostics were not a single group, nor did they have a single set of beliefs, but they all seemed to fall under the category of Gnosticism in the early Church. Irenaeus appears to use the term τῆς ψευδωνύμου γνώσεως, "the knowledge falsely called," found in 1 Timothy 6:20, to describe the various heresies that were circulating in the early Church.[18] Irenaeus notes in *Haeresis* 1.11.1 and 1.25.6 that members of the group (*Gnostike haeresis*) called themselves *Gnostikoi*. However, this was not the only group that he identified in this category; others included the Valentinians. He argues in *Haeresis* 1.23.2 that this false knowledge originated with Simon Magus in Acts 8:9–24 (although there is nothing in the Acts text that suggests this is the case). This would suggest then that stories were circulating about Simon the Magician that Irenaeus appears to cite in his work. Apparently, Simon taught that it was him who appeared among the Jews as the Son, and he appeared as the Father to the Samaritans and as the Holy Spirit to the Gentiles (1.23.1). He identified himself as "the Being who is the Father" as well as "the Great Power of God," a false claim among early Christians. Simon gained followers who were later known in the second century as the Simonians. His teachings were centered in his cosmology, which suggested that "Fire" was the first of all things and it encompassed both genders. This dual-gendered "Fire" was able to give birth to the universe, which was made up of six components: mind, thought, reason, reflection, voice, and name. From this, mind and thought gave birth to six other elements: Heaven, Earth, Air, Water, Sun, and Moon; all of these, interestingly, are part of the cosmology of the Greeks (1.23.2).

The Simonians believed that creation began with "first thought" (*Ennoia*) of the "Father's" mind, which created the angels. These angels then allegedly created the material world. The so-called "first thought" apparently was unable to return to God because the path was blocked by the same angels. This Ennoia passed through humanity through possession of female

---

17. See Hector M. Scerri, "Augustine the Manichaean and the Problem of Evil," *Augustinian Panorama* 5–7 (1988–90): 76–86.
18. See Birger A. Pearson, "Early Christianity and Gnosticism in the History of Religions," *Studia Theologica* 55 (2001): 81–106, here, 97.

bodies, including such figures as Helen of Troy, until it took possession of Helena, the consort of Simon Magus. From these tales, the Ennoia is understood as the "lost sheep." According to Simonism, Simon was the Father, who in human form wanted to unite with Ennoia in order to bring redemption to humanity.

Many people followed the teachings of Simon forming many churches in the second century. The group had its own mystic priests who practiced magic arts performing exorcisms and incantations (1.23.4). Simon's successor was named Menander, also a Samaritan magician. He too claimed to be a Messiah who gives knowledge that is used to overcome the angels who created the world. Other Gnostic heretics identified by Irenaeus included Saturninus and Basilides, who both promoted the idea that angels were the ones who created the cosmos and also humanity. It was these angels who declared, "Let us make man after our image and likeness" (1.24.1), but it was the "power above" that gave the human the spark of life to walk upright and have life. Saturninus suggests an angelic role for the satan figure, who was the "enemy of the creators of the world" and "especially of the God of the Jews" (1.24.2). In *Haeresis* 1.25–31, Irenaeus goes on to discuss the Gnosticism of Carpocrates, Cerinthus, the Ebionites, the Nicolaitanes, Cerdo, Marcion, Taitan, the Encratites, the Barbeliotes, the Ophites, the Sethians, and the Cainites. Irenaeus contends that the groups "manifested like mushrooms growing out of the ground" (1.29.1). Each group offered variations of the creation myth, the Father, the angels, the creation of humanity, and the coming of the Messiah. Significant in all the doctrines of these groups is the presence of the "first angel" who sends forth the Holy Spirit, also known as Sophia (the mother of the first angel). She appears to have formed the lower regions of creation that included inferior angels, the firmaments, and all things on the earth (1.29.4). The first angel united with Authadia (audacity) and produced wickedness, emulation, envy, fury, and lust. When these were created, Sophia departed from the angel and returned to the heavens. The angel, after being left alone as the "only being in existence," declared, "I am a jealous God, and besides me there is no one." Irenaeus contends these "are the falsehoods which these people [Gnostics] invent" (1.29.4) and the early Church had to challenge in order to establish its orthodox theology.

Apostolic Fathers

Thomas J. Farrar has identified 160 "certain or probably references to Satan, under various designations" in the Apostolic Fathers and other Jewish Christian / Christian literature dated circa 100–150 CE. These works include the Ascension of Isaiah, Apocalypse of Peter, Odes of

Solomon, Gospel of Truth, Ptolemy's Letter to Flora, and the writings of Justin Martyr.[19] Farrar identifies numerous terms or phrases such as the familiar "the adversary" (ὁ ἀντικείμενος),[20] "the devil" (ὁ διάβολος),[21] "the satan" (ὁ σατανᾶς),[22] and "the Ruler of This Age" (ὁ ἄρχων τοῦ αἰῶνος τούτου).[23] He identifies numerous others as either certain or probable references to the satan figure.[24] Farrar estimates there are over three hundred references to the satan figure, including those in the NT, "in extant Christian literature through the mid-second century CE."[25] In what follows, we will attempt to address the more prominent terms in the writings of the early Church, which are familiar to most readers.

CLEMENT OF ROME

The earliest figure of note in the AF who addresses the issue of a devil-*type* figure is Clement of Rome, who wrote his "Epistle of Clement" (1 Clem.) to the Corinthians around 96 CE. He only makes one reference to such a figure in 1 Clement 51:1, in which he speaks of seeking forgiveness of transgressions that were brought on by "suggestions of the adversary" (διά τινας τῶν τοῦ ἀντικειμένου).[26] The term he uses, ἀντικειμένου, is not the NT term used for the devil or the satan (διάβολος, σατανᾶς); rather, a form of this term appears in the NT eight times and is used in the sense of a human adversary rather than a spiritual adversary (Luke 13:17; 21:15; 1 Cor 16:9; Gal 5:17; Phil 1:28; 1 Tim 1:10; 5:14; 2 Thess 2:4, "the antichrist";[27]). It is similarly used in the LXX to describe a human adversary twelve times (Exod 23:22, צרר; 2 Sam 8:10, לחם; Esth 8:11; 9:2; 1 Macc 14:7; 2 Macc 10:26; 3 Macc 7:9; Job 13:26, איב; Isa 41:11, חרה; 45:16, צרר; 51:19, קרא; 66:6, איב). It appears in the infinitive form, ἀντικεῖσθαι, in LXX Zechariah 3:1, translating the Hebrew לשטן, "to be an adversary," the one who is opposing the appointment of Joshua as the high priest. Interestingly, the LXX of Zechariah 3:1 uses the term ὁ διάβολος to translate the Hebrew השטן, "the adversary," rather than the term ἀντικειμένος.

It appears from Clement's argument that there is a group within the Corinthian community who are causing disruption (acting as adversaries) in the Church. Clement's epistle to the Corinthians suggests that some believers have fallen away and committed sins on account

---

19. See Farrar, "Intimate and Ultimate Adversary."
20. See 1 Clem. 51.1.
21. See 2 Clem. 18.2; Ignatius, *Eph.* 10.3; *Trall.* 8.1; *Rom.* 5.3; *Smyrn.* 9.1; Polycarp, *Phil.* 7.1; *Martyr Polycarp* 2.4.
22. See Ignatius, *Eph.* 13.1; Polycarp, *Phil.* 7.1.
23. See Ignatius, *Eph.* 17.1, 19.1; *Magn.* 1.2; *Trall.* 4.2; *Rom.* 7.1; *Philad.* 6.2.
24. See table 1 in Farrar, "Intimate and Ultimate Adversary," 522–33.
25. Farrar, 522–33.
26. See Francis X. Gokey, "The Terminology for the Devil and Evil Spirits in the Apostolic Fathers" (PhD diss., Catholic University of America, 1961), 68.
27. See Burke, "Satan and Demons," 142.

of the one who opposes the church (1 Clem. 51:1). The "opposer" here is the ἀντικειμένου, the "adversary" who apparently is causing great jealousy among those in the community (see 1 Clem. 3).[28] 1 Clement 14.1 suggests this jealousy may be the result of the actions of a group who are sowing dissent among the community (see 1 Clem. 15:5; 46:8–9; 47:5–6); the "adversary" could be understood as the leader of this group rather than the supernatural "divine" adversary, the devil. Considering the extent of Clement's first letter, sixty-five chapters, it is surprising that he makes no clear references to the work of Satan in a church with such dissent. In addition, the author attributes sin to the lusts of the "evil heart" rather than a supernatural being like the devil.[29]

2 Clement

The second-century (ca. 100–120 CE) pseudepigraphal writing titled 2 Clement was not written by the author of 1 Clement, but it often follows it in manuscripts. It is considered "a 'word of exhortation' by an anonymous presbyter" in 17:3.[30] It seems likely that 2 Clement was preached at Corinth in an effort to call the people "to repentance, purity, and steadfastness."[31]

Despite the author's use of Matthew 25:31–46 (esp., 25:41: "You being cursed, depart from me into the eternal fire, the one being prepared for the devil and his angels"), there is no mention of the devil and his fallen angels. There is only one reference to the devil (τοῖς ὀργάνοις τοῦ διαβόλου, "the instruments of the devil") in 2 Clement 18:2, which may be referring to a supernatural being with the author's statement that he has "not yet fled temptation of the works of the devil," but the context does not make clear if this is a human or spiritual adversary. Burke contends it is unlikely due to the preceding content in 17:4–7, in which the author discusses "an ethical dualism in an eschatological context, without any reference to supernatural evil."[32] However, particularly telling is 17:7, which describes how the righteous, "having done well and endured torments and hated the pleasures of the soul . . . observe those who have deviated from the right path and denied Jesus through their words or deeds and are punished with terrible

---

28. Interestingly, Clement, in his rebuke of the Corinthians, appears to cite a section of Wis 2.24 but omits the phrase φθόνῳ δὲ διαβόλου, "envy of the devil," and contends their jealousy is due to "the lusts of their heart," which resulted in death entering into the world.
29. Burke, "Satan and Demons," 142.
30. Michael W. Holmes, ed. and trans., *The Apostolic Fathers: Greek Texts and English Translations* (Grand Rapids, MI: Baker Academic, 2007), 132. Burke describes it as an "eschatological commentary which uses Isa 66:18, 24; Matt 3:12; 13:37–43; 25:31–46; Mark 9:43, 48; and Luke 3:17."
31. Holmes, *Apostolic Fathers*, 132–33. The author cites such biblical texts as Isa 3:5; 54:1; and Ezek 6:8 along with various sayings of the Lord. Four of the quotations are not from the NT, and one of them (12:2) is from the Gospel of Thomas, saying #22.
32. Burke, "Satan and Demons," 155.

torments in a fire." The torments here are not directly attributed to the devil, which is generally the case in writings from the early second century, but the inclusion of an eternal fire suggests the devil is in the picture somewhere.

The author also notes his previous pagan practice of idol worship, which he ascribes to ignorance rather than a demonic influence behind the idols, which one would expect to be the case ("we worshipped, stone and wood, and gold and silver and brass, works of humans"; 1:6). The author's etiology of sin is contrary to that of other AF in that his is without a clear attestation directed at a supernatural being as the cause but rather follows a dualistic worldview that speaks of this age versus the one to come. For the author, the present age is one that speaks of adultery, corruption, greed, and deceit, and the other age renounces these things (6:3–4). He is suggesting a life of ethical choices in which one must choose the perishable or the imperishable. The audience is warned to keep its "baptism pure and undefiled" (6:9). He says humanity must pursue virtue and "abandon that evil mindset, the forerunner of our sins, and flee ungodliness lest evil things overtake us." There is no threat from a supernatural devil; rather, other humans (heretics?) "persist in teaching evil to innocent souls" (10:5). In chapter 15, he gives the admonition to choose a life of self-control, which with righteousness and holiness one may remain true to God's will (15:4).

In 2 Clement 18:2, the author states that he is "utterly sinful and has not yet escaped from temptation." He notes that "even though I am surrounded by the instruments of the devil/ adversary (τοῖς ὀργάνοις τοῦ διαβόλου), I make every effort to pursue righteousness." As mentioned previously, this διαβόλου could indicate a supernatural being, but it may perhaps refer to the flesh of the author or other humans that surround the community, teaching evil things to the Church. It is interesting that within an exhortation about living the righteous life in the midst of sin and temptation, the author does not raise the issue of the temptations and trials of the devil or even the work of evil spirits except possibly here.

IGNATIUS OF ANTIOCH

The next figure we will examine is Ignatius of Antioch, circa 50–117 CE (died sometime between 98–117), who served as the third bishop of Antioch following the apostle Peter and Evodius.[33] The seven epistles of Ignatius are thought to have been written between 110 and 117 CE, although Russell contends he was martyred in 107.[34] Ignatius entered into a debate primarily with the Docetists, who argued that Jesus only appeared to be human, which inspired their

---

33. See Eusebius, *Church History* 2.3.22.
34. See Russell, *Satan*, 34.

name the "illusionists."³⁵ This understanding of Jesus was also part of other groups belonging to the circle of Gnosticism and later Manichaeism. Ignatius's argument with Docetism came to light in his epistle to Smyrna (ca. 107 CE), in which he defended the full incarnation of Christ.³⁶ Concerning the figure of the devil,³⁷ in chapters 8 and 9 of the epistle to Smyrna, he stresses the issue of obedience to the bishop, saying that nothing should be conducted in the Church without the bishop (8:1). This included administering the Eucharist, conducting baptisms, or funeral feasts, although these sacraments may be conducted by someone who has been granted authority by the bishop (8:2). Anyone who does any of these acts secretly without the knowledge of the bishop, "serves the devil" (ch. 9; τῷ διαβόλῳ λατρεύει). This suggests that the devil may hold sway over all who are operating outside of the orthodox liturgical doctrine of the Church that is upheld by the bishop—that is, the heretics.

In Ignatius's epistle to the Ephesians 10:3, he suggests the devil has a role in the purity (ἁγνείᾳ|) or impurity of an individual and their self-control (σωφροσύνη|). Each person is to be an imitator of Christ (physically and spiritually, σαρκικῶς καὶ πνευματικῶς) "in order that no weed of the devil may be found in you" (ἵνα μὴ τοῦ διαβόλου βοτάνη τις εὑρεθῇ ἐν ὑμῖν). The term βοτάνη (weed) may be referring to the Parable of the Tares, although the Greek used in Matthew 13:25–40 is ζιζάνια. A second use of the term τοῦ διαβόλου is found in his letter to the Trallians 8:1, in which he warns the people that he "foresees the plots/traps of the devil" (προορῶν τὰς ἐνέδραη τοῦ διαβόλου; this may be an allusion to the "traps of Belial"). The snares of the devil appear to be such things as "holding a grudge" or giving opportunity to the pagans through one's folly to blaspheme the Lord. In Trallians 9, he goes on to identify the ways in which the pagans will blaspheme the Lord. He emphasizes the reality of Jesus's persecution under Pontius Pilate, "who really was crucified and died," "who really was raised from the dead"; all of these were ways in which the Docetists were denying the humanity of Christ.

A third use of τοῦ διαβόλου is found in the epistle to the Romans 5:3 in a discussion of martyrdom in rather gruesome terms in which he attributes his torture to the "evil punishments of the devil" (κακαὶ κολάσεις τοῦ διαβόλου). This passage seems to attribute significant power

---

35. See Clement of Alexandria, *Stromata* 3.13; 4.17. The founder of the group is thought to be Julius Cassianus, also a disciple of Valentinian. See also Hippolytus, *Philosophumena* VIII, i–iv, X, xii.
36. In chapter 2, he contended that all those who believe in this illusion, when they die, will be mere evil spirits (or "phantom-like"). Ignatius argued these heretics were not true Christians and with the denial of the humanity (fleshly body) of Christ, they were denying the physical resurrection of Christ (ch. 5) and thus their own.
37. Ignatius uses other terminology that may make reference to a supernatural evil being or force. He uses "ruler of this age" in Ign. Eph. 17:1, in reference to teaching (heretical); Ign. Eph. 19:1, birth of Christ; Ign. Magn. 1, abuse by the "ruler"; Ign. Rom. 7:1, being captive of the "ruler"; Ign. Phil. 6:2, evil tricks and traps of the "ruler."

to the devil, but what seems more likely in Ignatius's thinking is that the devil was at work behind the scenes rather than that this is the devil's work. Ignatius is one of the earliest theologians to identify the satan figure with the "ruler of this age." He writes in Ephesians 17, "Do not let yourself be anointed with the foul smell of the teaching of the ruler of this age [τοῦ ἄρχοντος τοῦ αἰῶνος τούτου] lest he capture you and rob you of the life to come." In his epistle to the Philadelphians 6.1–2, he uses the phrase "ruler of this age," in what could be understood as an anti-Jewish polemic, in a warning not to listen to those who speak of Judaism without Christ, for this is the deceit and plot of the "ruler of this age."

The writings of Ignatius suggest that the devil stands as a supernatural spiritual opponent to the believers in the late first to early second century CE. The devil does not appear to be a personification of the internal human struggle with sin and temptation, but rather the devil is a major part of the etiology of sin and evil in his epistles to the various communities. However, one cannot rule out completely that the "ruler"[38] represents the human governments, pagan groups, or Jews who were opposed to Christianity. In addition, he sees the devil behind the teachings of the various heretical groups with which he is in debate.

POLYCARP OF SMYRNA

Polycarp of Smyrna was a disciple of John the apostle and friend to Ignatius of Antioch. Like Ignatius, Polycarp was in an ongoing debate with the Docetists. He lived approximately 69–155 CE and died a martyr's death in 155 while residing as bishop of Smyrna.[39] His is the earliest recorded account of a martyr being burned alive, although it is alleged that the flames would not harm him, and so he was stabbed to death. Only one of his writings survive, his epistle to the Church at Philippi, but we do have a letter written to him by Ignatius and also the account of his martyrdom written by eyewitnesses (see Mart. Pol. 15:1).

Polycarp's purpose in writing the Letter to Philippi was to address the improper behavior of certain members of the Church, which he argues was a result of their wrong beliefs.[40] He uses the term *devils* (διάβολοι) in his epistle to the Philippians 5:2, in which his concern surrounds

---

38. In the NT, the title "ruler" appears to be used for a leading evil figure: "ruler of demons" in Matt 12.24–29; Mark 3.22–27; Luke 11.15–21; "ruler of this world" in John 12.31; 14.30; 16.11; "ruler of the authority of the air" in Eph 2.2; "evil ruler" in the Epistle of Barnabas 4.13, "ruler of the present time of lawlessness" in the Epistle of Barnabas 18.2; and "unrighteous ruler" in Martyrdom of Polycarp 19.2 (this could be referring to the local governor).
39. Holmes, *Apostolic Fathers*, 298.
40. Holmes, 274. It is argued that the letter was two letters written at different times: that chapters 13–14 were written after Ignatius left Philippi, and chapters 1–12 around 135–37 due to its anti-Marcionite elements; see P. N. Harrison, *Polycarp's Two Epistles to the Philippians* (Cambridge: Cambridge University Press, 1936). This idea is still up for debate—see Holmes, 275–76.

the office of deacon, but in this case, it appears to be used for human "adversaries" or possibly "slanderers." The text contends that deacons must be blameless, *not slanderers* (μὴ διάβολοι), not insincere (μὴ δίλογοι, "of two words/reasons"); the context certainly suggests this is speaking of humans and not heavenly beings. Philippians 7:1 is an argument against the Gnostics (Docetists) and their belief that Christ did not come in the flesh. Whoever believes this is an antichrist (note, it is not *the* antichrist) and "whoever does not acknowledge the testimony of the cross is from the devil" (ὃς ἂν ὁμολογῇ τὸ μαρτύριον τοῦ σταυροῦ ἐκ τοῦ διαβόλου ἐστίν). Granted the "devil" here could be a human adversary, perhaps the leader of the Gnostics in the Church, but that he calls that individual "a firstborn of the Satan" (οὗτος πρωτότοκός ἐστι τοῦ σατανᾶ) may suggest he has in mind a supernatural figure. No matter how Polycarp means to use the two terms, it certainly appears he employs *devil* and *satan* synonymously; thus, the phrase "firstborn of the satan" could be referencing one who has been chosen by "the satan" to serve him or the leader of a heretical group in the church. He contends that anyone who does not acknowledge the words of Christ concerning the resurrection or judgment, a characteristic of the Docetists heresy, "is the firstborn of satan."[41] Polycarp, in all but one occasion, appears to use forms of the terms ὁ σατανᾶς and ὁ διαβόλος to refer to a heavenly adversary who is attempting to interfere in the lives of the faithful ones.[42] The issues to which he connects these figures all seem to be related to the heretical beliefs of Gnostic groups, likely the Marcionites or the Docetists. On each occasion, the adversarial figure is attempting to cause disruption within one or more Church. This raises an interesting point as to the "omnipresence" of the devil or the satan figure in the early Church. To this point in Jewish and Christian traditions, the figure has not had the ability to be in more than one place at a time. His role thus far is to test the faith of individuals on the earth and incorporate a group of evil spirits (likely the spirits of the giants from the Enoch Watcher tradition) into his ongoing role upon the earth as the adversary to humanity. It appears now, in the late first and early second centuries CE, that the figure has the ability to interfere with multiple churches and meddle in the lives of untold numbers of individuals throughout the known world, but most likely by using willing individuals (false teachers) or other evil spirits on his

---

41. Interesting here is his use of the term *prototokos* in relation to the satan figure. This term is only used in the NT to refer to Christ in his human form or his postresurrection form, both of which suggest he is the first of more to come. One might ask if this is how Ignatius is using it, suggesting there will be many to follow the heresies of the Gnostics or "the deep things of the satan."
42. The use of the term *teaching* could suggest he is warning against the teaching of the Gnostics (the epistle is warning against being corrupted by evil teachings, which corrupt one's faith in God); if this is the case, then Polycarp, and other AF, appear to see the satan figure behind the teachings of the various Gnostic groups.

side. This may signal the beginning of the understanding of this figure as a semiautonomous or even autonomous force of evil on the earth.

Martyrdom of Polycarp

Our next examination concerns the text the Martyrdom of Polycarp, which records the death of Polycarp (ca. 155–60 CE)[43] and was written by eyewitnesses to his death from the Church at Smyrna and written to the Church at Philomelium.[44] The theological issues of the letter surround the Lord Jesus versus the Lord Caesar (see 10:1). The Christians were viewed as disloyal to the empire, which resulted in an edict concerning the worship of the emperor.[45] Polycarp would serve as a model martyr for the many Christians that would follow his path.

The first instance of the term ὁ διάβολος is found in 2:4, which follows the description of many of the torturous things the martyrs went through, which the author contends were brought about by the devil: "for many things the devil devised against them" (πολλὰ γὰρ ἐμηχανᾶτο κατ' αὐτῶν ὁ διάβολος). However, according to Burke, the majority reading for 2:4 includes the term ὁ τύραννος, "the tyrant," making it the subject of the verb for "devised" rather than "the devil."[46] This would then identify the instigator of the martyrdoms as a government official (see 3:1, the proconsul), also identified as "the adversary" of the Church. In 3:1, the author notes that despite the torturous acts against them "the devil [not in the Greek; implied from 2:4[47]] did not prevail against any of them" (κατὰ πάντων γὰρ οὐκ ἴσχυσεν, "for he was not strong against all of them"). One might assume this meant they did not renounce their faith in Christ (in chapter 4, it appears Quintus [and others] renounced his faith and offered a sacrifice to Caesar; see 8:2); only if they did so would the devil have prevailed. If this is the case, then we see a continuation of the devil's/satan's task of testing and trying the faith of believers in the early Church. It appears that he is using nonbelievers/pagans to assist him in this task. One might also consider that the author of the Martyrdom of Polycarp, in using the term *devil*, may be referring to the Roman emperor or the local governor who has been

---

43. Holmes, *Apostolic Fathers*, 301–2.
44. Holmes, 298.
45. Holmes, 298.
46. Burke, "Satan and Demons," 153. Burke contends the Martyrdom of Polycarp is modeled after the martyrology of 4 Macc. Similar terminology is used in 1 Macc 1:36, which uses the phrase ὁ διάβολος πονηρός, "the evil adversary," in reference to "the opponents of the Jews under Apollonius." Burke also suggests the use of πονηρός here may have influenced its use, as well as "jealous and envious," in Martyr. 17:1, which describes the proconsul (cf. 1 Clem. 5.1–6.2).
47. Holmes, *Apostolic Fathers*, 308–9.

instructed to force the Christians to bow to Caesar—or at best, that the author understands the devil is behind the actions of the empire.[48]

In chapter 17, the author then appears to identify the satan figure as "the adversary, the jealous one, and the evil one" (ὁ δε ἀντίζηλος καὶ βάσκανος καὶ πονηρός—each name is definite, provided the article ὁ is governing all three nouns), all of which leads up to the figure being called "the one in opposition" (ὁ ἀντικείμενος) of the race of the righteous. The author then states in 17:2 that this figure (ὁ ἀντικείμενος) influences Nicetes to appeal to the magistrate not to allow the believers to take Polycarp's body for fear that they may begin to worship him rather than Christ. There is a decidedly anti-Jewish tone in 13:1, 17:2, and 18:1, in which they (the Jews) are the ones instigating the magistrate's and centurion's actions concerning the burning of Polycarp and the disposal of his body. The Jews are accused of having the custom of burning people in 13:1, and they are behind the refusal to give over the body to the believers in 17:2 and 18:1. These actions, along with the notion that the "adversary" was influencing Nicetes to refuse to allow the body to be turned over, suggests that the author may have thought the Jews too were being influenced by the adversary (ὁ ἀντικείμενος). Eusebius, in recording this story, goes as far as to remove "evil one" from 17:1 and inserts "certain ones," perhaps suggesting in 17:2 that the Jews incited Nicetes to ask the magistrate (τῷ ἄρχοντι), thus identifying the opponents of the Church as humans—that is, the Jews.

Epistle of Barnabas

The Epistle of Barnabas offers a few comments on the satan/devil figure. The epistle is dated sometime between 70 and 135 CE, and according to Holmes; it is difficult to be more precise.[49] James N. Rhodes contends the purpose of the epistle, despite its Jewish polemical tone, is to help the audience maintain its covenant fidelity in the midst of the growing strain between Judaism and Christianity.[50] David Flusser contends the author is drawing on an early Jewish source that holds a strong dualistic worldview, which is clear in chapter 18 with the use of such language as

---

48. See Sophie Lunn-Rockliffe, "Diabolical Motivations: The Devil in Ecclesiastical Histories from Eusebius to Evarius," in *Shifting Genres in Late Antiquity*, ed. Geoffrey Greatrex and Hugh Elton (Burlington, VT: Ashgate, 2015), 119–34, here, 123. See also E. Leigh Gibson, "The Jews and Christians in the Martyrdom of Polycarp: Entangled or Parted Ways?," in *The Ways That Never Parted: Jews and Christians in Late Antiquity and the Early Middle Ages*, ed. Adam H. Becker and Annette Yoshiko Reed (Tübingen, Germany: Mohr Siebeck, 2003), 145–58, here, 154–55. Gibson contends the varying difficulties of the text in chapter 17, which apparently lacked clarity in its original form and the transcribers thought to correct some of the ambiguity. She notes that two manuscripts omit 17:2d and 17:3.
49. Holmes, *Apostolic Fathers*, 373. See also the discussion in James N. Rhodes, *The Epistle of Barnabas and the Deuteronomic Tradition* (Tübingen, Germany: Mohr Siebeck, 2004), 75–87.
50. See Rhodes, *Epistle of Barnabas*, 180.

"two ways of teaching and power, one of light and one of darkness . . . For over the one [way] are the light-giving angels of God . . . and over the other [way] the angels of the satan."[51] This may suggest the author's familiarity with the tradition of the Treatise of the Two Spirits in 1QS.

The Epistle of Barnabus 2:1 offers the first allusion to the satan figure (without naming it) in the author's claim that the people are living in evil days and "the one who is at work has the power" (καὶ αὐτοῦ τοῦ ἐνεργοῦντος ἔχοντος τὴν ἐξουσιαν). As a result, the people are told to be on guard and seek out the righteousness of the Lord. The audience is warned in 2:10 to walk with care "so that the evil one does not work a creeping error in us" (ἵνα μὴ ὁ πονηρος παρείσδυσιν πλάνης ποιήσας ἐν ἡμῖν). This passage seems to suggest the satan figure is tasked with testing individuals (or groups) with the temptation to sin, in this case to offer false oaths against one's neighbor (2:8). The author is using another name for this same figure in 4:9, where he states that believers must keep their guard up during the age of lawlessness "so that *the black [dark?] one* does not have opportunity to sneak in." This wording may be used to describe the satan figure, although it may be describing a human figure—that is, "the evil ruler" (ὁ πονηρός ἄρχων). This phrase is offered in the midst of a warning not to fall asleep in sin or one may be cast out of the Kingdom of the Lord. Perhaps another instance in which the author speaks to this figure (the satan figure) is found in 9:4 in a discussion about the circumcision of the Jews, although once again, the context may allow for a human figure. The author states that the Lord had told the people that circumcision of the flesh was no longer required, but the people continued to do so "because an evil angel enlightened (ἐσόφιζεν) them"; however, this could be understood as an "evil messenger" (ἄγγελος πονηρὸς) rather than a heavenly being, who could be speaking heresy to the community—that is, saying that circumcision is still necessary to enter the Kingdom (9:6). The author contends that it is the circumcision of the heart that matters, for "every Syrian and Arab and all the idol-worshipping priests are also circumcised; does this mean that they too belong to their covenant?"

The Epistle of Barnabus 18:2 offers the clearest mention of a satan figure within the author's discussion of the "two ways." He suggests there are two paths to follow, one of light guarded by "light-giving angels/messengers of God" (φωταγωγοὶ ἄγγελοι τοῦ θεοῦ) and one of darkness, watched over by "angels/messengers of the satan" (ἄγγελοι τοῦ σατανᾶ); again, both of these "angels" could be human messengers. The satan is identified in 18:2 as the one opposed to

---

51. David Flusser, *Judaism of the Second Temple Period: The Jewish Sages and Their Literature* (Grand Rapids, MI: Eerdmans, 2009), 2:233; Flusser suggests that the Jewish work "The Two Ways" and the Epistle of Barnabas share a source but that the latter, in its original form, "was essentially identical with 'The Two Ways'—save a few minor differences." The satan in this case is identified as "the ruler of the present age of lawlessness" (ὁ δὲ ἄρχων καιροῦ τοῦ νῦν τῆς ἀνομίας), perhaps alluding to the dominion of Belial.

the Lord and is "the ruler of the present time of lawlessness" (ὁ δὲ ἄρχων καιροῦ τοῦ νῦν τῆς ἀνομίας); one might suggest this is referring to the period in which Belial/wickedness rules, as seen in the Dead Sea Scrolls.

The next possible reference to the/a satan figure is found in 19:11 in the context of a description of the "way of light" (19:1–12). Following a long list of dos and don'ts (more don'ts than dos), the reader is instructed that "to the end you shall hate *the evil one*" (εἰς τέλος μισήσεις τὸν πονηρόν). In this context, it appears the role of this "evil one" is to try to cause the people to do the "don'ts" and thus turn away from "the way of light." In 20:1, the satan figure is once again called "the black one." He is the one overseeing the "way of darkness" that is crooked and completely cursed, and anyone who follows it will meet eternal death. The characteristics of people on this path are the opposite of those on the way of light. Those on the "way of darkness" commit idolatry, hypocrisy, adultery, murder, robbery; they are guilty of pride, sorcery, and magic, among many other sins, culminating in a lack of fear of the Lord (this list continues in 20:2, describing how these sinful actions manifest in actions toward others).

A reference to "the evil one," likely synonymous with the/a satan figure, is found in 21:3, which describes the end of days "in which everything will perish together with the evil one" (ἐν ᾗ συναπολεῖται πάντα τῷ πονηρῷ|). It appears that during this time the final Judgment will take place and "the evil one" will meet the Lord and God's recompense will be handed out to the righteous and the wicked. The author of the Epistle of Barnabus uses other appellations that seem to be identifying a supernatural evil being; however, considering the persecutions that were being carried out during the suggested time of the writing of the Epistle of Barnabus, the author may have been referring to the Roman emperor or a local government official. In 2:1, he is "the ruler who is at work in the age of evil"; he is the "evil one" in 2:10; 19:11; and 21:3; the "evil ruler" in 4:13; the "lawless one" in 15:5; and somewhat enigmatically, "the black one" in 4:9 and 20:1. It appears that the satan figure is the key source for the author's etiology of evil and sin and is part of the author's understanding and expectations during the eschaton and the time of lawlessness.

Shepherd of Hermas

According to Michael Holmes, the Shepherd of Hermas (SH) "is one of the more enigmatic documents to have survived from the postapostolic period."[52] The book likely circulated in two sections, chapters 1–24 and 25–114. The first, 1–24, may have been written in the late first

---

52. Holmes, *Apostolic Fathers*, 442.

century to early second century, and the second, 25–114, toward the mid-second century.[53] No author can be firmly identified. The book offers a description of a series of visions given to the author that were mediated to him by an angelic figure (the shepherd), not unusual for the period in which the genre of apocalyptic flourished. The author presents various discussions concerning the issue of "repentance and forgiveness of postbaptismal sin" of a believer in light of God's justice and mercy.[54] In addition, the author contemplates the issue of social and economic justice or the lack thereof within his community. The Shepherd of Hermas was widely accepted as Scripture by some prominent ECF, including Clement of Alexandria, Origen, and Tertullian. It was included in the canon of Didymus the Blind in the fourth century and, along with the Epistle of Barnabas, the Shepherd of Hermas is included in the Codex Sinaiticus following John's Apocalypse.[55]

The language of the author's diabology is scattered throughout the three sections of Shepherd of Hermas; it contains twenty-four instances of ὁ διάβολος or a form of it, although there is no reference to the term ὁ σατανᾶς (the satan) in the 114 chapters. In addition, there is no mention of a devil figure or evil spirits in chapters 1–24 (Visions), the suggested earliest independent section of the book. Evil spirits are mentioned two times in chapter 33, three times in chapter 34, once in chapter 40, and once in chapter 95. The term διάβολος, while significant in the Visions and the Mandates, is found only once in the Parables (69:6).

The etiology of evil in the world in Shepherd of Hermas is anthropogenic in 6:2, in which the Shepherd Angel tells Hermas that all his children "have rejected God and blasphemed the Lord by their great evil." As a result, temptation and sin, normally attributed to the devil, is blamed on the "human passions" in 1:8; "evil desire" in 2:4; the "desire for riches" in 14:6; "licentious desires and evil deeds" in 15:2; and "weakness of the flesh" in 17:3.[56] However, the devil (ὁ διάβολος) is still the one who comes "to test" (ἐκπειράζων, "the one testing") the

---

53. Holmes, 447; Burke, "Satan and Demons," 143; see also Russel, *Satan*, 43n36. Gokey contends that the Visions 1–4 (chs. 1–24) were likely written toward the end of the first or early/mid-second century CE, which, Gokey argues, reflect the content of the Didache, 1 Clement, and the Adamic etiology of sin. The remainder of the Shepherd of Hermas reflects the views of evil that are found in texts dated from the late second century CE, in which "a supernatural evil tempter" is at work in the world. See Gokey, *Terminology for the Devil*, 148.
54. Holmes, *Apostolic Fathers*, 443.
55. Holmes, 444–45.
56. Burke, "Satan and Demons." 145. This is a similar line of argument for many Alexandrian theologians, including Philo of Alexandria, a Jewish exegete. Following a similar line as the T12 Patr., the Shepherd of Hermas suggests the "vices" are demons, or better yet, δαιμόνια; for example, "slander" and "vain confidence" are identified as *daimonian*. In 27:3, the author speaks of "slander" as a "restless demon" (ἀκατάστατον δαιμόνιόν), and in 99:3, "vain confidence" and "self-will" are identified as great demons (μέγα . . . δαιμόνιόν). This personification of vices as demons in the Shepherd of Hermas is not seen in other AF's writings, but the author is often inconsistent in his dialogue about evil spirits (this may be an idea that could be part of Philo's or an Alexandrian demonology, although Philo does not make this connection). See Gokey, *Terminology for the Devil*, 127.

servants of God (48:4), but according to 48:2, he cannot overcome the believer if they resist (cf. Jas 4:7). At the same time, if the person is "completely empty," then they will fear the devil and the devil will overcome them (48:7). In addition to a nonsupernatural evil power, the way of salvation is not attributed to an eschatological supernatural being; rather, it is accomplished through ethical instruction in 3:2, self-control in 6:1–2, repentance from double-mindedness in 6:4, walking in innocence and sincerity in 7:2 and 9:9, walking in righteousness in 9:6, and charity and almsgiving in 17:4–6.[57] Of course, all of these actions/characteristics are part of the teachings of Jesus in the Gospels.

The first reference to the devil is found in 31:4, in the midst of a discussion about forgiveness and repentance of sins in which the author warns of "the cunning of the devil" (τὴν πολυπλοκίαν τοῦ διαβολοῦ), which can overcome the weakness of an individual. The shepherd tells Hermas that God knows the weakness of humans and that the devil behaves wickedly toward God's servants by doing some evil act to them, but that person has the opportunity to repent and be forgiven. There is no mention as to the authority of the devil to afflict these individuals, although one might suggest that because the Lord knows the weaknesses of individuals, he may want their faith tested in these areas, and he permits the devil to test them. In 31:6, the author may be alluding to the idea that the Lord has granted permission to the devil to test humanity (τις ἐκπειρασθείς); the shepherd states that should that person fail the test, they have one opportunity to repent of the sin. If a person repeatedly sins and repents, it is of no use to them, as they will attempt this with difficulty, perhaps suggesting they will live a hard life.

The second reference to the devil is found in 37:2 in the context of a discussion of keeping the Lord's commandments. One's ability to resist the testing of the devil is accomplished by a healthy "fear of the Lord." If one has this, then they need not fear the devil but will be able to rule over the devil because the devil has no power/authority of his own. The shepherd says that if one rejects the devil then the devil has no power/authority over that individual (cf. the Trials of Jesus in the Wilderness, Matt 4 and Luke 4). In 37:3, the shepherd warns that a person should "fear the works of the devil, for they are evil." In contrast, when a person fears the Lord, they will know to fear the works of the devil and avoid them. Interestingly, there is no mention as to what these works are or the actual role of the devil in this context.

---

57. It appears the author of Shepherd of Hermas may have been influenced by the Letter of James and the idea of faith without works is not much good and that failure to follow the acts of righteousness allows an open door for trial by the adversary, the satan. See Oscar J. F. Seitz, "The Relationship of the Shepherd of Hermas to the Epistle of James," *JBL* 63, no. 2 (1944): 131–40; Patrick J. Hartin, *James*, Sacra Pagina Series 14 (Collegeville, MN: Liturgical Press, 2003).

The next reference to the devil is found in 39:11 in a discussion about being double-minded (διψυχίαν, "two souls"). The shepherd warns that "double-mindedness . . . is evil and senseless" and has caused many to lose faith; it is "a daughter of the devil and does much evil to God's servants" (39:9). In 39:11, double-mindedness (doubt) is described as "an earthly spirit from the devil that has no power" in contrast to faith that is from the heavenly realm (39:12). This idea seems to suggest the influence of a spirit that is working alongside the devil to bring confusion to an individual; what is interesting is that here there is no mention of a spirit from the Lord to counter this evil spirit until we get to chapter 43.

Chapter 43 presents a discussion on false prophets and the spirit from the devil and the divine spirit. In 43:3, the shepherd states that the false prophet is filled with emptiness, lacking the divine spirit, and gives empty answers to the double-minded who ask him to prophecy to them. Interestingly, the prophet does speak some true words, "for the devil fills him with his own spirit, to see if he will be able to breakdown any of the righteous." This perhaps alludes to the task of the devil, testing the faithful. Contrary to the actions of the false prophet, the true prophet operates in the power of the divine spirit (τῆς δυνάμεος τοῦ θείου πνεύματος; 43:5). He will never prophesy from a question of another person but will only speak when the Spirit wants him to speak (43:8). In 43:17, Hermas is warned to put his trust in the spirit from God and not in the earthly spirit that is from the devil and lacks power. This idea may reflect the "lying spirit" concept (from the Ahab story) and add to the image of the devil being the father of lies.

The next occurrence of the devil is found amid a discussion of evil and good desires. In 45:1–2, the shepherd warns of the evil desire for foolish luxuries that include unneeded wealth, needless eating and drinking, and lustful desires for another person's spouse. All these excesses are foolish and empty to the servants of God and should be avoided at all cost. Like the lying spirit, this "evil desire" or lust for luxury or extravagance is "a daughter of the devil" (ἡ ἐπιθυμία ἡ πονηρά τοῦ διαβόλου θυγάτηρ ἐστίν). In 45:4, the author seems to personify "evil desire": "If the evil desire perceives that you are fully armed with fear of God and you are resisting it (the evil desire), it will flee far from you." This resembles the idea that if one follows after God and his Law, the devil or Belial must flee from you. This phrase "daughter of the devil" may be an epithet for an evil spirit that is working with the devil.

In chapter 47, the shepherd returns to a discussion about keeping the commandments of the Lord. Only those people with the Lord in their hearts are able "to have power over" (κατακυριεῦσαι) the commandments (47:3; and everything under heaven, 47:2); those with the Lord only on their lips and hard-hearted (double-minded?; 47:4) will not master the commandments. In 47:5–7, he states that those who do not walk in the Lord's commandments walk in the devil's commandments (οἱ ταῖς ἐντολαῖς πορευόμενοι τοῦ διαβόλου; 47:6), "which are difficult, bitter, wild and licentious," but there is no mention as to what these commandments are. Still, all those who walk in them are commanded to turn from them (repent, ἐπιστράφητε) and "be not afraid of him [the devil], and he will flee from you" (47:7). This language seems to reflect the Qumran idea that if one turns back to the Torah and follows God's commands, the adversary must flee, similar to the wilderness test of Jesus in the Gospels. In verse 45:7, the shepherd identifies himself as the "angel of repentance" who has power over the devil who, according to the shepherd, can only cause fear for the individual, but it is a fear without power. The description of the devil suggests that he is under the power of this angel and that his power is limited to a fear that will prevent individuals from having a fear of the Lord.

Verses 48:1–2 seem to support this idea by suggesting that even attempts by those who desire to keep God's commandments are made difficult as "the devil is hard, and he oppresses them" presumably to test their faith. In verse 48:2, the shepherd states that "the devil can wrestle against, but he is not able to overthrow [them] if one resists him." If one is able to resist the test, then the devil must flee in shame. Only those "who are empty fear the devil as if he had power." "Empty" here seems to suggest a lack of holy spirit or faith, as suggested in verse 4, which further supports the idea that the task of the devil is to test the servants of God (ὁ διάβολος ἔρχεται ἐπι πάντας τοὺς δούλους τοῦ θεοῦ ἐκπειράζων αὐτούς, "the devil comes upon all the servants of God, testing them"). He goes on to state that those full of faith resist him, and he leaves and pursues those who are empty or partially empty: "he enters into them" (εἰσπορεύεται εἰς αὐτούς), which suggests possession, but surely this cannot be speaking of the singular devil, as he is only one spirit. Rather, the author must have in mind the evil spirits that are under the devil's authority. Or is the author attributing, perhaps unknowingly, a sense of omnipresence to the devil figure? Can he "possess" more than one person at a time?

In 49:1, the author states that the "angel of repentance" was sent to strengthen the faithful and encourage them not to fear the devil. This angelic figure seems to reflect some of the characteristics or tasks that are attributed to the Angel of Light in the DSS in such texts as 1QS, 11Q13, among others. In chapter 63, the author introduces Hermas to the "angel of punishment" (ὁ ἄγγελος τῆς τιμωρίας), one of the angels of righteousness. Those who wander away from God are handed over to this angel in an effort to bring them back. One might ask if this is the angel that Paul speaks of when he hands individuals over to the devil in order to destroy the flesh and save the person's soul (e.g., 1 Cor 5; 1 Tim 1:20).[58] This would support the idea that the devil is an angel of punishment

---

58. See discussion of the satan as "the attacker" in Stokes, *Satan*, 205–7.

who God uses to purify the wicked. The punishments inflicted seem quite harsh: tortures, loss, illnesses, every kind of disturbance, affliction by worthless people. The shepherd states in 49:2 that forgiven believers who practice righteousness (do righteous acts) have power over the devil's works and will not fear the threat of the devil. In 49:4, Hermas states the angel of repentance will shred all power of the devil, giving believers power to overcome him, if their hearts are pure (49:5).

The final reference to the devil in Shepherd of Hermas is found in chapter 69. Here, in a discussion of the Parable of the Willow Tree, Hermas (Angel of Punishment) continues his discussions with the shepherd (Angel of Repentance). The tree is identified as the Law of God (νόμος θεοῦ), and the Law is the Son of God (ὁ υἱὸς τοῦ θεοῦ). In the midst of this discussion is the Angel of the Lord (ὁ ἄγγελος οὗ κυρίου, 69:1), who appears to be later identified as "the great and glorious angel Michael" (69:3), who has authority over God's people and is "the one setting the Law in the hearts of the ones who are faithful." The shepherd tells of sticks that are from the tree that represent people. Some sticks have been sent to the Tower and other sticks have been left with the shepherd (Angel of Repentance?) with hopes they will repent. In 69:6, the shepherd states that those who have been crowned and sent to the Tower are those who have been faithful and have wrestled with the devil and have conquered him (οἱ μετὰ τοῦ διαβόλου παλαίσαντες καὶ νικήσαντες). This scenario suggests that the faithful will need to endure the testing and trials of the devil for the sake of the Law (i.e., the Son).

Excursus: *The "Two Spirits" in the Shepherd of Hermas*

The author of the Shepherd of Hermas appears to adopt an anthropological dualism similar to that which is present in the DSS. At least four markers of dualism are found in the text: two paths, straight and crooked; two spirits, good and evil;[59] two cities, the Lord's and that of those opposed to him; and

---

59. There is some indication of the presence of the "evil inclination" in Shepherd of Hermas, although it is slightly ambiguous as to its exact meaning. The Jewish concept of "double-mindedness" is found in chapters 39–43, in which the author speaks of asking God for all things without hesitation (cf. Jas 1:5–8), for hesitation will result in receiving nothing (39:5). Jeffrey Russell suggests this double-mindedness has its roots in the human inclination to choose the path of good or evil. The spirituality of the Shepherd of Hermas is ambiguous, as the author often intermingles the literal and figurative while identifying human virtues and vices with good and evil spirits, which can be taken literally or symbolically as a good or evil inclination in the human heart. See Russell, *Satan*, 43. Gokey contends that the term διψυχία, the author's favorite when speaking of "double-mindedness" (e.g., 39:9, 12), has its roots in the rabbinic tradition of two hearts or two inclinations—*yetserim*, which the author also uses the Greek word ἐπιθυμία. See Gokey, *Terminology for the Devil*, 122. In Shepherd of Hermas, the author uses the term ἐπιθυμία to convey the idea of the Hebrew *yetser* in chapters 44–46, in which he speaks of two desires, one evil and one good: "Remove from yourself of all evil desire (πᾶσαν ἐπιθυμίαν πονηράν) and put on the desire that is good and holy (τὴν ἐπιθυμίαν τὴν ἀγαθὴν καὶ σεμνήν)." In 45:5, the author states that "if you serve the good desire and submit to it, you will be able to have power over the evil desire and control it if you wish."

two angels (messengers?), of righteousness and of evil; although, it is unclear at times if the angels are cosmic in nature or personal. In 33:1–2, the author identifies two spirits that can dwell in the human person, the "holy spirit" (τὸ πνεῦμα τὸ ἅγιον) and an "evil spirit" (πονηροῦ πνεύματος). If the "evil spirit" attempts to encroach on the human space, the holy spirit seeks to leave to find an uncontaminated place (33:3). The author states that if this occurs, then the holy spirit is unable "to serve the Lord" as it desires. There is no sense that this is the Divine Holy Spirit, but rather it is a spirit of holiness, although in each instance the definite article is present. If both spirits continue to dwell together in the person, "it is unfortunate and evil for that person" (33:4). The individual is able to assist the holy spirit and in turn overcome the evil spirit by practicing patience and understanding (33:1); in doing so, they will "overcome all evil works and will accomplish all righteousness." Similar to the "two spirits" in 1QS, there is language that refers to the spirits as actual angels. In 36:1, the author notes, "There are two angels with a person, one of righteousness and one of wickedness." One should keep in mind the "angels" here, ἄγγελοι, could indicate "messengers" rather than heavenly beings. However, there is no sense that the ἄγγελοι are "in" the person; rather, they are "with" (μετὰ τοῦ ἀνθρώπου) that person. This seems to suggest an external influence on a person rather than possession (36:2); this follows the similar line in 1QS. Nonetheless, the language in 36:3 is ambiguous about the physical positioning of the angel of righteousness. The author states that the angel "advances toward/upon your heart" (ἐπὶ τὴν καρδίαν σου ἀναβῇ) and speaks words concerning righteousness, purity, holiness, and contentment; when these things "come upon (enters into?) one's heart" (εἰς τὴν καρδίαν σου ἀναβῇ), a person can know the angel of righteousness is with them. There is certainly a different intention in the language used concerning the angel/messenger and the "thoughts" inspired by the angel. The opposite thoughts will come upon a person when the angel of wickedness is with them. This angel is ill-tempered, bitter, and foolish, and his works are evil and always trying to overthrow the servant of the Lord (36:4). The author warns Hermas that when he recognizes the works of this angel, "know that he is in you" (γίνωσκε ὅτι αὐτός ἐστιν ἐν σοί); although the Greek preposition ἐν can mean "with," we have seen previously the author use the preposition μετὰ to signify an external position in relation to the "angel of righteousness." There appears to be an ongoing struggle for the human heart/soul between these two angels/messengers, a struggle in which the person must choose which angel to follow (36:10), a similar battle to the one we see in the DSS.

PAPIAS OF HIERAPOLIS

Papias was the bishop of Hierapolis in Asia Minor and allegedly lived around the same time as Polycarp (ca. 70–155 CE). According to Irenaeus (in Fragments of Papias, frag. 14; see below), Papias knew the apostle John. Since this is a collection of fragments, it is nearly impossible to date them as they come from not only Papias's writings but those of Irenaeus, who allegedly cites him.[60] In the Fragments of Papias, Papias provides some of the earliest testimony concerning the authorship of Matthew, Mark, John, and John's Apocalypse.[61] Perhaps one of the more significant items one can gather from Papias's writings is that "even after [the] gospels were written, oral traditions continued to circulate and to influence the written text."[62] This would suggest that there may have been some significant editorial work done to the Gospels we now possess.

The first mention of the devil/satan figure is found in fragment 11;[63] here it is noted that "Papias says, word for word: 'Some of them'—obviously meaning those angels that once were holy—'he assigned to rule over the orderly arrangement of the earth, and commissioned them to rule well.'" This is likely an allusion to the Watchers in the Watcher tradition of 1 Enoch (or possibly the Seventy Shepherds tradition). The fragment follows with a quote from Papias, "But as it turned out, their administration came to an end [lit. 'died']. And the great dragon, the ancient serpent, the one being called devil and the satan, was cast out; the one deceiving the whole world was cast down to the earth and his angels." This quote from John's Apocalypse 12:9 is certainly not speaking of the Watcher tradition, so it leaves one wondering how Papias was making the connection (if he was) between the angels who were appointed to rule over the earth and the satan figure and his alleged fallen angels in Revelation 12:9.

In fragment 24:1–11, which survives in the Armenian translation of Constantine of Hierapolis,[64] Papias is cited speaking on Revelation 12:7–9, in which he describes the "fall

---

60. Holmes suggests Papias's major work, *Expositions of the Sayings of the Lord* (see frag. 3.1), was written around 130 CE; see Holmes, *Apostolic Fathers*, 722.
61. Holmes, 722.
62. Holmes, 723. See also James D. G. Dunn, *Jesus Remembered* (Grand Rapids, MI: Eerdmans, 2003), 173–254, for a discussion of "oral tradition" in the early Church.
63. See Andrew of Caesarea, *On the Apocalypse*, ch. 34, serm. 12, noted in Holmes, *Apostolic Fathers*, 749n10.
64. Holmes, *Apostolic Fathers*, 762–63; F. Siegert, "Unbeachtete papiaszitate bei armenichen Schriftstellern," *New Testament Studies* 27 (1981): 605–14.

of satan." In addition, he appears to speak of the fall of satan in 24:2: "Heaven did not endure his earthly intentions, because it was impossible for light to communicate with darkness."[65] It must be assumed *light* is heaven and *darkness* is the satan figure; however, there is no further mention of the name satan until 24:8, nor in the preceding thirteen chapters, but this is likely due to the fragmentary nature of the work. The fall of the satan figure is described as one that takes place prior to the creation of humanity as he states in verse 24:3: "He fell to earth, here to live; and when humanity came here, where he was, he did not permit them to live in natural passions; on the contrary, he led them astray into many evils."[66] So Andrew of Caesarea suggests that Papias understood that this figure, possibly the satan, existed on the earth prior to the creation of humanity, despite no evidence of this in Genesis, although we know from Jubilees that the heavenly beings were created by God prior to humanity.

In verse 24:4, the reader is told that Michael and his legions of angels are also on the earth helping humanity, although this appears to be after the expulsion from the Garden during the period of the giving of the Torah and the days of the prophets (Dan 10, 12); this could be an allusion to the original tasks of the Watcher angels in Jubilees prior to the fall of the group from the Enochic tradition. In verse 5, the author shares that there is now a war against the dragon (not the satan figure) in an effort to stop it from setting stumbling blocks for humanity—this is a description of one of the functions of the figure, but there are no specific actions described. In verse 6, the "battle crosses over into heaven, to Christ himself," this is an apparent allusion to the battle in Revelation 13–14. But 24:7 then states, "Yet Christ came, and the Law, which was impossible for anyone else, he fulfilled in his body."[67] It appears from this reading that there is a battle occurring on the earth prior to Christ coming to the earth in bodily form, but in Revelation 12, we are told a battle occurs after Jesus has ascended to heaven following the resurrection.

In verse 8, the author states that Christ "defeated sin and condemned Satan, and through his death he spread abroad his righteousness over all."[68] Then in verse 9 we have an allusion to the incident of Revelation 12 in which Michael defeats the dragon and he is cast down to earth defeated; this casting down, according to Papias in verse 24:10, is what we find in Luke 10 when Jesus said, "I saw Satan fallen from heaven like a lightning bolt."[69] If this is the case, then Papias may be suggesting that the dragon/satan is battling Michael in the heavens (Rev 12) while Christ is on the earth in human form. But what then was the role of the dragon/satan figure

65. Holmes, *Apostolic Fathers*, 763.
66. Holmes, 763.
67. Holmes, 763.
68. Holmes, 763.
69. Holmes, 763.

on earth prior to the battle breaking out between him and Michael? It seems from verse 24:5 that he was putting humanity through trials and perhaps got carried away with this authority, which brought on the battle in verse 6 prior to Christ coming to the earth.

In 24:11, Papias appears to identify two falls of the satan figure; the first one is a spatial fall from heaven (wherever that might be) and the second fall is judgment and the expected punishment for perhaps exceeding his authority. However, when one examines the 2TP Jewish texts and the function of the satan figure, there are not two falls that correspond to what the Papias fragments say. One might suggest two falls if one is in Revelation 12 and the other in the Life of Adam and Eve at the creation of Adam. What might be worth considering is that the satan figure began to extend his authority beyond what God had granted him at some point in the late first century CE if one wants to take the battle in Revelation 12–14 as a literal battle between heavenly forces and the forces of the satan figure.

EPISTLE TO DIOGNETUS

This epistle is a clear Christian apologetic in which the author has very little respect for the Jews and their customs. The date of the letter ranges widely from 117 to 313 CE with a tighter range offered by Lightfoot, Meecham, and Frend between 150 and 225,[70] although these suggestions are not much better. There is very little known of the author or the recipient of the letter. The epistle is not helpful in determining much about the satan figure other than that the serpent in the Garden is not identified as the devil in the three times it is mentioned (12:3, 6, 8). He also maintains an Adamic etiology of sin in the Garden brought about by the deceit of the serpent.

SUMMARY OF APOSTOLIC FATHERS

As we have seen in the writings of the AF, these individuals should be understood as moralists who are attempting to instruct the early Church as to the presence of a devil and evil spirits. They do not, however, give a significant role to the devil in their theology, unlike the soon-to-follow ECF and apologists of the faith. The AF are concerned with the devil's role in the factionalism of the Church, the heresies being spoken in the communities, and the right behavior of the righteous. The AF categorize the heretics such as Judaizers (see Ignatius, the Martyrdom of Polycarp, and Epistle of Barnabas), the Docetists (see Ignatius and the epistle of Polycarp), and those refusing to obey the bishop (Ignatius) as "tools of the devil."[71] We do see the devil and his evil spirits apparently functioning in a similar role as seen in 2TP Jewish literature, as the tester

---

70. Holmes, 689n3. Frend offers the earliest date: no later than 150.
71. See Gokey, *Terminology for the Devil*, 175.

of the righteous who attempts to lead believers into sin and manifesting vices, but these episodes are few in number. The attacks that the righteous face seem to fall under the issue of ethical dualism, which can be controlled by a sound mind and righteous living. There is not a strong presence of a satanology in the AF; rather, they seem, although with a few exceptions, more inclined to follow the Jewish "two ways" worldview, in which humans have the responsibility to choose the right spirit to follow and allow that spirit to influence them.

Early Church Fathers

In the first or second decade of the second century CE, apologists for the Christian faith began defending the doctrines of the early Church due to a variety of opponents, the most prominent being the various heretical groups, in particular those of the Gnostic persuasion. Two of these very early apologists included Aristides and Quadratus, who both presented their defense of the faith to the Roman emperor Hadrian around 124 CE.[72] The Gnostics and their unorthodox beliefs were a growing issue for the young Church and many individuals entered the fray of defending the faith. One of the more prominent among this group was the apologist Justin Martyr.

JUSTIN MARTYR

Tradition tells us that Justin Martyr was born circa 114 CE in Samaria, near modern-day Nablus. He was a follower of Socrates and Plato before converting to Christianity.[73] He was likely martyred in 165 CE during the rule of Marcus Aurelius. Although much of his writing has been lost, his very significant works, *1* and *2 Apologies* and his *Dialogue with Trypho*, survive.[74]

Justin Martyr appears to the be the first ECF to connect the devil/satan with the serpent in the Garden. In *1 Apology* 28.1 he notes, "Among us the chief [ruler] of the wicked demons [ὁ ἀρχηγέτης τῶν κακῶν δαιμόνων] is called the serpent, and satan, and devil, as you can learn from looking into our writings." This is the only mention of the satan figure in Justin's *1 Apology* and *2 Apology*. It is clear that this figure is on the earth to lead astray those willing to follow him but by their own choice of vices or virtues.

---

72. Robert M. Grant, "Aristides," in *Anchor Bible Dictionary*, ed. David Noel Freedman (New Haven, CT: Yale University Press, 1992), 1:382.
73. Russell, *Satan*, 63.
74. Leslie William Barnard, trans., *St. Justin Martyr: The First and Second Apologies* (Leuven, Belgium: Peeters, 1997), 3–5.

In *Dialogue with Trypho* 45, he states, "The serpent that sinned from the beginning, and the angels like him, may be destroyed," likely alluding to the serpent in the Garden—that is, the satan in his mind is the serpent in the Garden (he identifies the satan as the serpent in *Dial.* 45, 79, 100, 124). According to Russell, Justin made the first major impact in discussing "the problem of evil in theological terms," inasmuch as he saw that the Church was in the midst of "a cosmic struggle" with the satan and his followers.[75] As mentioned previously, in *2 Apology*, he is very much aware of the Fallen Watcher tradition of 1 Enoch, or at least a variation of it.[76] In *2 Apology* 5, he states that God appointed angels to watch over humanity, but the angels transgressed the Laws of the Cosmos and begat children with the daughters of humanity and produced offspring whom he calls demons (*2 Apol.* 5, cf. 1 En. 9.9; 19.1). These demons[77] (Justin skips the giants and immediately calls the offspring demons) subdue humanity and lead them into sin and idolatry and all wickedness. In addition, these demons have convinced humanity that they (the demons) are pagan gods (see *2 Apol.* 5).[78] He appears to suggest though that the Fallen Watchers are working alongside the demons to corrupt humankind, which, as we know, is not the case in the Book of Watchers; the Watchers have been bound in the pit along with 90 percent of the evil spirits of the giants, according to Jubilees 10. He argues in *2 Apology* 7 and *Dialogue* 140–41 that humans and angels are created with free will and can choose to follow God or reject him; interestingly, in *Dialogue* 141, he seems to suggest that the angels who have sinned, along with the humans, can still repent and know God; that would include the satan figure.

In *1 Apology* 54, Justin contends that demons, the pagan gods, are responsible for the Greek myths of Bacchus, Bellerophon and his horse Pegasus, Perseus, Heracles, and Aesculapius, due to the prophecies foretold by the prophets of the coming Christ, intending to show they (the prophecies) were "mere marvelous talks, like the things which were said by the poets." The idea that δαιμόνια are pagan gods is found in such biblical texts as Psalm 96:5, "for all the gods of the nations are idols" (אלילים, "idols"; LXX 95:5, δαιμόνια, "demons"), and Deuteronomy 32:17, "They sacrificed to demons (לשדים, 'demons'; LXX, δαιμονίοις, 'demons'), not God, to deities (אלהים, θεοῖς) they did not know." This idea that the pagan gods were demons was promoted by Justin and quickly adopted in the early Church in an effort to direct people to the

---

75. Russell, *Satan*, 63–64.
76. See Yoshiko Reed, "Trickery," 141–53; also Forsyth, *Old Enemy*, 351. This connection is also addressed by Athenagoras (ca. 133–90) in *An Embassy for the Christians* 25, in which he contends the fallen angels had intercourse with the virgins and begot the "so-called giants." However, Athenagoras veers from the Watcher tradition to suggest that the fallen angels haunt the air and the earth and "they are the demons which wander about the world" and are servants of the Prince of Matter (the satan).
77. See Justin Martyr, *2 Apol.* 5.4, in which Justin may be referring to the fallen angels as demons.
78. He blames the same demons for the death of Socrates, who attempted to tell people that they were demons and not gods.

true God of Israel. It may have been driven by Justin's early polemical interpretations of these texts in relation to the Jews and their rejection of Christ.[79] In addition to the Jewish question, Justin argued in *1 Apology* 56 that the evil demons (οἱ φαῦλοι δαίμονες, the pagan gods) were attempting to replace the Christ with other individuals such as Simon and Menander, who performed magic and claimed a divine status, and also Marcion, who denied God was the creator of all things, who deceived many from following the Christ.

In the *Dialogue with Trypho* (160 CE), Justin offers a very different understanding of the origins of evil. Why are the etiologies in *2 Apology* and *Dialogue* so different? Yoshiko Reed rightly suggests that *1* and *2 Apologies* and *Dialogue* are directed toward two different non-Christian audience. The *Apologies* are targeted at a pagan audience, probably Roman elite, in which he was "promoting Christianity as the true philosophy" while demonstrating similar Greco-Roman and Christian values.[80] The *Dialogue* is directed toward the Jews and offers Justin's argument that the Church is the true Israel and has since displaced the Jews from their legitimate heritage.

Throughout the *Dialogue*, Justin offers his understanding of sin and the origins of evil by contrasting Christian piety and Jewish sinfulness.[81] With less emphasis on the fallen angel tradition to address sin (see *Dial.* 79),[82] he goes to the Garden scene and the disobedience of Adam and Eve for his explanation. In *Dialogue* 88.22–23; 10.36–43; and 125.21–29, Justin makes what is likely the earliest connection between the satan and the serpent in the Garden. He draws the parallel between the serpent and the satan figure whom in 124.18, he identifies as one of the princes (ἀρχόντων—this seems to imply a "heavenly being"). He argues the satan figure was apostate from the will of God (125.26) and was a sinner (as the serpent) from the beginning (*Dial.* 45: ὁ πονηρευσάμενος τὴν ἀρχὴν ὄφις); a similar accusation is made concerning the Fallen Watchers in *2 Apology* (see also *Dial.* 100, in which he groups the serpent, the angels, and men who are like the satan into a category of evil). As a result, the satan convinces Adam and Eve to turn away from God's will in the Garden, which results in the eventual wickedness of humanity and, according to Yoshiko Reed, has particularly dire consequences for the Jews for

---

79. Forsyth, *Old Enemy*, 352.
80. See Yoshiko Reed, "Trickery," 154. Yoshiko Reed also suggests that perhaps the two approaches to the origins of sin were already circulating in the likes of Jubilees and 3 Baruch (159).
81. See the discussion in Judith Lieu, *Image and Reality: The Jews in the World of Christians in the Second Century* (Edinburgh: T&T Clark, 1999), 177–82.
82. In *Dial.* 79, Trypho responds to Justin by calling his idea that the angels sinned against God blasphemy. Justin replies that evil angels dwell in Tanis Egypt. The princes of Tanis are evil angels, but it is unclear what the position or role the princes hold in Tanis; however, Justin clearly sees them as demonic: "The gods of the nations are demons." Justin cites Isa 30:1–5 in stating the evil angels are in Tanis. Here, the MT text reads, "For his [Pharaoh's] princes [likely political leaders] and his messengers [מלאכיו] were in Tsoan." This connection between the princes and the evil angels appears again in 124.18 (ἀρχόντων).

their entire history.[83] However, Justin does not offer any reason as to how or why he makes this connection between the serpent and the satan in the midst of this polemic against the Jews (see esp. *Dial.* 132–33). In the *Dialogue* he offers a story of Jewish history that reveals their ongoing disobedience and the punishment they faced from God.[84] The satan has deceived the Jews into thinking that they will be saved due to the fact they are the fleshly seed of Jacob (125.37), but this redemption is negated by their rejection of Jesus as the Messiah and their role in his death (*Dial.* 16.4; 17.1; 32.3; 93.4; 103.2; 104.1; 133.6).[85] In *Dialogue* 119, he accuses them of acting like the nations in Deuteronomy 32:17, which "sacrificed to demons which were not gods" (cf. LXX Ps 105.37 in *Dial.* 19: "They sacrificed their sons and daughters to the demons"; τοῖς δαιμονίοις).

Justin has identified both the pagans and the Jews in the persecution of Christians. The pagan persecution has been directed by the demonic forces behind the pagan religions in *1* and *2 Apologies* (their gods are demons), while in *Dialogue* 17.4–5, it is the Jews who direct the persecution against Christians, and Justin goes as far as to blame the Jews for "crucifying the only blameless and righteous man." He also accuses the Jews of sending out men from Jerusalem to accuse Christians of heresy against God among the Gentiles. Also, behind the Jewish persecutions is the devil and his host of demons who have inflicted death upon the Christians (*Dial.* 131.14–15). He clearly sees the devil has a central role in the persecution of Christians since the crucifixion and the death of Christ; however, he does not identify the devil in the Fallen Watcher tradition in *2 Apology*, as other early Church theologians who follow after him will.

Athenagoras

Athenagoras was an Athenian philosopher and apologist who wrote in the second half of the second century. Only two of his writings survive, *Plea for the Christians* (176–77 CE) and *Treatise on the Resurrection* (176–80). The *Plea* was addressed to the Roman emperor Marcus Aurelius and his son Commodus, asking that justice be shown to Christians. *Resurrection* is possibly the first treatise on the Christian doctrine of the resurrection of the body, which Athenagoras attributes to the power of God or perhaps just the nature of the human body.[86]

In our discussion in relation to the satan figure, we begin with *Plea* 24, in which Athenagoras speaks of the belief in one God among the poets and philosophers. For them, he argues, there were several gods; some were thought to be demons (δαιμόνων), others "matter" (ὕλης),

---

83. See Yoshiko Reed, "Trickery," 155.
84. See Justin's condemnations of Israel in *Dial.* 19 and 92 on circumcision; 20 on dietary laws; see also Yoshiko Reed, 156.
85. See Yoshiko Reed, 156.
86. Leslie Barnard, "Notes on Athenagoras," *Latomus* 31, no. 2 (1972): 413–32, http://www.jstor.org/stable/41503808.

while still others believed these gods were once men (*Plea* 26). In the midst of this cosmology, Athenagoras contends that the heavenly angels were created by the Logos, and the so-called devil was one of these good-natured angels (*Plea* 24). Although Athenagoras does not use the terms ὁ διάβολος or ὁ σατανᾶς, in *Plea* 25, he does speak of a figure that could align with the satan figure, which, in writing his views on physical matter (much like the Gnostics),[87] he identifies as the "ruler of matter" (τῆς ὕλης ἄρχων),[88] who is in control of the things that are outside of the "spirit" issues related to God, and interestingly, he operates in this arena with God's permission (*Plea* 25).[89] This "ruler's" original task, along with all other angels, was to exercise providence over creation and keep it and humanity in correct order for God; this sounds like the original task of the Watchers in Jubilees. Athenagoras is also the first of the ECF to use the term ἀντίθεον, which is not something hostile to God; if it was, it would cease to exist (*Plea* 24), but rather the ruler of matter (the Satan?) controls the matter that is surrounded by the good that is God.[90] The adverse spirit (presumably the ruler of matter) attempts to move people and nations in various ways, some according to the things of matter and some according to things divine. The character of each person and the direction they might take in life (good or evil) is affected by the attention given to them by the spirit and the demons pursuing them.

Athenagoras may be one of the earliest theologians to identify the satan as one who tells many lies, but interestingly, he is not quoting Jesus from John 8:44. He quotes Hesiod's muses in *Theogony* 27 (cf. Homer's *Odyssey* 19.203). This idea would of course make the connection to the pagan polytheism that has been associated with the demons in the second century CE.[91]

In *Plea for the Christians*, Athenagoras contends that the fallen angels (the ruler of matter included) had the same freedom of choice over moral excellence and evil as do humans. Some of the angels, by their own accord, remained faithful in watching over what God made and ordained, while other angels corrupted the essence of their nature and the realm entrusted to them and followed after their lust for the human women and created the giants of the Watcher tradition. In *Plea* 25, Athenagoras discusses these two categories of spirits similar to those in the writings of Justin Martyr: the fallen angels and the souls of the giants (αἱ τῶν γιγάντων ψυχαί)

---

87. See Forsyth, *Old Enemy*, 353.
88. Athenagoras uses the term ἄρχων in reference to the devil four times in *Legatio pro Christianis*: 24.24, 27; 25.4, 25.
89. Athenagoras acknowledges the existence of other powers (δυνάμεις) that exercise dominion over matter, but there is one that is opposed to God (although nothing is really opposed to God because it would cease to exist; *Plea* 24). This is an interesting term in this context. Besides hostile or opposed to God, it can also mean equal to the gods or godlike. This could suggest the divine nature of the satan figure. Athenagoras is clear that God created this "spirit that is over matter" along with all the other angels, some of which rebelled against their nature (*Plea* 24).
90. See G. Ruhbach, "Zum Begriff ἀντίθεος in der alten Kirche," *TU* 92 (1966): 372–84. Ruhbach contends the epithet was later applied to the devil.
91. See Forsyth, *Old Enemy*, 354.

from the Enochic Watcher tradition. In the discussion of this tradition, unlike Justin, Athenagoras contends the gods of the pagans are not demons but men known from history (ἱστορίας εἰδέναι ἄνθρωποι γεγόνασιν; *Plea* 26—perhaps alluding to the οἱ γίγαντες in LXX Gen 6:4, "men of renown"); however, for Athenagoras, the demons are at work behind the names of these gods.

In *Plea* 25, Athenagoras contends that the angels who fell from heaven still haunt the earth and the air and cannot rise again to the heavenly realm. Similarly, the spirits of the giants are the demons (δαίμονες) that wander the earthly realm (see 1 En. 6–16). He does suggest that along with the spirits of the giants, the fallen angels haunt the air and the earthly realm, which would not align with the fate of the Watcher angels in 1 Enoch, who are bound up in the pit, awaiting judgment. Athenagoras seems to be mixing the tradition of the Watchers with that of the fall of the satan figure in John's Apocalypse chapter 12, in which we are told angels fell to earth with the satan (cf. Latin Life of Adam and Eve). In addition, Athenagoras alludes to the Ezekiel 28 "cherub" tradition by suggesting the fallen angel was dwelling in the "first firmament" of the earthly realm on the "holy mountain of God." Later Church theologians interpret Ezekiel 28 and Isaiah 14 as the fall of the satan figure due to his pride.[92]

From this brief discussion, we can say two things about the satan figure in the world of Athenagoras: (1) he does not appear to be a spirit being that is in direct opposition to God, and (2) he is not operating autonomously in the material/earthly realm.

Irenaeus

Irenaeus was born around 140 CE in Asia Minor and died as a martyr in approximately 202.[93] He served as the bishop of Lyon in Gaul. His key writings focus on his conflict with the Valentinian Gnostics as recorded in the work titled *Against Heresies* (*Haeresis*, ca. 180 CE). For Irenaeus, all heretics are part of the satan's army that is in a war against Christ (*Haeresis* 1.25.3). The Gnostic contention that the created world was a result of an evil creator, the Demiurge (δεμιουργόν), was completely rejected by Irenaeus (*Haeresis* 1.5), as neither the prophets nor the apostles identified another god involved in creation, only YHWH. The converse and far superior being, the true Creator, was the Logos (*Haeresis* 1.5; 4). In discussing the creation story, Irenaeus, citing John 1:3, states that the heavenly beings (angels) are created good by God;

---

92. Forsyth, 353–55. Athenagoras connects the Fallen Watchers and the evil spirits of 1 Enoch as servants of the satan due to the idea that negligence and forgetfulness were the causes of the fall of the satan, which Forsyth argues were factors in later interpretations of the Ezek 28 and Isa 14 stories of the "fall of the satan." See Origen, *De Prin.* 2.8.3; 2.9.2.
93. Russell, *Satan*, 80.

since he considered the satan an angel, he too was created good (*Haeresis* 3.8.3). The dualistic cosmology of the Gnostics is thus nullified in that the satan (the Demiurge for the Gnostics) is inferior to God and the satan is not a god. Irenaeus does identify the satan as a liar (*Haeresis* 5.22–24), the Adversary (3.18.7; 5.22.1), a serpent (4.40.3), murderer (3.8, 18; 5.22), apostate (3.23.3; 4.40.1; 5.25), and the devil (3.8.2; 4.40.1). He granted less power to the satan than that given by the Gnostics and other ECF.[94]

Instead of raising the independence of the satan in the realm of sin, Irenaeus places the majority of answerability for sin on humanity.[95] This does not relieve the satan figure of all responsibility in the process; in fact, he describes the task of the satan in similar terms as the figure in the 2TP Jewish texts and the NT, although often under different names. He is testing humans in an effort to persuade them to turn from God and stop following the Law, thus "emphasizing human responsibility for sin."[96] This does not, however, set up a cosmic dualism of the satan as the enemy of God but portrays him as the adversary of corrupt humanity (*Haeresis*, 4.41.1–3; 5.24.2), although even then his power over humanity is limited, as he is only operating under the authority that belongs to God (5.24.3). Following the story line of the satan in the Life of Adam and Eve, the Satan figure is envious of humanity, Adam in particular, because God put creation under Adam's authority (*Haeresis*, 3.23; 4.40; 5.21, 24). Russell contends that due to this envy, the satan figure fell from heaven following the creation of humans (*Apostolic Preaching* 17: the "rebel angel" caused the sin in the Garden and caused Cain to slay Abel), but the apostate angels fell prior to the Flood, in the time of Enoch. Irenaeus argues in *Haeresis* 4.16.2 (also *Apostolic Preaching* 18) that the story of the fall of the Watcher angels in 1 Enoch, along with their teachings that corrupted humanity, are events we learn from Scripture,[97] perhaps alluding to the acceptance of 1 Enoch in the early Church.[98]

In *Haeresis* 3.23.3, Irenaeus, although in a convoluted way, contends that the devil either took on the form of a serpent or spoke through the serpent when Eve and Adam were tempted in the Garden. He quotes Jesus's words about the fire that is prepared for the devil and his angels, claiming that the devil is the one who beguiled Adam to sin. However, Irenaeus argues that the

---

94. Russell, 81.
95. Also, Theophilus, Bishop of Antioch (ca. 169), emphasized human responsibility over demonic influence in a work now lost—"Discourse to Autolycus." He writes in 2.28 that the devil was at first an angel who envied humanity. See Russell, 78–79.
96. Russell, *Satan*, 81.
97. See Saint Irenaeus, *Proof of the Apostolic Preaching*, trans. Joseph P. Smith (London: Longmans, Green, 1952), 58, 155–56n100.
98. Russell, *Satan*, 81–82. In *Haeresis* 3.23.3, Irenaeus suggests that the devil and the angels fell at the Garden episode, but the eternal fire had been prepared for the devil and the apostate angels and not humanity. However, in this text, there does not appear to be a connection to the Enochic Watcher story.

devil did not compel the couple to sin; it was their own choice and weakness, which, strangely enough, Irenaeus attributes at least partially to God.[99] As a result of this human weakness, the satan empowers people to perform magic, create false doctrines, worship idols, and follow the stars; he does all this by one of the Fallen Watchers, Azazel from 1 Enoch (*Haeresis* 1.15.6), once again maintaining the Enochic Watcher tradition's role in the origins of evil in the latter part of the second century CE.

For Irenaeus, the end of evil in the world will begin when the antichrist appears, and all who follow the devil will follow the antichrist (see *Haeresis* 5.25–30).[100] In the final battle, the antichrist will be defeated and the satan and his demons will be cast into the eternal fire.

TERTULLIAN

Tertullian was born around 155 CE in the city of Carthage into a wealthy family. He is identified as "the first great Latin theologian." No fewer than thirty-one works in Latin attributed to him survive, dating from 196–212.[101] He is thought to have converted to Christianity sometime prior to 196 CE. Even though he strongly rejected the Gnostic cosmological dualism of two gods involved in creation (God versus the satan), he asserted a form of Jewish ethical dualism that permeated his writings. As such, he stressed that an austere and regimented ethical lifestyle, avoiding all the wiles of the devil, would be the only thing to assist one in resisting the devil (*De spec.*, 1, 26).

Tertullian contends that the physical world belongs to God, contrary to the Gnostics, while the sin in the world is a result of worldliness, which belongs to the devil—that is, loving the things of this world (*De spec.* 15). He also understands that the devil is like the Destroying Angel of YHWH. In this role, he carries out the opposite of what God is doing in the world but with God's permission (*De anima* 57). He is not the ruler of the cosmos but has been given dominion over the earth, or at least the part of it that he has corrupted (cf. Matt 13:18–30; see *De anima* 16, in which he connects the weeds in the parable to the heresy of the Gnostics). But according to Tertullian, the dominion of the satan over the earth was not enough. In *Adversus Marcionem* 5.17, speaking on the actions of the satan, he draws on Isaiah 14:14, although not quoting the biblical text exactly (a mix of 14:13 and 14): "I will set my throne in the clouds, I will be like unto the Most High." Tertullian states that the devil has set himself up as a deity: "this must be the

---

99. See Russell, *Satan*, 82n10.
100. Russell, 88.
101. Russell, 88–89. See especially 88–89n24.

devil . . . we shall recognize as the god of this world."[102] However, as mentioned previously, I see no overt identifying markers for the satan figure in Isaiah 14 until we meet up with Tertullian and later ECF and their interpretations of this passage and Ezekiel 28.

He takes a very hard line on the devil, whom he identifies as the primary cause of the fall in the Garden. In *Adversus Marcionem* 2.5–10, we are told that the satan corrupted the image of God in Adam, even though, according to Tertullian elsewhere, they could have resisted by their own will; they failed to stay on God's path and did not resist the temptation of the satan. What is interesting in Tertullian's Garden scene is that there is no concept of the satan testing the faith of Adam and Eve, even though he does confess that the satan is given permission by God to do all that he does. Tertullian calls him a lying angel who corrupted humanity from the beginning (*De spec.* 2.12), but the satan doesn't stop with humans; he then turns to his fellow heavenly beings in an effort to turn them from God.

In *Adversus Marcionem* 2.9.3–4, Tertullian contends that the soul (נפש, ψυχή) is just a reflection of the "spirit"—that is, the spirit that is from God. As such, humans are just a reflection of the image of God, for if they were the image of God, then God would also be capable of corruption. He argues this makes humans of a lower quality than God, but at the same time, they have the ability to choose to do God's will. It is from here that he argues that angels are lower than humans because there is no mention that they too are created "in the image of God."

He begins with stating in *Adversus Marcionem* 2.10 that angels are inferior to humans as they are not created in God's image, unless of course one argues that God is speaking to the angels in Genesis 1:26: "Let us make humanity in *our* image, according to *our* likeness." According to Jubilees 2.2, the spirits that serve before him (ἄγγελοι) were the only other beings in existence at the time. He goes on to say in 2.10 that God did not make the devil the devil, but rather the Adversary/Accuser was made by himself, not created, but became evil by self-transformation due to his choices. This began with his accusation against God to Eve about forbidding them from eating from every tree in the Garden (*Ad. Marc.* 2.10.2–3). This idea, of course, posits that the serpent is the devil. It is here that Tertullian turns to an allegorical interpretation of the Old Testament. The satan was originally a good angel full of wisdom who then, Tertullian claims (citing Ezekiel 28 and the story of the king of Tyre), chose to corrupt himself (2.10.2). Evans suggests in his translation that even though the devil, as an angel, was created in the "likeness" (assuming "of God"), he then annulled/unsealed

---

102. Tertullian, *Tertullian: Adversus Marcionem*, trans. Ernest Evans (Oxford: Oxford University Press, 1972), 617.

the likeness.[103] Tertullian goes on to describe the devil as an archangel who was dwelling upon God's holy mountain but then sinned. He contends that this is the description of the angel's transgression and not the king's, for no human was born in God's paradise, not even Adam, who Tertullian argues was "translated there" (2.10.3), which seems to contradict the biblical account of the creation of Adam in the Garden. Nor was any human in the heights of heaven (if one takes into consideration the "heavenly journeys" of Jewish apocalyptic texts, a person in the heights of heaven is a possibility), which he argues is where the satan figure fell from when he was cast down (2.10.3). Tertullian argues in 2.10.5 that God precondemned the satan figure prior to the final judgment because he departed from his created nature of goodness due to his own free will.

In *Apology* 22,[104] Tertullian describes the relationship between demons, the satan figure, and humans. He suggests that each human has a demon watching over them (see *De anima* 57).[105] He contends that God allowed evil spirits to put humans to the test within the boundaries he had set for the evil spirits (*De fuga* 1.1). However, at the onset of the passion of Christ, followers of Christ were granted authority over the evil spirits and given the ability to repel them during their continued testing and persecution until the final judgment (*Apol.* 27). In *Adversus Marcionem* 5:17, Tertullian turns Marcion's description of his god of this world toward that of the satan figure, whom Marcion thinks is "the Creator" of creation, the Demiurge. He describes the satan as the "god of this world," the "prince of the power of the air," and "a worker of disbelief." Here, Tertullian turns to the Isaiah 14:14 text to identify the satan as the prince of Tyre who has "filled the whole world with his lying pretense of deity."[106]

In the midst of Tertullian's diabology, people were invoking demons' names (idols or gods) when offering a curse and, in doing so, were actually invoking the name of the satan, whom Tertullian identifies as the "ruler of evil spirits" (a possible connection to Mastema in Jubilees). Following the ideas of Justin Martyr, Tertullian links the demons to corrupt angels, who appear to be from the Watcher tradition of 1 Enoch. He argues these fallen angels are demons, led by their prince, and their primary task is to bring about the ruin of humanity.[107] All of their

---

103. Evans, *Adversus*, 116–17. See particularly 116n1, in which Evans argues Tertullian contends the angels were created at the same time as the animals in Gen 2:18–20.
104. William Reeve, *The Apology of Tertullian* (London: Griffith, Farran, Okeden & Welsh, 1709). Interestingly, here, in *Apol.* 22, Tertullian appears to refer to the Enochic Watcher story as "sacred literature," perhaps hinting at his view of its place in the church.
105. Russell, *Satan*, 97.
106. Evans, *Adversus*, 617.
107. Tertullian offers an analogy between a pandemic that infected the air and the deadly potion that is scattered throughout the world as a "contagion that walks in the darkness," claiming that so also do demons and evil angels "blast the minds of men." See Reeve, *Apology*, 71.

actions are meant to lead people to idolatry and to turn them away from seeking the true God, the same role we saw for evil spirits in the 2TP Dead Sea Scrolls.[108]

CLEMENT OF ALEXANDRIA

Clement of Alexandria, named Titus Flavius Clemens, was born circa 150 CE in Athens (see Epiphanius, *Heresies* 32.6). He converted to Christianity at some point, but the date is not noted in any of his writings (see *Paed.* 1.1.1; 2.8.62).[109] He died around 210 CE.[110]

Clement's work was broadly Stoic in its philosophical outlook and allegorical. Some argue it was at times gnostic in its cosmology.[111] He argued that when the philosophy of the pagans was properly understood, it pointed to Christ and that the Christian life should be examined through divine revelation.[112] His explanation of the satan figure starts with his view that evil was a contradiction to God's creation and offered an explanation of it "within a coherent philosophical system."[113] For Clement, the satan exists metaphorically and objectively, but perhaps more significantly, he sees him as the evil activity in the human soul. But the satan is also active as an outside force or influence, perhaps a view influenced by the Jewish *yetser ra* in 2TP texts and early rabbinic thought. As a result, Clement stressed the "nonbeing" presence of evil rather than the personified evil being—that is, the satan figure. As with many other early Christian theologians, he suggested a view that could be categorized as a gnostic dualism in that it posited that Jesus came to disclose "the hidden deity to a select few and teach them saving knowledge."[114] However, his view of evil was in direct conflict with the gnostic dualism of the time.

Clement's view of evil emerges out of his understanding of "being." Humans exist as beings, but evil is a result of its lack of being. As Russell argues, Clement's explanation appears to be a result of a Platonic and Gnostic emanationism, in which all things flow from a first principle—in Clement's case, God's being.[115] For Clement, God is absolute, total, and perfectly good, but *only* God is perfect. The rest of creation was created ἐκ μὴ ὄντος, not *ex nihilo*, but from matter not yet formed; as a result, it is inevitably less real and less good. For Clement and other Neoplatonists,

---

108. See Reeve, 72. He contends that "every spirit, angel, and demon . . . may be said to be winged for they can be here and there and everywhere in a moment" giving the illusion that they are omnipresent.
109. John Ferguson, *Clement of Alexandria* (New York: Twayne, 1974), 13. Translation consulted for works of Clement: A. Cleveland Coxe, *Ante-Nicene Fathers: The Writings of the Fathers down to A.D. 325*, 2 vols. (Peabody, MA: Hendrickson, 2004).
110. Russell, *Satan*, 107.
111. Russell, 107.
112. Russell, 108.
113. See W. E. G. Floyd, *Clement of Alexandria's Treatment of the Problem of Evil* (London: Oxford University Press, 1971).
114. Salvatore R. C. Lilla, *Clement of Alexandria: A Study in Christian Platonism and Gnosticism* (Eugene, OR: Wipf & Stock, 2005).
115. Russell, *Satan*, 109.

this meant that the more real something is the more spiritual it is, while the more material something is the less real it is.[116] Because God was the only being in existence, he chose to create the natural world and all that is in it, but it was not wholly good or wholly real. If this is the case, then one might ask, Why does God declare it good in the process of creating the world? Within this created world, there is a sliding scale of reality and spirituality, which resulted in a hierarchy of beings and matter rather than a pure dichotomy of good versus evil. The angels are the closest to the idea of "being" as God is; they are followed by humans, animals, other things in creation and finally unformed matter, "which is least real, least good, least spiritual, most deprived of being, and consequently most evil."[117] This resulted in the Gnostic view that matter was evil due to its distance from God and thus was created by an evil god. Because creation was created out of unformed matter (ὕλη—"nonbeing"), and the lowest point on the scale is matter, it is evil, and because matter exists, creation cannot exist without evil. As Russell suggests, "If evil is merely the deprivation of good, why do morally free agents choose it in preference to good?"[118] However, if we look at this on Clement's sliding scale, then there is some measure of good even in the evil elements in the cosmos. This uncovers the problem in Clement's thinking: the devil cannot be high on the ontological scale and morally the lowest of all because, as a created being, he does exist. But if one approaches the issue of the satan from the 2TP perspective that he is functioning as one of God's officials, as an adversary, then his actions are not evil and immoral but in line with the hierarchy of beings suggested by Clement (see *Paed.* 1.8).

Clement argued in *Stromata* 5.14 that the devil was the first to choose by his own free will (he is also able to repent; *Strom.* 1.17) and he is the leader of demons (*Strom.* 5.14). He contends that the devil generated evil nature (τῶν κακῶν φύσιν γεννήσας), and the angels and humanity followed him. The idea that the devil was able to "generate (give birth to) the evil nature" seems to suggest he was able, in some sense, to create, which does not fit into Clement's theology of the "Principle Being"; rather, it would fit better in the Gnostic view of a second "evil" creator god.

Like others before him, Clement acknowledged the Watcher tradition of the fallen angels without the devil having a role in it (*Paed.* 3.2; *Strom.* 3.7; 5.1; 7.7). In *Stromata* 3.7, he states that in the past, a group of angels saw the beauty of human women and desired to have offspring, and they fell to the earth. Similar to the cosmic and anthropological dualistic struggles in the Qumran demonology, there are two groups of spiritual beings (likely angels) who are in a battle for the

---

116. Russell, 109n8.
117. Russell, 110. Russell suggests Clement has drawn on a version of the Platonist view of the spiritual world of God and the angels and the material world of humans and their inferiors.
118. Russell, 111.

human soul (see *Rich Man* 42.16–18).[119] However, in *Stromata* 5.14, Clement identifies demons as those types mentioned in Socrates, which are meant as guides in life for each individual, and fails to mention the evil spirits of the giants from 1 Enoch. In the same passage, he identifies the devil as the prince of demons and a wicked spirit that appears to operate in a heavenly realm along with principalities, powers, and spiritual things that are in opposition to good spiritual beings (cf. Eph 6:12). In *Stromata* 2.20, Clement connects demons to idolatry and claims that the human soul is full of the powers of the devil and these unclean spirits, which results in the individual doing things that are opposed to God. However, the devil only has the authority to test and try, "no power to compel humans to sin" (*Strom.* 4.12). Clement suggests in *Stromata* 2.13, 20; 3.15; and 5.14 some of the ways in which evil spirits attempt to drive people away from God. The spirits test individuals with idols, the spreading of heresy, use of magic, persecution, and the temptation of vices.[120]

Clement leaned toward a universal salvation that included the redemption of the satan figure despite the idea that the satan sinned from the beginning. He argued that because of God's mercy, there exists "salvation for all free and intelligent beings," along with the idea that free-willed beings can opt for good at any time (*Strom.* 1.17: "Now the devil being possessed of free will, was able to repent and to steal"). This idea of *apocatastasis* would be further developed by Origen in the early third century CE.

ORIGEN OF ALEXANDRIA

Origen was born in approximately 185 CE in Alexandria to a wealthy family, and as a result, he was well educated. During his late teens, his city came under severe persecution, during which his father, Leonides, was imprisoned and eventually martyred in 202 CE. Origen became the head of the household and had to provide support for his mother and brothers; his previous education allowed him to become a teacher and find support from a generous female benefactor who helped him establish a school in Alexandria.[121] Eusebius records that he suffered torture under Decius in 251 and later died when Gallus was made ruler in 253 (*Church History* 6.39.5 and 7.1.1).

Origen is well known for his allegorical commentaries on Scripture. He is recognized as the first ECF to speak of the three hypostases in the concept of the Trinity.[122] As a Platonist,

---

119. Clement appears to identify the devil with Belial in *Strom.* 3.8, in which he cites 2 Cor 6:15 in a list of contrasting issues of good and evil: righteousness and lawlessness, fellowship of light and darkness, and harmony between Christ and Belial.
120. Russell, *Satan*, 115n22.
121. See Eusebius, *Church History* 6.3.1; 6.7–8.1. Mark Edwards, "Origen of Alexandria," in *The Wiley Blackwell Companion to Patristics*, ed. Ken Perry (Oxford: Wiley Blackwell, 2015), 98–110.
122. See Mark Edwards, "Origen," in *Stanford Encyclopedia of Philosophy*, ed. Edward N. Zalta et al. (Palo Alto, CA: Stanford University Press, 2018), 1–35.

Origen identifies his bodiless God with *nous*, or intellect. Plato at times used the term *nous* in reference to the Demiurge, which was subordinate to the first *nous*, which was Plato's *Good*. Origen's God can only be known by his *dunamis*, by which he has interaction with other beings (*On Prayer* 25.3). All *dunamis* exhibited by any created being has its source in the *dunamis* of God (*Commentary on John* 1.39.291). In *Contra Celsum* 5.45, Origen claims that the *dunamis* of the Father (ὁ θεός) is mediated in the heavens and on the earth by the second person of the Trinity (θεός), who provides the "food of the celestial *dunameis* who have remained true to the Creator," while the satan is described as "the food of those who have fallen."[123]

Origen discusses the fall of creation and the beings that occupy it in light of what were once pure intellects who dwelled in the presence of God (sounding very much like Philo, *De Gigantibus*). However, these beings, through their free will, sought a greater measure of satisfaction (κόρος; *De Prin.* 1.4.1) but, as a result of original sin, fell to various levels of "being." The least fallen were angels, followed by humans, and the worst of all to fall were demons (something Philo does not acknowledge).[124]

Origen's primary attack on the Gnostics is centered on his idea of an "ambitious angel," which he argues is already a prominent feature in the views of the Church in the early third century.[125] His purpose is to try to establish a consistent story of the origin of evil. In *De principiis* 6, he contends that the "most widespread opinion in the church, however, is that the devil was an angel, and that once he became a rebel, he persuaded the greatest number of angels possible to revolt." It is here where we find the "replacement" for the Fallen Watcher myth. Despite carrying his own Gnostic ideas, his ongoing fight with pagans and Gnostics resulted in him establishing clear doctrines concerning the origins of evil in an effort to refute the Gnostic heresies of the Demiurge. As a result of his teachings on the satan figure concerning universal redemption—that is, the satan could be redeemed[126]—Origen was later condemned for heresy, as these were considered Gnostic ideas.[127]

Origen refuted Celsus, a second-century Greek philosopher who was a strong critic of early Christianity in his nonextant *The True Word*. Celsus argued that Christianity perverted the words of the philosopher Plato and that the Jewish/Christian God was not all-knowing or all-powerful.

---

123. Edwards, 14.
124. In Origen, *De Prin.* 3.5.6, in which he discusses Eph 1:4, he alludes to the soul's descent from God's hand, although not in the sense of a fall due to sin. This idea of the descent of the soul follows a similar track to Philo of Alexandria and the separation of souls from the Divine. See Philo of Alexandria, *Heir of Divine Things* 240.
125. Forsyth, *Old Enemy*, 358.
126. See Mark J. Edwards, "The Fate of the Devil in Origen," *Ephemerides theologicae Lovanienses* 86, no. 1 (2010): 163–70.
127. He was condemned by Justinian in 543 and also at the Second Council of Constantinople in 553; see Forsyth, *Old Enemy*, 359.

He argued that either the satan figure was a mortal fabrication thought up by Christians to scare others into believing their doctrines or, if he did exist, then God was not all-powerful, but a weak lesser god.[128] However, Origen contended that people like Celsus were under the influence of the devil and, as a result, are unable to comprehend God or Scripture. He argued that all knowledge of the devil needs to be collected from Scripture and properly examined (*basanos*, "to test the validity of one's interpretation"). He claimed the heretics were examining Scripture in a tortured fashion—a secondary meaning for *basanos*. According to Forsyth, Origen may have struggled with the idea that he had tortured the text "to extract the doctrine of Satan" from Scripture.[129] In other words, he felt he did not hold the correct interpretive key to establishing a proper doctrine of the devil. The idea of the "correct interpretive key" sounds very Gnostic and may reveal Origen's gnostic roots.

Origen's thoughts on the origins of evil evolve through three periods in his life. In the early stage, his view seems to be influenced by the Watcher tradition and such writers as Clement of Alexandria (*Strom.* 3.7; 5.1; 7.7) and Philo of Alexandria (*De Gigantibus*). The middle stage of development is found in *De principiis*, in which he presents a detailed discussion on the precosmos fall of the satan figure, which comes about in his refutation of the Gnostic view of the satan; the final stage is presented in *Contra Celsum*, a defense of the doctrine against the claim that Christianity was a primitive dualism that includes the Fallen Watchers. In 5.52, we are to understand that Celsus complained that Christians believed there were "many angelic visitations other than Christ's . . . even sixty or seventy at a time, who were perverted and for punishment were chained under the earth." Origen refutes Celsus saying that he is misreading the book of Enoch or that it "is not generally held to be divine among the churches."[130] He then appears to allude to Philo's doctrine of the soul (*De Gigantibus* 2.2–18, citing Gen 6:1–4) and its descent to live in a human body (*Contra Celsum* 5.55).

Origen turns to the prophets Ezekiel and Isaiah to clarify the position of the devil in the hierarchy of rational (freewill) creatures. He draws on Ezekiel 28 in support of his rebellion motif in relation to this evil power. He claims that the words of the prophet cannot be speaking of a man but rather a divine being who was cast from the heavens due to his change in nature, not his decision to change (*De Prin.* 1.5.5; this appears to also be the cause of the Watchers' fall). He uses the Isaiah 14 passage to argue against the Gnostic belief that the devil was evil

---

128. See Celsus, *On the True Doctrine: A Discourse against the Christians*, trans. Joseph Hoffman (Oxford: Oxford University Press, 1987). One might ask how much truth lies behind this suggestion by Celsus; should we accept Origen's criticism of Celsus or give it careful consideration?
129. Forsyth, *Old Enemy*, 361.
130. Forsyth, 368.

at his creation, saying he had once been light but was now a creature of darkness. He contends that Isaiah calls him the "prince of this world" and that he has power over all who follow his wickedness (1 John 5:19). Again, we see Origen using his understanding of the satan figure as a rebellious being in order to refute the Gnostic view that he was created with an evil nature. Thus, he substitutes the lustful Watcher motif with the rebellious motif of the satan figure with the use of the Ezekiel 28 and Isaiah 14 passages. However, one should remember that the Watcher motif was also one of rebellion, involving a band of angels versus the single angel of the satan.

In addition to the prophets, Origen draws on the words of Christ in his refutation of the Gnostics. He suggests that Luke 10:18 requires that Satan was once a creature of light who fell as lightning from heaven. He argues the Lord is stating that the satan once shared in the light as an angel of light. This passage of course can be argued as a prophetic vision given by Christ when he sees the satan falling from heaven in the future and not a previous event, but it does say that the satan figure was created with a good nature and not an evil one as the Gnostics argued.

Origen attempts to connect the satan figure with Belial in his reading of Judges 19:22 and 20:13. However, one should keep in mind that there is no personification of the term *Belial* in the Hebrew Bible. The story concerns the "sons of belial," which is understood to be "sons of worthlessness or wickedness." Origen simply states, "Who other than he [the devil] can be the one whose sons they are said to be because of their wickedness?"

Origen sums up his idea of the satan figure and the origins of evil in *De principiis* 1.8.1–4 and 1.6.1–3:

> Before the [Gnostic] eons, all spirits were pure, demons, souls, and angels, serving God and fulfilling his commandments. The devil, who is one of them, having free will, wanted to oppose God and God threw him out. All the other powers fell with him, and the ones who had sinned a lot became demons; the others who had sinned less, angels; those who had sinned even less, archangels: thus, each received his lot according to his own sin. Only those souls [humans] were left who had not sinned enough to become demons, nor so lightly as to be angels. God therefore made the present world and bound the soul to the body in order to punish it.

We see here a mix of a biblical "fall" myth and the Platonic view of the fall of the soul as espoused by philosophers such as Philo of Alexandria, all in an effort to counter the Gnostic narratives of the origins of evil.

Augustine, Bishop of Hippo

Augustine, the Bishop of Hippo, was one of the most influential figures in the development of the satan tradition in the ECF. He was born in 354 CE in Thagaste, in Roman Africa, to a mother who was a devout Christian.[131] A number of Augustine's theological arguments were due to his confrontation with the teachings of Mani and the group called the Manicheans. The primary doctrine of Manichaeism was that of the divided cosmos that involved the struggle between a good spirit and an evil spirit. Mani followed the tightly knit dualistic worldview that was perpetuated in the ethical and eschatological teachings found in such texts as the Dead Sea Scrolls and the NT: light versus darkness and the cosmic figures behind them. Mani was born to Persian parents, which may have influenced his worldview (i.e., Zoroastrianism), but he was raised in a Jewish Christian Gnostic community known as the Elchasites.[132] He took up the Enochic book of Giants and its allusions to ANE myths such as Gilgamesh and Huwawa in developing his Zoroastrian Jewish/Gnostic Christianity. This was very much a "universalist" Christianity that included Eastern as well as Western aspects of religion.[133] Unfortunate for Mani, he was disliked by the Romans, the Christians, and the Eastern rulers located in Persia and was executed in circa 276 for apostasy against Zoroastrianism.

Mani contended that in the beginning, light and darkness, good and evil, and God and matter were separate. The darkness sought to fulfill hate and strife for itself, but at some point, the powers within darkness met light and, through its envy of light, went on the attack. Light was unable to repel the attack, and God was "forced to create a new divine hypostasis more suitable for combat"; he called this figure "Primal Man." The knowledge of the Primal Man was part of the Gnostic secret knowledge.[134] The Manichaeans named this figure "Ormazd," similar to the god of light in the Persian Zoroastrianism, Ahura Mazda, who was opposed to Ahriman, the god of darkness. During the battle between light and darkness, the Primal Man was defeated by the Satan figure, and light and darkness mixed, but the light had the adverse effect of making the darkness more evil. At the same time, the Primal Man of light was saved by the spirit of light—in the NT world, the event of the crucifixion.

The next phase of this Manichaean story describes how the so-called Prince of Darkness created Adam and Eve (Gen 1:27) to imprison part of the divine light. As a result, humanity is the major arena in which the forces of Light and Darkness battle, much like the situation in

---

131. Christian Tornau, "Saint Augustine," in Zalta et al., *Stanford Encyclopedia of Philosophy*, 424–27.
132. Forsyth, *Old Enemy*, 390.
133. Forsyth, 390–91.
134. Forsyth, 391–92.

Zoroastrianism, the Community Rule texts of Qumran, and the possession stories in the NT. Interestingly, the procreation of humanity in Mani's theology resulted in a dissipation of the Light in humanity. Adam must be warned and messengers are sent; one takes on the form of a serpent, which Jesus speaks through to warn Adam and convince him to eat from the tree of knowledge to begin his trek toward salvation through the revelation of many who would follow after him: Seth, Enoch, Noah, Buddha, Zarathustra, Jesus Christ, and finally Mani.[135] It is these teachings that Augustine will attack head-on in his various works.

Augustine set the standard of orthodoxy for several major doctrinal issues, including "original sin," which involved the satan figure.[136] In *City of God* 11.13–15, he examines whether or not the satan figure was evil from the beginning of his existence. He cites John 8:44 in establishing that he was a murderer from the beginning of humanity in that he deceived Adam and caused his death and that from his creation he did not stand in the truth, nor was truth in him. The other angels were blessed because they submitted themselves to their creator (see Latin LAE). The Manichaeans argued that the devil was created out of an evil nature, while Augustine insisted that he chose not to abide in the truth of his creator. He argues in stanza 14 that because he does not aid in the truth, there is no truth in him, not the other way around. The devil had the opportunity to abide in the truth, but his pride would not permit him.

In stanza 15, he rejects the Manichaean idea that 1 John 3:8, "the devil sinned from the beginning," means that "the devil was made with a sinful nature"; he maintains that if "sin is natural, then it is not sin." Augustine's early understanding of evil is seen through the nature of the devil's sin. In attacking Mani, Augustine argues that sin precedes evil and is the cause of evil; Mani on the other hand argued that evil is the cause of sin, with each being an expression of the power of darkness. In addition, Augustine attacked the Manichaean and Gnostic idea that matter itself was evil by stating "that evil is corruption, not substance."[137] If matter were

---

135. Forsyth, 393.
136. See Augustine, *Confessions* 2.4.9. Augustine still needed to offer reasons for sin and suffering among humanity. In doing so, he challenged the Manichaean idea that evil dwelt in humanity by insisting that humanity was responsible for sin through the exercise of free will and not by a cosmic power (e.g., of darkness; *De duabus animabus* 10.14). However, in the years to follow, Augustine would realize that free will was not the sole cause of sin in humanity. This change in his thinking was brought about by reading Rom 5:12: "Death came into the world through one man and death through sin." Augustine continually mistranslated the last part of the verse, which reads, "in that all men sinned" (ἐφ' ᾧ πάντες ἥμαρτον); Augustine translated it as "in whom [Adam] all men sinned" (see *Contra Julianum* 1.3.10; 1.4.11). Thus, Augustine argued that original sin is transmitted through sexual intercourse, and as a result, a person is damned from birth. See Kenneth Wilson, *Augustine's Conversion from Traditional Free Choice to "Non-free Free Will": A Comprehensive Methodology* (Tübingen, Germany: Mohr Siebeck, 2018), 93, 127, 140, 146, 231–33, 279–80. This seems contrary to God's command to go forth and populate the world—this would seem to suggest that God wanted to intentionally spread sin and death. According to Augustine, self-gratification causes one to turn away from God, which causes guilt, which causes sin. Because the devil is the cause of this sin, then the entire human race is in servitude to the devil.
137. Forsyth, *Old Enemy*, 399.

evil, then it would have to be evil to everything and everyone; thus, fire, air, earth, and water would always be evil. It appears he has made this argument to counter the Gnostic idea of the Demiurge, a divine being who is responsible for creating the material world. If this is the case, how then is the satan figure able to enter into the divine council in Job and have a conversation with God? If from the beginning he has rebelled, how is he able to remain in the role he has under God's authority?

Augustine asks how the Manichaeans could not recognize the nature of the devil in Isaiah 14 and Ezekiel 28, which, he asserts, describe the fall of the satan figure (*City of God* 11.15). He uses these prophetic texts to argue against those who believe the devil was created with a sinful nature (the Manichaeans). Thus, according to Augustine, the devil was not created with a sin nature but rebelled by his own free will. Augustine is the first to identify the satan as "the fallen one, Lucifer, son of the morning" in Isaiah 14:12: "O how you fell from heaven, shining one,[138] son of the dawn" (איך נפלת משמים הילל בן שחר; ὡς ἐξέπεσεν ἐκ τοῦ οὐρανοῦ ὁ ἑωσφόρος ὁ πρωὶ ἀνατέελλων). Augustine combines this line with Ezekiel 28:13 and argues that the satan is the one who was in the Garden of God and every precious stone was his covering; he suggests that Ezekiel is saying that at some point in his existence, the satan figure was without sin: "You were perfect in your ways from the day you were created, until iniquity was found in you" (Ezek 28:15).

In the *City of God* 11–13, he contends for two sets of angelic beings—good and evil—but that all originally were created light (11.11). Some angels have turned from the light and have lost the blessed and wise life; they do, however, maintain a life of reason, but it is one of darkened folly, which, he argues, will bring an end to the lives of the evil angels. He argued the angels were of the same ontological existence—they all have wisdom and reason—but then suggests that beings of equal wisdom and with an eternal position in the heavenly hierarchy could not rebel against God while the others remained steadfast. Of those who remained steadfast, the good angels, he maintains that no new devil will arise from them (11.13). He maintains that the angels who fell were never granted the same characteristics (wisdom and reason) or assurances that the good angels obtained (11.13). Interestingly, in his discussion of the "evil" angels in chapter 11, he does not identify their function among humanity or in any other realm.

As for Adam and Eve, Augustine argues that the sin of pride, one of the vices of the devil (14.13), was the cause of the fall of Adam. The result of this pride was the soul being "enamored

---

138. ὁ ἑωσφόρος, "morning star," likely signifies the planet Jupiter. A form of this word (φωσφόρος) is used in 2 Pet 1:19 to refer to Jesus as the morning star that rises in one's heart, which leaves the question if this can be referring to the satan figure in Isa 14:12.

of its own power" (including the fallen angels; 12.8; 11.33). This suggests that the fall of the satan figure was the result of pride, but what was the origin of the satan's pride? Was it due to his free will or was he created with pride? If it is through free will, this suggests the act of choosing to be prideful was the fall. Adam then becomes a victim of the satan figure's pride and not his own will, as Augustine states in 13.14. Nevertheless, Augustine suggests in 14.13 that Adam had already chosen "to live for himself," and thus he was not actually deceived (14.11). Who, then, is at fault in this mythic event? The satan figure or the first Adam? Or is it simply to be laid at the feet of "free will"?

The theological and philosophical views of Augustine appear to have been the primary source that finally established what would be the understanding of the satan figure in the early Church. With the conversion of the Roman Empire to Christianity and the end to the persecution by the empire, Christians had to look elsewhere for an oppressor. Augustine turned to the spirit realm in order to set as doctrine a belief that early Christians had yet to solidify—where did the evil satan figure come from? He claimed, in the *City of God*, that the devil was originally a sinner—that is, the satan refused to accept the righteousness of God. In *City of God* 11.13, Augustine also contends the satan was originally good but that he, along with some other angels, fell away from the light of goodness. Augustine's apparent contradictions in matters concerning Christian doctrine lead to the question as to how we can trust that what he did ascertain as orthodox belief is actually what is true according to Scripture.

Summary

The understanding of the function of the satan figure AF and ECF texts is based primarily on the understanding that God is not the cause of evil (countering Valentinian and Manichaean doctrines of the origins of evil), a doctrine established by Augustine. But Scripture states otherwise in Amos 3:7, which suggests that if there is calamity in a city, then it was certainly a result of the Lord's doing. The Gnostic groups argued another divine figure nearly equal in power to YHWH, the Demiurge, was responsible for the evils in the world. The ECF and others were attempting to counter the Gnostic views by pressing the issue that the devil, created good, turned to evil through the sin of pride. As a result, the devil was trying to draw all humanity to himself and away from God. This autonomous or semiautonomous evil figure is a significant shift away from the satan figure that operated in the HB, 2TP Judaism(s), and NT Gospels.

Conclusion

For centuries, religious groups around the world have identified some sort of personified spirit figure as the primary cause of evil in the world. This examination has focused on how the Judeo-Christian traditions have identified, understood, and transmitted this personified evil through roughly the last three millennia and how those traditions have evolved. Our goal was to understand if this figure (or figures) played a part in solving the so-called problem of evil in the literature of ancient Israel (Jewish Scriptures), of various texts from 2TP Judaism(s), the writings of the New Testament, and the literature of the apologists and theologians of the early church. It is clear from this examination that the understanding or role of this evil figure evolved through the centuries in part due to the influences of the worldviews of other cultures as expressed in the literature of these cultures. In addition, it appears the relationship between Israel and their God YHWH had a particularly important part in the emergence of a personified evil figure.

As discussed in chapter 1, some points of contact, although no direct parallels, in the literature and imagery of the cultures of the Ancient Near East may have played a role in the development of the personified evil figure in later Jewish and Christian traditions. Many of the figures identified in the various cultures appeared to strike fear into the hearts of humanity because they were in some kind of conflict or battle with one or more of the "good" gods of their particular cultures. In addition, some of the functions or activities of these "evil" figures were developed further by the Jewish and Christian traditions into what some call "personified evil." The stories in which we find these figures attempted to answer such questions as these: Why is death part of the human existence? Why do people suffer? and Who or what is responsible for this suffering? As such, these figures and their functions in the world helped the people of a culture contend with the ideas of suffering, evil, and sin.

It appears that following the Israelites' time of exile in Babylon—during which they were influenced by the traditions of Zoroastrianism, in particular its cosmological dualism—the nation's understanding of YHWH's role in the evil they were facing day to day evolved. The literature from the 2TP suggests that there was a concerted effort to separate the God of Israel, YHWH, from the problem of evil or the instigation of evil against Israel and/or the various sects within the Judaism(s) in the Second Temple Period. It may be argued that this separation of YHWH from evil was the primary cause of the emergence of several entities within the worldviews of the Jews, including evil spirits, fallen angels, unclean spirits, and a leader or leaders (human or otherworldly) of these evil entities. It also may be suggested that at the time of the appearance of this growing presence of entities, some, if not all, of these spirit figures were operating under the authority of YHWH, including hasatan, belial, the devil, and various other epithets that are identified in the diverse collections of literature.

Chapter 2, on the Hebrew Bible and LXX, identified and discussed the major passages that include the terms שטן (*satan*) or διάβολος (*diabolos*) in the Hebrew and Greek Scriptures. Four major texts were addressed, including Numbers 22:22–35; Job 1–2; Zechariah 3:1–7; and 1 Chronicles 21:1–22:1. As discussed, scholars have argued for and against the idea that the השטן, "the satan," in each of these passages is in some way related to the later Christian "Satan" figure, which is understood as a somewhat semiautonomous evil being who apparently opposes everything that is the will of God. Within the presentation of these texts, a brief etymological study of the relevant terms was offered that defined the terms *the satan* and *the devil* as "the one who persecutes, opposes, or acts as an adversary." The results revealed that the terms used in these passages can identify either a heavenly adversary or a human adversary in the various contexts. The terms are used in other biblical texts to identify a human adversary, something that we see in later 2TP literature and the NT. The final discussion of the terms in the HB and LXX focused on additional three texts that interpreters have attempted to connect to the "satan" figure, Genesis 3:1–15; Isaiah 14:12–17; and Ezekiel 28:11–19. A plausible conclusion from this examination suggests that within the worldview of the Israelites in the preexilic and postexilic biblical texts there is no "Satan" figure similar to the autonomous or semiautonomous figure allegedly found in the later Christian tradition.

In chapter 3, similar to the situation in the HB and LXX, one encounters some difficulty when trying to identify the "satan" figure in the Dead Sea Scrolls. As can be understood from the discussion on the satan figure in the DSS, the evidence of the term/figure *satan* is quite limited. Only a few fragmentary references to the satan are extant in the collection. However, one must keep in mind the fragmentary nature of the scrolls; it may be possible or even likely that the term appeared in other material that is no longer extant. In each identified occurrence, the term suggests some sort of adversary, either a spirit or a human figure, but the extant scrolls offer little context by which one can make a definitive conclusion as to its use. It is likely that the term is not used in the sense of a proper name, but rather it describes the function of the satan figure. The use of this term in the scrolls reveals the authors intended to shift, to some degree, the so-called blame for the problem of evil away from the God of Israel, while at the same time, the role of the figure suggests he/it was acting as an adversary that may not require permission from God for each individual action it takes against an individual or the nation.

We also discovered in the scrolls that the idea of the names of heavenly figures are not fixed; although the prominent name for the so-called personified evil being is Belial, it may be otherwise known as the Angel of Darkness, Melchiresha, or Mastema. These figures, among others, are responsible for the problem of evil in the 2TP Jewish worldviews. We identified various dualisms in the Qumran worldview, which influenced the concept of evil in the 2TP; this is due to Zoroastrian dualism(s), which speaks of a cosmic good-versus-evil dichotomy. This resulted in an ongoing battle between light and dark, righteousness and evil, a spirit of truth and a spirit of darkness, and the eschatological war between the Sons of Light led by the archangel Michael and the Sons of Darkness who are led by the Angel of Darkness. Five main figures were identified in the scrolls that may be related to the "chief" evil being, the satan: Melchiresha, the Angel of Darkness, S/satan, Mastema, and Belial.

In chapter 4 and the discussion of the texts identified as Pseudepigrapha, one can suggest that the concept of "the satan/devil" was fluid during the Second Temple Period. As the examination shows, there are a significant number of Pseudepigrapha that employ the term *the satan*. Some of the texts examined reveal the function of the satan figure is to draw people away from God with testing, similar to what we saw in the HB and the DSS (e.g., T. Dan). The satan figure does not appear to be autonomous in that he is working at his own charge; rather, several contexts reveal he is working under the authority or permission of God (although with some freedom to act independently). In the Testament of Gad, for example, we discovered that the satan figure is working in collaboration with a group of spirits, in this case the spirit of hatred, to lead astray humanity, away from the plan of God. Similar to the HB, the noun *satan* is used with the article *the*, suggesting this is perhaps a title for the being—"the adversary"—rather than the proper name. The term *the satan*, and its synonym *the devil*, is functioning in ways similar to the satan figure in the biblical book of Job. In the Testament of Job, he is a figure whose task is to test and deceive humanity, in this case Job, but the figure can only do this under the authority / with the permission of God.

With several of these texts, one might ask why the term *the devil* does not receive the identification of a personal name, as does *the satan*—in the majority of occasions that it is used, ὁ διάβολος is not used as a proper name as many have attempted to do with ὁ σατανᾶς. The words have identical meanings—"the adversary"—but only the satan is identified by translators and scholars in the sense of a proper name.

The author of the Apocalypse of Sedrach explains the task of the devil among humanity in a way that is significantly different from other texts from the 2TP. The author suggests the devil "enters the hearts of humanity like a smoke and teaches them every sin." This may suggest the possibility of satanic possession, along the lines of the tradition of the satan entering the heart of Judas in the Gospels. The Lord then tells Sedrach that humanity has the ability to resist and make the right choices when approached by the devil; this understanding follows the tradition in CD 16 and also in 1 Peter 5:8–9.

The Life of Adam and Eve (GLAE and VITA) offers a significantly different story surrounding the satan figure. Here, he is depicted as a rebellious angel who draws Eve and Adam into sin against God. However, there is no evidence to suggest he is autonomous; rather, he may simply be doing the same task he performed in Job—that is, performing the function of the heavenly adversary—and could also be understood to be executing in Jubilees. However, the author of LAE also offers a reason for the satan's fall from heaven: he refused to follow God's command and bow down to Adam.

As can be understood from the discussion above, the authors of several of the Pseudepigrapha texts reveal that the satan/devil figure is functioning in a heavenly office called "the adversary" or "the accuser." We also discovered that some texts suggest that there were multiple satans functioning within a particular author's worldview (see, e.g., Enochic Similitudes).

We examined the figure of the satan/devil in the HB, the DSS, and the Pseudepigrapha and found he/it is present but is not necessarily aligned with the early Christian understanding of the "Satan," nor does their view of the figure help in identifying or clarifying the one responsible for the problem of evil in the lives of the Jewish people during the 2TP. In chapter 5, we noted in the discussion of the scrolls that there are other names by which a satan-type figure may have been known to the Jewish people. The difficulty one has in exploring this literature is finding direct parallels between the variety of terms found in the DSS, the Pseudepigrapha, and other literature. Some scholars have suggested these terms—Belial, Beliar, Mastema, and some of the other heavenly or human beings—are interchangeable with one another; however, as noted, this does not appear to be the case. This may suggest that the various names found in the scrolls and the Pseudepigrapha (in particular the T12 Patr.) are beings that held specific roles in the 2TP, some of them overlapping. If this is correct, then one can suggest there was no single being operating in a role similar to the later

Christian Satan, but rather these beings were functioning in much the same role as the satan figure in the biblical book of Job.

In addition to the other names in the DSS, we identified the primary figure of evil in the Pseudepigrapha and other 2TP Jewish texts as Beliar, perhaps synonymous with Belial. The T12 Patr. identifies Beliar as an instigator and leader of a group of evil spirits under his authority whose task is to afflict humanity in an attempt to draw them away from the Lord. Similar to the scrolls, there are strong dualistic components in the T12 Patr. (ethical, anthropological, cosmological), which are reflected in nine main concepts: (1) the two spirits, (2) the two inclinations, (3) the two sets of seven spirits, (4) a messianic figure in opposition to Beliar, (5) the Law of the Lord and the law of Beliar, (6) the Angel of the Lord and the spirit of Beliar, (7) the Angel of Peace and the spirit of Beliar, (8) light and darkness, and (9) the will of God and the will of Beliar. The evidence revealed in T12 Patr. points to the strong possibility of the belief in the existence of a spirit being that influences the evil activities that take place in the human realm—but under the sovereignty and authority of God.

In addition to the T12 Patr., the book of Jubilees is one the significant texts that present the issues of the problem of evil in the midst of a detailed angelology in the 2TP that, in particular, portrays angels as mediators between God and humanity. Not the least significant is Jubilees' inclusion of the Watcher tradition found in 1 Enoch. Jubilees portrays angels and evil spirits as having specific tasks within the human realm. There are good angels who help control the forces of nature, assist humanity, and act as intermediaries between humans and God, while the evil spirits in Jubilees are the author's way of dealing with the problem of evil in his worldview. For the author of Jubilees, evil reveals the omnipotence and goodness of God. It is understood to be a spiritual force that has emerged out of the heavenly realm, but the question is, Was it created by God? Significant to this discussion is Jubilees' presentation of a chief spiritual being identified as Mastema that has a portion of the evil spirits of the giants from the Watcher tradition working with it.

In chapter 6, the authors of the NT suggest a few roles for "the satan" such as a leader or chief over a group of evil spirits, an accuser of humanity, and one who tests the faith of individuals, including Jesus. In addition to the terms *the satan* or *the devil*, other names emerged in the NT, which many have suggested are related to if not the same figure as the satan. Such titles include Beliar (rather than the familiar Belial), used once in 2 Cor 6:15, Ruler of This World, Angel of Darkness, the Wicked One, the Serpent, the great red dragon. However, just as in the Jewish literature of the 2TP previously discussed (one exception: the Angel of Darkness becomes synonymous with the satan figure in the early Church), it is unclear if all these names relate to the same single figure, the satan (though in the NT, this is not quite as murky).

What is interesting about these other names is that they were not part of the nomenclature of the alleged personified evil being of earlier 2TP literature and that the nomenclature related to evil beings of the previous literature dropped out of use in the NT. One might ask what caused the shift of the use of the term *the satan* and *the devil* in the HB/LXX, to a seemingly less pronounced role in the 2TP, and then a return to prominence in the NT. A similar question might be asked of the term(s) *Belial/Beliar* and others that had a prominent use in the 2TP but seem to drop from use in the NT. We discovered that some of the characterizations of the satan figure in the NT echo a few from the 2TP, such as "the ruler of the demons/evil spirits," "Ruler of This Age," "Ruler of This World," "the Great Dragon," and "the Angel of the Pit." In addition, a variety of other figures may be closely tied with the satan in his role as the adversary, although not clearly identified as the same figure. These include the "lawless one" in 2 Thessalonians, the two beasts in Revelation 13, and the antichrist figure in 1 John 2:18 (one of many). One of the most significant similarities between the names of the evil figures in the earlier 2TP literature and those in the NT is the use of these names in identifying human religious leaders or governmental figures of the periods. It seems some authors saw spirits at work behind and within various human groups that were in opposition to God's plan and his people.

We discovered in the writings of the Apostolic Fathers that these individuals should be understood as moralists who are attempting to instruct the early Church as to the presence of a devil and evil spirits. They do not, however, suggest a precise theological role for the devil, unlike the Early Church Fathers and apologists of the faith. The AF are concerned with the devil's role in the factionalism of the Church, the heresies being spoken in the communities, and the right behavior of the righteous. The AF categorize the heretics such as Judaizers, the Docetists, and those refusing to obey the bishop as "tools of the devil." We do see the devil, with his evil spirits, apparently functioning in a similar role as in 2TP Jewish literature as the tester of the righteous who attempt to lead believers into sin while manifesting vices, but these episodes are few in number. The attacks that the righteous face seem to fall under the issue of ethical dualism, which can be controlled by a sound mind and righteous living by the individual. There is not a strong presence of a satanology in the works of the AF; rather, they seem, although with a few exceptions, more inclined to follow the Jewish "two ways" worldview, in which humans have the responsibility to choose the right spirit to follow and allow that spirit to influence them.

The understanding of the function of the satan figure in the AF and ECF writings is based primarily on the understanding that God is not the cause of evil, a doctrine established by Augustine. But Scripture states otherwise in Amos 3:7, which suggests that if there is calamity is in a city, then it was certainly a result of the Lord's doing. The Gnostic groups argued that another divine figure nearly equal in power to YHWH, the Demiurge, was responsible for the evils in the world. The ECF and others were attempting to counter the Gnostic views by pressing the issue that the devil, created good, turned to evil through the sin of pride rather than being created evil. As a result, the devil was trying to draw all humanity to himself and away from God. This autonomous or semiautonomous evil figure is a significant shift away from the satan figure that operated in the HB, 2TP Judaism(s), and the NT Gospels.

So what can we conclude from this study about the "problem of evil" and "the satan figure(s)?" It is clear that during the period of the AF and ECF, there was a shift in the theological understanding of the role or function of the satan or the devil in the world. Unlike his role in the HB/LXX and the 2TP literature, including the NT, he was seen as a heavenly evil being in direct opposition to the God of Israel and the Church—and in some worldviews, nearly as powerful.

But the question is, Can we accept the views of these people of the early church and the doctrines they established in the early centuries of the Christian movement? I would suggest that we should reconsider some of their views; after all, they were only human. Some of the doctrines were, and are, quite troubling when one considers the omnipotence of YHWH in the worldviews of Judaism and Christianity, not to mention other major world religions. In particular, the power that has been granted to this "personified evil being" is disturbing: his near omnipotence to turn anyone away from God, his omnipresence in afflicting multiple people at the same time all around the world, and his authority as the ruler of this world. How is this conceivable in the mind of a follower of the God of Abraham, Isaac, and Jacob? Can there be such a figure that is capable of ruling the world, or is it simply the case that this satan figure is at work in the principalities and powers that are behind the governments of this world?

As has been seen throughout the history of the human race, beginning with the myth of Adam and Eve, the story of the Fallen Watchers in 1 Enoch, Judas in the Gospels, and the numerous evil figures in human history, evil is a choice of one's will, whether human or divine (like the Watcher angels). It is clear from the literature that the satan figure(s) performed a function on the earth—the testing of individuals (and nations) as to their faithfulness to God (including Jesus)—but this testing was conducted under the authority and sovereignty of the God of Israel. Failure to pass the test resulted in pain and suffering, sometimes to the point of death or exile. Evil is something that is initiated by one's choices/decisions, which are their own responsibility (see Philo's *De Gigantibus*). This view is part of the ever-present "two ways" philosophy that has been found in the theological literature of humanity since the beginning. The path of evil or good exists in the cosmos, and our decisions or choices are being influenced by spiritual forces on the earth—good and evil.

However, if the evil is ever-present, from where did the evil originate? Did it come from God? Did it originate in the work of the Demiurge, as the Gnostics would have us believe? Or is it simply part of human nature / the human psyche? Humanity has always been searching for an answer to the problem of evil, usually always beyond itself. There has to be a cause for the evil we see, true—but is it an external evil force or is the real cause within ourselves? Like the early theologians had to blame something for the evils of humanity and the world they lived in: for the Gnostics, it was the Demiurge; for the Church Fathers, the satan/devil figure. In the case of the sin of Adam, it is the serpent and, in the end, the satan figure.

But what if the tree in the Garden was only a test of Adam and Eve's faithfulness? What if the Trial of Jesus in the Wilderness was just a test of his willingness to be the Messiah? Both were conducted by the same heavenly figure, the satan, but while one was a failure that caused the suffering of humanity and the unleashing of evil in the world, the other was a success that we hope is bringing about the end of that evil. As Anne Frank said, "How wonderful it is that nobody need wait a single moment before starting to improve the world"[139]

---

139. Anne Frank, *Tales from the Secret Annex: A Collection of Her Short Stories, Fables, and Lesser-Known Writings* (New York: Bantam, 2003).

Bibliography

Primary Texts

Baillet, Maurice. *Qumrân Grotte 4*. Vol. 3. DJD 7. Oxford: Clarendon, 1982.

Celsus. *On the True Doctrine: A Discourse against the Christians*. Translated by Joseph Hoffman. Oxford: Oxford University Press, 1987.

Charles, Robert H. *The Ascension of Isaiah: Translated from the Ethiopic Version, Which, Together with the New Greek Fragment, the Latin Versions and the Latin Translation of the Slavonic*. London: A&C Black, 1900.

———. *The Assumption of Moses*. London: A&C Black, 1897.

———. *The Ethiopic Version of the Hebrew Book of Jubilees*. Oxford: Clarendon, 1895.

———. *The Greek Versions of the Testaments of the Twelve Patriarchs: Edited from Nine Mss., Together with the Variants of the Armenian and Slavonic Versions and Some Hebrew Fragments*. Oxford: Clarendon, 1908.

Coxe, A. Cleveland, ed. *Ante-Nicene Fathers: The Writings of the Fathers down to A.D. 325*. 2 vols. Peabody, MA: Hendrickson, 2004.

Denis, Albert-Marie, ed. *Fragmenta pseudepigraphorum quae supersunt graeca una cum historicorum et auctorum Judaeorum hellenistarum fragmentis*. PVTG 3. Leiden: Brill, 1970.

Duhaime, Jean. "War Scroll (1QM; 1Q33; 4Q491–496 = 4QM 1–6; 4Q497)." In *Damascus Document, War Scroll, and Related Documents*, edited by James H. Charlesworth, 80–203. Vol. 2 of *The Dead Scrolls: Hebrew, Aramaic, and Greek Texts with English Translations*. Tübingen, Germany: Mohr Siebeck, 1995.

García Martínez, Florentino, and Eibert J. C. Tigchelaar, eds. *The Dead Sea Scrolls Study Edition*. 2 vols. Leiden: Brill, 1999.

García Martínez, Florentino, Eibert J. C. Tigchelaar, and Adam S. Van Der Woude. *Qumran Cave 11*. DJD 23. Oxford: Clarendon, 1998.

Godley, A. D. *Herodotus, with an English Translation*. Cambridge, MA: Harvard University Press, 1920.

Holmes, Michael W., ed. *The Apostolic Fathers: Greek Texts and English Translations*. 3rd ed. Grand Rapids, MI: Baker Academic, 2007.

Irenaeus. *Proof of the Apostolic Preaching*. Translated by Joseph P. Smith. London: Longmans, Green, 1952.

Justin Martyr. *The First and Second Apologies*. Translated by Leslie William Barnard. Leuven, Belgium: Peeters, 1997.

Levey, Samson H. *The Targum of Ezekiel*. Edinburgh: T&T Clark, 1999.

Mangan, Céline. "The Targum of Job." In *The Targums*, vol. 15 of *The Aramaic Bible*, edited by Kevin Cathcart, Michael Maher, and Martin McNamara, 24–27. Edinburgh: T&T Clark, 1991.

Milik, J. T. *The Books of Enoch: Aramaic Fragments of Qumrân Cave 4*. Oxford: Clarendon, 1976.

Origen. *On First Principles*. Translated by G. W. Butterworth. London: SPCK, 1936.

Pritchard, James B., ed. *Ancient Near Eastern Texts Relating to the Old Testament with Supplement*. Princeton, NJ: Princeton University Press, 1969.

Qimron, Elisha, and James H. Charlesworth. *Rule of the Community and Related Documents*. Tübingen, Germany: Mohr Siebeck, 1994.

Reeve, William. *The Apology of Tertullian*. London: Griffith, Farran, Okeden & Welsh, 1709.

Sanders, J. A. *The Psalms Scroll of Qumran Cave 11 (11QPs^a)*. DJD IV. Oxford: Clarendon, 1965.

Schaff, P., et al., eds. *A Select Library of the Nicene and Post-Nicene Fathers of the Christian Church*. Peabody, MA: Hendrickson, 1994.

Sukenik, E. L., ed. *The Dead Sea Scrolls of the Hebrew University*. Jerusalem: Magnes, 1955.

Tertullian. *Adversus Marcionem*. Translated by Ernest Evans. Oxford: Oxford University Press, 1972.

Tov, Emanuel, ed. *Qumran Cave 4: Parabiblical Texts Part 1*. DJD 13. Oxford: Clarendon, 1994.

Reference Works

Brown, Francis, S. R. Driver, and Charles A. Briggs. *The Brown, Driver, Briggs Hebrew and English Lexicon*. 1906. Reprint, Peabody, MA: Hendrickson, 2005.

Joüon, Paul. *Grammaire de l'Hébreu biblique*. Rome: Pontifical Biblical Institute, 1923.

Leslau, Wolf. *Comparative Dictionary of Ge'ez*. Wiesbaden, Germany: Harrassowitz Verlag, 2006.

Other Works

Agourides, S. "Apocalypse of Sedrach." In *The Old Testament Pseudepigrapha*, 2 vols., edited by James H. Charlesworth, 1:605–613. New York: Doubleday, 1983.

Aland, Kurt. "The Problem of Anonymity and Pseudonymity in Christian Literature of the First Two Centuries." *Journal of Theological Studies* 12 (1961): 39–49.

Alexander, Philip S. "Demonology of the Dead Sea Scrolls." In *The Dead Sea Scrolls after Fifty Years*, 2 vols., edited by Peter W. Flint and James C. VanderKam, 2:331–354. Leiden: Brill, 1999.

Allen, Leslie C. *Psalms 101–150*. WBC 21. Waco, TX: Word Books, 1983.

Andreasen, Niels-Erik. "Adam and Adapa: Two Anthropological Characters." *Andrews University Seminary Studies* 19, no. 3 (1981): 179–194.

Aubet, María E. *The Phoenicians and the West: Politics, Colonies, and Trade*. Cambridge: Cambridge University Press, 2001.

Aune, David E. *Revelation 1–5*. WBC 52A. Dallas: Word Books, 1997.

———. *Revelation 6–16*. WBC 52B. Nashville: Thomas Nelson, 1998.

Bahr, Gordon J. "The Subscriptions in the Pauline Letters." *Journal of Biblical Literature* 87 (1968): 27–41.

Bamberger, Bernard J. *Fallen Angels: The Soldiers of Satan's Realm*. New York: Jewish Publication Society, 1952.

Barnard, Leslie. "Notes on Athenagoras." *Latomus* 31, no. 2 (1972): 413–432. http://www.jstor.org/stable/41503808.

Barr, James. "'Thou Art the Cherub': Ezekiel 28:14 and the Post-Ezekiel Understanding of Genesis 2–3." In *Priests, Prophets and Scribes: Essays on the Formation and Heritage of Second Temple Judaism in Honour of Joseph Blenkinsopp*, edited by Eugene Ulrich et al., 212–223. JSOTSS 149. London: Bloomsbury, 1992.

Barrett, C. K. *The Gospel according to St. John: An Introduction with Commentary and Notes on the Greek Text*. 2nd ed. London: SPCK, 1978.

Bauckham, Richard J. "Pseudo-Apostolic Letters." *JBL* 107 (1988): 469–494.

Bauckham, Richard, James Davila, and Alex Panayotov, eds. *Old Testament Pseudepigrapha: More Noncanonical Scriptures*. Grand Rapids, MI: Eerdmans, 2013.

Baynes, Leslie. "Introduction to the Similitudes of Enoch." In *Early Jewish Literature: An Anthology*, 2 vols., edited by Brad Embry, Ronald Herms, and Archie T. Wright, 2:256–263. Grand Rapids, MI: Eerdmans, 2018.

Bickerman, Elias J. "The Date of the Testaments of the Twelve Patriarchs." *JBL* 69, no. 3 (September 1950): 245–260.

Birnbaum, David. *God and Evil: A Jewish Perspective*. Hoboken, NJ: KTAV, 1989.

Blenkinsopp, Joseph. *Ezekiel*. Louisville, KY: Westminster John Knox, 1990.

Block, Daniel. *The Book of Ezekiel Chapters 25–48*. Grand Rapids, MI: Eerdmans, 1998.

Boccaccini, Gabriele. *Beyond the Essene Hypothesis: The Parting of the Ways between Qumran and Enochic Judaism.* Grand Rapids, MI: Eerdmans, 1998.

Bovon, François. *Luke 1: A Commentary on the Gospel of Luke 1:1–9:50.* Hermeneia. Minneapolis: Fortress, 2002.

———. *Luke 2: A Commentary on the Gospel of Luke 9:51–19:27.* Hermeneia. Minneapolis: Fortress, 2013.

———. *Luke 3: A Commentary on the Gospel of Luke 19:28–24:53.* Hermeneia. Minneapolis: Fortress, 2012.

Bowen, Nancy R. *Ezekiel.* AOTC. Nashville: Abingdon, 2010.

Boyce, Mary. *Zoroastrians: Their Religious Beliefs and Practices.* 2nd ed. London: Routledge, 2001.

Brand, Miryam T. *Evil Within and Without: The Source of Sin and Its Nature as Portrayed in Second Temple Literature.* JAJS 9. Göttingen, Germany: Vandenhoeck & Ruprecht, 2013.

Brown, Raymond E. *The Gospel according to John (I–XII).* ABC 29. Garden City, NY: Doubleday, 1966.

Bruce, F. F. *1 & 2 Thessalonians.* WBC 45. Nashville: Thomas Nelson, 1982.

Brueggemann, Walter. *Isaiah 1–39.* Louisville, KY: Westminster John Knox, 1998.

Burke, Jonathan. "Satan and Demons in the Apostolic Fathers: A Minority Report." *Svensk Exegetisk Årsbok* 81 (2016): 127–168.

Capelli, Piero. "The Outer and Inner Devil on Representing the Evil One in Second Temple Judaism." In *The Words of a Wise Man's Mouth Are Gracious (Qoh 10:12)*, edited by Mauro Perani, 139–152. Berlin: Walter de Gruyter, 2005.

Charles, Robert H, ed. *The Apocrypha and Pseudepigrapha of the Old Testament.* 2 vols. Oxford: Clarendon, 1913.

Charlesworth, James H. *The Good and Evil Serpent: How a Universal Symbol Became Christianized.* New Haven, CT: Yale University Press, 2010.

———. *The History of the Rechabites.* Vol. 1, *The Greek Recension.* TT 17. PS 10. Chico, CA: Scholars Press, 1982.

———. "History of the Rechabites." In *The Old Testament Pseudepigrapha*, 2 vols., edited by James H. Charlesworth, 2:443–461. 1st ed. New York: Doubleday, 1985.

———, ed. *The Old Testament Pseudepigrapha.* 2 vols. 1st ed. New York: Doubleday, 1983–1985.

———, ed. *The Old Testament Pseudepigrapha.* 2 vols. 2nd ed. Carol Stream, IL: Tyndale House, 2010.

Chazon, Esther. "A Liturgical Document from Qumran and Its Implications: 'Words of the Luminaries' (4QDibHam)." PhD diss., Hebrew University, 1991.

Clines, David J. A. *Job 1–20.* WBC 17. Nashville: Thomas Nelson, 1989.

Cohen, A., and A. J. Rosenberg. *The Twelve Prophets.* Vol. 8 of *Soncino Books of the Bible.* Brooklyn, NY: Soncino, 1994.

Collins, John J. "Sibylline Oracles." In *The Old Testament Pseudepigrapha*, 2 vols., edited by James H. Charlesworth, 1:317–472. 1st ed. New York: Doubleday, 1983.

Collins, Matthew A. *The Use of Sobriquets in the Qumran Dead Sea Scrolls*. LSTS. London: T&T Clark, 2009.

Conybeare, F. C. "The Testament of Solomon." *JQR* 11 (1898): 1–45.

Coogan, Michael. *Stories from Ancient Canaan*. Philadelphia: Westminster John Knox, 1978.

Coogan, Michael, and Mark S. Smith, eds. *Stories from Ancient Canaan*. 2nd ed. Louisville, KY: Westminster John Knox, 2012.

Crawford, Sidnie White, and Cecilia Wassen, eds. *The Dead Sea Scrolls at Qumran and the Concept of a Library*. STDJ 116. Leiden: Brill, 2015.

Cross, Frank M. "The Council of Yahweh in Second Isaiah." *JNES* 12 (1953): 274–277.

Davidson, A. B. *A Commentary, Grammatical and Exegetical, on the Book of Job, with Translation*. Vol. 1. London: Williams and Norgate, 1862.

Davidson, Maxwell J. *Angels at Qumran: A Comparative Study of 1 Enoch 1–36, 72–108 and Sectarian Writings from Qumran*. JSPSS 11. Sheffield: Sheffield Academic, 1992.

Davies, Philip. *1QM, the War Scroll from Qumran: Its Structure and History*. BibOr 32. Rome: Pontifical Biblical Institute, 1977.

Day, Peggy L. "Abishai the Satan in 2 Sam 19:17–24." *CBQ* 49 (1987): 543–547.

———. *An Adversary in Heaven: Satan in the Hebrew Bible*. Atlanta: Scholars Press, 1988.

DeMoor, Johannes C. *The Rise of Yahwism: The Roots of Israelite Monotheism*. Leuven, Belgium: Leuven University Press, 1990.

Diestel, Ludwig. "Set-Typhon, Asahel und Satan: Ein Eeitrag zur Religionsgeshichte des Orients." *Zeitschrift für die historische Theologie* 30, no. 2 (1860): 158–217.

Dimant, Devorah. "Between Qumran Sectarian and Non-sectarian Texts: The Case of Belial and Mastema." In *The Dead Sea Scrolls and Contemporary Culture*, edited by Adolfo D. Roitman, Lawrence H. Schiffman, and Shani Tzoref, 235–256. STDJ 93. Leiden: Brill, 2010.

Dirksen, Peter B. *Historical Commentary on the Old Testament: 1 Chronicles*. Leuven, Belgium: Peeters, 2005.

Donahue, John R., and Daniel J. Harrington. *The Gospel of Mark*. Sacra Pagina 2. Collegeville, MN: Liturgical Press, 2002.

Drawnel, Henryk. *An Aramaic Wisdom Text from Qumran*. Leiden: Brill, 2004.

Duling, D. C. "Testament of Solomon." In *The Old Testament Pseudepigrapha*, 2 vols., edited by James H. Charlesworth, 1:935–987. 1st ed. New York: Doubleday, 1983.

Dunn, James D. G. *Jesus Remembered*. Grand Rapids, MI: Eerdmans, 2003.

Dupont-Sommer, A. *The Essene Writings from Qumran*. Translated by G. Vermes. Oxford: Blackwell, 1961.

———. "L'instruction sur les deux Esprits dans le 'Manuel de Discipline.'" *RHR* 142, no. 1 (1952): 296–316.

Ebeling, Erich. *Tod und leben nach den vorstellungen der Babylonier*. Berlin: Walter de Gruyter, 1931.

Edwards, Mark. "The Fate of the Devil in Origen." *Ephemerides theologicae Lovanienses* 86, no. 1 (2010): 163–170.

———. "Origen." In *Stanford Encyclopedia of Philosophy*, edited by Edward N. Zalta et al., 1–35. Palo Alto, CA: Stanford University Press, 2018.

———. "Origen of Alexandria." In *The Wiley Blackwell Companion to Patristics*, edited by Ken Perry, 98–110. Oxford: Wiley Blackwell, 2015.

Eichrodt, Walther. *Ezekiel: A Commentary*. Translated by Cosslett Quin. London: SCM, 1970.

Elgvin, Torleif. "Belial/Beliar/Devil/Satan." In *Dictionary of New Testament Backgrounds*, 153–157. Downers Grove, IL: InterVarsity, 2000.

Embry, Brad, Ron Herms, and Archie T. Wright, eds. *Early Jewish Literature: An Anthology*. 2 vols. Grand Rapids, MI: Eerdmans, 2017–2019.

Eshel, Esther. "Apotropaic Prayers in the Second Temple Period." In *Liturgical Perspectives: Prayer and Poetry in Light of the Dead Sea Scrolls*, edited by Esther Chazon, 69–88. STDJ 48. Leiden: Brill, 2003.

———. "Genres of Magical Texts in the Dead Sea Scrolls." In *Die Dämonen: Die Dämonologie der israelitisch-jüdischen und frühchristlichen Literatur im Kontext ihrer Umwelt*, edited by Armin Lange, Hermann Lichtenberger, and K. F. Diethard Römheld, 395–414. Tübingen, Germany: Mohr Siebeck, 2003.

———. "Mastema's Attempt on Moses' Life in the 'Pseudo-Jubilees' Text from Masada." *DSD* 10, no. 3 (2003): 359–364.

Eshel, Esther, J. C. Greenfield, and M. E. Stone, eds. *The Aramaic Levi Document*. SVTP 9. Leiden: Brill, 2004.

Evans, Craig A. "Jesus and Psalm 91 in Light of the Exorcism Scrolls." In *Celebrating the Scrolls: A Canadian Contribution*, edited by Peter W. Flint, Jean Duhaime, and Kyung S. Baek, 541–555. Atlanta: SBL, 2011.

———. *Mark 8:27–16:20*. WBC 3B. Nashville: Thomas Nelson, 2001.

Fabry, Heinz-Josef. "'Satan'—Begriff und Wirklichkeit: Untersuchung zur Dämonologie der altestamentlichen Weisheitsliterture." In *Die Dämonen: Die Dämonologie der israelitisch-jüdischen und frühchristlichen Literatur im Kontext ihrer Umwelt*, edited by Armin Lange, Hermann Lichtenberger, and K. F. Diethard Römheld, 269–291. Tübingen, Germany: Mohr Siebeck, 2003.

Falk, Daniel. *Daily, Sabbath & Festival Prayers in the Dead Sea Scrolls.* STDJ 7. Leiden: Brill, 1998.

Farrar, Thomas J. "The Intimate and Ultimate Adversary: Satanology in Early Second-Century Christian Literature." *JECS* 26, no. 4 (2018): 517–546.

———. "New Testament Satanology and Leading Opponents in Second Temple Jewish Literature: A Religio-historical Analysis." *JTS* 70, no. 1 (2019): 21–68.

Ferguson, John. *Clement of Alexandria.* New York: Twayne, 1974.

Fisch, Solomon. *Ezekiel.* London: Soncino, 1950.

Fitzmyer, Joseph A. *The Gospel according to Luke (I–IX).* ABC 28. New York: Doubleday, 1970.

———. *Luke the Theologian: Aspects of His Teaching.* London: Paulist, 1989.

Flint, Peter W. "Psalms and Psalters at Qumran." In *Early Jewish Literature: An Anthology*, 2 vols., edited by Brad Embry, Ronald Herms, and Archie T. Wright, 1:150–161. Grand Rapids, MI: Eerdmans, 2018.

Floyd, W. E. G. *Clement of Alexandria's Treatment of the Problem of Evil.* London: Oxford University Press, 1971.

Flusser, David. *Judaism of the Second Temple Period: The Jewish Sages and Their Literature.* Vol. 2. Grand Rapids, MI: Eerdmans, 2009.

———. "Qumran and 'Apotropaic' Prayers." In *Judaism and the Origins of Christianity*, 214–215. Jerusalem: Magnes, 1988.

Forsyth, Neil. *The Old Enemy: Satan and the Combat Myth.* Princeton, NJ: Princeton University Press, 1987.

———. *The Satanic Epic.* Princeton, NJ: Princeton University Press, 2003.

France, R. T. *The Gospel of Mark.* NIGTC. Grand Rapids, MI: Eerdmans, 2002.

Frank, Anne. *Tales from the Secret Annex: A Collection of Her Short Stories, Fables, and Lesser-Known Writings.* New York: Bantam, 2003.

Frey, Jörg. "Different Patterns of Dualistic Thought in the Qumran Library." In *Legal Texts and Legal Issues*, edited by Moshe Bernstein et al., 275–335. STDJ 23. Leiden: Brill, 1997.

———. *Qumran, Early Judaism, and New Testament Interpretation.* Edited by Jacob N. Cerone. WUNT 424. Tübingen, Germany: Mohr Siebeck, 2019.

———. "The Rule of the Community." In *Early Jewish Literature: An Anthology*, 2 vols., edited by Brad Embry, Ronald Herms, and Archie T. Wright, 2:95–115. Grand Rapids, MI: Eerdmans, 2018.

Friesen, Steven J. "The Beast from the Land: Revelation 13:11–18 and Social Setting." In *Reading the Book of Revelation*, edited by David L. Barr, 49–64. Atlanta: SBL, 2003.

Fröhlich, Ida. "Evil in Second Temple Texts." In *Evil and the Devil*, edited by Ida Fröhlich and Erkki Koskenniemi, 23–50. LNTS 481. London: Bloomsbury, 2013.

———. "Invoke at Anytime." *Biblische Notizen* 137 (2008): 41–74.

Galling, Kurt. *Die Bücher der Chronik, Ezra, Nehemia*. Göttingen, Germany: Vandenhoeck & Ruprecht, 1954.

Gammie, John. "The Angelology and Demonology in the Septuagint of the Book of Job." *Hebrew Union College Annual* 56 (1985): 1–19.

García Martínez, Florentino. "Qumran Origins and Early History: A Groningen Hypothesis." *Folio Orientalia* 25 (1988): 113–136.

Garrett, Susan R. *The Demise of the Devil: Magic and the Demonic in Luke's Writings*. Minneapolis: Fortress, 1989.

———. *The Temptations of Jesus in Mark's Gospel*. Grand Rapids, MI: Eerdmans, 1998.

Gerstenberger, Erhard. *Israel in the Persian Period: The Fifth and Fourth Centuries B.C.E.* Translated by Siegfried S. Schatzmann. Atlanta: SBL, 2014.

Gibson, E. Leigh. "The Jews and Christians in the Martyrdom of Polycarp: Entangled or Parted Ways?" In *The Ways That Never Parted: Jews and Christians in Late Antiquity and the Early Middle Ages*, edited by Adam H. Becker and Annette Yoshiko Reed, 145–158. Tübingen, Germany: Mohr Siebeck, 2003.

Gokey, Francis X. "The Terminology for the Devil and Evil Spirits in the Apostolic Fathers." PhD diss., Catholic University of America, 1961.

Golb, Norman. *Who Wrote the Dead Sea Scrolls?* New York: Scribner, 1995.

Grant, Robert M. "Aristides." In *Anchor Bible Dictionary*, edited by David Noel Freedman, 1:382. New Haven, CT: Yale University Press, 1992.

Grelot, P. "Isaïe XIV 12–15 et son Arrière-plan Mythologique." *RHR* 149 (1956): 18–48.

Guelich, Robert A. *Mark 1–8:26*. WBC 34A. Nashville: Thomas Nelson, 1989.

Gurtner, Daniel M. *Introducing the Pseudepigrapha of Second Temple Judaism: Message, Context, and Significance*. Grand Rapids, MI: Baker Academic, 2020.

Hagner, Donald A. *Word Biblical Commentary: Matthew 1–13*. WBC 33A. Dallas: Word Books, 1993.

Hall, Isaac H. "The Lives of the Prophets." *JBL* 7 (1887): 28–40.

Handy, Lowell K. "The Authorization of Divine Power and the Guilt of God in the Book of Job: Useful Ugaritic Parallels." *JSOT* 60 (1993): 107–118.

———. "Dissenting Deities or Obedient Angels: Divine Hierarchies in Ugarit and the Bible." *BR* 35, no. 1 (1990): 18–35.

Hanneken, Todd R. "The Book of Jubilees." In *Early Jewish Literature: An Anthology*, 2 vols., edited by Brad Embry, Ronald Herms, and Archie T. Wright, 1:510–541. Grand Rapids, MI: Eerdmans, 2018.

Hare, D. R. A. "The Lives of the Prophets." In *The Old Testament Pseudepigrapha*, 2 vols., edited by James H. Charlesworth, 2:379–399. New York: Doubleday, 1985.

Harkins, Angela Kim. "Hodayot." In *Early Jewish Literature: An Anthology*, 2 vols., edited by Brad Embry, Ronald Herms, and Archie T. Wright, 2:450–458. Grand Rapids, MI: Eerdmans, 2018.

Harkins, Angela Kim, Kelley Coblentz Bautch, and John C. Endres, eds. *The Fallen Angels Traditions: Second Temple Developments and Reception History*. CBQMS 53. Washington, DC: Catholic Biblical Association of America, 2014.

Harrington, Daniel J. *The Gospel of Matthew*. Sacra Pagina 1. Collegeville, MN: Liturgical Press, 2007.

Harrison, P. N. *Polycarp's Two Epistles to the Philippians*. Cambridge: Cambridge University Press, 1936.

Hartin, Patrick J. *James*. Sacra Pagina 14. Collegeville, MN: Liturgical Press, 2003.

Henze, Matthias, and Liv Ingeborg Lied, eds. *The Old Testament Pseudepigrapha: Fifty Years of the Pseudepigrapha Section at the SBL*. SBLEJL 50. Atlanta: SBL, 2019.

Herms, Ronald. "Testament of Moses." In *Early Jewish Literature: An Anthology*, 2 vols., edited by Brad Embry, Ronald Herms, and Archie T. Wright, 2:639–646. Grand Rapids, MI: Eerdmans, 2018.

Herrmann, W. "Baal Zebub." In *Dictionary of Deities and Demons in the Bible*, edited by Karel Van der Toorn, Bob Becking, and Pieter W. van der Horst, 154–156. Leiden: Brill, 1999.

Hölscher, Gustav. *Geschichte der israelitisch-jüdischen Religion*. Leipzig: Alfred Töpelmann, 1922.

Hooker, Morna D. *The Gospel according to Saint Mark*. BNTC 2. London: A&C Black, 1991.

How, W. W., and Joseph Wells. *A Commentary on Herodotus*. Oxford: Clarendon, 1912.

James, M. R. *Apocrypha Anecdota: A Collection of Thirteen Apocryphal Books and Fragments*. Texts and Studies, vol. 2, no. 3. Cambridge: Cambridge University Press, 1893.

Japhet, Sara. *The Ideology of the Book of Chronicles and Its Place in Biblical Thought*. Frankfurt: Peter Lang, 1989.

Jastrow, Marcus. "A Babylonian Parallel to the Book of Job." *JBL* 25 (1906): 135–191.

Jastrow, Morris, and Albert T. Clay. *An Old Babylonian Version of the Gilgamesh Epic: On the Basis of Recently Discovered Texts*. Cambridge: Cambridge University Press, 2015.

Jerome. *Commentary on Isaiah*. CCL 73. Swindon, UK: Bible Society, 2019.

Johnson, M. D. "Life of Adam and Eve." In *The Old Testament Pseudepigrapha*, 2 vols., edited by James H. Charlesworth, 2:249–295. New York: Doubleday, 1985.

Kaupel, Heinrich. *Die Dämonen im Alten Testament*. Augsburg, Germany: Benno Filser, 1930.

Kee, Howard C. "Testaments of the Twelve Patriarchs." In *The Old Testament Pseudepigrapha*, 2 vols., edited by James H. Charlesworth, 1:775–828. New York: Doubleday, 1983.

Kelly, Henry Ansgar. "The Devil in the Desert." *CBQ* 26 (1964): 190–220.

———. *Satan: A Biography*. Cambridge: Cambridge University Press, 2006.

Kinet, D. "The Ambiguity of the Concepts of God and Satan in the Book of Job." In *Job and the Silence of God*, edited by C. Duquoc and C. Floristán, 30–35. Edinburgh: T&T Clark, 1984.

King, L. W. *Enuma Elish: The Epic of Creation*. Whitefish, MT: Kessinger, 2010.

Klein, Ralph W. *1 Chronicles*. Minneapolis: Augsburg Fortress, 2006.

Klein, S. "*Al ha-seper* Vitae Prophetarum." In *Sefer Klozner*, edited by H. Torczyner, 189–208. Tel Aviv: Vaad Ha-yovel, 1937.

Kluger, Rivkah Schärf. *Satan in the Old Testament*. Translated by Hildegard Nagel. Evanston, IL: Northwestern University Press, 1967.

Knibb, Michael A. "Martyrdom and Ascension of Isaiah." In *The Old Testament Pseudepigrapha*, 2 vols., edited by James H. Charlesworth, 2:143–176. New York: Doubleday, 1985.

Kobelski, Paul J. *Melchizedek and Melchiresha*. CBQMS 10. Washington, DC: Catholic Biblical Association of America, 1981.

Koester, Craig R. *Revelation*. ABC 38A. New Haven, CT: Yale University Press, 2014.

Kugel, James. "How Old Is the Aramaic Levi Document?" *DSS* 14, no. 3 (2007): 291–312.

Kugler, Robert. *From Patriarch to Priest: The Levi-Priestly Tradition from Aramaic Levi to Testament of Levi*. SBLEJL 9. Atlanta: Scholars Press, 1996.

———. *Testaments of the Twelve Patriarchs*. Sheffield: Sheffield Academic, 2001.

Kulik, Alexander. *Retroverting Slavonic Pseudepigrapha*. Atlanta: SBL, 2004; Leiden: Brill, 2005.

Kushner, Harold S. *When Bad Things Happen to Good People*. New York: Schocken Books, 1981.

Landersdorfer, Simon. "Eine babylonische Quelle für das Buch Job?" *Bibl. Studien* 16 (1911): 55–59.

Lange, Armin. "Considerations concerning the 'Spirits of Impurity' in Zech 13:2." In *Die Dämonen: Die Dämonologie der israelitisch-jüdischen und frühchristlichen Literatur im Kontext ihrer Umwelt*, edited by Armin Lange, Hermann Lichtenberger, and K. F. Diethard Römheld, 331–353. Tübingen, Germany: Mohr Siebeck, 2003.

Lange, Armin, Eric M. Meyers, Bennie H. Reynolds III, and Randal Styers, eds. *Light against Darkness*. Göttingen, Germany: Vandenhoeck & Ruprecht, 2011.

Langton, Edward. *Essentials of Demonology*. London: Epworth, 1949.

Leibniz, Gottfried. *Theodicy: Essays on the Goodness of God, the Freedom of Man, and the Origin of Evil*. Translated by E. M. Huggard. London: Routledge & Kegan Paul, 1951.

Levison, John R. "Adam and Eve in Romans 1.18–25 and the Greek *Life of Adam and Eve*." *NTS* 50 (2004): 519–534.

———. *The Greek Life of Adam and Eve*. CEJL. Berlin: Walter de Gruyter, forthcoming.

———. "The Life of Adam and Eve." In *Early Jewish Literature: An Anthology*, 2 vols., edited by Brad Embry, Ronald Herms, and Archie T. Wright, 1:445–461. Grand Rapids, MI: Eerdmans, 2018.

Licht, J. "Taxo, or the Apocalyptic Doctrine of Vengeance." *JJS* 12 (1961): 95–103.

Lieu, Judith. *Image and Reality: The Jews in the World of Christians in the Second Century*. Edinburgh: T&T Clark, 1996.

Lilla, Salvatore R. C. *Clement of Alexandria: A Study in Christian Platonism and Gnosticism*. Eugene, OR: Wipf & Stock, 2005.

Ling, Trevor. *The Significance of Satan*. London: SPCK, 1961.

Lunn-Rockliffe, Sophie. "Diabolical Motivations: The Devil in Ecclesiastical Histories from Eusebius to Evarius." In *Shifting Genres in Late Antiquity*, edited by Geoffrey Greatrex and Hugh Elton, 119–134. Burlington, VT: Ashgate, 2015.

Mach, Michael. *Entwicklungsstadien des Jüdischen Engelglaubens in Vorrabbinischer Zeit*. Tübingen, Germany: Mohr Siebeck, 1992.

Manson, William. *The Gospel of Luke*. London: Hodder & Stoughton, 1930.

Martone, Corrado. "Evil or Devil? Belial between the Bible and Qumran." *Henoch* 26, no. 2 (2004): 115–127.

Mason, Steve. "The Writings of Flavius Josephus." In *Early Jewish Literature: An Anthology*, 2 vols., edited by Brad Embry, Ronald Herms, and Archie T. Wright, 1:252–358. Grand Rapids, MI: Eerdmans, 2018.

McCown, C. C. "The Christian Tradition as to the Magical Wisdom of Solomon." *JPOS* 2 (1922): 1–8.

McKay, J. W. "Helel and the Dawn Goddess: A Re-examination of the Myth in Isaiah XIV 12–15." *VT* 20 (1970): 451–464.

McKenzie, John L. "Mythological Allusion in Ezek 28:12–18." *JBL* 75, no. 4 (December 1956): 322–327.

McKinion, Steven A. *Isaiah 1–39*. ACCS, Old Testament 10. Downers Grove, IL: InterVarsity, 2004.

McNeile, A. H. *The Gospel according to St. Matthew*. London: Macmillan, 1915.

Meyer, W. "Vita Adae et Evae." *Abhandlungen der koeniglichen Bayerischen Akademie der Wissenschaften, Philsophisch-philologische Klasse* 14, no. 3 (1878): 185–250.

Meyers, Carol, and Eric Meyers. *Haggai, Zechariah 1–8*. ABC 25B. Garden City, NY: Doubleday, 1987.

Milgrom, Jacob. *Numbers*. JPSTC. Philadelphia: Jewish Publication Society, 2003.

Milik, J. T. "Milkî-sIedeq et Milkî-reša' dans les anciens écrits juifs et chrétiens." *JJS* 23 (1972): 95–144.

Mitchell, Alan C. *Hebrews*. Sacra Pagina 13. Collegeville, MN: Liturgical Press, 2009.

Morgenstern, Julian. "The Mythological Background of Psalm 82." *Hebrew Union College Annual* 14 (1939): 29–126.

Morris, Michael J. *Warding off Evil*. WUNT 2 451. Tübingen, Germany: Mohr Siebeck, 2017.

Mounce, Robert H. *Matthew*. Peabody, MA: Hendrickson, 1991.

Mounce, William D. *Pastoral Epistles*. WBC 46. Nashville: Thomas Nelson, 2000.

Müller, Ulrich B. "Vision und Botschaft: Erwägungen zur prophetischen Struktur der Verkündigung Jesu." *ZThK* 74 (1977): 416–448.

Murphy-O'Connor, Jerome. *Paul the Letter-Writer: His World, His Options, His Skills*. Collegeville, MN: Liturgical Press, 1995.

Myers, Jacob M. *1 Chronicles*. ABC 12. Garden City, NY: Doubleday, 1965.

Newsom, Carol A. "'Sectually Explicit' Literature from Qumran." In *The Hebrew Bible and Its Interpreters*, edited by David Noel Freedman, Baruch Halpern, and William H. C. Propp, 167–187. Winona Lake, IN: Eisenbrauns, 1990.

Neyrey, Jerome H. *2 Peter, Jude: A New Translation with Introduction and Commentary*. ABC 37C. New Haven, CT: Yale University Press, 1993.

Nickelsburg, George W. E. "An Antiochan Date for the Testament of Moses." In *Studies on the Testament of Moses*, edited by George W. E. Nickelsburg, 33–37. Atlanta: SBL, 1973.

———. *1 Enoch 1*. Minneapolis: Fortress, 2001.

———. "A Translation of the Similitudes of Enoch (1 Enoch 37–71)." In *Early Jewish Literature: An Anthology*, 2 vols., edited by Brad Embry, Ronald Herms, and Archie T. Wright, 2:264–296. Grand Rapids, MI: Eerdmans, 2018.

Nickelsburg, George W. E., and James C. VanderKam. *1 Enoch 2: A Commentary on the Book of 1 Enoch Chapters 37–82*. Minneapolis: Fortress, 2012.

Niditch, Susan. *The Responsive Self: Personal Religion in the Biblical Literature of the Neo-Babylonian and Persian Periods*. New Haven, CT: Yale University Press, 2015.

Nolland, John. *The Gospel of Matthew*. NIGTC. Grand Rapids, MI: Eerdmans, 2005.

———. *Luke 1–9:20*. WBC 35A. Dallas: Word Books, 1989.

———. *Luke 9:21–18:34*. WBC 35B. Nashville: Thomas Nelson, 1993.

———. *Luke 18:35–24:53*. WBC 35C. Nashville: Thomas Nelson, 1993.

Noth, Martin. *Numbers: A Commentary*. Translated by James D. Martin. Philadelphia: Westminster John Knox, 1968.

Notley, R. Steven. "The Melchizedek Scroll." In *Early Jewish Literature: An Anthology*, 2 vols., edited by Brad Embry, Ronald Herms, and Archie T. Wright, 1:490–497. Grand Rapids, MI: Eerdmans, 2018.

Orlov, Andrei A. *Dark Mirrors: Azazel and Satanael in Early Jewish Demonology*. Albany, NY: SUNY Press, 2011.

———. *Demons of Change: Antagonism and Apotheosis in Jewish and Christian Apocalypticism*. Albany, NY: SUNY Press, 2020.

———. *Divine Scapegoats: Demonic Mimesis in Early Jewish*. Albany, NY: SUNY Press, 2015.

Pagels, Elaine. *The Origin of Satan*. New York: Vintage Books, 1995.

Patmore, Hector M. *Adam, Satan, and the King of Tyre: An Interpretation of Ezekiel 28:11–19 in Late Antiquity*. Leiden: Brill, 2012.

Pearson, Birger A. "Early Christianity and Gnosticism in the History of Religions." *Studia Theologica* 55 (2001): 81–106.

Pierce, Chad T. "Satan and Related Figures." In *Eerdmans Dictionary of Early Judaism*, edited by John C. Collins and Daniel C. Harlow, 1196–1200. Grand Rapids, MI: Eerdmans, 2010.

Plantinga, Alvin. *God, Freedom, and Evil*. Grand Rapids, MI: Eerdmans, 1977.

Poirier, John C. "An Illuminating Parallel to Isaiah XIV 12." *VT* 49, no. 3 (July 1999): 371–389.

Pope, Marvin H. *El in the Ugaritic Texts*. VTSup 2. Leiden: Brill, 1955.

———. *Job: A New Translation with Introduction and Commentary*. ABC 15. New Haven, CT: Yale University Press, 1973.

Priest, J. "Testament of Moses." In *The Old Testament Pseudepigrapha*, 2 vols., edited by James H. Charlesworth, 1:919–934. New York: Doubleday, 1983.

Ramsay, W. M. *St. Paul the Traveller and the Roman Citizen*. London: Hodder & Stoughton, 1920.

Reed, Annette Yoshiko. *Fallen Angels and the History of Judaism and Christianity: The Reception of Enochic Literature*. Cambridge: Cambridge University Press, 2005.

———. "The Trickery of the Fallen Angels and the Demonic Mimesis of the Divine: Aetiology, Demonology, and Polemics in the Writings of Justin Martyr." *JECS* 12, no. 2 (2004): 141–171.

Rengstorf, Karl Heinrich. *Hirbet Qumrân and the Problem of the Library of the Dead Sea Caves*. Translated by J. R. Wilkie. Leiden: Brill, 1963.

Reventlow, Henning Graf, and Yair Hoffman, eds. *The Problem of Evil and Its Symbols in Jewish and Christian Tradition*. JSOTSS 366. London: T&T Clark, 2004.

Rhodes, James N. *The Epistle of Barnabas and the Deuteronomic Tradition*. Tübingen, Germany: Mohr Siebeck, 2004.

Richards, E. Randolph. *The Secretary in the Letters of Paul*. Tübingen, Germany: Mohr Siebeck, 1991.

Robinson, H. W. "The Council of Yahweh." *JTS* 45 (1943): 151–157.

Rogers, Robert W. *Cuneiform Parallels to the Old Testament*. New York: Eaton & Mains, 1912.

Rönsch, H. *Das Buch der Jubiläen oder die kleine Genesis*. Tübingen, Germany: Leipzig, 1874.

Rosenberg, Ruth. "The Concept of Biblical 'Belial.'" In *Proceedings of the World Congress of Jewish Studies*, vol. 8/A. Leiden: Brill, 1982.

Rosen-Zvi, Ishay, *Demonic Desires: Yetzer Hara and the Problem of Evil in Late Antiquity*. Philadelphia: University of Pennsylvania Press, 2011.

Ruhbach, G. "Zum Begriff ἀντίθεος in der alten Kirche." *TU* 92 (1966): 372–384.

Russell, Jeffrey B. *The Devil: Perceptions of Evil from Antiquity to Primitive Christianity*. Ithaca, NY: Cornell University Press, 1987.

———. *The Prince of Darkness: Radical Evil and the Power of Good in History*. London: Thames and Hudson, 1989.

———. *Satan: The Early Christian Tradition*. Ithaca, NY: Cornell University Press, 1981.

Sacchi, Paolo, ed. *Apocrifi dell'Antico Testamento*. Vol. 1. Turin, Italy: Unione tipografico-editrice torinese, 1981.

———. *The History of the Second Temple Period*. JSOTSS 285. Sheffield: Sheffield Academic, 2000.

———. *Jewish Apocalyptic and Its History*. Translated by W. J. Short. JSPSup 20. Sheffield: Sheffield Academic, 1990.

Sailhamer, John. "1 Chronicles 21:1—a Study in Inter-biblical Interpretation." *TJ* 10 (1989): 33–48.

Sarna, Nahum. *Genesis*. JPSTC. Philadelphia: Jewish Publication Society, 1989.

Scerri, Hector M. "Augustine the Manichaean and the Problem of Evil." *Augustinian Panorama* 5–7 (1988–1990): 76–86.

Schlier, Heinrich. *Principalities and Powers in the New Testament*. New York: Herder & Herder, 1961.

Schreiber, Stefan. "The Great Opponent: The Devil in Early Jewish and Formative Christian Literature." In *Deuterocanonical and Cognate Literature Yearbook, 2007: Angels the Concept of Celestial Beings*, 437–458. Berlin: Walter de Gruyter, 2007.

Schuller, Eileen M., and Carol A. Newsom. *The Hodayot (Thanksgiving Psalms): A Study Edition of 1QH^a*. SBLEJL 36. Atlanta: SBL, 2012.

Schultz, Brian. "The War Scroll." In *Early Jewish Literature: An Anthology*, 2 vols., edited by Brad Embry, Ronald Herms, and Archie T. Wright, 2:349–358. Grand Rapids, MI: Eerdmans, 2018.

Segal, Alan F. *Two Powers in Heaven: Early Rabbinic Reports about Christianity and Gnosticism*. Leiden: Brill Academic, 2002.

Segal, Michael. *The Book of Jubilees: Rewritten Bible, Redaction, Ideology and Theology*. Leiden: Brill, 2007.

Seitz, Oscar J. F. "The Relationship of the Shepherd of Hermas to the Epistle of James." *JBL* 63, no. 2 (1944): 131–140.

Sekki, A. E. *The Meaning of Ruah at Qumran*. SBLDS 110. Atlanta: Scholars Press, 1989.

Siegert, F. "Unbeachtete papiaszitate bei armenichen Schriftstellern." *New Testament Studies* 27 (1981): 605–614.

Simpson, David. *Judas Iscariot: The Man of Mystery, History, and Prophecy*. Waterloo, IA: H. Cedarholm, 1943.

Slotki, I. W. *Isaiah*. London: Soncino, 1967.

Smith, Mark S. *The Early History of God: Yahweh and the Other Deities in Ancient Israel*. San Francisco: Harper & Row, 1990.

Speiser, E. A. *Genesis: Introduction, Translation, and Notes*. 3rd ed. ABC 1. Garden City, NY: Doubleday, 1983.

Sperling, S. D. "Beliar." In *The Dictionary of Deities and Demons in the Bible*, edited by K. van der Toorn, B. Becking, and P. van der Horst, 169–171. Leiden: Brill, 1999.

Spittler, R. P. "Testament of Job." In *The Old Testament Pseudepigrapha*, 2 vols., edited by James H. Charlesworth, 1:829–868. New York: Doubleday, 1983.

Steudel, Annette. "God and Belial." In *The Dead Sea Scrolls Fifty Years after Their Discovery: Proceedings of the Jerusalem Congress, July 20–25, 1997*, edited by E. Tov, J. C. VanderKam, and G. Marquis, 332–340. Jerusalem: Israel Exploration Society, 2000.

Stokes, Ryan. "Belial." In *Eerdmans Dictionary of Early Judaism*, edited by John J. Collins and Daniel Harlow, 435–436. Grand Rapids, MI: Eerdmans, 2010.

———. "The Devil Made David Do It . . . or Did He? The Nature, Identity, and Literary Origins of the Satan in 1 Chronicles 21:1." *JBL* 128, no. 1 (2009): 91–106.

———. *The Satan: How God's Executioner Became the Enemy*. Grand Rapids, MI: Eerdmans, 2019.

Stone, Michael, and J. C. Greenfield. "The Prayer of Levi." *JBL* 112 (1993): 247–266.

Stuckenbruck, Loren T. "Demonic Beings and the Dead Sea Scrolls." In *Definitions and Development*, 121–144. Vol. 1 of *Explaining Evil*, edited by J. Harold Ellens. Denver: Praeger, 2011.

———. "The Demonic World of the Dead Sea Scrolls." In *Evil and the Devil*, edited by Ida Fröhlich and Erkki Koskenniemi, 51–70. London: Bloomsbury, 2013.

———. *Myth of the Rebellious Angels*. WUNT 335. Tübingen, Germany: Mohr Siebeck, 2014.

———. "Pleas for Deliverance from the Demonic in Early Jewish Texts." In *Studies in Jewish Prayer*, edited by C. T. R. Hayward and Brad Embry, 55–74. JSSup 17. Oxford: Oxford University Press, 2005.

———. "Satan and Demons." In *Jesus among Friends and Enemies*, edited by Chris Keith and Larry W. Hurtado, 173–197. Grand Rapids, MI: Baker, 2011.

Suter, David. "Fallen Angel, Fallen Priest: The Problem of Family Purity in 1 Enoch." *Hebrew Union College Annual* 50 (1979): 115–135.

Tàrrech, Armand Puig. "LC 10, 18: La Visió de la Caiguda de satanàs." *Revista Catalana de Teologia* 3 (1978): 217–243.

Tate, Marvin. "Satan in the Old Testament." *Review & Expositor* 89, no. 4 (Fall 1992): 461–474.

Terrien, Samuel. *The Book of Job: Introduction and Exegesis*. Nashville: Abingdon, 1954.

Tigchelaar, Eibert. "'These Are the Names of the Spirits of . . .': *4QCatalogue of Spirits (4Q230)* and New Manuscript Evidence for the *Two Spirits Treatise.*" *RevQ* 84, no. 4 (2004): 543–545.

Tornau, Christian. "Saint Augustine." In *Stanford Encyclopedia of Philosophy*, edited by Edward N. Zalta et al., 424–427. Palo Alto, CA: Stanford University Press, 2018.

Torrey, C. C. *The Lives of the Prophets.* JBLMS 1. Philadelphia: SBL, 1946.

———. *Pseudo-Ezekiel and the Original Prophecy.* New Haven, CT: Yale University Press, 1930.

Turnage, Marc. "Hodayot (1QH^a)." In *Early Jewish Literature: An Anthology*, 2 vols., edited by Brad Embry, Ronald Herms, and Archie T. Wright, 2:459–501. Grand Rapids, MI: Eerdmans, 2018.

Tur-Sinai, N. H. *The Book of Job.* Rev. ed. Jerusalem: Kiryat Sefer, 1967.

———. *The Book of Job: A New Commentary.* Jerusalem: Kiryat Sefer, 1981.

Twelftree, Graham H. "Exorcism and the Defeat of Beliar in the Testaments of the Twelve Patriarchs." *Vigiliae Christianae* 65 (2011): 170–188.

———. *In the Name of Jesus: Exorcism among Early Christians.* Grand Rapids, MI: Baker, 2007.

———. *Jesus the Exorcist: A Contribution to the Study of the Historical Jesus.* Eugene, OR: Wipf & Stock, 2011.

VanderKam, James C. *The Book of Jubilees.* 2 vols. Leuven, Belgium: Peeters, 1989.

———. "The Origins and Purposes of the Book of Jubilees." In *Studies in the Book of Jubilees*, edited by M. Albani, J. Frey, and A. Lange, 3–24. TSAJ 65. Tübingen, Germany: Mohr Siebeck, 1997.

———. *Textual and Historical Studies in the Book of Jubilees.* Missoula, MT: Scholars Press, 1977.

Van der Ploeg, J. "Fragments d'un manuscrit de Psaumes de Qumrân (11QPs^b)." *RB* 74 (1967): 408–413.

Van Ruiten, Jacques. "Angels and Demons in the Book of Jubilees." In *Angels: The Concept of Celestial Beings: Origins, Development and Reception*, edited by F. V. Reiterer, T. Nicklas, and K. Schöpflin, 585–609. Berlin: Walter de Gruyter, 2007.

Vollenweider, Samuel. *Ich sah den satan wie einen Blitz vom Himmel fallen (Lk 10:18).* WUNT 144. Tübingen, Germany: Mohr Siebeck, 2002.

Von der Osten-Sacken, Peter. *Gott und Belial: Traditionsgeschichtliche Untersuchungen zum Dualismus in den Texten aus Qumran.* SUNT 6. Göttingen, Germany: Vandenhoeck & Ruprecht, 1969.

Von Rad, Gerhard. *Genesis: A Commentary.* Translated by John H. Marks. London: SCM, 1961.

Wacholder, Ben Zion, trans. "The Damascus Document." In *Early Jewish Literature: An Anthology*, 2 vols., edited by Brad Embry, Ronald Herms, and Archie T. Wright, 2:135–159. Grand Rapids, MI: Eerdmans, 2018.

Wassen, Cecilia. "Angels in the Dead Sea Scrolls." In *Angels: The Concept of Celestial Beings: Origins, Development and Reception*, edited by Friedrich V. Reiterer, Pancratiius C. Beentjes, and Nura Calduch-Benages, 499–523. Berlin: Walter de Gruyter, 2007.

———. "The Damascus Document." In *Early Jewish Literature: An Anthology*, 2 vols., edited by Brad Embry, Ronald Herms, and Archie T. Wright, 2:128–134. Grand Rapids, MI: Eerdmans, 2018.

Watson, W. G. E. "Helel." In *Dictionary of Deities and Demons in the Bible*, edited by Karel van der Toorn, Bob Becking, and Pieter W. van der Horst, 392–394. Grand Rapids, MI: Eerdmans, 1999.

Watts, John. *Isaiah 1–33*. WBC 24. Waco, TX: Word Books, 2005.

Weinberg, Steven. *Dreams of a Final Theory*. New York: Pantheon Books, 1992.

Weiss, Meir. *The Story of Job's Beginning: Job 1–2: A Literary Analysis*. Jerusalem: Magnes, 1983.

Wernberg-Møller, P. "A Reconsideration of the Two Spirits in the Rule of the Community (1 Q *Serek* III, 3–IV, 26)." *RevQ* 3, no. 3 (1961): 413–441.

Whybray, Norman. *The Heavenly Counselor in Isaiah xl 13–14*. SOTSMS 1. Cambridge: Cambridge University Press, 1971.

———. *Job*. Sheffield: Sheffield Academic, 1998.

Wikenhauser, Alfred. *Die Offenbarung des Johannes*. RegensNT 9. Regensburg, Germany: Pustet, 1959.

Williams, Anthony J. "The Mythological Background of Ezekiel 28:11–19?" *BTB* 6 (1976): 49–61.

Williamson, H. G. M. *1 and 2 Chronicles*. Grand Rapids, MI: Eerdmans, 1982.

Wilson, Kenneth. *Augustine's Conversion from Traditional Free Choice to "Non-free Free Will": A Comprehensive Methodology*. Tübingen, Germany: Mohr Siebeck, 2018.

Wintermute, O. S. "Jubilees: A New Translation and Introduction." In *The Old Testament Pseudepigrapha*, 2 vols., edited by James H. Charlesworth, 2:35–142. New York: Doubleday, 1985.

Witmer, Amanda. *Jesus the Galilean Exorcist*. New York: T&T Clark, 2012.

Wray, T. J., and Gregory Mobley. *The Birth of Satan: Tracing the Devil's Biblical Roots*. New York: Palgrave Macmillan, 2005.

Wright, Archie T. "The Book of Watchers: 1 Enoch 1–36 as a Background for the Demonic Pericopes in the Gospels." *Henoch* 28 (2006): 189–207.

———. "The Demonology of 1 Enoch and the New Testament Gospels." In *Enoch and the Synoptic Gospels: Reminiscences, Allusions, Intertextuality*, edited by Loren T. Stuckenbruck and Gabriele Boccaccini, 215–244. Atlanta: SBL, 2016.

———. "Evil Spirits in Second Temple Judaism: The *Watcher Tradition* as a Background to the Demonic Pericopes in the Gospels." *Henoch* 28, no. 1 (2006): 189–207.

———. "The Life of Adam and Eve and Revelation 12:1–17: The Rebellion of the Satan Figure." In *Reading Revelation in Context: John's Apocalypse and Second Temple Judaism*, edited by Ben C. Blackwell et al., 109–115. Grand Rapids, MI: Zondervan, 2019.

———. *The Origin of Evil Spirits: The Reception of Genesis 6:1–4 in Early Jewish Literature*. Rev. ed. Minneapolis: Fortress, 2015.

———. "Social and Economic Injustice: Apocalyptic Themes in the Epistle of Enoch and the Apocalypse of John." In *The Blessings of Enoch: 1 Enoch and Contemporary Theology*, edited by Philip F. Esler, 70–88. Eugene, OR: Wipf & Stock, 2017.

Wright, John W. "The Innocence of David in 1 Chronicles 21." *JSOT* 60 (1993): 87–105.

Wright, N. T. *Evil and the Justice of God*. Downers Grove, IL: InterVarsity, 2006.

———. *Paul and the Faithfulness of God*. Grand Rapids, MI: Fortress, 2013.

Yarbro Collins, Adela. "Insiders and Outsiders in the Book of Revelation and Its Social Context." In *To See Ourselves as Others See Us: Christians, Jews, "Others" in Late Antiquity*, edited by Jacob Neusner and Ernest S. Frerichs, 187–218. Chico, CA: Scholars Press, 1985.

———. *Mark: A Commentary on the Gospel of Mark*. Hermeneia. Minneapolis: Fortress, 2007.

———. "Pergamon in Early Christian Literature." In *Pergamon: Citadel of the Gods*, edited by Helmut Koester, 163–184. Harrisburg: Trinity, 1998.

———. "Vilification and Self-Definition in the Book of Revelation." *HTR* 79 (1986): 308–320.

Zimmerli, Walter. *Ezekiel 1: A Commentary on the Book of the Prophet Ezekiel, Chapters 1–24*. Hermeneia. Philadelphia: Fortress, 1979.

———. *Ezekiel 2: A Commentary on the Book of the Prophet Ezekiel, Chapters 25–48*. Hermeneia. Minneapolis: Fortress, 1983.

Zimmern, H. *Die Keilinschriften und das Alte Testament*. 2 vols. Berlin: Reuther und Reichard, 1902.

Subject Index

1 Enoch, 9, 20, 25, 70, 81, 84, 85, 86, 91, 117, 124, 128, 139, 146, 157, 190, 193, 198, 199, 200, 221, 225, 229, 230, 231, 233, 236, 249, 251
2 Enoch, 40, 190, 200

Abaddon, 110
　spirit of, 114
Abimelech, 12
Abishai, 12, 13
Abraham, 12, 83, 120, 121, 143, 155, 156, 159, 167, 168, 170, 191, 251
abyss, 82, 86, 192, 193
accuse(r), 2, 12, 14, 15, 18, 20, 23, 25, 58, 85, 86, 88, 121, 140, 144, 145, 147, 148, 151, 162, 191, 194, 232, 248, 249
Adam(ic), 1, 27, 33, 43, 44, 45, 46, 47, 49, 73, 74, 75, 76, 77, 78, 79, 80, 81, 82, 88, 199, 200, 215, 223, 226, 230, 232, 233, 240, 241, 242, 243, 248, 251, 252
Adapa, 45, 48
adversary, 5, 6, 12, 13, 14, 15, 16, 18, 19, 21, 22, 23, 26, 29, 32, 49, 56, 58, 59, 60, 61, 63, 65, 69, 71, 72, 78, 79, 80, 83, 85, 87, 88, 90, 96, 99, 113, 114, 116, 127, 147, 149, 150, 152, 153, 154, 154, 155, 157, 158, 159, 160, 165, 166, 170, 171, 173, 174, 176, 177, 178, 179, 180, 181, 182, 184, 195, 205, 206, 207, 210, 211, 212, 216, 218, 230, 232, 235, 246, 247, 248, 250

agent(s) of YHWH, 21
Ahura Mazda, 4, 5, 6, 91, 240
Akedah, 143, 144
Amram, 91, 92
Anat, 6
ancient Near East (ANE), 8, 21, 27, 28, 41, 240
angel(s), 4, 14, 18, 19, 20, 24, 27, 29, 32, 33, 40, 46, 47, 48, 52, 56, 59, 65, 66, 67, 70, 71, 72, 73, 74, 76, 77, 78, 79, 80, 82, 84, 85, 86, 88, 91, 93, 101, 102, 106, 107, 108, 113, 114, 115, 119, 120, 121, 124, 136, 139, 142, 143, 144, 146, 150, 152, 153, 154, 155, 156, 159, 170, 183, 186, 189, 190, 191, 193, 194, 195, 199, 203, 204, 206, 213, 215, 218, 219, 220, 221, 222, 225, 226, 228, 229, 230, 232, 233, 234, 235, 237, 239, 241, 242, 243, 249, 251
　of Darkness, 51, 53, 90, 91, 93, 94, 98, 101, 102, 105, 108, 113, 121, 145, 147, 152, 154, 194, 247, 249
　of destruction, 102, 103, 105, 108, 120, 144, 175
　fallen, 38, 41, 43, 46, 48, 82, 84, 86, 90, 91, 198, 199, 206, 221, 225, 226, 228, 229, 233, 235, 243, 246
　of lawlessness, 135, 136
　of light, 93, 108, 176, 218
　of the Lord (YHWH), 18, 19, 20, 26, 73, 85, 121, 128, 130, 133, 144, 146, 183, 219, 231, 249

272 | Subject Index

angel(s) (*continued*)
   of Mastema, 52, 91, 100, 115, 119, 120, 147, 150
   of Peace, 65, 130, 132, 133, 146, 249
   of the Pit, 114, 147, 250
   of the Presence, 82, 140, 142
   of punishment, 85, 86, 218, 219
   of repentance, 218, 219
   of righteousness, 218, 220, 221
   of the satan, 2, 72, 130, 213
animosity, 14, 119
anti-God, 129, 133, 148
Antiochus IV Epiphanes, 26, 82, 115, 178
Apocalypse, 27, 28, 29, 62, 74, 75, 84, 88, 90, 154, 155, 163, 184, 185, 187, 188, 189, 190, 191, 192, 193, 194, 199, 204, 215, 221, 248
apotropaic prayers, 54, 55, 56
Aramaic, 51, 56, 57, 62, 66, 83, 84, 90, 101, 133, 148
archangels, 29, 68, 69, 80, 82, 85, 90, 98, 108, 128, 135, 142, 157, 183, 184, 190, 233, 239, 247
archdemons, 97, 98
army (armies), 2, 12, 13, 27, 33, 105, 106, 107, 108, 113, 125, 137, 138, 140, 144, 193, 229
astray, 57, 64, 67, 70, 86, 87, 93, 111, 129, 141, 142, 148, 155, 157, 160, 162, 190, 191, 193, 222, 224, 247
Athtar, 39, 40
atonement, 104, 117
   Day of, 22
Authadia, 204
authority, 8, 38, 42, 57, 60, 61, 63, 67, 67, 80, 83, 92, 93, 94, 103, 114, 119, 120, 124, 125, 127, 129, 130, 140, 141, 142, 143, 145, 148, 152, 156, 158, 161, 162, 163, 164, 165, 166, 167, 169, 173, 174, 180, 186, 187, 189, 191, 192, 198, 202, 208, 209, 216, 218, 219, 223, 230, 233, 236, 249, 251
   of God, 3, 17, 21, 55, 67, 80, 84, 87, 97, 101, 102, 124, 127, 133, 142, 143, 144, 146, 150, 152, 154, 155, 159, 160, 161, 162, 166, 167, 169, 179, 184, 190, 201, 230, 242, 246, 247, 249, 251
   autonomous(ly), 2, 3, 19, 22, 30, 49, 63, 87, 88, 97, 202, 211, 229, 243, 246, 247, 248, 251
Azazel, 86, 155, 231

Ba'al, 3, 6, 39, 41, 43, 45
Balaam, 14, 18, 19, 26, 27
bastard spirits, 59
Beelzeboul, 151, 152, 154, 157, 160, 166, 169
Behemoth, 16, 156, 192
Belial, 51, 53, 56, 59, 63, 89, 90, 91, 92, 93, 94, 95, 96, 97, 99, 100, 101, 102, 103, 104, 105, 106, 107, 107, 110, 111, 112, 118, 121, 122, 135, 145, 147, 151, 152, 154, 155, 161, 163, 165, 166, 172, 174, 176, 180, 181, 185, 188, 190, 191, 195, 197, 198, 208, 213, 214, 217, 236, 239, 246, 247, 248, 249, 250
   children/sons of, 95, 116, 153, 170, 173, 239
   congregation of, 109, 186
   lot of, 92, 103, 105, 121, 173
   spirit(s) of, 52, 56, 105
   torrents of, 110, 111
   troops of, 107
Beliar, 63, 64, 65, 70, 71, 89, 122, 123, 124, 125, 126, 127, 128, 129, 130, 131, 132, 134, 135, 136, 137, 138, 139, 140, 141, 145, 146, 147, 152, 167, 171, 188, 193, 194, 197, 248, 249, 250
   lot of, 127
   spirit(s) of, 57, 123, 126, 127, 128, 129, 131, 132, 140, 141, 146, 249
bene haElohim, 6

Canaan, 3, 6, 41, 69, 83
Canaanites, 3, 6, 7, 37, 39, 45, 46, 48
cherub, 5, 46, 47, 229
chief, 22, 38, 45, 82, 83, 91, 94, 107, 110, 113, 114, 119, 120, 121, 122, 123, 125, 126, 128, 131, 132, 135, 136, 139, 141, 142, 146, 147, 152, 154, 157, 159, 163, 166, 167, 168, 171, 174, 183, 184, 194, 195, 198, 224, 247, 249

children. *See* son(s)
Christ, 13, 28, 66, 70, 119, 125, 137, 154, 159, 160, 162, 164, 165, 173, 174, 178, 179, 181, 190, 191, 201, 202, 208, 209, 210, 211, 212, 222, 223, 225, 226, 227, 229, 233, 234, 236, 239, 241
congregation, 59, 98, 105, 106, 109, 110, 185, 186, 198
council, 22, 109, 116, 198, 237
  divine, 21, 23, 24, 25, 116, 117, 242
court, 12, 13, 20, 21, 22, 43, 71, 136, 183, 184
  divine, 5, 191
  heavenly, 13, 18, 19, 38, 58, 79, 81
creation, 1, 3, 46, 47, 48, 69, 80, 81, 82, 93, 123, 140, 142, 161, 165, 182, 195, 197, 202, 203, 204, 222, 223, 228, 229, 230, 231, 233, 234, 235, 237, 239, 241
curses, 87, 104

Day of Judgment, 22, 38, 82, 85, 93
Dead Sea Scrolls (DSS), 23, 26, 49, 51, 52, 53, 56, 61, 63, 82, 84, 87, 89, 91, 93, 94, 96, 98, 100, 108, 110, 118, 119, 122, 124, 125, 136, 147, 152, 158, 159, 170, 173, 174, 195, 218, 219, 221, 246, 247, 248, 249
deceit, 31, 111, 114, 125, 126, 127, 133, 173, 207, 209, 223
  men of, 109
deceiver, 24, 27, 31, 111, 138, 171, 172, 179, 188, 191
defile, 102, 115
Demiurge, 136, 202, 229, 230, 233, 237, 242, 243, 251, 252
demon(s), 140, 141, 143, 147, 151, 152, 154, 155, 156, 157, 158, 160, 164, 165, 166, 168, 169, 171, 173, 195, 198, 199, 201, 207, 209, 215, 224, 225, 226, 227, 228, 229, 230, 231, 233, 234, 235, 236, 239, 250
demonology, 166, 199, 215, 235
destruction, 5, 8, 16, 17, 35, 48, 55, 63, 86, 91, 100, 102, 103, 104, 105, 106, 107, 108, 109, 110, 111, 114, 120, 123, 124, 126, 132, 137, 141, 145, 175, 178, 179, 181, 199
deuterocanonical texts, 49, 61
devil, 2, 27, 29, 30, 31, 32, 34, 49, 51, 53, 61, 65, 66, 67, 68, 69, 70, 71, 72, 73, 74, 75, 76, 77, 78, 79, 80, 81, 82, 84, 87, 88, 89, 94, 129, 147, 148, 149, 150, 152, 153, 154, 155, 160, 161, 162, 163, 165, 167, 169, 170, 171, 172, 173, 174, 177, 179, 180, 181, 182, 183, 184, 185, 188, 190, 191, 192, 193, 194, 195, 197, 198, 199, 200, 201, 202, 205, 206, 207, 208, 209, 210, 211, 212, 215, 216, 217, 218, 219, 221, 223, 224, 227, 228, 230, 231, 232, 233, 235, 236, 237, 238, 239, 241, 242, 243, 246, 247, 248, 249, 250, 251
devilishness, 110
devilish schemes, 109, 111
devilish things, 111
devilish words, 111
devilry, 111
Docetism, 208
dominion, 92, 94, 102, 103, 104, 106, 108, 109, 114, 115, 118, 119, 123, 142, 158, 195, 198, 213, 228, 231
double heart, 111
dragon, 3, 28, 29, 31, 147, 184, 185, 186, 188, 189, 190, 192, 193, 194, 221, 222, 249, 250
dualism, 4, 8, 16, 49, 53, 90, 91, 93, 95, 124, 130, 145, 206, 224, 231, 238, 245, 250
  anthropological, 64, 65, 129, 219
  cosmic, 53, 90, 96, 101, 104, 230, 231
  cosmological, 64, 65, 93, 118, 153, 245
  eschatological, 153
  gnostic, 234
  psychological, 93
  social, 96, 101, 103
dunamis, 237
early Church Fathers (ECF), 197, 200, 202, 203, 215, 223, 224, 228, 230, 232, 236, 240, 243, 250, 251
Egypt, 3, 7, 13, 16, 62, 83, 92, 121, 131, 138, 143, 144, 145, 226

El, 6, 8, 41, 45, 118
Elim, congregation of, 105, 106
Eliphaz, 24, 25
Elohim, 6, 33, 116
Elymas, 31, 173, 174
Elyon, 40, 41, 45
enemy, 13, 22, 25, 27, 28, 80, 90, 107, 114, 128, 149, 153, 172, 177, 204, 230
Enki, 5, 6
Enlil, 5, 6
Ennoia, 203, 204
Enoch, 56, 63, 84, 85, 86, 91, 125, 129, 157, 163, 199, 210, 230, 238, 241
Enochic, 52, 56, 61, 82, 85, 86, 88, 91, 93, 118, 125, 128, 163, 191, 193, 198, 199, 200, 222, 229, 230, 231, 233, 240, 248
Enuma Elish, 3, 28
eschatological, 85, 90, 97, 103, 104, 118, 126, 138, 139, 145, 153, 178, 206, 216, 240, 247
Ethiopic, 26, 55, 56, 71, 72, 73, 81, 82, 83, 84, 85, 133, 135, 136, 140, 141, 143
etiology, 56, 107, 199, 207, 209, 214, 215, 223
etymological, 16, 49, 246
Eve, 1, 27, 33, 70, 73, 74, 76, 77, 78, 79, 80, 82, 88, 135, 170, 185, 190, 199, 226, 230, 232, 240, 242, 248, 251
evil, 1, 2, 3, 4, 5, 7, 8, 9, 17, 19, 20, 21, 22, 23, 24, 25, 26, 27, 28, 32, 33, 34, 35, 49, 51, 53, 55, 57, 58, 60, 63, 64, 65, 67, 72, 74, 76, 81, 82, 83, 84, 89, 90, 91, 93, 94, 95, 96, 97, 99, 101, 104, 107, 110, 112, 115, 118, 120, 122, 123, 124, 125, 126, 127, 128, 130, 131, 132, 133, 134, 135, 136, 139, 140, 141, 142, 143, 145, 146, 152, 154, 155, 159, 163, 165, 166, 169, 171, 172, 174, 175, 177, 180, 181, 182, 183, 184, 186, 194, 195, 197, 198, 199, 200, 202, 206, 207, 208, 209, 210, 211, 213, 214, 215, 217, 219, 220, 225, 226, 228, 231, 232, 234, 235, 236, 238, 239, 240, 241, 242, 243, 245, 246, 247, 248, 249, 250, 251, 252
angel(s), 93, 107, 170, 213, 226, 233, 242
force, 63, 86, 106, 211
inclination, 54, 56, 57, 93, 111, 130, 219
nature, 235, 239, 241
one, 13, 64, 83, 130, 147, 153, 154, 182, 194, 212, 213, 214, 239
origins of, 95, 199, 226, 231, 237, 238, 239, 243
personified, 14, 53, 59, 97, 98, 100, 101, 102, 105, 106, 108, 109, 114, 118, 131, 132, 137, 145, 148, 149, 183, 194, 234, 245, 250, 251
spirit(s), 14, 55, 56, 58, 59, 61, 63, 65, 66, 70, 74, 82, 83, 90, 91, 93, 94, 95, 98, 99, 100, 102, 104, 105, 106, 107, 108, 109, 110, 112, 115, 116, 117, 118, 121, 122, 123, 125, 127, 128, 130, 139, 140, 141, 142, 143, 145, 146, 147, 148, 152, 156, 157, 159, 164, 165, 166, 167, 168, 169, 171, 177, 184, 193, 194, 195, 199, 203, 207, 208, 210, 215, 216, 217, 218, 219, 220, 223, 225, 226, 228, 233, 234, 236, 240, 246, 249, 250
ex nihilo, 234
exorcism, 55, 104, 152, 155, 158, 164, 166, 173, 204

faithful(ness), 48, 67, 83, 98, 120, 121, 138, 148, 149, 154, 155, 156, 171, 175, 186, 210, 217, 218, 219, 228, 234, 251, 252
falsely, 13, 14, 18, 72, 101, 203
Flood, 2, 5, 91, 193, 230
fornication, 100, 101, 124, 125, 126, 128, 140, 180, 187
free will, 1, 2, 4, 33, 225, 233, 235, 236, 237, 239, 241, 242, 243

Gabriel, 85, 86
Garden, 11, 27, 29, 30, 31, 33, 37, 45, 47, 73, 74, 77, 78, 79, 80, 82, 87, 185, 190, 198, 199, 200, 222, 223, 224, 225, 226, 230, 232, 233, 242, 252
Ge'ez, 26, 61, 81, 83, 84, 135, 140, 142
giants, 56, 59, 82, 91, 93, 118, 124, 140, 141, 210, 225, 228, 229, 236, 240, 249

Gilgamesh, 5, 240
    Epic of, 5, 6, 7, 32
Gnostics, 136, 182, 197, 201, 202, 203, 204, 210, 224, 228, 229, 230, 231, 237, 239, 252
Gospels, 70, 88, 148, 164, 169, 170, 172, 177, 216, 218, 221, 243, 248, 251
Greece, 3, 41
Greek, 7
grudge, 14, 137, 208

Habayu, 6
Hadad, 13
Hades, 7, 38
Hahyah, 91
halakhic, 52
hasatan, 8, 9, 11, 18, 20, 21, 24, 25, 246
Hasmonean, 57, 59, 69, 116
Hebrew Bible (HB), 8, 9, 11, 12, 14, 15, 16, 17, 19, 20, 26, 43, 46, 47, 51, 52, 55, 56, 95, 98, 99, 106, 110, 111, 113, 115, 118, 119, 126, 141, 144, 145, 147, 149, 162, 190, 191, 192, 195, 243, 246, 247, 248, 250, 251
Helel ben Shahar, 34, 62
Hellenistic, 69, 82
Heracles, 43, 186, 225
Hermes, 7, 186
Herodotus, 15, 43
hierarchy, 6, 20, 168, 235, 238
    demonic, 52, 166
    heavenly beings, 116, 242
    of spirits, 140, 141
Hobabish, 91
Horus, 7, 188
host, 35, 86, 110, 189, 190, 199, 227
hostile, 12, 14, 92, 119, 128, 228
Humbaba, 5, 7

ideology, 1
idiom(s), 23, 40, 98
idol(s), 66, 67, 72, 124, 129, 187, 188, 199, 207, 213, 225, 231, 233, 236
idolatry, 129, 142, 188, 192, 214, 225, 234, 236

incantation, 55, 204
influence, 2, 3, 4, 7, 8, 16, 34, 40, 63, 71, 84, 90, 91, 92, 94, 102, 104, 106, 118, 125, 127, 129, 131, 133, 136, 145, 146, 153, 160, 164, 167, 171, 172, 184, 194, 200, 202, 207, 211, 212, 216, 217, 220, 221, 224, 230, 234, 238, 240, 245, 247, 249, 250, 251
injustice, 47, 185
insanity, 14
interpolation(s), 26, 40, 62, 70, 73, 122, 123, 125, 128, 129, 130, 131, 132, 136, 137, 189, 197
Israel, 2, 12, 13, 16, 19, 20, 21, 22, 25, 26, 27, 30, 35, 36, 37, 41, 48, 56, 62, 83, 84, 95, 99, 100, 101, 102, 103, 104, 105, 106, 107, 110, 111, 112, 113, 114, 116, 118, 120, 126, 127, 128, 131, 132, 135, 138, 139, 140, 141, 144, 149, 150, 155, 156, 160, 161, 167, 185, 226, 227, 245, 246, 247, 251
Israelite(s), 2, 3, 4, 12, 17, 20, 22, 27, 28, 30, 39, 49, 69, 72, 105, 131, 134, 140, 141, 144, 245, 246

Jerusalem, 20, 26, 68, 69, 72, 73, 104, 114, 115, 128, 136, 150, 153, 155, 162, 227
    priesthood, 96, 101, 115
    temple, 20, 97, 107, 178
Jezebel, 187, 191
Joab, 13, 25, 26
Job, 13, 15, 16, 17, 21, 22, 23, 24, 25, 26, 66, 67, 81, 87, 88, 120, 148, 155, 157, 160, 161, 168, 182, 242, 247, 248, 249
Jobab, 66, 67
Joshua, 13, 19, 20, 22, 48, 68, 85, 91, 121, 183, 205
Jubilees, 9, 14, 57, 61, 81, 82, 83, 88, 91, 118, 122, 139, 140, 141, 142, 144, 145, 146, 147, 150, 152, 159, 164, 199, 222, 226, 228, 233, 248, 249
Judaism, 1, 4, 5, 8, 20, 21, 40, 52, 95, 101, 109, 123, 143, 149, 151, 152, 163, 166, 209, 212, 243, 245, 246, 251

Judaizers, 179, 223, 250
Judas Iscariot, 75, 167, 168
Judeo-Christian, 1, 3, 4, 80, 122, 139, 148, 152, 245
judgment, 19, 22, 33, 36, 41, 69, 70, 83, 86, 91, 110, 117, 118, 138, 143, 175, 183, 210, 223, 229
   day of, 22, 38, 82, 85, 93, 102, 125, 199
   final, 153, 154, 214, 233
justice, 1, 24, 215, 227

kingdom(s), 7, 29, 35, 37, 41, 44, 47, 62, 83, 128, 142, 149, 151, 152, 153, 158, 159, 160, 161, 162, 163, 164, 166, 176, 177, 188, 189, 194, 201, 213
   of the Cosmos, 161
   of darkness, 92, 103, 113, 152, 154, 161
   of the enemy, 128
   of God, 152, 158, 159, 160, 165, 168, 171, 174, 175, 190
   of satan, 152, 158
king of iniquity, 137
Kittim, 105, 108

Latin, 34, 39, 40, 68, 69, 70, 71, 79, 80, 84, 133, 135, 140, 151, 231, 241
lawless one(s), 132, 147, 195, 201, 202, 214, 250
Leviathan, 16, 28, 189, 192
Levites, 103, 104, 107, 128
liar, 27, 30, 230
light bearer, 34
Logos, 228, 229
Lot, 92, 93, 99, 103, 104, 105, 106, 107, 108, 109, 113, 114, 115, 116, 117, 118, 121, 122, 171, 173, 239
Lucifer, 11, 34, 39, 40, 242

Mahaway, 91
malevolent, 1, 2, 4, 56, 101, 119, 120, 121
Manasseh, 70, 71, 72, 135, 136, 137, 167, 171
Mani, 202, 240, 241

Manichaean(s), 202, 203, 208, 240, 241, 242, 243
manuscript(s), 4, 6, 53, 57, 60, 65, 68, 69, 71, 75, 79, 81, 84, 93, 95, 122, 129, 130, 133, 135, 137, 141, 187, 206, 212
Marduk, 3, 28
Masada, 81, 121
Masoretic Text (MT), 12, 13, 14, 18, 21, 24, 25, 27, 29, 30, 41, 47, 54, 116, 190
Mastema, 14, 51, 52, 53, 55, 56, 63, 82, 83, 84, 90, 91, 93, 94, 97, 98, 100, 107, 113, 114, 118, 119, 120, 121, 122, 126, 128, 139, 140, 141, 142, 143, 144, 147, 147, 150, 152, 154, 156, 159, 164, 168, 191, 197, 233, 247, 248, 249
   angel, the, 52, 91, 100, 107
   Angel(s) of, 52, 91, 100, 107, 115, 119, 120, 147, 150
   Chief of, 120, 121
   Prince, 82, 91, 93, 120, 142, 143
   spirits of, 56
Melchiresha, 51, 53, 90, 91, 92, 94, 97, 108, 136, 145, 147, 152, 154, 190, 247
Melchizedek, 41, 46, 90, 91, 92, 94, 98, 108, 117, 118, 190
Melqart, 43
Mesopotamia, 3, 5, 6, 15, 20, 41, 45, 46
messenger(s), 20, 51, 100, 106, 107, 108, 114, 115, 119, 152, 176, 213, 220, 221, 226, 241
   of YHWH/God, 14, 19, 33
Messiah, 93, 133, 138, 139, 147, 150, 151, 153, 156, 157, 159, 160, 161, 165, 166, 169, 170, 171, 188, 193, 204, 227, 252
Michael (archangel), 29, 68, 69, 72, 80, 82, 85, 86, 90, 91, 98, 108, 113, 128, 145, 183, 184, 188, 190, 219, 222, 223, 247
military, 13, 25, 26, 27, 60, 192
Mot, 6, 7, 45
myth/mythology, 3, 7, 28, 34, 37, 39, 40, 43, 44, 45, 46, 47, 48, 95, 132, 188, 190, 192, 198, 200, 201, 204, 225, 237, 239, 240, 243, 251

Subject Index | 277

nachash, 27
Nergal, 7
nonsectarian, 55, 80
nouns
  abstract, 100, 105, 108, 109, 110
  proper, 11, 12, 26, 34, 54, 72, 99, 100, 101, 102, 104, 109, 111
nous, 237

offspring, 13, 18, 31, 66, 84, 86, 90, 91, 92, 104, 142, 192, 198, 199, 225, 235
'Ohyah, 91
Olympus, 7
omnipotent, 2, 143
omniscient, 2
oppose, 2, 11, 12, 20, 24, 49, 58, 93, 98, 108, 112, 113, 117, 155, 173, 174, 180, 182, 183, 185, 186, 187, 201, 206, 209, 213, 219, 236, 239, 240, 246

Palestine, 16, 21, 62, 133, 157
Pan, 7
paradise, 5, 28, 31, 32, 76, 77, 78, 79, 233
persecute, 12, 14, 49, 80, 131, 137, 246
Persia, 3, 4, 8, 90, 113, 202, 203, 240
personified, 6, 7, 14, 27, 59, 64, 72, 90, 95, 97, 98, 101, 105, 106, 109, 110, 114, 117, 118, 131, 132, 137, 145, 149, 183, 194, 234, 245, 247, 250, 251
Pesher, 37, 100, 116
pestilence, daughter of, 95
Phaeton, 39, 40
Phanuel (archangel), 85, 86
Philistines, 12, 25, 26, 30
Pit, 6, 44, 46, 82, 100, 110, 114, 119, 147, 199, 225, 229
  Angel of the, 250
plague, 55, 67, 144
plan, 14, 20, 39, 63, 101, 111, 113, 114, 119, 121, 124, 135, 148, 159, 160, 170, 171, 176, 177, 184, 194
  of Belial, 113, 121, 122

evil, 107, 121
God's, 3, 19, 64, 72, 81, 87, 118, 119, 134, 144, 148, 153, 155, 156, 160, 169, 170, 171, 184, 195, 247, 250
of hatred, 107
of Mastema, 114
of Sammael, 136
sinful, 92, 107
of wickedness, 111, 112
plotter, 13
Pluton, 7
possession (demonic), 29, 54, 66, 88, 133, 134, 135, 157, 166, 167, 168, 171, 172, 173, 203, 204, 218, 220, 241, 248
postexilic, 2, 4, 5, 17, 20, 21, 24, 49, 95, 246
priest, 42, 46, 95, 104, 118, 128, 204, 213
  chief, 107, 159, 167
  high, 19, 46, 85, 101, 104, 107, 108, 117, 152, 205
  Wicked, 96, 97, 101, 103, 109, 110, 114, 115, 117
priesthood, 18, 46, 96, 101, 101, 102, 107, 114, 115, 128, 138
Primal Man, 240
prince, 42, 48, 93, 102, 108, 113, 119, 120, 136, 142, 155, 157, 167, 171, 198, 200, 201, 226, 233, 236
  of animosity, 52
  of Darkness, 102, 122, 240
  of Light(s), 90, 93, 94, 98, 101, 102, 107, 108, 152, 190
  Mastema, 83, 91, 93, 120, 142, 147
  of matter, 225
  of this world, 70, 239
Pseudepigrapha, 49, 61, 62, 81, 87, 88, 89, 122, 132, 145, 206, 247, 248, 249
Pseudo-Jubilees, 120, 121

Raphael (archangel), 85, 86
Ras Shamra, 6, 7
rebellion, 29, 39, 40, 52, 79, 80, 81, 83, 123, 178, 198, 201, 238, 239

Rechabites, 62, 73
reign, 28, 59, 82, 115
Resheph, 6, 7
roam (about), 15, 22, 49
Roman Empire / Roman(s), 159, 160, 168, 173, 178, 181, 185, 186, 188, 190, 192, 194, 198, 226, 240, 243
    emperor, 137, 188, 190, 192, 211, 214, 224, 227
ruach, 25
rule, 36, 37, 39, 51, 54, 56, 57, 83, 90, 92, 93, 94, 98, 102, 103, 108, 113, 114, 115, 120, 121, 123, 127, 130, 140, 141, 142, 149, 165, 179, 214, 216, 221
    Community, 59, 93, 96, 97, 103, 241
ruler, 43, 44, 45, 47, 55, 63, 91, 94, 97, 125, 128, 141
    of demons, 141, 151, 157, 158, 166, 209
    of matter, 228
    of this Age, 195, 197, 198, 205, 208, 209, 250
    of this World, 135, 136, 147, 161, 191, 194, 201, 209, 249, 250, 251

Sabbath, 120, 140, 167, 169
satan
    synagogue of, 188
    throne of, 187, 193
Satanail, 200
sectarian, 4, 52, 55, 60, 93
Semitic, 6, 15, 68, 73, 133, 157
serpent, 3, 11, 19, 27, 28, 29, 30, 31, 32, 33, 74, 76, 77, 78, 82, 110, 135, 185, 188, 190, 191, 192, 193, 194, 221, 223, 224, 225, 226, 227, 230, 232, 241, 249, 252
Set/Seth, 7, 16, 17
Shemihazah, 90, 91
Sheol, 37, 38, 41, 48, 110
Shimei, 12, 13
Shining One, 34, 38, 39, 242
Simonians, 203
Simon Magus, 139, 203, 204

Sitnah, 12
sobriquet, 97, 106, 107, 111, 117
son(s), 12, 13, 29, 34, 38, 39, 41, 43, 45, 62, 63, 64, 65, 100, 105, 120, 122, 127, 135, 141, 143, 152, 166, 203, 227, 242
    of Belial, 95, 96, 114, 116, 153, 154, 170, 173, 178, 239
    of Darkness, 90, 97, 98, 104, 105, 108, 109, 145, 247
    of a devil, 31, 172, 173
    of God, 6, 22, 70, 149, 150, 155, 156, 160, 161, 162, 182, 187, 192, 198, 201, 203, 219
    of Light, 90, 92, 93, 94, 98, 104, 105, 106, 109, 118, 145, 247
    of Man, 22, 28, 85, 153, 154, 159
Sophia, 204
sovereignty, 1, 20, 35, 80, 115, 133, 143, 144, 146, 201, 249, 251
spirit(s), 4, 5, 6, 14, 24, 25, 47, 48, 51, 53, 54, 55, 56, 57, 58, 60, 63, 64, 65, 67, 70, 71, 75, 82, 84, 89, 91, 91, 92, 93, 94, 99, 101, 102, 104, 105, 106, 107, 108, 109, 110, 112, 113, 114, 116, 117, 118, 121, 123, 124, 131, 141, 142, 143, 146, 152, 161, 175, 177, 181, 195, 201, 202, 203, 217, 220, 224, 228, 232, 236, 239, 240, 249, 250
    of anger, 63, 127
    bastard, 59
    of Belial, 52, 56, 99, 102, 104, 105, 107, 108, 114, 117, 121, 122
    of Beliar, 57, 123, 126, 127, 128, 129, 131, 132, 133, 140, 247
    chief of the, 83
    of darkness, 90, 94, 145, 247
    of deception, 25, 125, 125, 127, 147
    of error, 63, 123, 129
    evil, 55, 56, 58, 59, 61, 63, 65, 66, 70, 74, 82, 83, 90, 93, 94, 95, 96, 97, 98, 99, 100, 102, 104, 105, 106, 107, 108, 109, 110, 112, 115, 116, 117, 118, 121, 122,

123, 125, 126, 127, 128, 129, 139, 145, 146, 147, 156, 157, 159, 163, 164, 165, 166, 169, 171, 177, 184, 193, 194, 195, 199, 208, 210, 215, 217, 218, 220, 223, 225, 233, 234, 236, 240, 246, 249
  of fornication, 123, 124, 128, 131
  of (the) giants, 56, 59, 82, 86, 91, 118, 141, 210, 229
  of hatred, 64, 87, 247
  of hearing, 123
  Holy, 31, 69, 147, 149, 155, 163, 169, 172, 174, 203, 204, 207, 218
  of impurity, 55, 58
  of iniquity, 93
  of jealousy, 125, 127
  of life, 123
  of light, 94
  Lord of the, 85, 86, 191
  of lust, 123, 131
  of lying, 25, 63, 111, 127
  of Mastema, 56, 82, 145
  of pride, 63
  of procreation, 123
  of sight, 123
  of sleep, 123
  of smell, 123
  of speech, 123
  of taste, 123
  of truth, 90, 93, 111, 123, 145, 247
  unclean, 54, 55, 56, 57, 58, 246
  of uncleanness, 167
  of unrighteousness, 123
  of wickedness, 65, 104, 105, 126, 132
suffering, 1, 2, 8, 13, 20, 21, 24, 57, 58, 143, 155, 159, 182, 185, 241, 245, 251, 252
Syriac, 40, 46, 69, 73, 81, 84, 133, 157

temptation, 27, 33, 70, 78, 124, 153, 161, 162, 175, 177, 181, 206, 207, 209, 213, 215, 232, 236
test(ing), 32, 33, 63, 66, 82, 87, 91, 98, 113, 120, 141, 143, 149, 150, 152, 155, 156, 157, 160, 161, 162, 163, 169, 175, 176, 177, 181, 184, 186, 191, 194, 211, 213, 215, 216, 217, 218, 219, 230, 232, 233, 247, 251
theodicy, 1, 2, 150, 202
Therapeutae, 66
Tiamat, 3, 28
Torah, 24, 28, 64, 92, 95, 102, 111, 113, 114, 115, 118, 119, 120, 128, 150, 161, 162, 163, 169, 177, 181, 182, 184, 218, 222
tradition, 16, 28, 38, 40, 41, 46, 48, 63, 71, 75, 76, 88, 92, 93, 116, 141, 163, 182, 213, 219, 224, 229, 248
  Christian, 3, 5, 22, 27, 28, 34, 37, 43, 49, 70, 246
  Enochic, 82, 86, 157, 191, 200, 222
  Jewish, 55, 70, 135, 156, 161, 165
  Judeo-Christian, 122, 135, 139, 148, 152
  oral, 40, 42, 162, 221
  satan, 3, 5, 8, 9, 56, 71, 82, 93, 240
  Seventy Shepherds, 221
  Watcher, 14, 24, 56, 59, 82, 86, 93, 124, 139, 140, 146, 191, 193, 198, 199, 210, 221, 225, 227, 229, 233, 235, 238, 249
transgress, 56, 74, 143, 225
traps, 100, 101, 102, 104, 110, 112, 115, 163, 172, 180, 184, 185, 208
trial, 32, 70, 73, 74, 78, 94, 152, 157, 159, 179, 184, 188, 207, 223
  of Jesus, 73, 74, 149, 155, 160, 161, 163, 169, 173, 216, 219, 252

Ugaritic, 6, 39, 40, 45

Valentinians, 203

Watcher(s)
  Book of, 25, 56, 81, 84, 86, 90, 93, 118, 124, 128, 157, 163, 198, 199, 225
  Fallen, 86, 90, 99, 117, 157, 163, 198, 199, 200, 225, 226, 229, 231, 238, 251

wickedness
    congregation of, 98, 186
    fruits of, 114
    lot of, 115, 173
    rule of, 98
    torrents of, 98
will
    of the devil, 65, 181
    of God, 2, 11, 49, 65, 129, 133, 145, 146, 178, 226, 246, 249
wisdom, 32, 33, 45, 47, 48, 53, 66, 98, 99, 152, 157, 201, 202, 232, 242
worldview(s), 2, 3, 4, 8, 17, 21, 49, 51, 52, 53, 59, 80, 84, 88, 90, 95, 96, 98, 101, 105, 109, 125, 129, 130, 136, 137, 139, 143, 145, 146, 202, 207, 212, 224, 240, 245, 246, 247, 248, 249, 251
    two ways, 250

Yahad, 52, 103, 114
yetser, 112, 219
    ra, 112, 124, 234
    tov, 124

Zion, 41, 60, 98
Zoroastrianism, 4, 5, 6, 90, 145, 202, 240, 241, 245
Zosimos, 73, 74

Scripture and Ancient Text Index

Ancient Near East

Epic of Gilgamesh	5	**Gathas**	4
Tablet 1, col. iv, lines 16–34	32		

Jewish Scriptures (Hebrew [Aramaic]/Greek)

Genesis		16:10	18
1–5	76	17:1	48
1:26	32, 232	22	120
2:12	46	26:21	12, 49
2:17	33	27:41	14, 119
3	27, 29, 30, 31, 32, 33	32:29	18
3:1–19	27	49:17	29
3:1–15	11, 17, 49	49:23	14, 119
3:1–5	31	50:15	14, 119
3:1	31, 77, 190		
3:2–5	32	**Exodus**	
3:5	32, 33	3:1	47
3:6	33	4:17	30
3:14	27, 29	4:24	143
3:15	29, 31	6:18	91
3:23–24	5	7:15	30
3:24	47	12:21–23	145
6:1–4	198	23:22 [LXX]	205
6:4 [LXX]	229	24:12–18	139
6:9	48	24:13	47
14:19–22	41	24:17	48

281

25:18–22	48	19:22	239		
34:1	48	20:13	95, 239		
37:7–9	48				

Leviticus

11:41–43	29		
19:15	47		
19:35	47		

Numbers

6:24	104
7:89	48
11:15	46
21	28, 30
21:8–9	28
22	18, 19, 26, 27
22:20	19
22:22–35	11, 18, 49
22:22	14, 17, 55
22:28	27
22:32	55
25:3	6

Deuteronomy

5:24	46
13:14	95
25:13–16	47
28:1	23
31:14	22
32:8	43
32:17	156, 225, 227
32:28	98, 101

Joshua

24:14	48

Judges

2:1–3	18
2:13	6
4:11	73
6:22	18
13:17–18	18

1 Samuel

1:16	95
4:4	48
4:6, 9	12
9:16	43
10:19	22
10:27	95
13:3	12
13:4	43
14:21	12
25:17	95
29:4	12, 17, 49

2 Samuel

6:2	48
7:11	112
8:10	205
14:17	33
16:5–7	13
19:17–24	12, 17
19:23	12, 49
19:36	32
22:5	95, 110
24	16, 18, 26
24:1	25, 27
24:16–17	19
24:16	102

1 Kings

3:9	32
5:4	59
5:16–20	13, 49
5:18	13, 55
11:14–25	13, 26, 49
11:14	27
11:23	13
14:35	43
16:32	6
18:20–40	43

18:27	43	30:7	16
19	156	34:14	156
21:13	95	37:16	48
22:19–23	21, 22, 25	41:11 [LXX]	205
22:53	6	45:7	3, 7, 53
		45:16 [LXX]	205
2 Kings		51:9	16
1:2–16	151	51:19	205
18:4	30	61:11	126
19:15	48	65:25	29
		66:6 [LXX]	205
Isaiah			
1–12	36	**Jeremiah**	
6	21	8:17	30
11:2	126	21:1	43
13–23	36	23:5	126
13–14	33, 40	33:15	126
13:6–13; 17–18	35	51:34	192
13:17–22	33		
13:17	37	**Ezekiel**	
13:19–22	35, 36	1:5–28	48
14	33, 35, 39, 40, 42, 85, 163, 178, 229, 238, 239, 242	9:3	48
		10:1–20	48
14:1–4a	36	17:12	44
14:3–21	33, 34	18:8	47
14:4	36, 37	26–27	42
14:5–6	37	27:33	44
14:7	38	28	37, 40, 42, 46, 48, 163, 178, 229, 233, 238, 239, 242
14:8	37		
14:9	38	28:1–10	42, 44
14:10–11	38	28:2–19	41
14:12–17	11, 17, 49, 190	28:2–10	41
14:12–14	34, 46	28:2	41, 43, 44, 47
14:12	34, 38, 242	28:3	47
14:13	40, 45, 231	28:6–8	44
14:14	231, 233	28:8	45
14:15–16	41	28:9	44
14:29	30	28:11–19	12, 17, 42, 44, 49
24	85	28:12–18	46
24:17	100	28:12–15	45
27:1	28	28:12	44, 45, 47
27:11	101	28:13–14	45

28:13	43, 45, 46, 242	3:1	19, 27, 162, 183, 205 [LXX]
28:14	45, 46	3:2	20, 58, 182
28:15	47, 48, 242	3:3	19
28:16	47, 48	3:4	20
28:17–20	46	3:8	126
28:17	44	4:3	20
29:2	44	4:10	15
31:8–9	37	6:5	22
32:2–3	192	6:12	126
34:5	156	13:2	54
34:8	156		
34:24	44	**Psalms**	
34:25	156	6:6	38
37:25	44	7:7–9	116
38:2–3	193	18:5	95, 110
38:8	193	22:11–21	156
43:10	44	29:1	21
		31:18	38
Hosea		38:21 [37:21, LXX]	13, 17, 49
9:7	119	41:9	95
9:8	14, 119	48:3	41
		55:4	14, 119
Joel		58:5	30
2:28–29	126	71:13 [70:13, LXX]	13, 17, 49
		74:13–14	189
Amos		74:14	192
5:19	30	76:13	44
		80:2	48
Micah		82	41, 45
7:17	29	82:1–2	116
		82:1	21, 45, 190
Nahum		87:4	192
2:1	95	88:12, 13	38
11:1	95	89:7	21
		89:10	16
Habakkuk		91	156
2:5	6	91:11–12	162
2:17	37	95:5	199
		96:5 [95:5, LXX]	225
Zechariah		97:4	16
3	8, 120, 190, 191	99:1	48
3:1–7	11, 13, 18, 49	101:3	95
3:1–2	55	105:37 [LXX]	227

106:28	6	18:13	6
109:1–6	13, 17	26:6	38
109:3	34	26:13	30
109:4–6 [108:4–6, LXX]	13, 49	30:21	119
109:6–7	19	34:18	95
109:20, 29 [108:20, 29, LXX]	13, 17, 49	38:32	34
115:17	38	40:15	156
119	58	42:7	25
119:33b	56		
119:113b	54	**Proverbs**	
119:133	56	6:12	95
140:4	30	22:29	22
		23:32	30
Job		30:19	30
1–2	3, 5, 6, 11, 16, 20, 23, 27, 49, 58, 74, 98, 116, 120, 149, 162, 190, 191	**Ecclesiastes**	
1:6–12	15, 55	10:8, 11	30
1:6–8	23		
1:6	6, 21, 22	**Esther**	
1:7	15	7:4 [LXX]	13
1:8	22, 23	8:11 [LXX]	205
1:10	23	9:2 [LXX]	205
1:12	24		
1:12, 13–19, 20–21	23	**Daniel**	
2:1–10	55	1–3	75
2:1–3b	23	2:22	188
2:1	22	2:38	38
2:3	23	4:13 [MT, v. 10]	21
2:5	24	4:17 [MT, v. 14]	21
2:6	24	4:23 [MT, v. 20]	21
2:7	24	7	85, 189, 192
2:9	24	7:2–8	192
4:7	24	7:9–14	21
4:12–21	24	7:25	192
4:12–19	24	8:10	189
4:15	25	9:25	43
4:16	25	10	222
7:9	38	11:22	43
9:11	25	12	222
11:17	34	12:7	192
13:26 [LXX]	205		
16:9	14, 119	**1 Chronicles**	
17:16	38	2:55	73

Scripture and Ancient Text Index | 285

9:20	43	11:11	43
13:1	43	13:1	43
13:6	48	13:7	95
21	16, 17, 18, 25, 26, 191	14:9–15	27
21:1–22:1	11, 49	16:9	15
21:1	15, 25, 27, 55, 59, 162	18:18–22	25
21:15–16	26	19:11	43
21:16	19	31:12	43
2 Chronicles		32:21	43
10:15	25		

Deuterocanonical/LXX

1 Maccabees		**4 Maccabees**	
14:7 [LXX]	205	18:8	29
2 Maccabees		**Sirach**	
4:18–20	43	21:27	87
10:26 [LXX]	205	**Wisdom of Solomon**	
		2:23–24	19, 181
3 Maccabees		2:24	29, 32, 87, 190
7:9 [LXX]	205	4:18–5:13	85

Pseudepigrapha

1 Enoch		24.1	46
1–36	84, 118	25.3	46
6–16	56, 229	37–71	84
8.1–3	86	40	85
9.9	225	40.7	20, 26, 57, 84, 85, 86
10	86	40.9	85
10.1	26	53.3	84, 85, 86
10.2	5	54	86
10.4–13	193	54.1–5	193
10.11	199	54.3	85
14.6	132	54.5	86
18.6–8	46	54.6	84
18.14	190	55	86
19.1	198, 225	65	86
21.3–6	190	65.1	20

65.3	86	5.2	75
65.5	84	5.3	62, 75
65.6	57, 86	5.5	75
69.6	190	5.6	75
72–82	84	6.1	75
83–90	84		
85–90	84	**History of the Rechabites**	
86.1–3	190	7.7–8	73
88.3	190	7.8	62, 73
91–105	84	11.1–12.9	73
91.1–10, 18, 19	84	12.9a–13.5c	73
106–7	84	16.1b–8	73
108	84	19–23	73
		19.1	62, 73
2 Enoch		19.2	62, 73
7	200	20.1	62, 73, 74
18	200	20.2	74
29.4–5	40, 190	20.3	74
29.4	193	20.4	74
31.6	190	21.1	62, 73, 74
		21.4	62, 73
2 Baruch		21.5	74
55:10–12	200	21.6	74
		21.7	74
3 Baruch		22.2	62, 73
4.8	62	22.4	74
16.3	132		
		Jubilees	
4 Ezra	75, 85, 199	1.20	56, 140, 141
		1.27	140
Apocalypse of Moses		2.2–3	57
15.3	62	2.2	82, 142, 232
16.1, 2, 5	62	3.17	82
17.1	62, 190	3.23	82
17.4–5	27	7	198
17.4	62	7.20	140
21.3	62	7.27	140
29.15	62	10	57, 63, 91, 225
39.2	193	10.1–2	141
		10.3–6	56
Apocalypse of Sedrach		10.3	141
4.5	62, 75	10.7–8	142

10.8–11	98
10.8	56, 82, 83, 100, 141, 142
10.9	142
10.11	26, 54, 142, 193
10.12	83
11	142
11.2–5	143
11.4	142
11.5	93, 142
11.11–14	159
11.11	83, 143
15.33	141
17	156, 168
17.15–16	83, 98, 143
17.17	143
18.9–12	98
18.12	143
19.28	56
23.29	26, 55, 83
40.9–10	83
46.2	55, 83
48	143, 144
48.2–4	143
48.2	83
48.4	144
48.5–8	144
48.9	83, 144
48.10	144
48.12	83, 144
48.15	144
48.18	144
49.1–8	145
49.2	145
50.5	55, 83

Life of Adam and Eve (Gk.)

13–16	40, 190
15.3	76, 77, 78
16	190
16.1	76
16.2	76, 77
16.3	190
16.5	76, 77, 78
17.1	76, 78
17.2	76
17.3	78
17.4	76, 77, 78
19.1	77, 78
19.3	77
21.2–3	78
21.2	78
21.3	76, 78

Life of Adam and Eve (VITA)

9.1	62
9.2	79
10.2	79
10.3	79
11.1	80
11.2	80
11.3	80
12–16	79
12.1	62, 80
12.3	80
13.1	80
14.1	80
14.2	80
15–30	79
15.1	80
17.1	80
17.2	80
29	79
33.2	80
47.3	193
51	79

Lives of the Prophets

4.6	134
4.7	134
4.21	134
17.2	134
17.3	134
17.4	134

Martyrdom and Ascension of Isaiah (Gk. MS A + Ethiopic)

1.1–3.12	70
1.8–9	135

1.9	62, 71, 135, 137	1.9	65
1.11	62, 71, 135	2	64
2.1–4	135	2.1–3.2	65
2.2	62, 71, 72, 135	3.2	130
2.3	135	6	183
2.4–4.4	71	6.4	62, 65, 130
2.4	135, 136	6.5	65, 130
2.7	62, 71, 136	6.6	65, 130
3.2	62, 72		
3.3	62, 72	**T. Benjamin**	
3.8	62, 72	3.3	131
3.11	136, 137, 171	3.8	131
3.13–4.22	70	6.1	131, 132
3.13	136	6.5–6	132
3.18	62	6.5	132
4.1	139	6.7	131, 132
4.2	136	7.1	131, 132
4.3	137	7.2	131, 132
4.14	137		
4.22	136	**T. Dan**	
5.1	137	1.7	63, 127
5.1–16	70	1.8	127
5.15–16	137	1.9	127
5.16	62	3.6	62, 63
6–11	70, 71	4.7	63, 127
7.9	62, 72	5.1	63, 127
10.29	136	5.5–6	63, 125, 128
11.23, 41, 43	62, 72	5.6	62, 63, 128
		5.7	128
Sibylline Oracles		5.9–10	126
2.167	138	5.10	63, 127, 128
3.63–69	138	5.11	63, 127, 128
3.63	138	6.1	62, 128
3.73	138	6.2	128
3.396–400	189	6.3	128
3.751	132	6.4	128
5.512–13	190	6.5	126
T. Asher		**T. Gad**	
1.2	64	2.2	63
1.3	64, 130	2.4	64
1.5	64, 130	3.1, 3	64
1.8	130	4.7	62, 64
1.8–9	64		

T. Issachar
6.1	126
7.2–4	126
7.5	126
7.6–7	126
7.7	126

T. Job
3.3	62, 191
3:5b	187
3.6	62, 66, 191
4.4–5	67
4.4	62, 66, 187
4.6	67
5.1–2	67
6.4	27, 62, 66, 67
7	67
7.1	62
7.6	62, 66, 67
7.12	62, 66, 67
8	67
16.2	66, 67
16.7	67
17.1	62
17.2	27
20.1	62, 66, 67
20.5	27
21–22	67
23.1	27
23.1, 3, 11	62, 66, 67
26.6	62
27.1	27, 62, 66, 67
27.6	62, 66, 67
41.5	62, 66

T. Joseph
7.4	131
7.7	131
20.2	131

T. Judah
19.4	125
20.1	123, 125
20.2	125
24	125
25.1–2	125
25.3	125, 193
25.5	126

T. Levi
3.3	125, 190
18.12	125
19.1	125

T. Moses
2, 8, 9, 10	62

T. Naphtali
2.6	129
2.7	129
3.1	65, 129
3.3	62, 129
3.5	129
4.1	129
8.4	62, 66
8.6	62, 66

T. Reuben
2.2	123, 124
2.3	123
3.1–7	123
3.2	123
3.3–6	123
3.3–4	125
4.6–7	124
4.11	124
5.1	124
5.6–7	124

T. Simeon
2.7	125
5.3	124

Scripture and Ancient Text Index | 291

T. Solomon		T. Zebulon	
3–16	151	9.7	126, 127
15.10	70	9.8	127
15.11	62, 70		

Ancient Authors

Herodotus
Histories
1.114 — 15

Hesiod
Theogonia
27 — 228
378 — 39

Homer
Odyssey
19.203 — 228

Josephus
Antiquities
8.141–49 — 43
9.2.1 — 151
10.40 — 193

Ovid
Metamorphosis
1.747–2.400 — 39

Philo of Alexandria
De Gigantibus
2.2–18 — 238

Dead Sea Scrolls

1QH^a	**97, 109, 110**	12.13–14	111
2.22	186	13.28	96, 111
4.6	26, 54, 58, 90	13.41	96, 111, 112
15.5–6	112	14.24	96, 111, 112
15.6	112	14.25	112
10.14	109	15.6	96, 112
10.18	96, 109	22.25	51, 58, 96
10.24	95, 109, 110	24.16	59
11	110	24.23	51, 58, 59, 96
11.19	110	24.26	59
11.27	110	45.3	26, 54, 58, 90
11.28	110		
11.29	96, 110	**1QM**	**97, 104**
11.30	96, 110	1.1	96, 105, 106, 107
11.33	96, 110	1.5	96, 106
11.35–37	110	1.6	106
12.7–9	111	1.10	105
12.11	111	1.13	96, 106, 109

1.14–15	106, 109	2.19–10.18	104
1.15	96	2.19	103, 104
3.9	106	3	183, 191
4.2	96	3.13–4.25	53, 93, 168
4.9	186	3:15–17	53, 94
11.8–9	107	3.18	93
11.8	96	3.19	111
11.16	193	3.20–21	93, 98, 108, 152
12.20	107	3.20	93
13.1–5	107	3.21	94
13.1	107	3.22–23	94
13.2	96	3.23	94, 121
13.4–5	107	3.24–25	94
13.4	96, 121	3.24	93
13.10–11	107, 108	3.25	53, 94
13.11–12	107	4.17	153
13.11	53, 96, 100, 107, 119	10.19	104
14.9	96, 108	10.21	103, 104, 114
14.10	109		
15	192	**1QSb**	
15.2	108	1.8	26, 54, 59, 90
15.3	96, 108		
15.17	96, 108	**1Q21**	57
16.11	96		
17.1	108	**4QDibre Hame'orot**	
17.4–6	108	1–2 iv 12	55
17.5–9	190		
17.5	108	**4Q161**	193
17.6	108		
18.1–3	108	**4Q163**	
18.1	96	frag. 8–10	37
18.3	96		
		4Q171 1 2ii.9–10	112
1QS	93, 96, 97, 181, 218		
1	191	**4Q174**	
1.18	59, 103	1 2i.8–9	112
1.22	103	1 2i.8	112
1.24	103	1 3ii.1–2	113
2.4	103, 153	4.3	113
2.5–9	92		
2.5	103, 104	**4Q177**	
2.7–8	103	1 4.8	113
2.11	104	1 4.10	113

10 11.4	113	**4Q286**	
12 13i.6–7	113	7ii.1–3	121
12 13i.11	113	7ii.1–5	114
		7ii.6	114
4Q201	84	7ii.7	114
4Q209	84	**4Q287**	
		6.2	121
4Q213a (Levi[b]**)**	58		
1 i 10	51, 56, 57, 90	**4Q386**	
1.17	55, 57	1ii.3–4	114
4Q214	57	**4Q387**	
		1.3–10	115
4Q215	65	2ii.12	120
		2iii.4	115, 120
4Q225	121		
2i.9–10	120	**4Q390**	
2i.10	120	1.8–9	120
2ii.6–7	120	1.11	120
2ii.6	119	2i.2	115
2ii.13–14	113, 120	2i.4	115
		2i.7	115, 120
4Q255–64	59		
		4Q398	
4Q260		14 17ii.5	115
5.2	114		
5.3	114	**4Q444**	
5.4	114	1–4 i + 5.8	56
4Q270		**4Q463**	
6ii.18	119	1.1–4	99
		2.1	92
4Q271		2.2–7	92
4ii.6	119	2.2	92
5i.18	114	2.3	99
4Q280 (*Curses*)		**4Q495**	
2.1	92	2.3	119
2.2–7	92		
2.2	92, 97	**4Q504**	59
		1_2 iv 12	51, 90
		1_2Riv 12–13	59

4Q505	59	**11Q13 (*Melchizedek*)**	92, 98, 116, 218
		2.10–12	116
4Q506	59	2.11	116, 117
		2.12	99, 116, 117
4Q509	59	2.13	116, 117
		2.22	116, 117
4Q511		2.24–25	117
18ii.5	115	2.25	116, 117
		3.7	116, 193
4Q543		5.3	116
5–9	91	9–15	190
4Q544	94, 152	**11Q19 (Temple Scroll)**	
1	91	55.3	118
2.13–16	91		
2.13–14	94	**Damascus Document (CD)**	
2.13	91, 97	1.7	126
3.1	94	3.24	93
3.21	94	4.12–18	93, 106, 108, 112
		4.12–13	100
4Q547		4.14–16	100
1–2 iii	91	4.14	100
		4.15	100
4Q548 (*Amram*)		4.17–18	100, 180
2.3	108	5	101, 103
		5.16–20	101
5Q11	59	5.17–18	93, 108
		5.18–19	101
11Q5 (11QPs^a; *Plea for Deliverance*)	56, 57	5.18	98, 100
16	57	7.19–20	126
19.1–18	54	8.2	100, 101, 102
19.13b–16a	54, 90	12.2	100, 102
19.15	51, 54, 56, 58	12.3	114
24.12	55	16	126, 127, 148, 149, 150, 181
27.4–6	54	16.2–4	81
27.10	55	16.5	119, 120
		19.14	100, 101, 102
11Q6	54		
		Cambridge Genizah	
11Q11 (Apocryphal Psalm)		Frag. T-S 16.94	57
2.2	121		
2.4	121		

Christian Testament

Matthew		4:4	159
4	149, 156, 191	4:11	159
4:1	149, 155	4:15	155, 158, 159
4:3–10	150	5	134, 173
4:3	149, 150	5:12	171
4:5	150	8:29	159
4:6	149, 156	8:33	155, 159, 160
4:8–9	150	8:34–9:1	160
4:10	150	13:19–22	165
4:11	153		
9:24	201	**Luke**	
12	157	4	173, 216
12:22–30	166	4:2	155, 160
12:23	151, 166	4:3	161
12:24	201	4:5–6	189
12:25	152	4:6	161
12:26	151, 152	4:8	162
12:27–28	152	4:9	162
13:18–30	231	4:10–11	156, 162
13:25–40	208	4:12	162
13:36–43	152	4:13	162
13:38–9	153	4:31–37	166
16:21	153	4:33	167
16:23	153	8:12	163, 172
25:31–46	206	8:13	163
25:41	154, 206	8:14	163
		8:15	163
Mark		8:30	171
1	156	10	222
1:12	155	10:2	164
1:13	66, 155	10:3	164
3	160	10:9	164
3:19	157	10:11	164
3:20–27	157	10:17–20	166
3:22–27	166	10:17	164
3:22–26	151	10:18	40, 163, 164, 239
3:22	201	11:14	166
3:23	155, 157, 158	11:15	151, 201
3:26	155, 158	11:17	166
3:27	159	11:18	166
4	216	11:20	166

11:22	166	8:9–23	139
12:12	165	10:38	173
13:16	167	13:10	31, 173
13:17	205	14:2	185
17–18	151	16:6–10	178
21:15	205	16:16	185
21:25–27	165	26:18	173
22	165		
22:3	167, 171, 172, 198	**Romans**	
22:31	168	1	76
22:32	168	1:13	178
22:53	198	3:5	178
		11:4	6
John		11:33	188
1:3	229	15:22	177
3:14–15	28	16:20	31, 174
6:48	169		
6:52	169	**1 Corinthians**	
6:53–56	169	2:6	201
6:70	169, 170	2:8	201
6:71	170	2:10	188
8:33	170	2:11	147
8:41	170	2:12	147
8:42	170	5	218
8:44	30, 170, 201, 228, 241	5:5	175, 175, 175
8:48	171	7:5	175, 191
12:1–9	28	7:8–9	175
12:31	191, 201	10:13	186
12:32	191	15:26	181
13	149	15:55	181
13:2	31, 171, 198	16:9	205
13:21	29		
13:27	169, 171, 172, 198	**2 Corinthians**	
14:30	201	2:11–15	176
16:11	191, 201	2:11	176, 177
		4:4	201
Acts		11:14	176
2:22	179	11:15	176
4:34	172	12:7	154, 176
5:3	31, 172	12:9	176
8:9–24	203	12:11	176

Galatians
5:7	178
5:17	205

Ephesians
2:2	201
4:26–27	177
4:27	148
6:11	147, 177
6:12	177, 236

Philippians
1:28	205

Colossians
13:33	111

1 Thessalonians
2:18	177, 198

2 Thessalonians
	147
2:3	178
2:4	205
2:7–12	201
2:9–11	179
2:9–10	147
2:9	177, 178
2:11	202

1 Timothy
1:10	205
1:19	179
1:20	179, 218
3:6	31, 179, 180
3:7	179, 180
3:8	180
3:11	179, 180
5:13	180
5:14	180, 205
5:15	180
6:20	200, 203

2 Timothy
2:17	179
2:26	180
3:2	181
3:3	180, 181
3:7	180

Hebrews
2:14	181

James
1:2	186
1:12	186
4:7	148, 181, 216

1 Peter
1:6–7	186
5:8	6, 15, 148, 198
5:9	182

2 Peter
1:19	34
2:1	201
2:4	193

1 John
2:18–19	202
2:18	147
3:4	182
3:8	31, 182, 202, 241
3:10	182
3:12	182
5:19	239

Jude
2, 8, 9, 10	69
6	193
9	68, 69, 183

Revelation
1:5	201
2:9	184, 185, 188

2:10	184, 186, 191, 198	12:14		185, 192
2:13	184, 186, 188, 191, 192	12:15		185
2:18	187	12:16		185, 192
2:20	187, 191	12:17		185, 192, 198
2:23	187	12:18		192
2:24	184, 187	13–14		222
3:7	188	13:1		192
3:9	184, 186, 188	13:2		185, 186, 192
3:10	188	13:4		185, 187, 193
12–14	223	13:7		187
12	28, 29, 81, 163, 187, 222, 223, 229	13:11–18		193
12:1–2	189	13:11		185, 193
12:3	185, 189	13:14		191, 193
12:4	185, 189	16:13		185
12:5	191	17:3		189
12:7–18	164	17:9–14		189
12:7–9	154, 221	19:20		191
12:7	185, 189	20:2		31, 184, 185, 193
12:8	190	20:3		191, 193
12:9	31, 184, 185, 190, 192, 221	20:7		184, 191, 193
12:10–11	191	20:8–9		193
12:10	191	20:8		191, 193
12:11	191	20:10		154, 184, 191, 193
12:12	184, 192	20:14		181
12:13	147, 185, 192	22:16		34

Church Fathers

Athenagoras
Plea for the Christians
24	227, 228	11.14		241
25	228, 229	11.15		241, 242
26	228, 229	11.33		243
		12.8		243
		13.14		243
		14.11		243
		14.13		242, 243

Augustine
Christian Instruction
3.37	34

Clement of Alexandria
Paedagogus

City of God
11–13	242	1.1.1		234
11.11	242	1.8		234
11.13–15	241	2.8.62		234
11.13	242, 243	3.2		235

Rich Man		18:2		213
42.16–18	236	19:1–12		214
Stromata		19:11		214
1.17	235, 236	20:1		214
2.13	236	20:2		214
2.20	236	21:3		214
3.7	235, 238			
3.15	236	**Epistle to Diognetus**		
4.12	236	12:3, 6, 8		223
5.1	235, 238			
5.14	235, 236	**Eusebius**		
7.7	235, 238	*Church History*		
		6.39.5		236
Clement of Rome		7.1.1		236
1 Clement				
3	206	**Ignatius of Antioch**		
14:1	206	*Epistle to the Ephesians*		
15:5	206	10:3		208
46:8–9	206	17		199, 208
47:5–6	206	*Epistle to Philadelphia*		
51:1	205, 206	6:1–2		208
2 Clement		6:1		188
1:6	207	8:2		188
6:3–4	207	*Epistle to the Romans*		
6:9	207	5:3		208
10:5	207	*Epistle to Smyrna*		
15	207	8–9		208
15:4	207	8:1		208
17:3	206	8:2		208
17:4–7	206	*To the Trallians*		
17:7	206	8:1		208
18:2	206, 207	9		208
		10		199
Epistle of Barnabas				
2:1	213, 214	**Irenaeus**		
2:8	213	*Apostolic Preaching*		
2:10	213, 214	17		230
4:9	213, 214	18		230
4:13	214	*Haeresis*		
9:4	213	1.5		229
9:6	213	1.11.1		203
15:5	214	1.15.6		230

1.23.1	203	*Dialogue with Trypho*	
1.23.2	203	10.36–43	226
1.23.4	204	16.4	227
1.24.1	204	17.1	227
1.24.2	204	17.4–5	227
1.25–31	204	19	227
1.25.3	229	32.3	227
1.25.6	203	45	225, 226
1.29.1	204	79	225, 226
1.29.4	204	88.22–23	226
3.8	230	93.4	227
3.8.2	230	100	225, 226
3.8.3	230	103.2	227
3.8.18	230	104.1	227
3.18.7	230	119	227
3.23	230	124	225
3.23.3	230	124.18	226
4	229	125.21–29	226
4.16.2	230	125.26	226
4.40	230	125.37	227
4.40.1	230	131.14–15	227
4.40.3	230	132–33	227
4.41.1–3	230	133.6	227
5.21	230	140–41	225
5.22–24	230		
5.22	230	**Martyrdom of Polycarp**	
5.22.1	230	2:4	211
5.24	230	3:1	211
5.24.2	230	8:2	211
5.24.3	230	10:1	211
5.25–30	231	13:1	212
5.25	230	17:1	212
		17:2	212
Justin Martyr		18:1	212
1 Apology			
28.1	199, 224	**Origen**	
54	225	*Contra Celsum*	
2 Apology		5.45	237
5	198, 199	5.52	238
5.3	198	5.55	238
5.4	198	*On First Principles*	
5.5	198, 225	1.4.1	237
7.1	199, 225	1.5	34

1.5.5	238	25–114	214, 215
1.6.1–3	239	31:4	216
1.8.1–4	239	33	215
3.2	68	33:1–2	220
4.3.9	34	33:1	220
6	237	33:3	220
On Prayer		33:4	220
25.3	237	34	215
		36:1	220
Papias of Hierapolis		36:2	220
Fragments of Papias		36:3	220
11	221	36:4	220
14	221	36:10	221
24:1–11	221	37:2	216
24:2	222	37:3	216
24:3	222	39:9	217
24:4	222	39:11	217
24:5	222, 223	39:12	217
24:6	223	40	215
24:7	222	43	217
24:8	222	43:3	217
24:10	222	43:5	217
24:11	223	43:8	217
		43:17	217
Polycarp of Smyrna		45:4	217
Epistle to Philippi		45:7	218
5:2	209	47	217
7:1	210	47:2	217
		47:3	217
Shepherd of Hermas		47:4	217
1–24	214, 215	47:5–7	217
1:8	215	47:6	218
2:4	215	47:7	218
3:2	216	48:1–2	218
6:1–2	216	48:2	216, 218
6:4	216	48:4	216, 218
7:2	216	48:7	216
9:6	216	49:1	218
9:9	216	49:2	219
14:6	215	49:4	219
15:2	215	49:5	219
17:3	215	63	218
17:4–6	216	69	219

69:1	219	*Apology*	
69:3	219	22	233
95	215	27	233
		De anima	
Tertullian		16	231
Adversus Marcionem		57	231, 233
2.5–10	232	*De fuga*	
2.9.3–4	232	1.1	233
2.10	232	*De spectaculis*	
2.10.2–3	232	1	231
2.10.2	232	2.12	232
2.10.3	233	15	231
2.10.5	233	26	231
5.17	231, 233		

Rabbinic Literature

Baba Bathra		**Targum of Genesis**	
16a	57	5:3	170
Berakhoth		**Targum of Job**	
16b	57	1:6	22
		1:7	22
Numbers Rabba		2:1	22
9.9	54		
Sotah			
3a	54		